𝕀𝕎orld's 𝔹est 𝕳istories

IRELAND

THE PEOPLE'S HISTORY
OF IRELAND

BY

JOHN F. FINERTY

PRESIDENT OF THE UNITED IRISH LEAGUE OF AMERICA

Illustrated

IN TWO VOLUMES

VOLUME ONE

NEW YORK AND LONDON
THE CO-OPERATIVE PUBLICATION SOCIETY

HISTORY OF IRELAND

VOLUME ONE

CONTENTS

BOOK I

Contents

BOOK II

Contents

Contents

BOOK III

Contents

BOOK I

DEALING WITH THE STORY OF THE IRISH PEOPLE
FROM THE EARLIEST PERIOD TO THE ADVENT OF
THE REFORMATION IN THE SIXTEENTH CENTURY

CHAPTER I

Prefatory—Territorial Divisions of Ireland—Physical Features of the Country—Peculiarities of Soil, Climate, and Scenery

THAT famous English Republican, Thomas Paine—whose political pamphlets have been admired quite as much as his theological works have been censured—uttered in "Common Sense," published in 1776, while he was serving under Washington in the Continental Army, this striking aphorism: "Europe, and not England, is the parent country of America." His object was to stimulate the patriotic pride of such American colonists—and they were many—as were not of English birth or descent, and to proclaim that the other great branches of the human race, settled in America, must, of necessity, have a vital interest in the successful issue of the War for Independence. No other great country of the world has a population made up of so many divers "previous nationalities," all combined into one gigantic political whole, as the United States of America. Most of the notable nations of the Old World are here represented not by hundreds or thousands, but by millions of citizens, "racy of the soil," and proud to call themselves Americans. A French patriot once said, speaking in the Chamber of Deputies: "There is no French race. France is a grand political entity which all true Frenchmen, of whatever race, worship." This fine sentiment can be even more

(3)

logically applied to America and Americans, for both are still in the formative period. Several centuries hence, perhaps, a race of people distinctively American in all respects may occupy this country, but while the great stream of European immigration continues to flow toward the setting sun there can not exist such a racial condition in this Republic, except in those remote districts in which the immigrant rarely seeks a home.

Most Americans have read something of the political misfortunes of Ireland, but very many among us have not made her history even a partial study, and have often taken their views of it, at second hand, from sources that could not fail to be partial and, therefore, prejudicial. We do not need to apologize for seeking to throw more light, in a simple yet comprehensive manner, on the history of that beautiful island the blood of whose exiled children flows in the veins of not less than 20,000,000 of the American people. The Irish race owes much to America, and America, in turn, owes much to it. Truly has it been said of the American Irish that they were with the Republic at its birth, guarded its infancy, rejoiced in its growth and prosperity, and will endure with it until the end, which comes, in the fulness of time, to even the greatest among nations. Thomas Francis Meagher (Mä'her or Marr)—the young Irish patriot and orator of 1848, and afterward a famous Union general of the Civil War—in one of the brilliant speeches he delivered in this country, said: "When, in 1849, I was a political captive on board an English battleship, I beheld, one bright morning, through the porthole of my cabin, while we were anchored in an Australian harbor, the Stars and

Stripes floating from the mast of a stately American frigate and hailed Liberty at my prison-gate!" And this is the sentiment of every honest immigrant who seeks the shelter of our flag.

Ireland, called poetically, because of its perennial verdure, the Emerald Isle, lies in the Atlantic Ocean, immediately westward of the larger island of Great Britain, from which it is separated by, in most parts, a wide and deep strait, varying in width from 14 miles, where the headlands of Antrim approach the western coast of Scotland, to about 125 miles, which is the maximum distance from the coast of England. This strait is called, running from north to south consecutively, the North Channel, the Irish Sea, and St. George's Channel. The high shore of Scotland is always visible, in clear weather, from the northeast coast of Ireland, and the mountains of Wales, about 65 miles distant, may be seen, under similar conditions, from Bray Head and other points on the Leinster coast, but no part of England can be seen at any time from the Irish shore. Ireland, considered geographically, is of an irregular rhomboidal shape, by some writers compared to an oblong shield, and is situated between Latitude 51° 26' and 55° 21' North, and Longitude 5° 21' and 10° 26' West, projecting farther into the Atlantic Ocean, to the westward, than any other portion of European soil. Its total area, including many small islands close to the coast, is about 32,500 square miles, or 19,000 less than England, 2,000 more than Scotland, 25,000 more than Wales, and nearly 2,000 less than our inland State of Indiana. Ireland would make, almost to a fraction, thirty-two States the size of Rhode Island, which has a Legislature of its own—a privilege the Green Isle does not, at present, enjoy.

The island is divided into four provinces—in ancient times it had five; namely, Leinster in the east, Ulster in the north, Connaught in the west, and Munster in the south. These are, again, divided into two-and-thirty counties—a system of Anglo-Norman, or English, invention, and, according to the learned Doctor Joyce, savant and historian, they generally represent the older native territories and sub-kingdoms. King John, "Lord" of Ireland, formed twelve of them in the twelfth century— Dublin, Kildare, Meath, Uriel (or Louth), Carlow, Kilkenny, Wexford, Waterford, Cork, Kerry, Limerick, and Tipperary. Henry VIII divided Meath proper into two counties and called one Westmeath. King's and Queen's Counties were formed in the reign of Mary I, who married Philip II of Spain, out of the old districts of Leix and Offaly. Hence their capitals are called, respectively, Philipstown and Maryborough. The county Longford was formed out of the territory of Annaly, by Deputy Sir Henry Sydney, about 1565. The same official divided Connaught into six counties—Galway, Mayo, Sligo, Roscommon, Leitrim, and Clare. The latter county, although situated on the Connaught bank of the river Shannon, was subsequently given to Munster, because it had formed a part of that province in ancient times. Antrim and Down were organized into counties early in the reign of Queen Elizabeth, and Lord Deputy Perrot, about 1584, formed seven others out of Ulster; namely, Armagh, Monaghan, Tyrone, Coleraine (now Derry), Donegal, Fermanagh, and Cavan. Dublin County, at first,

included Wicklow, but, in 1605, during the reign of
James I, Sir Arthur Chichester made the latter a separate county.

The existing division of the counties among the prov-
inces is as follows: Munster comprises Clare, Cork, Kerry,
Limerick, Tipperary, and Waterford; Ulster contains
Antrim, Armagh, Cavan, Donegal, Down, Fermanagh,
Derry, Monaghan, and Tyrone; Connaught has Galway,
Leitrim, Mayo, Roscommon, and Sligo; Leinster com-
prises Carlow, Dublin, Kildare, Kilkenny, King's County,
Longford, Louth, Meath, Queen's County, Westmeath,
Wexford, and Wicklow.

The reader ought to know, however, that a majority
of the Ulster and Connaught counties, and some in Leinster and Munster, did not recognize their English designations, or yield to English law, in any shape, until after
the accession of James I to the British throne, in 1603.
They were governed by their own princes, chiefs, and
judges, under the old Brehon law, until "the Peace of
Mellifont" in that year.

While the Irish counties differ very materially in extent, the provinces show the following proportions: Munster, 6,064,579 acres; Ulster, 5,475,458; Leinster, 4,871,-
118; Connaught, 4,392,043. The island is further subdivided into 316 baronies, 2,532 parishes, and 60,760
townlands, which average about 300 acres each. These
are figures with which every student of Irish history
should be familiar.

The country is, in general, very fertile, and grows
cereals luxuriantly. The green crops, such as turnips,
parsnips, cabbages, and kindred vegetables, are unex-

celled. Its grazing capacity is very great, and Irish
horses, horned cattle, sheep, and swine are among the
choicest in Europe. Apples, pears, plums, and the smaller
fruits grow abundantly in the mild, moist climate, but the
Irish sun will not ripen peaches, grapes, or tomatoes, unless they are under glass. Poultry thrive wondrously,
and there is a large exportation of fowl and eggs to the
British markets. Irish butter ranks high also. Yet the
country is poor, chiefly because of the scarcity of manufactures, and for other reasons that will be explained as
we proceed.

The Irish climate is equable, but, in general, damp,
when compared with that of America. Neither summer
heat nor winter cold produces discomfort, except at very
rare intervals. Violent storms are infrequent, except
along the western coast, and electrical disturbances are
much rarer than in our atmosphere. Only one cyclonic
storm, that of January 6, 1839, visited Ireland during the
nineteenth century, and it is known to this day as "the Big
Wind."

Irish scenery is peculiar in character—soft, yet bold of
outline, as regards its mountain regions. The cliffs on
the Connaught, Ulster, and Munster coasts are tall and
beetling—those of Moher, in Clare, and those that flank
the Giants' Causeway—a remarkable basaltic formation
in Antrim—being the most notable. All the elevations
that rise above a thousand feet are clothed with the
heather, which is also peculiar to Scotland, and this
plant changes its hue with every season so that
there is a constant shifting of color, which adds much
to the charm of the landscape. The Irish sky, too,

is changeful, so much so that an Irish poet, in paying tribute to the beauty of his wife, wrote:

"Eyes like the skies of dear Erin, our mother,
Where shadow and sunshine are chasing each other!"

Snow generally disappears from the summits of the Irish mountains about the second week of May. The mildness of the climate in a latitude so far toward the north is due to the powerful influence of the warm Gulf Stream, and this also explains the verdure of the country at almost all periods of the year. A striking characteristic of the Irish mountains is that they, in general, rise abruptly from the plain, which gives them an appearance of greater altitude than they really possess; the highest peak in the island—that of Carn Tual in Kerry—being only a trifle over 3,400 feet. There is still another peculiarity of the Irish mountain system which strikes all tourists—the highland chains, for the most part, rise near the coast, and follow its course, thus making it one of the boldest and grandest in Europe, while some detached groups, such as the Galtee and Slieve Bloom ranges in Munster and Leinster, the Curlews in Connaught and Slieve Snacht (Snowy range) in Ulster, seem to be independent formations.

The Irish lakes are numerous and, in general, picturesque. Lough Neagh (Nay) in the north, Lough Corrib in the west, and Lough Dearg—an expanse of the Shannon—are the largest, but the most famed for scenery are those of Killarney in Kerry, Lough Dan in Wicklow, and Lough Gill in Sligo. The Irish rivers are many, and, in the main, beautiful streams. The Shannon is the greatest river in the realm of Great Britain and Ireland, while the Suir, the Barrow, the Nore, the Slaney, the Corrib, the Erne, the Foyle, the Boyne, and the Liffey are also considerable rivers and possess enough waterpower, were it scientifically utilized, to turn the wheels of the world's machinery. The Munster Blackwater, celebrated, like its sister river, the Suir, in the charming poetry of Edmund Spenser, is called, because of its peculiar loveliness, "the Irish Rhine." After a winding and picturesque course through the south of Munster, it falls into the ocean at Youghal—a town of which the famous Sir Walter Raleigh, of Queen Elizabeth's Court, was once mayor.

One-seventh of the surface of Ireland is computed to be under bogs—semi-spongy formations, claimed by some naturalists to be the decomposed relics of mighty forests with which Ireland was covered in remote ages. The aspect of these "moors," as they are called by the British, is dreary enough in winter, but at other periods they have their charms; the heather and mosses with which they are, in many places, thickly clothed, changing hue, as on the mountains, with every season. Nearly all of these bogs are capable of being reclaimed for agricultural uses, but the people do not desire their reclamation, for the reason that they furnish cheap fuel to most of the rural districts, where there is neither coal nor timber supply. Owing to the mildness of the climate, the cut and dried sods of "peat," called "turf," which resemble brown bricks, take the place of coal and wood, and make quite a comfortable fire. "Stone turf," produced by artificial pressure, and an extra drying process, makes almost as hot a fire as anthracite, but is much dearer than the ordinary article, which is softer and lighter. Indeed, the common Irish turf would be almost useless in our fierce winter weather. These fuel "reservoirs" can not be exhausted for ages to come. It is claimed that, by some mysterious process of nature, they renew themselves from time to time, after they have been "given a rest" by the turf-cutters. Many large bogs occupy the summits and sides of the mountains, and seem to be of the same character as those on the level land. Occasionally the high morasses shift their positions, like glaciers, only with a much quicker movement, and overwhelm, like the avalanche, everything in their path. These are called "the moving bogs." The last phenomenon of the kind occurred in the County Kerry a few years ago, when much property was destroyed and several lives were lost. Scientists claim that these bogs are undermined by bodies of water, which, when flooded, lift the crust and carry it with them, in their effort to find their natural level. It is well known in Ireland that several small, but deep, lakes now occupy places that were formerly covered by these strange formations. We will devote a separate chapter to other features of this interesting country.

CHAPTER II

Further of the Characteristics and Resources of the Island—Present Form of Government

GOLD, silver, copper, lead, iron, and other malleable minerals are found in Ireland. The gold is discovered in small quantities, at least in modern times, but the beautiful ornaments, composed of that precious metal, and much used by the ancient Irish nobility, preserved in the Museum of the Royal Irish Academy, Dublin, and elsewhere in Ireland and Great Britain, would indicate that it was at one time plentiful in the island. Silver is found in paying quantities in several districts, and silver mines are now in operation in the northern portion of Munster. The lead, copper, and iron deposits have never been seriously worked, and, therefore, it is impossible to arrive at any satisfactory estimate of their extent. Coal is found in many counties, but the most extensive fields are in Ulster. Much light is thrown on this subject by Kane's "Resources of Ireland," which can be found, most likely, in the public libraries. It gives most interesting statistics, but they would be far too heavy for our more condensed narrative.

Ireland possesses over seventy harbors. Fourteen are of the first class and can shelter the very largest seagoing vessels, whether naval or mercantile. Unhappily, excepting those of Dublin, Cork, Limerick, and Belfast, they are comparatively little used for commerce, for reasons that will present themselves in succeeding chapters.

Although in olden times a thickly wooded country, Ireland of to-day is rather bare of forests. There are numerous luxuriant groves and woodlands, and many of the highroads are bordered with stately trees. The "quick-set hedges," planted with thorn shrubs, give, particularly in summer, a well-furnished appearance to the country, except in a few rather barren districts, where stone walls, as in portions of New England, are quite common. Irish farms are nearly all divided and subdivided by these formidable fences, quick-set or stone, so that, when viewed from any considerable height, the surrounding country looks like a huge, irregular checker-board—a much more picturesque arrangement of the landscape than our American barbed-wire obstructions, but at the cost of a vast amount of good land, in the aggregate.

The island contains many populous, finely built cities, well governed under local municipal rule. Dublin, the capital, contains, including suburbs, about 300,000 people, and is considered a very handsome metropolis. It is surrounded by enchanting hamlets, and the sea-bathing resorts in the neighborhood are delightful. Belfast, the great commercial city of Ulster, is almost as populous as Dublin, and has many of the thrifty characteristics of an American municipality. Cork, Waterford, Limerick, Galway, Sligo, Londonderry, and Drogheda are still places of much importance, although some of them have greatly declined, both in wealth and population, during the last century.

Owing to persistent agitation, and some fierce upris-

ings, which caused the imperial government to listen
to the voice of reason, the social and political conditions
of the Irish people have been somewhat improved of
late years. The Irish Church was disestablished by the
Gladstone Ministry, in 1869, and, under the leadership
of Isaac Butt, Parnell, Davitt, and other Irish patriots,
Protestant as well as Catholic, the harsh land laws have
been greatly modified, and the Irish people have a better
"hold on their soil," and are much less subject to the
capricious will of their landlords than formerly. They
are, also, much better lodged and fed than in the last
generation, and education, of a practical kind, has become almost universal. The national school system has
many features in common with our own, and is improv-
ing year by year. In the higher branches of education,
Ireland is well supplied. Trinity College, Dublin, the
Alma Mater of many celebrated men, has existed since
the reign of Queen Elizabeth, but, until the end of the
eighteenth century, was not open to Catholics. Maynooth College, in Kildare, is the great Catholic ecclesiastical seminary of Ireland, and there is also a Catholic
university in Dublin. Carlow, Kilkenny, Wexford, and
other cities have Catholic colleges, and there are Protestant seats of learning in Ulster and other provinces.
Cork, Belfast, and Galway have each branch universities, called "Queen's Colleges," which are conducted on
a non-sectarian basis. These are only a few of Ireland's
educational institutions, but they serve to illustrate the
agreeable fact that a dearth of opportunity for acquiring
learning is no longer a reproach to the Irish people, or,
rather, to their English law-makers. The taxes which sup-

port the institutions maintained by Government are paid by Ireland into the Imperial Treasury, so that Great Britain is not burdened by them, as many suppose. Recently, a commission appointed by the British Parliament to inquire into the financial relations between Great Britain and Ireland reported back that the latter country was overtaxed annually to the amount of $15,000,000. This grievance, although complained of by all classes, has not yet been redressed. Dublin, Belfast, and other leading Irish cities possess very choice and extensive libraries. That of Trinity College, in the first-mentioned city, is considered one of the best in Europe, and it is particularly rich in ancient Irish manuscripts, some of which have been translated from the original Gaelic into English by the late Dr. John O'Donovan, Professor Eugene O'Curry, and other Irish savants. There are many large circulating libraries in all the principal municipalities, and most of the smaller towns. These are patronized, in the main, by poor people of literary taste, who can not afford satisfactory libraries of their own. There is now a revival of Irish literature in Great Britain as well as in Ireland itself. Many English and Scotch firms have taken to printing Irish prose and poetry in the English tongue, so that Irish authors are no longer confined, as they were, with a few exceptions, of old, to an insular constituency. Irish literary work of merit, when not strongly patriotic, sells readily in Great Britain to-day. This is due, partly, to a growing appreciation of Irish talent among the more liberal classes of the English people, and still more, perhaps, to the very large Irish population that has developed itself on the soil of "the predominant partner" within the last half of the nineteenth century. There is a strong Chartist, or republican, element in England friendly to the Irish claim of legislative independence, and this element, which we hear comparatively little of in America, for reasons it is not necessary to discuss in this history, is growing more powerful as time rolls by, and some day, not very distant, perhaps, is bound to greatly modify the existing governmental system of the British Empire, and render it more popular.

Ireland is very rich in monastic and martial ruins. The round towers which sentinel the island are declared by many antiquaries to antedate the Christian period, and are supposed to have been pagan temples dedicated to the worship of the sun, which, some historians claim, was Ireland's chief form of the Druidic belief.

> "The names of their founders have vanished in the gloom,
> Like the dry branch in the fire, or the body in the tomb,
> But to-day, in the ray, their shadows still they cast—
> These temples of forgotten gods, these relics of the past."

The grass-grown circular raths, or "forts," as the peasantry call them, varying greatly in diameter, are supposed to be remnants of the Danish invasion, but many archæologists place them at a much earlier date, and give them not a Danish but a Danaan origin—the latter tribe being claimed as among the first settlers of Ireland. The largest "fort" or "dun" in the island is that near Downpatrick, which is sixty feet high and three-quarters of a mile in circumference. Much of the stately architecture seen in the ruins of abbeys, churches, and chapels belongs to the Anglo-Norman period, as does also the military architecture, which survives in such types as the keeps of Limerick, Nenagh, and Trim; but the Celtic type of church construction is preserved, after the lapse of more than a thousand years, in its primitive purity, at Glendalough in Wicklow, Clonmacnois in King's County, and Cong in Galway.

Three hundred years of warfare with the pagan Danes, and five hundred with the Anglo-Normans and Anglo-Saxons, made Ireland the Island of Ruins, as well as the Island of Saints and Scholars.

Before January 1, 1801, Ireland was a distinct and separate kingdom, having a Parliament of her own and connected with Great Britain by what has been called "the golden link of the crown." How that Parliament was, unfortunately for all concerned, abolished will appear in its proper order. Since 1801 Ireland has been governed by the Imperial Parliament, sitting in London, composed of representatives from England, Scotland, Ireland, and Wales—670 in all, of whom 103 are Irish members. Of these latter, 82 are Nationalists, or Repealers of the Act of Union, while 21 are Unionists, or adherents of the present political connection. The preponderating vote of Great Britain hopelessly overwhelms the Irish representation, and hence the work of reform, as far as Ireland is concerned, is slow and difficult. The executive functions are intrusted to a Lord Lieutenant, who is appointed by each succeeding Ministry, to represent the monarch of Great Britain. He is assisted in his duties by a Chief Secretary, two Under Secretaries, a Lord Chancellor, a Lord Chief Justice, a Master of the Rolls, a Chief Baron of the Exchequer, many less prominent officers, and a Privy Council, which comprises several of the officials mentioned, together with the leading supporters of the crown in the capital and throughout the country. Some of the official members of this Council are not natives of Ireland; and the Lord Lieutenant himself is almost invariably an English or Scotch aristocrat of high rank and liberal fortune. No Catholic can fill the office of Viceroy of Ireland. The authority of the latter is, to all intents and purposes, absolute. In seasons of political agitation, even when there is no violence, he can suspend the ordinary law without having recourse to Parliament. This power has been frequently exercised even in this generation. The Lord Lieutenant's official residence is Dublin Castle, but he has also a commodious viceregal lodge in the Phœnix Park. His salary is $100,-000 per annum—just twice that of our President—but, in general, he spends much more out of his private fortune, as he is, nearly always, chosen for his wealth as much as for his rank. When he goes among the people, he is, almost invariably, attended by a strong cavalry escort and a dashing staff of aides-de-camp, glittering in silver, steel, and gold. The military garrison of Dublin is strong, not often under 10,000 men, and at the Curragh Camp, about twenty miles distant, in Kildare, there is a much larger force. Most of the large towns are also heavily garrisoned. Thus, after an occupation, either nominal or actual, of seven and one-third centuries, England still finds it expedient to govern Ireland as a military district—a sad commentary on the chronic misgovernment of ages.

CHAPTER III

The Original Inhabitants of Ireland

VAGUE poetical tradition flings a mystical veil over
the origin of the earliest inhabitants of Ireland.
The historian, McGee, who would seem to have made a
serious study of the subject, says that the first account
given by the bards and the professional story-tellers attributes the settlement of the island to Parthalon of the
race of Japhet, who, with a number of followers, reached
it by way of the Mediterranean and Atlantic, "about
three hundred years after the Universal Deluge." The
colonists, because of the unnatural crimes of their leader,
were, we are told, "cut off to the last man by a dreadful
pestilence."

The second colony, also a creature of tradition, was
said to have been led by a chief called Nemedh from the
shores of the Black Sea across Muscovy to the Baltic,
and from that sea they made their way to the Irish
shore. In Ireland, they encountered a stronger race, said
to have been of African origin, called Formorians, with
whom they had many severe battles and were by them
finally defeated and either killed or driven from the
country, to which some of their descendants returned in
after years.

After Nemedh came the Firbolgs, or Belgæ, under the
five sons of their king, Dela, who divided the island into
five parts and held it undisputedly until the Tuatha de

Danaans, said to be descended from Nemedh, and having magical power to quell storms, invaded the island, carrying with them the "lia fail," or "Stone of Destiny," from which Ireland derived its fanciful title of "Innis fail," or the "Island of Destiny." The Danaans are said to have been of the Greek family. In any case, it is claimed, they subdued the Belgæ and made them their serfs. They ruled mightily, for a time, but, in turn, were compelled to give way to a stronger tide of invasion.

This was formed by a people who called themselves, according to most Irish annalists, Gaels, from an ancient ancestor; Milesians, from the appellation of their king, who ruled in distant Spain, and Scoti, or Scots, from Scota, the warlike mother of King Milesius. These Milesians are said to have come into Spain from the region of the Caucasus, and all agree that they were formidable warriors. Tradition says that Ireland was first discovered, as far as the Milesians were concerned, by Ith, uncle of the Spanish king, who, while on a voyage of exploration, sighted the island, and, attracted by its beauty, landed, but was attacked by the Danaans and mortally wounded. His followers carried him to his galley, and he died at sea, but the body was brought back to Spain. His son, Loci, who had accompanied Ith, summoned all the Milesian family to avenge their kinsman's death and conquer the Promised Island of their race. Milesius, or Miledh, had expired before Loci's return, but his sons, Heber the Fair, Amergin, Heber the Brown, Colpa, Ir, and Heremon rallied to the call of vengeance and conquest, set sail for Ireland, landed there, and, in spite of Danaan witchcraft and Firbolgian valor, beat down all opposition and became masters of the

beautiful island. Thomas Moore, in his immortal Irish
Melodies, thus deals with this legendary event:

> "They came from a land beyond the sea,
>   And now o'er the Western main,
> Set sail in their good ships gallantly
>   From the sunny land of Spain.
> 'Oh, where's the isle we've seen in dreams,
>   Our destined home or grave?'
> Thus sang they as, by the morning's beams,
>   They swept the Atlantic wave.
>
> "And, lo, where afar o'er ocean shines
>   A sparkle of radiant green,
> As though in that deep lay emerald mines
>   Whose light through the wave was seen.
> ''Tis Innisfail! 'tis Innisfail!'
>   Rings o'er the echoing sea,
> While bending to heaven the warriors hail
>   That home of the brave and free.
>
> "Then turned they unto the Eastern wave,
>   Where now their Day-God's eye
> A look of such sunny omen gave
>   As lighted up sea and sky,
> Nor frown was seen through sky or sea,
>   Nor tear on leaf or sod,
> When first on their Isle of Destiny
>   Our great forefathers trod."

The migration of those Celto-Iberians to Ireland is
generally placed at from 1500 to 2000 years before the
birth of Christ; but there is not much certainty about the
date; it stands wholly on tradition. On one point, at
least, a majority of Irish annalists seem to be agreed—
namely, that the Milesians were of Celtic stock and Scyth-
ian origin, but the route they took from Scythia to Spain,
as well as the date of their exodus, remains an unde-
termined question. Celtic characteristics, both mental
and physical, are still deeply stamped on the Irish peo-

ple, notwithstanding the large admixture of the blood of
other races, resulting from the numerous after invasions,
both pagan and Christian.   Thomas Davis, the leading
Irish national poet of the middle of the nineteenth century, sums up the elements that constitute the present
Irish population, truly and tersely, thus:

> "Here came the brown Phœnician,
>   The man of trade and toil;
> Here came the proud Milesian
>   A-hungering for spoil;
> And the Firbolg, and the Kymry,
>   And the hard, enduring Dane,
> And the iron lords of Normandy,
>   With the Saxons in their train.
>
> And, oh, it were a gallant deed
>   To show before mankind,
> How every race, and every creed,
>   Might be by love combined;
> Might be combined, yet not forget
>   The fountains whence they rose,
> As filled by many a rivulet
>   The stately Shannon flows!"

And the fine verses of the Irish poet may be applied
with almost equal propriety to the cosmopolitan population of the United States—more varied in race than
even that of Ireland.   No good citizen is less of an
American simply because he scorns to forget, or to allow his children to forget, "the fountains whence they
rose." Anglo-Americans never forget it, nor do Franco-
Americans, or Americans of Teutonic origin; or, in fact,
Americans of any noted race.   Americans of Irish birth
or origin have quite as good a right to be proud of their
cradle-land and their ancient ancestry as any other element in this Republic; and the study of impartial Irish

history by pupils of all races would do much to soften
prejudices and remove unpleasant impressions that slan-
derous, partial historians have been mainly instrumental
in creating.

The language—Gaelic, or Erse, as it is called in our
day—spoken by the Milesian conquerors of Ireland so
many thousand years ago, is not yet nearly extinct on
Irish soil; and it is often used by Irish emigrants in various parts of the world.   More than thirty centuries
have faded into eternity since first its soft, yet powerful,
accents were heard on Ireland's shore, but still nearly a
million people out of four and a half millions speak it, and
hundreds of thousands have more or less knowledge of
the venerable tongue in its written form.   Great efforts
have been put forth of late years to promote its propaga-
tion throughout the island, and it is a labor of love in
which all classes, creeds, and parties in Ireland cordially
work together.   It is not intended, of course, to supplant
the English language, but to render Gaelic co-equal with
it, as in Wales—a thoroughly Celtic country, in which the
native language—Kymric—has been wondrously revived
during the past and present century.

CHAPTER IV

The Religion of Ancient Ireland—Many Writers say it was Worship of the Sun, Moon, and Elements

WE have mentioned that sun-worship was one of the forms of ancient Irish paganism. There is much difference of opinion on this point, and the late learned Gaelic expert, Professor Eugene O'Curry, holds that there is no reliable proof of either sun-worship or fire-worship in antique Irish annals. On the other hand, we have the excellent historian, Abbé McGeoghegan, chaplain of the famous Franco-Irish Brigade of the seventeenth and eighteenth centuries, supported by other authorities, instancing the sun as, at least, one of the objects of Irish pagan adoration. Other writers, including the painstaking McGee, seem to accept the startling assertion that human victims were occasionally sacrificed on the pagan altars. This, however, is open to doubt, as the Irish people, however intense in their religious convictions, have never been deliberately cruel or murderously fanatical. We quote on these sensitive subjects— particularly sensitive where churchmen are concerned— from McGeoghegan and McGee, both strong, yet liberal, Catholic historians. On page 63 of his elaborate and admirable "History of Ireland," McGeoghegan remarks: "Great honors were paid to the Druids and Bards among the Milesians, as well as to those among the Britons and Gauls. The first, called Draoi in their language, performed the duties of priest, philosopher, legislator, and judge. Cæsar has given, in his Commentaries, a well-detailed account of the order, office, jurisdiction, and doctrine of the Druids among the Gauls. As priests, they regulated religion and its worship; according to their will, the objects of it were determined, and the 'divinity' often changed; to them, likewise, the education of youth was intrusted. Guided by the Druids, the Milesians generally adored Jupiter, Mars, Mercury, Apollo, the sun, moon, and wind; they had also their mountain, forest, and river gods. These divinities were common to them and to other nations of the world. . . . According to the Annals of Ulster, cited by Ware, the antiquarian, the usual oath of Laegore (Leary) II, King of Ireland, in the time of St. Patrick, was by the sun and wind."

McGee, writing of the same subject, on pages 5 and 9 of his "Popular History of Ireland," says: "The chief officers about the kings, in the first ages, were all filled by the Druids or pagan priests; the Brehons, or judges, were usually Druids, as were also the Bards, the historians of their patrons. Then came the Physicians, the Chiefs who paid tribute to or received annual gifts from the sovereign, the royal Stewards, and the military leaders, or Champions. . . . Their religion in pagan times was what the moderns call Druidism, but what they called it themselves we now know not. It was probably the same religion anciently professed by Tyre and Sidon, by Carthage and her colonies in Spain; the same religion which the Romans have described as existing in great part of Gaul, and, by their accounts, we learn the awful fact that it sanctioned, nay, demanded, human sacrifices. From the few traces of its doctrines which Christian zeal has permitted to survive in the old Irish language, we see that

Belus or Crom, the god of fire, typified by the sun, was its chief divinity—that two great festivals were held in his honor on days answering to the first of May and last of October. There were also particular gods of poets, champions, artificers, and mariners, just as among the Romans and Greeks. Sacred groves were dedicated to these gods; priests and priestesses devoted their lives to their service; the arms of the champion and the person of the king were charmed by them; neither peace nor war was made without their sanction; their own persons and their pupils were held sacred; the high place at the king's right hand and the best fruits of the earth and the water were theirs. Old age revered them, women worshiped them, warriors paid court to them, youth trembled before them, princes and chiefs regarded them as elder brethren. So numerous were they in Erin, and so celebrated, that the altars of Britain and Western Gaul, left desolate by the Roman legions, were often served by hierophants from Ireland, which, even in those pagan days, was known to all the Druidic countries as the Sacred Island."

The two greatest battles fought in Ireland during the early Milesian period were that near Tralee, in Kerry, where the Milesian queen-mother, Scota, perished, and the conflict at Taltean, in Meath, where the three Danaan kings, with their wives and warriors, were slain. After these events, Heber and Heremon divided Ireland between them, but eventually quarreled. A battle ensued, in which Heber fell, and Heremon was thereafter, for many years, undisputed monarch of all Ireland. A large majority of the Celtic families of the island are descended from the two royal brothers and bitter rivals. Their most famous Milesian successors in pagan times were

Tuathal (Too-hal), the Legitimate, who formed the royal province of Meath, which existed for many ages, and is now represented, but on a much smaller scale, by the modern counties of Meath and Westmeath. The province itself was dismembered centuries ago, and, since then, Ireland has had but four provincial divisions instead of five. Tuathal is also credited with having originated the Borumah (Boru) or "Cow Tribute," which he imposed on Leinster as a penalty for a crime committed against two of his daughters by the king of that province. This tribute was foredoomed to be a curse to the Irish nation at large, and its forceful imposition by successive Ard-Righs caused torrents of blood to be shed. It was abolished toward the end of the seventh century by the Christian king of all Ireland, Finacta II, surnamed the Hospitable. "Conn of the Hundred Battles" made a record as a ruler and a warrior. Cormac Mac-Art, because of his great wisdom, was called the Lycurgus of Ireland. Niall of the Nine Hostages—ancestor of the O'Neills—was a formidable monarch, who carried the terror of his arms far beyond the seas of Ireland. His nephew, King Dathi (Dahy) was also a royal rover, and, while making war in northern Italy, was killed by a thunderbolt in an alpine pass. Dathi was the last king of pagan Ireland, but not the last pagan king. His successor, Leary, son of the great Niall, received and protected St. Patrick, but never became a Christian. After Leary's death, no pagan monarch sat on the Irish throne.

Ancient Ireland was known by several names. The Greeks called it Iernis and Ierni; said to have meant "Sacred Isle"; the Romans Hibernia, the derivation and

meaning of which are involved in doubt, and the Milesians Innisfail, said to mean "the Island of Destiny,"
and Eire, or Erinn, now generally spelled Erin, said to
signify "the Land of the West." Many learned writers
dispute these translations, while others support them.
Within the last six centuries, the island has been known
as Ireland, said to signify West, or Western, land, but,
as the savants differ about this translation also, we will
refrain from positive assertion.

The Roman legions never trod on Irish soil, although
they conquered and occupied the neighboring island of
Britain, except on the extreme north, during four hundred years. Why the Romans did not attempt the conquest of the island is a mystery. That they were able
to conquer it can hardly be doubted. Strange as the
statement may seem to some, it was unfortunate for Ireland that the Romans did not invade and subdue it.
Had they landed and prevailed, their great governing
and organizing genius would have destroyed the disin-
tegrating Gaelic tribal system, which ultimately proved
the curse and bane of the Irish people. They would also
have trained a nation naturally warlike in the art of
arms, in which the Romans had no superiors and few
peers. With Roman training in war and government,
the Irish would have become invincible on their own
soil, after the inevitable withdrawal of the Legions from
the island, and the Anglo-Normans, centuries afterward,
could not have achieved even their partial subjection.

CHAPTER V

Advent of St. Patrick—His Wonderful Apostolic Career in Ireland
—A Captive and a Swineherd for Years, he Escapes and be-
comes the Regenerator of the Irish Nation

A MAJORITY of learned historians claim that Christianity was introduced into Ireland by Catholic missionaries from the continent of Europe long before the advent of the accepted national apostle, St. Patrick, who, in his boyhood, was captured on the northern coast of Ireland, while engaged in a predatory expedition with the Gauls, or some other foreign adventurers. In regard to this period of the future apostle's career, we are mainly guided by tradition, as the saint left no memoirs that would throw light on his first Irish experience. Such expeditions were not uncommon in the age in which he lived, nor were they for ages that followed. It seems certain that his captors offered him no bodily harm, and he was sent to herd swine amid the hills of Down. This inspired boy, destined to be one of the greatest among men and the saints of God, remained a prisoner in the hands of the pagan Irish—whom he found to be a generous, and naturally devotional, people—for many years, and thus acquired a thorough knowledge of their laws, language, and character. Whether he was finally released by them, or managed to escape, is a question of some dispute, but it is certain that he made his way back to Gaul—now known as France—which, according to many accounts, was his native land, although Scotland claims him also, and thence proceeded to Rome, where, having been ordained a priest, he obtained audience of Pope Celestine, and was by him encouraged and commissioned to convert the distant Irish nation to Christianity. Filled with a holy zeal, Patrick repaired as rapidly as possible to his field of labor, and, after suffering many checks and rude repulses, at last, about the year 432, found himself back in Ulster, where he fearlessly preached the Gospel to those among whom he had formerly lived as a serf, with miraculous success. Afterward, he proceeded to the royal province of Meath, and on the storied hill of Slane, "over against" that of Tara, where the Irish monarch, Leary, was holding court, lighted the sacred fire in defiance of the edict of the Druid high-priest, who worshiped the fires of Baal and forbade all others to be kindled, and, by its quenchless flame, flung the sacred symbol of the Cross against the midnight skies of pagan Ireland. The pagan king summoned the daring apostle to his presence, and asked him concerning his sacred mission. Patrick explained it, and, having obtained the royal consent, proceeded to preach with an eloquence that dazzled king, princes, chiefs, and warriors. He even captivated some of the Druid priests, but the high-priest, who dreaded the apostle's power of words, would have stopped him at the outset, had not King Leary extended to him his favor and protection, although he himself remained a pagan to the end of his life. The saint, having made a deep impression and converted many of high and low degree, took to baptizing the multitude, and tradition says that the beautiful river Boyne was the Jordan of Ireland's great apostle. It was while preaching at Tara that St. Patrick's presentation of the mystery of the Blessed Trinity was challenged by the Druid priests. He immediately stooped to the emerald sod, plucked therefrom a small trefoil plant called the shamrock—some say it was the wood sorrel—and, holding it up before the inquisitive and interested pagans, proved how possible it was to an infinite Power to combine three in one and one in three. Since that far-distant day, the shamrock has been recognized as the premier national symbol of Ireland, although the "sunburst" flag, emblematic of the Druidic worship, it is presumed, precedes it in point of antiquity. The harp, which is another of Ireland's symbols, was adopted at a later period, in recognition of her Bardic genius.

St. Patrick, or rather Patricius, his Roman name, which signifies a nobleman, lived and labored for many, many years after he preached at Tara, and made many circuits of the island, adding tribe after tribe to the great army of his converts. So deep was the impression he made in the country that now, after the lapse of fourteen hundred years, which were perioded by devastating wars and fearful religious and social persecutions, his memory is as green and as hallowed as if he had died but yesterday. Mountains, rivers, lakes, islands, and plains are associated with his name, and thousands of churches, in Ireland and throughout the world, are called after him, while millions of Ireland's sons are proud to answer to the glorious name of Patrick. He died at a patriarchal age, in the abbey of Saul, County Down, founded by himself, A.D. 493, and the anniversary of his departure from this life is celebrated by Irishmen of all creeds, and in every land, on each 17th day of March, which is called, in his honor, St. Patrick's Day.

It is no wonder that the Irish apostle is so well remembered and highly honored. Since the disciples preached by the shores of the Galilee, there has been no such conversion of almost an entire people from one form of belief to another. The Druid priests, with some exceptions, struggled long and bitterly against the rising tide of Christianity in Ireland, but, within the century following the death of the great missionary, the Druidic rites disappeared forever from the land, and "Green Erin" became known thenceforth, for centuries, as the Island of Saints. Romantic tradition attributes to St. Patrick the miracle of driving all venomous reptiles out of Ireland. It is certain, however, that neither snakes nor toads exist upon her soil, although both are found in the neighboring island of Great Britain.

According to Nennius, a British writer quoted by Dr. Geoffrey Keating, St. Patrick founded in Ireland "three hundred and fifty-five churches, and consecrated an equal number of bishops; and of priests, he ordained three thousand." "Let whomsoever may be surprised," says Dr. Keating, "at this great number of bishops in Ireland, contemporary with St. Patrick, read what St. Bernard says in his Life of St. Malachias, as to the practice in Ireland with regard to its bishops. He there says that 'the bishops are changed and multiplied at the will of the metropolitan, or archbishop, so that no single diocese is trusting to one, but almost every church has its own proper bishop.' " After this statement of St. Bernard no one can be astonished at the number of prelates mentioned above, for the Church was then in its young bloom. The number of bishops there mentioned will appear less wonderful on reading her domestic records. In them we find that every deaconry in Ireland was, formerly, presided over by a bishop. Irish annals show, also, that St. Patrick consecrated in Ireland two archbishops, namely, an archbishop of Armagh, as Primate of Ireland, and an archbishop of Cashel. After the great apostle's death, a long and illustrious line of native Irish missionaries took up his sacred work and completed his moral conquest of the Irish nation. Nor did their labors terminate with the needs of their own country. They penetrated to the remotest corners of Britain, which it is said they first converted to the Christian faith, and made holy pilgrimages to the continent of Europe, founding in every district they visited abbeys, monasteries, and universities. Ireland herself became for a long period the centre of knowledge and piety in insular Europe, and the ecclesiastical seminaries at Lismore, Bangor, Armagh, Clonmacnois, and other places attracted thousands of students, both native and alien, to her shores. Gaelic, the most ancient, it is claimed by many savants, of the Aryan tongues, was the national language, and continued so to be for more than a thousand years after the era of Patrick; but Latin, Greek, and Hebrew formed important parts of the collegiate curriculum, and the first-named tongue was the ordinary means of communication with the learned men of other countries.

The art of illuminated writing on vellum was carried to unrivaled perfection in the Irish colleges and monasteries, and the manuscripts of this class preserved in Dublin and London, facsimilies of which are now placed in many American public libraries, as well as in those of European universities, bear witness to the high state of civilization attained by the Irish people during the peaceful and prosperous centuries that followed the coming of St. Patrick and continued until the demoralizing Danish invasion of the eighth century.

The roll of the Irish saints of the early Christian period is a large one, and contains, among others, the names of St. Colomba, or Columbkill, St. Finn Barr, St. Brendan, the Navigator; St. Kieran, of Ossory; St. Kevin, of Glendalough; St. Colman, of Dromore; St. Canice, of Kilkenny; St. Jarlath, of Tuam; St. Moling, of Ferns; St. Comgall, of Bangor; St. Carthage, of Lismore; St. Finian, of Moville; St. Kiernan, of Clonmacnois; St. Laserian, of Leighlin; St. Fintan; St. Gall, the Apostle of the Swiss; St. Columbanus, the Apostle of Burgundy; St. Aidan, Apostle of Northumbria; St. Adamnan, Abbot of Iona; St. Rumold, Apostle of Brabant; St. Feargal, Bishop of Salzburg. These are only a few stars out of the almost countless galaxy of the holy men of ancient Ireland. Of her holy women, also numerous, the chief were St. Bridget, Brighid, or Bride, of Kildare; St. Monina, St. Ita, St. Syra, St. Dympna, and St. Samthan. The premier female saint was, undoubtedly, St. Bridget, which signifies, in old Gaelic, "a fiery dart." Modern slang often degrades the noble old name into "Biddy." Although thought to be a purely Irish appellation, it has been borne by, at least, two English women of note. The Lady Bridget Plantagenet, youngest daughter of King Edward IV, and "Mistress," or Miss, Bridget Cromwell, daughter of the Lord Protector of the English Commonwealth. Lady Plantagenet, who, in addition to being the daughter of a monarch, was the sister of Edward V and Elizabeth, Queen of Henry VII; the niece of Richard III and the aunt of Henry VIII, died a nun in the convent of

Dartford, England, long after the House of York had ceased to reign. "Mistress" Cromwell became the wife of one of her father's ablest partisans, and lived to see the end of the Protectorate, from which her brother, Richard, was deposed, and the restoration of the House of Stuart to the English throne.

CHAPTER VI

Ancient Laws and Government of the Irish

IRELAND, ages before she was Christianized, possessed a legal code of great merit, generally called the Brehon Laws. These remained more or less in force, from the earliest historic period down to the days of James I, who, because of the wars and conquests of the armies of his predecessor, Queen Elizabeth, was the first of the English monarchs that succeeded in thoroughly breaking up the old system of Irish law and government. The Brehon Laws were of Irish origin and contained many provisions more in harmony with humanity and wisdom than some of the boasted English enactments. In common with many other ancient countries of Europe, Ireland did not impose the death penalty on a homicide, but, instead, collected an eric, or blood fine, from him and his relatives, for the benefit of the family of the man slain by his hand. The best and briefest work on these interesting laws, which need more attention than they can be given in a general history, was recently issued by an English publishing house for the industrious author, Lawrence Ginnell, lawyer, of the Middle Temple, London. In writing of the ancient form of Irish monarchy, which, as we have already noted, was elective, Mr. Ginnell says: "The Irish always had a man, not an assembly, at the head of the state, and the system of electing a Tanist (heir-apparent) while the holder of the office was living, in addition to its making for peace on the demise of the Crown, made an interregnum of more rare occurrence than in countries which had not provided a Tanist in advance." The same author divides the classes of Irish kings thus: The lowest was the Righ-Inagh (Ree-eena) or king of one district, the people of which formed an organic state. Sometimes two or three of these, nearly related and having mutual interests, did not hesitate to combine for the public good under one king. The next in rank was the Righ-Mor-Tuah (Ree-More-Tooa), who ruled over a number of districts, and often had sub-kings under him. The next class of monarch was the Righ-Cuicidh (Ree-Cooga), a title which signified that he had five of the preceding class within his jurisdiction. This was the rank of a provincial king. And, highest of all, as his title implied, was the Ard-Righ (Ard-Ree), meaning High, or Over, King, who had his seat of government for many ages at the national palace and capital, established on the "royal hill of Tara" in Meath. The king of each district owed allegiance and tribute to the Righ-Mor-Tuah. The latter owed allegiance and tribute to the Righ-Cuicidh; and he, in turn, owed allegiance and tribute to the Ard-Righ.

Although the ancient Irish monarchy was, except where forceful usurpation occasionally prevailed, elective, the candidate for the Tanistry, or heir-apparency, was required to be of the "blood royal." Minors were seldom or never recognized as being eligible. At rare intervals one might win popular recognition by displaying a precocious wisdom, or prowess. The ablest and bravest male member of the reigning family was almost invariably chosen Ard-Righ, and the provincial and district rulers were chosen on the same principle. Meath was the High King's own province, and the lesser monarchs swayed over Ulster, Munster, Leinster, and Connaught, subsidiary to, yet in a measure independent of, the Ard-Righ, who held his court at Tara until A.D. 554, when St. Ruadan, because of sacrilege committed by the reigning monarch, Dermid, in dragging a prisoner from the saint's own sanctuary and killing him, pronounced a malediction on the royal hill and palaces. Thenceforth Tara ceased to be the residence of the Ard-Righs of Ireland, and total ruin speedily fell upon it. All that now remains of its legendary splendor is comprised in the fast vanishing· mounds on which once stood the palaces, assembly halls, and other public buildings of Ireland's ancient monarchs. No man or woman of Irish race can gaze unmoved on the venerable eminence, rising proudly still above the rich plains of Meath, which has beheld so many fast succeeding vicissitudes of a nation's rise, agony, and fall.

> "No more to chiefs and ladies bright
>   The harp of Tara swells;
> The chord alone which breaks at night
>   Its tale of ruin tells:
> Thus, Freedom now so seldom wakes,
>   The only throb she gives
> Is when some heart indignant breaks
>   To show that still she lives."

The most famous and powerful of the royal families of Ireland were the O'Neills of Ulster, who enjoyed the High Kingship longest of all; the O'Briens of Munster, the O'Conors of Connaught, the MacMurroughs of Leinster, and the McLaughlins of Meath. Their descendants are simply legion, for all the Irish clansmen were kindred to their kings and chiefs, and assumed, as was their blood right, their surnames when these came into fashion. When the Irish septs, about the end of the tenth century, by the direction of King Brian the Great, chose their family designations, the prefix "Mac" was taken as indicating the son, or some immediate descendant of the monarch, prince, or chief of that particular tribe, while that of "Ui" or "O," as it is now universally written in English, signified a grandson or some more remote kinsman of the original founder of the name. Thus, the families bearing the prefix "Mac" generally hold that they descend from the elder lines of the royal family, or the leading chiefs, while those who bear the "O" descend from the younger lines. And so it has come to be a national proverb, founded on more than mere fancy, that every Irishman is the descendant of a king. The Irish prefixes, however, are a genuine certificate of nobility, if by that term is meant long descent. An old rhyme puts the matter in homely but logical manner thus:

> "By 'Mac' and 'O' you'll surely know
> True Irishmen, they say;
> But if they lack both 'O' and 'Mac'
> No Irishmen are they."

Many families of Irish origin in this and other countries have foolishly dropped the Celtic prefixes from their names, and thus destroyed their best title to respectability. They should remember that "Mac" and "O" indicate a longer and nobler pedigree than

either Capet, Plantagenet, Tudor, Stuart, Guelph, or
Wettin—all distinguished enough in their way, but quite
modern when compared with the Gaelic patronymics.
The Scotch Highlanders, who are of the junior branch
of the Irish race, according to the most reliable historians, use the "Mac" very generally, while the "O" is
rarely found among them. On this account, as well as
others, some of the Scottish savants have attempted to
argue that Ireland was originally peopled by immigrants
from Scotland, but this argument is fallacious on its face,
because Ireland was known to the ancients as "Scotia
Major" — greater or older Scotland; while the latter
country was designated "Scotia Minor" — smaller or
younger Scotland. The Irish and Scotch were alike called
"Scots" until long after the time of St. Patrick, and the
kindred nations were close friends and helpful allies,
from the earliest historical period down to the reign of
Edward III of England, and even later. It was in Ireland that Robert Bruce, his brother Edward—afterward
elected and crowned king of that country—and their
few faithful retainers sought and found friends and a
refuge just before their final great victory at Bannockburn, A.D. 1314. Sir Walter Scott mentions this fact
in his graphic "Tales of a Grandfather," and also in his
stirring poem, "The Lord of the Isles." Keating quotes
Bede, who lived about 700 hundred years after Christ,
as saying in his "History of the Saxons," "Hibernia is
the proper fatherland of the Scoti" (Scots). So also
Calgravius, another ancient historian, who, in writing
of St. Columba, says: "Hibernia (Ireland) was anciently called Scotia, and from it sprang, and emigrated, the nation of the Scoti, which inhabits the part

of Albania (Scotland) that lies nearest to Great Britain (meaning England), and that has been since called Scotia from the fact."

"Marianus Scotus, an Alban (*i.e.* Scotch) writer," says Keating, "bears similar testimony in writing on the subject of St. Kilian. Here are his words: 'Although the part of Britannia which borders upon Anglia (England) and stretches toward the north, is at present distinctively called Scotia (Scotland), nevertheless, the Venerable Bede (already quoted) shows that Hibernia was formerly known by that name; for he informs us that the nation of the Picti (Picts) arrived in Hibernia from Scythia, and that they found there the nation of the Scoti.'

"Serapus, in certain remarks which he makes in writing about St. Bonifacius, is in perfect accord with the above cited writers. He says that 'Hibernia, likewise, claimed Scotia as one of her names, but, however, because a certain part of the Scotic nation emigrated from this same Hibernia and settled in those parts of Britannia in which the Picti were then dwelling, and was there called the nation of the Dal-Riada, from the name of its leader, as the Venerable Bede relates, and because this tribe afterward drove the Picti from their homes, and seized upon the entire northern region for themselves, and gave it the ancient name of their own race, so that the nation might remain undivided; in this manner has the name of Scotia become ambiguous—one, the elder, and proper, Scotia being in Hibernia, while the other, the more recent, lies in the northern part of Britannia.' From the words of the author I draw these conclusions: (1) that the Irish were, in strict truth, the real Scoti;

(2) that the Dal-Riada was the first race, dwelling in Scotland, to which the name of Scoti was applied; (3) that Ireland was the true, ancient Scotia, and that Alba (Scotland) was the New Scotia, and also that it was the Kinéscuit, or Tribe of Scot, that first called it Scotia."

There were numerous after invasions of Alba by the Milesian Irish, who established new colonies—the most formidable of which was that founded by the brothers Fergus, Andgus, and Lorne in the beginning of the sixth century. For nearly a hundred years this colony paid tribute to Ireland, but, in 574, the Scotch King Aedan, who was brother to the King of Leinster, declined to pay further tribute. A conference of the monarchs was held—all being close kindred of the Hy-Nial race—and St. Columba, their immortal cousin, came from his monastery in Iona to take counsel with them. The result was a wise and generous abrogation of the tribute by the Irish nation, and Scotland became independent, but remained, for long centuries, as before stated, the cordial friend and ally of her sister country. The Scots then became paramount in Scotia Minor, and brought under subjection all the tribes who were hostile to the royal line, founded by Fergus, from whom descended the Stuarts and other monarchical houses of Great Britain. This convention also lessened the number and power of the Bards, who had become arrogant and exacting in their demands upon the kings, princes, and chiefs, who feared their sarcastic talent, and paid exorbitant levies, rather than endure their abuse and ridicule.

After the abandonment of Tara as a royal residence, in the sixth century, the High Kings held court at Tailltenn, now Telltown, and Tlachtga, now the Hill of Ward, in Meath, and at Ushnagh (Usna) in Westmeath. The Ulster monarchs had seats at Emain, near Armagh (Ar'-ma') Greenan-Ely, on the hill of Ailech, in Donegal; and at Dun-Kiltair—still a striking ruin—near Downpatrick. The kings of Leinster had their palaces at Naas in Kildare, Dunlavin in Wicklow, Kells in Meath, and Dinnree, near Leighlin Bridge, in Catherlough (Carlow). The Munster rulers held high carnival, for ages, at Cashel of the Kings and Caher, in Tipperary; at Bruree and Treda-na-Rhee—still a most picturesque mound, showing the ancient Celtic method of fortification, in Limerick; and at Kinkora, situated on the right bank of the Shannon, in Clare. The O'Conors, kings of Connaught, had royal residences at Rathcroaghan (Crohan) and Ballintober—the latter founded by "Cathal Mor of the Wine Red Hand," in the thirteenth century—in the present county of Roscommon; and at Athunree, or Athenry—Anglice, "the Ford of the Kings," in Galway. Ballintober, according to tradition, was the finest royal residence in all Ireland, and the remains of Cathal Mor's castle are still pointed out in the vicinity of the town. It was to it Clarence Mangan alluded in his "Vision of Connaught in the Thirteenth Century," thus:

"Then saw I thrones and circling fires,
    And a dome rose near me as by a spell,
Whence flowed the tone of silver lyres
    And many voices in wreathèd swell.
        And their thrilling chime
        Fell on mine ears
Like the heavenly hymn of an angel band—
        'It is now the time
        We are in the years
Of Cathal Mor of the Wine Red Hand."

One of the great institutions of ancient Ireland, vouched for by Dr. Geoffrey Keating and many other learned historians, was the Fiann, or National Guard, of the country, first commanded by Finn MacCumhail (MacCool), "the Irish Cid" of pagan times. This force was popular and lived by hunting, when not actively engaged in warfare, to preserve internal government, or repel foreign aggression. When so engaged, they were quartered upon and supported by the people of the localities in which they rendered service. Their organization was simple, and bore much resemblance to the regimental and company formations of the present day. Their drill and discipline were excessively severe. Four injunctions were laid upon every person who entered this military order. The first was "to receive no portion with a wife, but to choose her for good manners and virtue." The second was "never to offer violence to any woman." The third enjoined on the member "never to give a refusal to any mortal for anything of which one was possessed." The fourth was "that no single warrior of their body should ever flee before nine champions."

Other stipulations were of a more drastic character. No member of the Fiann could allow his blood, if shed, to be avenged by any other person than himself, if he should survive to avenge; and his father, mother, relatives, and tribe had to renounce all claim for compensation for his death.

No member could be admitted until he became a Bard and had mastered the Twelve Books of Poesy.

No man could be allowed into the Fiann until a pit or trench deep enough to reach to his knees had been dug in the earth, and he had been placed therein, armed with his shield, and holding in his hand a hazel staff of the length of a warrior's arm.   Nine warriors, armed with nine javelins, were then set opposite him, at the distance of nine ridges; these had to cast their nine weapons at him all at once, and then, if he chanced to receive a single wound, in spite of his shield and staff, he was not admitted to the Order.

Another rule was that the candidate must run through a wood, at full speed, with his hair plaited, and with only the grace of a single tree between him and detailed pursuers.   If they came up with him, or wounded him, he was rejected.

He was also rejected "if his arms trembled in his hands"; or if, in running through the wood, "a single braid of his hair had been loosened out of its plait."

He was not admitted if, in his flight, his foot had broken a single withered branch.   Neither could he pass muster "unless he could jump over a branch of a tree as high as his forehead, and could stoop under one as low as his knee, through the agility of his body."   He was rejected, also, if he failed "to pluck a thorn out of his heel with his hand without stopping in his course." Each member, before being admitted to the Order, was obliged to swear fidelity and homage to the Righ-Fein-nedh (Ree-Feena) or king of the Fenians, which is the English translation of the title.

There were also other military bodies—not forgetting the more ancient "Red Branch Knights," whom Moore has immortalized in one of his finest lyrics, but the Fenians and their redoubtable chief hold the foremost place of fame in Irish national annals.

It would seem that a kind of loose federal compact existed, from time to time, between the High King and the other monarchs, but, unfortunately, there does not appear to have been a very strong or permanent bond of union, and this fatal defect in the Irish Constitution of pre-Norman times led to innumerable disputes about succession to the Ard-Righship and endless civil wars, which eventually wrecked the national strength and made the country the comparatively easy prey of adventurous and ambitious foreigners. The monarchical system was, in itself, faulty. Where a monarchy exists at all, the succession should be so regulated that the lineal heir, according to primogeniture, whether a minor or not, must succeed to the throne, except when the succession is, for some good and sufficient reason, set aside by the legislative body of the nation. This was done in England in the case of Henry IV, who, with the consent of Parliament, usurped the crown of Richard II; and also in the case of William and Mary, who were selected by the British Parliament of their day to supplant James II, the father-in-law and uncle of the former and father of the latter. The act of settlement and succession, passed in 1701, ignored the male line of the Stuarts, chiefly because it was Catholic, and placed the succession to the throne, failing issue of William and Mary and Anne, another daughter of the deposed King James, in a younger, Protestant branch of the female line of Stuart—the House of Hanover-Brunswick—which now wears the British crown. But, in general, as far as the question of monarchy is concerned, the direct system of succession has proven most satisfactory, and has frequently prevented confusion of title and consequent civil

war. We can recall only one highly important occasion
when it provoked that evil—the sanguinary thirty years'
feud between the kindred royal English, or, rather, Norman-French, Houses of York and Lancaster. Even in
that case the quarrel arose from the original bad title of
Henry IV, who was far from being the lineal heir to the
throne. Our own democratic system of choosing a chief
ruler is, no doubt, best of all. We elect from the body
of the people a President whose term of office is four
years. In some respects he has more executive power
than most hereditary monarchs, but if at the end of his
official term he fails to suit a majority of the delegates
of his party to the National Convention, some other
member of it is nominated in his stead. The opposition
party also nominates a candidate, and very often succeeds in defeating the standard-bearer of the party in
power. Sometimes there are three or more Presidential
candidates in the field, as was the case in 1860, when
Abraham Lincoln was elected. Succession to the Presi-
dency, therefore, is not confined to any one family, or
its branches, in a republic, and the office of President of
the United States may be competed for by any eligible
male citizen who can control his party nomination. The
example of Washington, who refused a third term, has
become an unwritten law in America, and it defeated
General Grant's aspiration to succeed Mr. Hayes in the
Republican National Convention of 1880. In France,
under Napoleon, every French soldier was supposed to
carry a marshal's baton in his knapsack. In the United
States, every native-born schoolboy carries the Presidential portfolio in his satchel.

CHAPTER VII

Period of Danish Invasion

THE Irish people, having settled down to the Christian form of worship, were enjoying "life, liberty, and the pursuit of happiness," building churches and colleges, and sending out a stream of saints and scholars to the rest of Europe, when, about the end of the eighth century, the restless Norsemen, universally called "Danes" in Ireland, swept down in their galleys by thousands on the Irish coasts, and, after many fierce conflicts, succeeded in establishing colonies at the mouths of many of the great rivers of the island. There they built fortified towns, from which they were able to sally forth by sea or land to change their base of operations and establish new conquests. Dublin at the mouth of the Liffey, Drogheda at the mouth of the Boyne, Wexford at the mouth of the Slaney, Waterford at the mouth of the Suir, and Limerick at the estuary of the Shannon, are all cities founded by the Danes, who were natural traders and fierce warriors. They did not confine their attentions exclusively to Ireland, but, about the same period, conquered Saxon England, ruling completely over it; and they established a strong colony on the north coast of France, which is called Normandy to this day, and from which sprang, by a combination of Scandian with Gallic blood, the greatest race of warriors —the Romans, perhaps, excepted—the world has known.

The native Irish met their fierce invaders with daunt-

less courage, but they had been so long at peace that
they were no longer expert in the use of arms, and the
Danes were all-powerful on the seas. Those Norsemen
were pagans, and had no respect for revealed religion,
literature, works of art, architecture, or, in short, anything except land-grabbing and plunder. It must be remembered that most of northern Europe, at the period
written of, was in a benighted state, and that Great Britain itself was barely emerging from the intellectual and
spiritual gloom of the Dark Ages. The Norse invaders,
whenever successful in their enterprises against the Irish
chiefs, invariably demolished the churches and colleges,
murdered the priests, monks, and nuns—often, however,
carrying the latter into captivity—and burned many of
the priceless manuscripts, the pride and the glory of the
illustrious scholarship of ancient Ireland. In the middle
portion of the ninth century—about 840—when Nial III
was Ard-Righ of Ireland, came the fierce Dane Turgesius,
at the head of an immense fleet and army. He at once
proceeded to ravage the exposed portions of the coast,
and then forced his way inland, laying the country under
tribute of all kinds as he advanced. He made prisoners
of Irish virgins and married them, by main force, to his
barbarous chiefs. He even occupied the celebrated monastery of Clonmacnois and its university as a headquarters, converted the great altar into a throne, and issued
his murderous edicts from that holy spot. Clonmacnois,
translated into English, means "the Retreat of the Sons
of the Noble," and was the Alma Mater of the princes
and nobility of Ireland. This crowning outrage, coupled
with insults offered to Irish ladies, finally aroused the
spirit of burning vengeance in the breasts of the Irish

people. Tradition says that thirty handsome young men, disguised as maidens, attended a feast given at Clonmacnois by Turgesius and his chiefs. When the barbarians were sated and had fallen into a drunken stupor, the youths rose upon and slew them all. The body of Turgesius, with a millstone tied around the neck, was thrown into a neighboring lake. Then the nation, under the brave Nial III, rose and drove the Norsemen back to the seacoast, where they rallied. Another raid on the interior of the island was attempted, but repelled. Sad to relate, the gallant King Nial, while attempting to save the life of a retainer who fell into the Callan River, was himself drowned, to the great grief of all Ireland. The name of the river in which he perished was changed to the Ownarigh (Ownaree) or King's River—a designation which, after the lapse of ages, it still retains.

A period of comparative repose followed. Many of the Danes became converts to Christian doctrine, and there was, probably, more or less of intermarriage among the higher classes of the rival races. But the Norsemen retained much of their old-time ferocity, and, occasionally, the ancient struggle for supremacy was renewed, with varying success. It is humiliating for an Irish writer to be obliged to admit that some of the Irish Christian princes, jealous of the incumbent Ard-Righ, did not remain faithful to their country, and actually allied themselves with the Danes, participating in their barbarous acts. This explains why, for a period of about three hundred years, in spite of repeated Irish victories, the Norsemen were able to hold for themselves a large portion of Ireland, especially the districts lying close to the sea, where they had no difficulty in receiving supplies and reinforcements from Denmark and Norway. Many of those old Irish princes were, indeed, conscienceless traitors, but the people, as a whole, never abandoned the national cause.

The feuds of the Munster chiefs, toward the end of the tenth century, had the unlooked for effect of bringing to the front the greatest ruler and warrior produced by ancient Ireland. Because of a series of tragedies in which the hero himself bore no blameful part, Brian of Kinkora, son of Kennedy and brother of Mahon, both of whom had reigned as kings of Thomond, or North Munster, ascended the throne of that province. Mahon, progenitor of the southern MacMahons—from whom descended the late President of the French Republic, Maurice Patrice MacMahon, Marshal of France and Duke of Magenta—was murdered by Prince Donovan, a faithless ally. His younger brother, Brian, afterward called Borumah or "Boru"—literally, "Brian of the Cow Tribute"—fiercely avenged his assassination on the treacherous Donovan, and on the Danish settlers of Limerick, who were the confederates of that criminal in his evil acts. Brian, young, powerful, and destitute of fear, after disposing of Donovan, killed with his own brave hand Ivor, the Danish prince, together with his two sons, although these fierce pagans had taken refuge in the Christian sanctuary on Scattery Island, in the Shannon, and then swept the remaining conspirators, both Irish and Danes, off the face of the earth. Prince Murrough, Brian's heir, then a mere boy, slew in single combat the villanous chief, Molloy, who, as the base instrument of Donovan and Ivor, actually killed his uncle, King Mahon. Afterward, Brian reigned for a brief period, quietly, as

King of Thomond. He had a profound insight and well knew that only a strong, centralized government could unite all Ireland against the foreigners, and he designed to be the head of such a government. He had only one rival in fame and ability on Irish soil—the reigning Ard-Righ, Malachy II. This monarch had scourged the warrior Northmen in many bloody campaigns. In one battle he slew two Danish princes, and took from one a golden collar, and from the other a priceless sword. The poet Moore commemorates the former exploit in the well-known melody, "Let Erin Remember the Days of Old."

Brian of Kinkora, fiery of mood, enterprising, ambitious, and, we fear, somewhat unscrupulous in pursuit of sovereignty, a born general and diplomat, as either capacity might suit his purpose, burned to possess himself of the supreme sceptre. His ambition led, as usual under such conditions, to acts of aggression on his part, and, finally, to civil war between Malachy and himself. A terrible struggle raged in Ireland for twenty years, until, at last, Ard-Righ Malachy was forced to capitulate, and his rival became High King of Ireland in his place. The Danes, naturally, took advantage of the civil strife to re-establish their sway in the island, and gained many advantages over the Irish troops. Moved by the danger of his country, the noble Malachy allied himself with Brian, and, together, they marched against the Norsemen and drove them back to their seacoast forts. But those bold and restless spirits did not, therefore, cease to war upon Ireland. Again and yet again they placed new armies in the field, only to be again baffled and routed by either the skilful Brian or the devoted Malachy.

CHAPTER VIII

Battle of Clontarf, A.D., 1014—Total Overthrow of the Danish Army
and Power in Ireland

MANY of the princes of Leinster, more especially
the MacMurroughs (MacMurro) were generally,
in some measure, allied to the Danes, and fought with
them against their own countrymen. After several years
of warfare, a peace was, at length, patched up with the
MacMurrough, and he became a guest of King Brian at
Kinkora. In those days chess was the national game
of the Irish princes and chiefs, and while engaged in it
with the Leinster guest, Prince Murrough (Murro),
Brian's eldest son, in a fit of anger, hurled a taunt at the
former in regard to his recent alliance with the invaders
of his country. This action was, of course, rude, and
even brutal, on the part of Prince Murrough, although
MacMurrough had been guilty of treasonable offences.
The Leinster potentate rose immediately from the table
at which they were playing, pale from rage, and, in a
loud voice, called for his horse and retainers. He was
obeyed at once and left the palace. The wise King Brian,
on learning of the quarrel and departure, sent messengers
after the King of Leinster to bring him back, but his
anger was so great that he would not listen to their representations, so that they went back without him to Kinkora. MacMurrough immediately re-allied himself with
the Danes, and so the flames of war were rekindled with a
vengeance. Many other princes and chiefs of Leinster

made common cause with their king and his foreign allies. Reinforcements for the latter poured into Ireland from Scandinavia, from Britain, from the neighboring islands, from every spot of earth on which an invader could be mustered—all inflamed against Ireland, and all expecting to wipe King Brian and his army from the Irish soil. But Brian had his allies, too; the armies of Munster, Connaught, part of Ulster, and most of the heroic clans of Leinster flocked to his standard, the latter led by the ever-faithful Malachy and his tributary chiefs. All of the MacMurrough interest, as already stated, sided with the Danes. A majority of the Ulster princes, jealous of Brian's fame and supreme power, held back from his support, but did not join the common enemy.

Brian was now an old man, and even his bold son, Murrough, the primary cause of the new trouble, was beyond middle age. The hostile armies hurried toward Dublin, the principal Danish stronghold, and on Good Friday morning, April 23, 1014, were face to face on the sands of Clontarf, which slope down to Dublin Bay. We have no correct account of the numbers engaged, but there were, probably, not less than thirty thousand men —large armies for those remote days—on each side. It was a long and a terrible battle, for each army appeared determined to conquer or die. Under King Brian commanded Prince Murrough and his five brothers: Malachy, Kian, Prince of Desmond, or South Munster; Davoren, of the same province; O'Kelly, Prince of Hy-Many, East Connaught; O'Heyne, the Prince of Dalaradia, and the Stewards of Mar and Lennox in Scotland.

The Danes and their allies were commanded by Brodar, the chief admiral of the Danish fleet; King Sitric, of

Dublin;* the Danish captains, Sigurd and Duvgall, and the warrior Norwegian chiefs, Carlos and Anrud. The Lord of the Orkney Islands also led a contingent, in which Welsh and Cornish auxiliaries figured.

Thus, it will seem, the cause was one of moment, as the fate of a country was to be decided, and the ablest captains of Ireland and Scandinavia led the van of the respective hosts. The struggle was long and murderous, for the armies fought hand to hand. Brian, too feeble to sit his war-horse and bear the weight of even his light armor, worn out, moreover, by the long march and the marshaling of his forces, was prevailed upon to retire to his pavilion and rest. He placed the active command of the Irish army in the hands of King Malachy and his son, Prince Murrough O'Brien. The conflict lasted from daylight until near the setting of the sun. Every leader of note on the Danish side, except Brodar, was killed—many by the strong hand of Prince Murrough and his brave young son, Turlough O'Brien, after his father the person most likely to be elected to the chief kingship of Ireland. On the Irish side there fell Prince Murrough, his gallant son, the Scottish chiefs of Mar and Lennox, who came, with their power, to fight for Ireland, and many other leaders of renown. King Brian himself, while at prayer in his tent, which stood apart and unguarded, was killed by Brodar, the flying Danish admiral, who was pursued and put to death by a party of Irish soldiers.

The slaughter of the minor officers and private men, on both sides, was immense, and the little river Tolka, on the banks of which the main battle was fought, was

---

* Sitric, according to some writers, was not in the battle.

choked with dead bodies and ran red with blood. But
the Danes and their allies were completely broken and
routed, and the raven of Denmark never again soared
to victory in the Irish sky. Many Danes remained in
the Irish seaport towns, but they became Irish in dress,
language, and feeling, and thousands of their descendants are among the best of Irishmen to-day.

Ireland, although so signally victorious at Clontarf, sustained what proved to be a deadly blow in the loss of her
aged king and his two immediate heirs. Brian, himself,
unwittingly opened the door of discord when he took the
crown forcibly from the Hy-Niall family, which had worn
it so long. His aim was to establish a supreme and per-
petual Dalcassian dynasty in himself and his descendants
—a wise idea for those times, but one balked by destiny.
Now all the provincial Irish monarchs aspired to the supreme power, and this caused no end of jealousy and
intrigue. Brian, in his day of pride, had been hard on
the Ossorians, and their chief, Fitzpatrick, Prince of
Ossory, basely visited his wrath, as an ally of the Danes,
on the Dalcassian contingent of the Irish army returning
from Clontarf encumbered by their wounded. But these
dauntless warriors did not for a moment flinch. The
hale stood gallantly to their arms, and the wounded, unable to stand upright, demanded to be tied to stakes placed
in the ground, and thus supported they fought with magnificent desperation. The treacherous Ossorian prince
was routed, as he deserved to be, and has left behind
a name of infamy. Many noble patriots of the house of
Fitzpatrick have since arisen and passed away, but that
particular traitor ranks with Iscariot, MacMurrough,
Monteith, and Arnold in the annals of treachery. Who

that has read them has not been thrilled by the noble lines
of Moore which describe the sacrifice of the wounded
Dalcassians?

> "Forget not our wounded companions who stood
>   In the day of distress by our side;
> When the moss of the valley grew red with their blood
>   They stirred not, but conquered and died!
> That sun which now blesses our arms with his light,—
>   Saw them fall upon Ossory's plain,
> O! let him not blush when he leaves us to-night
>   To find that they fell there in vain."

The glorious King Malachy, although ever in the
thickest of the battle, survived the carnage of Clontarf.
Unable to agree upon a candidate from any of the provincial royal families because of their bitter rivalries,
the various factions, having confidence in Malachy's wisdom and patriotism, again elected him High King of
Ireland, the last man who held that title without dispute.
He reigned but eight years after his second elevation to
the supreme throne of his country and died at a good
old age about the middle of September, 1022, in the
odor of sanctity, and sincerely lamented by the Irish
nation, excepting a few ambitious princes who coveted
the crown his acts had glorified. In the whole range of
Irish history he was the noblest royal character, and his
name deserves to be forever honored by the nation he
sought to preserve.

After the good king's death, a younger son of Brian
Boru, Prince Donough (Dunna), made an attempt to be
elected Ard-Righ, and, failing in that, sought to hold
the crown by force. But the provincial monarchs refused
to recognize his claims, as he did not appear to inherit
either the military prowess or force of character of his

great father. After some futile attempts to maintain his assumed authority, he was finally deposed by his abler nephew, Turlough O'Brien, who occupied the throne, not without violent opposition, for a period. Poor Donough proceeded to Rome and presented his father's crown and harp to the Pope, probably because he had no other valuable offerings to bestow. This circumstance was afterward made use of by the Anglo-Normans to make it appear that the presentation made by the deposed and discredited Donough to the Pontiff carried with it the surrender of the sovereignty of Ireland to his Holiness. No argument could be more absurd, because, as has been shown, the crown of Ireland was elective, not hereditary, except with well understood limitations, which made the blood royal a necessity in any candidate. Donough, in any case, was never acknowledged as High King of Ireland, and could not transfer a title he did not possess. In fact all the Irish monarchs may be best described not as Kings of Ireland, but Kings of the Irish. They had no power to alienate, or transfer, the tribe lands from the people, and held them only in trust for their voluntary subjects. Modern Irish landlordism is founded on the feudal, not the tribal, system. Hence its unfitness to satisfy a people in whom lingers the heredity of the ancient Celtic custom. King Brian, the most absolute of all the Irish rulers, is described by some annalists as "Emperor of the Irish."

CHAPTER IX

Desolating Civil Wars Among the Irish

FROM the deposition of Donough O'Brien down to the period of the Norman invasion of the island—about a century and a half—Ireland was cursed by the civil wars which raged interminably, because of disputes of royal succession, between the McLoughlins of Ulster —a branch of the Hy-Niall dynasty—and the descendants of King Brian of Kinkora, in which the latter were finally worsted. Then the successful family fell out with royal O'Conors of Connaught. One of the latter, a brave and ambitious man, called Turlough Mor, aimed at the chief sovereignty and proved himself an able general and a wise statesman. He reigned in splendor over Connaught, and terrorized his enemies of Ulster and Munster by his splendid feats of arms. He held his court at Rathcroghan, in Roscommon, and often entertained as many as 3,000 guests on occasions of festival. His palace, fortified after the circular Celtic fashion, dominated more than four hundred forts, or duns, which were the strongholds of his chiefs, in the territory of Roscommon alone; he founded churches and was generous to the clergy and to the poor. In spite of all this, however, he was unable to attain to the High Kingship, and only succeeded in paving the way to the national throne for his son and successor, Rory, commonly called Roderick, O'Conor, whose reign was destined to behold the Anglo-Normans in Ireland. Dr. Joyce, in dealing with this troubled period of Irish history, says that during the one hundred and fifty years comprised in it, there were eight Ard-Righs "with opposition"—that is, some one of the provinces, perhaps more, would refuse to recognize their jurisdiction. There was also chaos among the minor royal families. As regarded the High King, it was not unusual to have two of them using that title at once, as was the case with Donal O'Loughlin, King of Ulster, and Murtough O'Brien, King of Munster. Both these claimants terminated their careers in monasteries. A similar condition existed, also, between Turlough Mor O'Conor, before mentioned, and Murtough O'Loughlin, King of Ulster, and the strife was only ended by the death of Turlough Mor, in 1156. His son, Roderick, then attempted to wrest the Ard-Righship from the Ulster monarch, but was defeated. On the death of the latter, in 1166, Roderick, who was not opposed by any candidate of influence, was elected High King—the last of the title who reigned over all Ireland.

It may be asked, why did not the clansmen—the rank and file of the Irish people—put a stop to the insane feuds of their kings, princes, and chiefs? Because, we answer, they were accustomed to the tribal system and idea. Doubtless, they loved Ireland, in a general way, but were much more attached to their family tribe-land, and, above all, they adored the head of their sept and followed where he led, asking no questions as to the ethics of his cause. Had they been more enlightened regarding the art of government, they might have combined against their selfish leaders and crushed them. But the tribal curse was upon them, and is not yet entirely lifted.

The Danes held the crown of England for about a quarter of a century after they were driven from power in Ireland. At last, after great difficulty, they were driven from the throne and the saintly Edward the Confessor, of the old Saxon line, was raised to the kingship of England. His successor, King Harold—a brave but, we fear, not a very wise man—is said by English historians to have "done homage"—an evil custom of those days—to William, Duke of Normandy, while on a visit to that country. At all events, William claimed the crown, which Harold, very properly, declined to surrender. William was an able and resolute, but fierce and cruel, warrior. He speedily organized a force of 60,000 mercenaries, mainly French-Normans, but with thousands of real Frenchmen among them, and, having provided himself with an immense flotilla—a wondrous achievement in that age of the world—succeeded in throwing his entire force on the English coast. Harold, nothing daunted, met him on a heath near Hastings, in Sussex, where the Saxon army had strongly intrenched itself, and would, perhaps, have been victorious had not it abandoned its position to pursue the fleeing Normans, who, with their accustomed martial skill, turned upon their disordered pursuers and repulsed them in return. The centre of the great conflict is marked by the ruins of Battle Abbey. The two armies were about equal in strength and fought the whole length of an October day before the combat was decided. Prodigies of valor were performed, but, at last, the brave Harold fell, and the remains of the Saxon army fled from that fatal field. William, soon afterward, occupied London. The Saxons made but small show of resistance, after Hastings, and, within a few years, "fair England" was parceled out among William's Norman-French captains, who thus laid the foundation of the baronial fabric that, with one brief interval, has dominated England ever since. A few of the Saxon nobles managed, somehow, to save their domains—probably by swearing allegiance to William and marrying their lovely daughters to his chiefs—but, as a whole, the Saxon people became the serfs of the Norman barons, and were scarcely recognized even as subjects, until the long and bloody wars with France, in the thirteenth, fourteenth, and fifteenth centuries, made them necessary, in a military sense, to the Plantagenet kings, who employed them chiefly as archers. Under Norman training, their skill with the deadly long bow made them perhaps the most formidable infantry of the Middle Ages.

The Normans in England, very wisely, accommodated themselves to the new conditions and made up their minds to live upon and enjoy the lands they had won by the sword. They rapidly became more English than Norman, and after the accession of the House of Anjou to the throne, in the person of Henry II, began to call themselves "Englishmen." Sir Walter Scott, in his noble historical romance of "Ivanhoe,". draws a splendidly vivid picture of that period.

In Ireland, as we have seen, the series of distracting civil wars, all growing out of questions of succession to the national and provincial thrones, still progressed, and, owing to the unceasing discord, prosperity waned, and some historians claim that Church discipline was relaxed, although not to any such extent as is asserted by the Norman chroniclers. But the reigning Pontiff, hearing of the trouble, summoned some of the leading hierarchs of the Irish Church to Rome, where they explained matters satisfactorily.

About the time that Henry II, in virtue of his descent from the Conqueror, through his mother, daughter of Henry I, assumed the English crown, the Papal chair was occupied by Adrian the Fourth, whose worldly name was Nicholas Breakspeare, an Englishman by birth, and the only man of that nationality who ever wore the tiara. He, too, had been informed by Norman agents of the disorders in Ireland, where, among other things, it was claimed that the people in general had neglected to pay to the Papacy the slight tribute known as "Peter's Pence." This circumstance, no doubt, irritated the Pontiff, and when Henry, who had his ambitious heart set on acquiring the sovereignty of Ireland, laid open his design, Pope Adrian, according to credible authority, gave him a document called a "bull," in which, it would appear, he undertook to "bestow" Ireland on the English king, with the understanding that he should do his utmost to reform the evils in Church and State said to exist in that country, and also compel the regular payment of the Papal tribute. All of which Henry agreed to do.

CHAPTER X

The Norman-Welsh Invasion of Ireland—Their Landing in Wexford

POPE ADRIAN'S "gift" of Ireland to Henry II, absurd as it may appear in this age, was not without precedent in the Middle Ages, when the Roman Pontiff was regarded as supreme arbiter by nearly all of Christendom. Such "gifts" had been made before the time of Adrian, and some afterward, but they were not considered bona fide by the countries involved. So also with the Irish people as a majority. They respected, as they still respect, the Pope in his spiritual capacity, but rightly conceived that he had no power whatever to make a present of their country to any potentate, whether native or alien, without their consent. An influential minority held otherwise, with most unfortunate results, as we shall see. Some superzealous Catholic writers have sought to discredit the existence of the "bull" of Adrian, but weight of evidence is against them, and, in any case, it was "confirmed," at Henry's urgent request, by Pope Alexander III. The king was engaged in civil war with his own sons—in every way worthy of their rapacious father—during most of his reign, for he held under his sway Normandy, Aquitaine, and other parts of France, which they wanted for themselves. Thus no chance to push his long meditated Irish scheme presented itself until about A. D. 1168. Fifteen years prior to that date, Dermid, or Dermot, MacMurrough

(Mac Murro), King of Leinster, a very base and dissolute ruler, had carried off the wife of O'Ruarc, Prince of Breffni, while the latter was absent on a pious pilgrimage. The lady was a willing victim, and added the dowry she brought her husband to the treasure of her paramour. When Breffni returned to his castle and found that his wife had betrayed him, he was overpowered by grief and anger, and, not having sufficient military force himself to punish his enemy, he called on Turlough Mor O'Conor, then titular Ard-Righ, to assist him in chastising MacMurrough. O'Conor did so to such purpose that, according to Irish annals, Dervorgilla, which was the name of O'Ruarc's wife, together with her dowry, was restored to her husband, who, however, discarded her, and she died penitent, it is said, forty years afterward in the cloisters of Mellifont Abbey. But Dermid's evil conduct did not end with his outrage against O'Ruarc. He entertained the most deadly animosity to the O'Conor family on account of the punishment inflicted on him by Turlough Mor, and when on the death in battle of Ard-Righ Murtagh McLaughlin, Roderick, son of Turlough Mor, claimed the national crown, MacMurrough refused him recognition, although nearly all the other sub-kings had acknowledged him as supreme ruler of Ireland. Incensed at his stubbornness, King Roderick, who had with him O'Ruarc and other princes of Connaught, marched against Dermid, who, seeing that he was overmatched, burned his palace of Ferns, and, taking to his galley, crossed the Irish Sea to England and sought out King Henry II at his Court of London. On arriving there he was informed that the king was in Aquitaine, and thither he at once proceeded. The politic founder of the Plantagenet dynasty received him quite graciously and listened complacently to his story. Henry was secretly well pleased with the treasonable errand of his infamous guest, which was to demand Anglo-Norman aid against his own monarch, regardless of the after consequences to the fortunes of his country. He enumerated his grievances at the hands of the O'Conors, father and son, and related how he had been the faithful ally of the former in his long war with one of the Thomond O'Briens. Turlough Mor, he considered, had treated him badly for the sake of O'Ruarc, and his son, Roderick, had been quite as hostile, forcing him to seek Henry's protection against further invasion of his hereditary patrimony. The Anglo-Norman king said, in reply, that he could not aid MacMurrough in person as he was then engaged in a war with one or more of his own sons, but he consented to give him commendatory letters to certain Norman chiefs, brave but needy, who were settled in Wales and the West of England, and had there made powerful matrimonial alliances. The traitor gladly accepted the letters, "did homage" to Henry, and took his leave elated at the partial success of his unnatural mission. Landing in Wales, he found himself within a short time in the presence of Richard De Clare, surnamed "Strongbow," a brave, adventurous, and unscrupulous Norman noble, who bore the title of Earl of Pembroke. He also made the acquaintance of other Norman knights—among them Robert Fitzstephen, Maurice De Prendergast, Maurice Fitzgerald, ancestor of the famous Geraldine houses of Kildare and Desmond; Meyler FitzHenry and Raymond Le Gros—all tried warriors, all in reduced circumstances, and all ready and willing to barter their fighting blood for the fair hills and rich valleys of Ireland. They listened eagerly while Mac-Murrough unfolded his precious plot of treason and black revenge. The daring adventurers seized upon the chance of fortune at once, and the traitor was sent back to Ireland to prepare his hereditary following for the friendly reception of "the proud invaders," his newly made allies. Before leaving Wales he had made bargains with the alien adventurers which were disgraceful to him as a native-born Irishman. In a word, he had, by usurped authority, mortgaged certain tracts of the land of Leinster for the mercenary aid of the Anglo-Normans, or, to be more historically exact, the Norman Welsh.

Soon after the departure of Dermid for Ireland, Robert Fitzstephen, the readiest of the warlike plotters, and the first of the invaders, sailed for that country at the head of thirty knights, sixty men in armor, and three hundred light-armed archers. In the fragrant ides of May, 1169, they landed on the Wexford coast, near Bannow, and thus, inconsequentially, began the Norman invasion of Ireland. De Prendergast arrived the following day with about the same number of fighting men. Only a few years ago, in removing some débris—the accumulation of ages—near Bannow, the laborers found the traces of the Norman camp-fires of 1169 almost perfectly preserved. The two adventurers sent tidings of their arrival to MacMurrough without delay, and he marched at once, with a powerful force of his own retainers to join them. All three, having united their contingents, marched upon the city of Wexford, many of whose inhabitants were lineal descendants of the Danes. They made a gallant defence, but were finally outmanœuvred, overpowered, and compelled to capitulate. Other towns of less importance submitted under protest to superior force. Indeed there seemed to be a total lack of military foresight and preparedness in all that section of Ireland in 1169. Fitzpatrick, Prince of Ossory, descended from that ally of the Danes who attacked the Dalcassians returning from Clontarf, alone opposed to the invaders a brave and even formidable front. He committed the mistake of accepting a pitched battle with MacMurrough and his allies, and was totally defeated. King Roderick O'Conor, hearing of the invasion, summoned the Irish military bodies to meet him at Tara. Most of them responded, but the Prince of Ulidia, MacDunlevy, took offence at some remark made by a Connaught prince, and, in consequence, most of the Ulster forces withdrew from the Ard-Righ. King Roderick, with the troops that remained, marched to attack MacMurrough at his favorite stronghold of Ferns, where he lay with the Normans, or a part of them, expecting a vigorous siege. Instead of assaulting the enemy's lines at once, when his superior numbers would, most likely, have made an end of the traitor and his Norman allies, O'Conor weakly consented to a parley with Dermid, who was a most thorough diplomat. The Ard-Righ consented, further, to a treaty with MacMurrough, who, of course, designed to break it as soon as the main body of the Normans, under Strongbow in person, should arrive from Wales. He did not, nevertheless, hesitate to bind himself by a secret clause of the treaty with the king to receive no more foreigners into his army, and even gave one of his sons as a hostage to guarantee the same. The Ard-Righ retired from Ferns satisfied that the trouble was ended.

The royal army was scarcely out of sight of the place when MacMurrough learned that Maurice Fitzgerald, at the head of a strong party of Normans, had also arrived on the Wexford coast. He now thought himself strong enough to lay claim to the High Kingship and negotiated with the Danes of Dublin for recognition in that capacity. Meanwhile, still another Norman contingent under Raymond Le Gros landed at the estuary of Waterford, on the Wexford side thereof, and occupied Dundonolf Rock, where they intrenched themselves and eagerly awaited the coming of Strongbow with the main body of the Norman army.

By this time Henry II began to grow jealous of the success of his vassals in Ireland. He wanted to conquer the country for himself, and, therefore, sent orders to Strongbow not to sail. But that hardy soldier paid no attention to Henry's belated command, and sailed with a powerful fleet and army from Milford Haven, in Wales, arriving in Waterford Harbor on August 23, 1171. The Normans, under Raymond Le Gros, joined him without loss of time, and the combined forces attacked the old Danish city. The Danes and native Irish made common cause against the new enemy and a desperate and bloody conflict occurred. The Normans were several times repulsed, with great loss, but, better armed and led than their brave opponents, they returned to the breach again and yet again. At last they gained entrance into the city, which they set on fire. An awful massacre ensued. Three hundred of the leading defenders were made prisoners, their limbs broken and their maimed bodies flung into the harbor. King MacMurrough, who had already pledged his daughter's hand to Strongbow—a man old enough to have been her father—arrived just after the city fell. In order to celebrate the event with due pomp and circumstance, he caused the Princess Eva to be married to the Norman baron in the great cathedral, while the rest of the city was burning, and the blood of the victims of the assault still smoked amid the ruins! An ominous and fatal marriage it proved to Ireland.

And now, at last, the blood of the native Irish was stirred to its depths and they began, when somewhat late, to realize the danger to their liberty and independence. In those far-off days, when there were no railroads, no electric wires, no good roads or rapid means of communication of any kind, and when newspapers were unknown, information, as a matter of course, traveled slowly even in a small country, like Ireland. The woods were dense, the morasses fathomless, and, in short, the invaders had made their foothold firm in the east and south portions of the island before the great majority of the Celtic Irish comprehended that they were in process of being subjugated by bold and formidable aliens. There had existed in Ireland from very ancient times five main roads, all proceeding from the hill of Tara to the different sections of the country. That called "Dala" ran through Ossory into the province of Munster. The road called "Assail" passed on toward the Shannon through Mullingar. The highway from Tara to Galway followed the esker, or small hill range, as it does in our own day, and was called "Slighe Mor," or great road; the road leading from Tara to Dublin, Bray, and along the Wicklow and Wexford coasts was called "Cullin"; the highway leading into Ulster ran, probably, through Tredagh, or Drogheda, Dundalk, Newry, and Armagh, but this is not positive. As it was the route followed by the English in most of their Ulster wars, it is quite probable that they picked out a well-beaten path, so as to avoid the expense and labor of making a new causeway. McGee tells us that there were also many cross-roads, known by local names, and of these the Four Masters, at different dates, mentioned no less than forty. These roads were kept in repair, under legal enactment, and the main highways were required to be of sufficient width to allow of the passage of two chariots all along their course. We are further informed that the principal roads were required by law to be repaired at seasons of games and fairs, and in time of war. At their best, to judge by the ancient chroniclers, most of them would be considered little better than "trails" through the mountains, moors, and forests in these times.

MacMurrough and Strongbow did not allow the grass to sprout under their feet before marching in great force on Dublin. King Roderick, leading a large but ill-trained army, attempted to head them off, but was outgeneraled, and the enemy soon appeared before the walls of Leinster's stronghold. Its Dano-Celtic inhabitants, cowed by the doleful news from Waterford, tried to parley; but Strongbow's lieutenants, De Cogan and Le Gros, eager for carnage and rich plunder, surprised the city, and the horrors of Waterford were, in a measure, repeated. The Danish prince, Osculph, and most of his chief men escaped in their ships, but the Normans captured Dublin, and the English, except for a brief period in the reign of James II, have held it from that sad day, in October, 1171, to this.

Roderick O'Conor, that weak but well-meaning prince

and bad general, retired into Connaught and sent word to MacMurrough to return to his allegiance, if he wished to save the life of his son, held as a hostage. The brutal and inhuman traitor refused, and King Roderick, although humane almost to a fault, had the unfortunate young man decapitated. This was poor compensation for the loss of Waterford and Dublin. Those pages of Irish history are all besmeared with slaughter.

Many of the Irish chroniclers, who are otherwise severe on Norman duplicity, relate a story of chivalry, worthy of any age and people, in connection with Maurice de Prendergast and the Prince of Ossory. Strongbow had deputed the former to invite the latter to a conference. The Irish prince accepted. While the conference was in progress, De Prendergast learned that treachery was intended toward his guest. He immediately rushed into Strongbow's presence and swore on the hilt of his sword, which was a cross, that no man there that day should lay hands on the Prince of Ossory. The latter was allowed to retire unmolested, and Prendergast and his followers escorted him in safety to his own country. De Prendergast has been known ever since in Irish annals as "the Faithful Norman," and his fidelity has made him the theme of many a bardic song and romantic tale.

CHAPTER XI

Superior Armament of the Normans—Arrival of Henry II

ALTHOUGH two of the chief Irish cities had fallen to the invaders, the struggle was not entirely abandoned by the Irish nation. Ulster and most of Connaught remained intact, and even in Munster and Leinster there was, from time to time, considerable, although desultory, resistance to the Anglo-Normans. The latter, clad in steel armor from head to foot, and possessing formidable weapons, had a great advantage over the cloth-clad Irish, although, of course, the latter greatly outnumbered them. The weapons of the Irish were the skian, or short-sword—resembling the Cuban machete— the javelin, and the battle-axe—the latter a terrible arm at close quarters; but even the axe could not cope with the ponderous Norman sword and the death-dealing long bow, with its cloth-yard shaft. In discipline and tactics, also, the Irish were overmatched. In short, they were inferior to their enemies in everything but numbers and courage. But all would have been redeemed had they but united against the common foe.

Why they did not may be justly, as we think, attributed to the tribal system which taught the clans and tribes to be loyal to their particular chiefs rather than to their country as a whole; the absence of a fully recognized federal head, and the vacillations of an honest and patriotic Ard-Righ, who, noble and amiable of character, as he undoubtedly was, proved himself to be a bungling

diplomat and an indifferent general. Had his able and
determined father, Turlough Mor, been on the Irish
throne, and in the vigor of his life, when Strongbow
landed, he would have made short work of the Norman
filibusters. The king seemed ever behind time in his
efforts to stem the tide of invasion. He had rallied still
another army, and gained some advantages, when he was
confronted by a new enemy in the person of Henry II.
This king, determined not to be outdone by his vassals,
had ordered Strongbow, who, because of his marriage
with Eva MacMurrough, had assumed the lordship of
Leinster, to return with all his chief captains to England,
the penalty of refusal being fixed at outlawry. Strongbow attempted to placate the wrathful king and sent to
him agents to explain his position, but the fierce and
crafty Plantagenet was not a man to be hoodwinked. He
collected a powerful fleet and army, set sail from England, in October, 1171, and, toward the end of that month,
landed in state at Waterford, where Strongbow received
him with all honor and did homage as a vassal. This was
the beginning of Ireland's actual subjugation, for had
the original Norman invaders refused to acknowledge
Henry's sovereignty, and, uniting with the natives,
kept Ireland for themselves, they would eventually,
as in England, have become a component and formidable
part of the nation, and proved a boon, instead of a curse,
to the distracted country. The landing of Henry put an
end to such a hope, and with his advent began that dependency on the English crown which has been so fatal
to the liberty, the happiness, and the prosperity of "the
most unfortunate of nations."

Henry having "graciously" received the submission of

Strongbow and his confederates, proceeded, at once—for he was a monarch of great energy—to make a "royal progress" through the partially subdued portions of Munster and Leinster. He took care, in doing this, to show Pope Adrian's mischievous "bull" to the Irish prelates and princes, some of whom, to their discredit be it confessed, bowed slavishly to the ill-considered mandate of the Pontiff. Many of the princes were even base enough to give Henry "the kiss of peace," when, instead, they should have rushed to arms to defend the honor and independence of their country. The prelates, trained to ecclesiastical docility, disgusted with the everlasting civil contentions of the country, and fearful of further unavailing bloodshed, had some feeble excuse for their ill-timed acquiescence, but what are we to say of those wretched Irish princes who so weakly and wickedly betrayed their nation to the foreign usurper? They were by no means ignorant men, as times went, but they were ambitious, vain, and jealous of the half-acknowledged authority of High King Roderick, who, poor man, seems to have been the Henry VI of Ireland. Those treasonable princes deserve enduring infamy, and foremost among them were Dermid McCarthy, King of Desmond, and Donald O'Brien, King of Thomond. Both lived to regret most bitterly their cowardice and treason.

Henry II was a politic monarch. He flattered the pliable Irish bishops and spoke to them gently about Church reforms, while he palavered the despicable Irish princes, and, at the same time, pretended to favor the common people and affected to check the rapacity of his Norman subjects. Hostilities ceased for a time, except on the borders of Leinster and Connaught, where King

Roderick, deserted by many of his allies, and deeply depressed at the absence of national union against the invaders, kept up an unavailing resistance. In this he was encouraged and aided by the patriotic Archbishop of Dublin, St. Lorcan O'Tuhill, who appears to have been the only man among the entire Irish hierarchy who comprehended the iron grip the Normans had on the throat of Ireland. Had all the prelates been like St. Lorcan, and preached a war of extermination against the invaders at the outset, Ireland could, undoubtedly, have thrown off the yoke, because the princes would have been forced by their people, over whom the bishops had great moral sway, to heal their feuds and make common cause for their country. King Roderick, despite his errors, deserves honor for his patriotic spirit. The Ulster princes, too, with few exceptions, stood out manfully against the foreigner, and a long period elapsed before the Anglo-Norman power found a secure footing amid the rugged glens and dense forests of the western and northern portions of the invaded island.

Geraldus Cambrensis, or Gerald Barry, a Norman priest of Welsh birth, accompanied, A.D. 1185, King Henry's son, John, as chronicler, to Ireland. Like nearly every man of his race, he hated the native Irish, but, occasionally, as if by accident, spoke well of some of them. In general, however, his book is a gross libel on the Irish Church and the Irish people. He purports to give Roderick O'Conor's address to his army on the eve of battle with the Anglo-Normans, and the concluding words of the speech are alleged to have been as follows: "Let us then," said the Irish king, "following the example of the Franks, and fighting bravely for our country, rush against our enemies, and as these foreigners have come over few in numbers, let us crush them by a general attack.   Fire, while it only sparkles, may be speedily quenched, but when it has burst into a flame, being fed with fresh materials, its power increases with the bulk, and it can not be easily extinguished.   It is always best to meet difficulties half way, and check the first approaches of disease, for (the Latin quotation of the king is here translated)

> " 'Too late is medicine, after long delay,
> To stop the lingering course of slow decay.

Wherefore, defending our country and liberty, and acquiring for ourselves eternal renown, let us, by a resolute attack, and the extermination of our enemies, though they are but few in number, strike terror into the many, and, by their defeat, evermore deter foreign nations from such nefarious attempts."

Henry's astute policy disarmed, for a time, even Roderick himself.   The Anglo-Norman monarch, who would have made an admirable modern politician, does not seem to have desired the absolute ruin of the Irish nation, but his greedy Norman captains were of a different mind, and when Henry, after having wined and dined the Irish princes to their hearts' content, in Dublin and other cities, at last returned to England, in the fall of 1173, the Norman leaders showed their teeth to the Irish people, and forced most of those who had submitted into fierce revolt.   As a result, the Norman forces were crushed in the field.   Strongbow, himself, was shut up in Waterford, and his comrades were similarly placed in Dublin, Drogheda, and Wexford.   Henry, incensed at this unlooked-for sequel to his Irish pilgrimage, sent over a commission to inquire into the facts. The result was that an Irish delegation went to London to explain, and, at Windsor, where Henry held his court, a treaty was entered into, finally, between King Roderick and himself, by which the former acknowledged Henry as "suzerain," and Roderick was recognized as High King of Ireland, except the portions thereof held by the Normans under Henry. This was a sad ending of Roderick's heroic beginning. As usual with English monarchs, when dealing with the Irish people, Henry, urged by his greedy dependants in Ireland, soon found means to grossly violate the Treaty of Windsor, as the compact between the representatives of Roderick and himself was called, thus vitiating it forever and absolving the Irish nation from observing any of its provisions. Another fierce rebellion followed, in which the southern and western Irish—the Anglo-Normans having now grown more numerous and powerful—were remorselessly crushed. Roderick's rascally son, Prince Murrough O'Conor, who thought his father should be satisfied with the titular High Kingship, and that he himself should be King of Connaught, rose in revolt and attempted to seize the provincial crown. The Connacians, indignant at his baseness, stood by the old king. Murrough was defeated and received condign punishment. This bad prince must have been familiar with the unseemly course pursued by the sons of Henry II in Normandy, for he allied himself with his country's, and his father's, enemies, the Anglo-Normans, under the treacherous De Cogan, and this act, more even than his filial impiety, inflamed the minds of his countrymen against the unnatural miscreant. King Roderick, unhappy man, whose pride was mortally wounded, and whose paternal heart, tender and manly, was wrung with sorrow at the crime of his son and its punishment—decreed by the Clans and not by himself—disgusted, besides, with the hopeless condition of Irish affairs, made up his mind to retire from the world, its pomps and vexations. He repaired to the ancient monastery of Cong, in Galway, and there, after twelve years of pious devotion, on the 29th day of November, 1198, in the 82d year of his age, this good and noble but irresolute monarch surrendered his soul to God. He was not buried at Cong, as some annalists have asserted, but in the chancel of the Temple Mor, or Great Church, of Clonmacnois, in the present King's County, where he was educated. Tradition has failed to preserve the location of the exact place of sepulture within the ruined shrine. And so ended the last Ard-Righ, or High King, that had swayed the sceptre of an independent Ireland.

King Henry's claim that the Irish Church needed great reformation is disproved by the enactments of his own reign in that connection, viz.: 1. That the prohibition of marriage within the canonical degrees of consanguinity be enforced.   2. That children should be regularly catechized before the church door in each parish.   3. That children should be baptized in the public fonts of the parish churches.   4. That regular tithes should be paid to the clergy, rather than irregular donations from time to time.   5. That church lands should be exempt from the exaction of livery and other burdens.   6. That the clergy should not be liable to any share of the eric, or blood fine, levied off the kindred of a man guilty of homicide.   7. A decree regulating the making of wills.

Surely, this was small ground on which to justify the invasion of an independent country and the destruction of its liberty!

CHAPTER XII

Prince John "Lackland" Created "Lord" of Ireland—Splendid Heroism of Sir Armoricus Tristram

HENRY II, whatever may have been his original intentions toward Ireland and the Irish, soon after his return to England assumed the tone of a conqueror and dictator. He forgot, or appeared to forget, the treaty he had concluded with King Roderick's representatives at Windsor, which distinctly recognized the tributary sovereignty of the Irish monarch, and left the bulk of the Irish people under the sway of their own native laws and rulers. Now, however, he, in defiance of the commonest law of honor, proclaimed his weakest and worst son, the infamous John, "Lord" of Ireland—a title retained by the English kings down to the reign of Henry VIII, who, being a wily politician, contrived to get himself "elected" as "King of Ireland." This title remained with the English monarchs until January 1, 1801, when the ill-starred legislative union went into effect, and George III of England became king of the so-called "United Kingdom of Great Britain and Ireland."

Henry II died in 1189, preceding the Irish king he had so deeply wronged to the grave by about nine years. His last hours were doubly imbittered by the discovery that his youngest son, John, who was also his favorite, and in whom he had concentred all his paternal love and confidence, was leagued with his enemies. An able, but thoroughly bad, man, Henry Plantagenet died a miserable death—his heart filled with rage against his own rebellious offspring, who, no doubt, only practiced the perfidious policy inculcated by their miserable father. The death scene occurred at Chinon, in Aquitaine, and his last words, uttered in the French tongue, and despite the vehement protests of the surrounding ecclesiastics, were, "Accursed be the day on which I was born, and accursed of God be the sons I leave after me!" His curse did not fall on sticks and stones. All of his guilty sons, except John, died violent and untimely deaths. Lackland, the exception, died of an overdose of pears and fresh cider, added to grief over the loss of his treasure, which sunk in a quicksand while he was marching with his guard along the English coast. Henry's curse remained with the Plantagenets to the end, and most of the princes of that family met a horrible doom, from Edward II, foully murdered in Berkeley Castle, to the last male Plantagenet, of legitimate origin, the Earl of Warwick, beheaded by order of Henry VII in 1499. Strongbow, Henry's chief tool in the acquirement of Ireland, died of a dreadful blood malady, which, the doctors said, resembled leprosy, some years before the king. He is buried in Christ Church Cathedral, Dublin, and beside him are said to rest the relics of his only son, killed by the ferocious father's hand, because he fled from the Irish in some border battle.

Before closing this chapter we may be allowed to remark that Richard III, when he had his nephews murdered in the Tower of London, in 1483, came legitimately by his cruel nature. John Lackland was the progenitor of all the Plantagenets who succeeded him on the English

throne, and, like his direct descendant, Richard Crook-
back, was a usurper, because Prince Arthur, son of his
elder brother, Geoffrey Plantagenet, was lineal heir to
the throne.   History and tradition agree in saying that
John caused Prince Arthur to be murdered, and some
historians say that he was the actual murderer.   He was
the only coward of his race, and was, also, frivolous and
deliberately ill-mannered.   When on a visit to Ireland, in
the supposed interest of his father, he caused a revolt
among the Irish chiefs who called upon him, by pulling
their long beards and otherwise insulting them.   Those
cringing chiefs deserved the treatment they received,
but John Lackland, as he was dubbed, is not, therefore,
excusable for having acted toward them as a boor and
a ruffian.   Later on, when he became King of England,
he again visited Ireland, and built many strong castles.
That of Limerick, called King John's Castle, is still almost
perfectly preserved, and is a superb relic of Norman military architecture.   As the Irish were not provided with
armament, or appliances, for making a successful siege,
the fortresses built by King John were, so far as they
were concerned, virtually impregnable.   Whenever the
Normans were vanquished in the field, they retired to
their castles, which were amply provisioned, and defied
the vengeance of their foes.

In the last year of the reign of Henry II, there occurred in Ireland one of those memorable combats which
deserve a lasting place in history, not so much because of
any important reform or social or political blessing of
any kind resulting from them, but as tending to show that
warrior men, in all ages, have often been chivalrous and
self-sacrificing.   The Norman race—glorious as has been

its record all over Europe and Palestine—never evinced greater bravery than on the bloody field of Knocktuagh (Nockthoo), "the Hill of Axes," in Galway, A.D. 1189. Sir John de Courcy, hard pressed in Ulster by the fiercely resisting septs of the north, asked aid from his sworn friend and comrade, Sir Armoricus Tristram—ancestor of the family of St. Lawrence, Earls of Howth—then serving in Connaught. Tristram had with him, according to some accounts, thirty knights, one hundred men-at-arms, mounted, and one hundred light-armed infantry; according to other statements, he had under his command thirty cavalry and two hundred foot. This force Cathal O'Conor, afterward known as "the Red-Handed," Prince of the royal house of Connaught—a most valiant and skilful general, who was younger brother, born out of wedlock, of King Roderick, then virtually in the retirement of the cloisters of Cong Abbey—led into an ambush, and attacked with a superior force. Sir Armoricus saw at a glance that escape was hopeless, and that only one refuge was left for him and his following—to die with honor. Some of his horsemen, tradition says, proposed to cut their way out and leave the infantry to their fate. Against this mean proposition Sir Armor's brother and other knights vehemently protested. "We have been together in many dangers," they said; "now let all of us fight and die together." Sir Armor, by way of answer, alighted from his steed, drew his sword and, with it, pierced the noble charger to the heart. All the other horsemen, except two youths, who were detailed to watch the fight from a distant hill, and report the result to De Courcy in Ulster, immediately followed their glorious leader's example. Tradition asserts that the two young men who made their escape, by order, were Sir Armoricus's son and the squire of De Courcy, who brought the latter's message to Tristram.   Having completed the slaughter of their horses, the little band of Normans formed themselves in a phalanx, and marched boldly to attack the outnumbering Irish.   The latter met the shock with their usual courage, but the enemy, clad in armor, cut their way deeply and fatally into the crowded ranks of their cloth-clad foes.   The Irish poet, Arthur Gerald Geoghegan (Geh'ogan), thus graphically and truthfully describes the dreadful encounter:

"Then rose the roar of battle loud, the shout, the cheer, the cry!
The clank of ringing steel, the gasping groans of those who die;
Yet onward still the Norman band right fearless cut their way,
As move the mowers o'er the sward upon a summer's day.

"For round them there, like shorn grass, the foe in hundreds bleed;
Yet, fast as e'er they fall, each side, do hundreds more succeed;
With naked breasts undaunted meet the spears of steel-clad men,
And sturdily, with axe and skian, repay their blows again.

"Now crushed with odds, their phalanx broke, each Norman fights
    alone,
And few are left throughout the field, and they are feeble grown,
But high o'er all, Sir Tristram's voice is like a trumpet heard,
And still, where'er he strikes, the foemen sink beneath his sword.

"But once he raised his visor up—alas, it was to try
If Hamo and his boy yet tarried on the mountain nigh,
When sharp an arrow from the foe pierced right through his brain,
And sank the gallant knight a corse upon the bloody plain.

"Then failed the fight, for gathering round his lifeless body there,
The remnant of his gallant band fought fiercely in despair;
And, one by one, they wounded fell—yet with their latest breath,
Their Norman war-cry shouted bold—then sank in silent death."

When Cathal Mor finally became King of Connaught, he caused a monastery, which he called "the Abbey of

Victory," but which has been known to the Irish of Connaught for ages as "Abbey Knockmoy," to be erected on or near the site of the battle.   Tradition, not a very reliable guide, fails to exactly define the scene of Cathal's victory over the Normans. Knocktuagh, an inconsiderable eminence, is within a few miles of the city of Galway, whereas Knockmoy, where stands the historic abbey, is fully twelve miles east of that ancient borough, on the highroad to Athlone. Cathal of the Red Hand fought many battles and won many splendid victories, although he occasionally sustained defeats at the hands of the Normans and their traitorous native allies; his greatest victory was won over his bitter rival, albeit his nephew, Caher Carragh O'Conor, whom he encountered somewhere in the county of Galway.   There was an awful slaughter on both sides, but Cathal prevailed, and, no doubt, built the abbey on the spot where Caher and his leading chieftains, Irish and Norman, fell. De Courcy was the only foreigner allied with Cathal Mor in this great battle. Abbey Knockmoy is one of the most interesting of Irish ruins, and contains friezes and frescoing most creditable to Irish art in the thirteenth century. The victory gave Cathal Mor the undisputed sway of Connaught.   Adopting the policy of the invaders, for the benefit of his country, he used Norman against Norman; allied himself with Meyler FitzHenry, the last of Strongbow's lieutenants, to punish Connaught's inveterate foe, William de Burgo, ancestor of the Clanricardes in Limerick, and to humble the pride of the ambitious De Lacys in Leinster.   In 1210, this gallant Irish monarch compelled King John of England to treat with him as an independent sovereign, and, while he lived, no

Norman usurper dared to lord it over his kingdom of Connaught. Like his royal father and brother, he was a champion of the Irish Church, and was a liberal founder and endower of religious houses. Had the Connacian kings who followed been of his moral and military calibre, the Normans could never have ruled in Connaught. Nor did this great Irishman confine himself to his native kingdom alone; he also assisted the other provinces in resisting foreign encroachment. Even in his old age, when the De Lacys tried to embarrass his reign by fortifying Athleague, so as to threaten him in flank, the dauntless hero, at the head of his hereditary power, marched from his palace of Ballintober, made two crossings of the river Suck, and, by a bold manœuvre, came on the rear of the enemy, compelling them to retreat in all haste across the Shannon into Leinster. He did not fail to raze their forts at Athleague to the ground. This was the last of his countless exploits. His time was drawing nigh, and, according to the Four Masters, "signs appeared in the heavens" which foretold his death. In 1223, Cathal's load of age and care became too heavy, and he resigned the crown of Connaught to his son, Hugh. The old king, assuming the habit of the Franciscans, retired to the Abbey of Knockmoy, and there expired, mourned by his country and respected by its enemies, A.D. 1224. Tradition still points to his tomb amid the majestic ruins of that venerable pile. His death was the signal for the rise of Norman power in Connaught, and for the final deposition by the alien De Burgos of the royal race of O'Conor.

CHAPTER XIII

Ireland Under the Earlier Edwards—The Younger Bruce Elected
King by the Irish—Battle of Athenry—Death of Bruce
at Faughart Hill

AFTER the death of King John, affairs in Ireland
proceeded tamely enough until the repeated encroachments of the Anglo-Norman settlers and their progeny,
who occupied chiefly a comparatively small district called
"the Pale," which consisted of most of the present counties of Dublin, Louth, Meath, Westmeath, Kildare, and
Kilkenny, forced the native Irish to rise "in rude but
fierce array" against them.   The Norman family of
De Lacy disputed supremacy in Leinster with the Fitzgeralds, or Geraldines, but the latter, finally, outshone
their rivals both in court and camp.   The De Courcys,
headed by the bold and chivalrous Sir John, "of that
ilk," made some impression on the coast of Ulster.   The
De Burgos, ancestors of all the Irish Burkes, became powerful in Connaught, and the old Irish, headed by the
O'Conors, fought against them fiercely from time to time.
But the gallant, if covetous, Norman captains beheld the
Irish maidens, and saw that they were fair.   Love-mak-
ing, despite frequent feuds, progressed between Norman
lord and Celtic virgin; and not uncommonly between
Irish prince and Norman lady.   Many "mixed mar-
riages" resulted, and, naturally, racial animosities became
greatly softened, "for love will still be lord of all."
Very soon the warrior Normans, who acknowledged but

a doubtful allegiance to the English monarch, began to assume Irish manners, wear the Irish costume, and speak in the Gaelic tongue. All this did not suit the English policy, and the Norman Irish were often described by their kindred across the sea as "Degenerate English." It was written of the Fitzgeralds, in particular, that they had grown "more Irish than the Irish." This alarmed England, for it began to look as if Norman and Celt in Ireland would soon make common cause against her power. But many Norman chiefs were land hungry, and many of the Irish princes were fierce and filled with a just wrath against their invaders. Gradually, therefore, the Geraldines swept all before them in Kildare and Desmond, for they were very warlike, and many native Irish joined their fortunes to theirs, because of "fosterage" and other interests. The Butlers possessed themselves of large tracts of country in the present counties of Kilkenny and Tipperary, and became Earls of Ormond; and the De Burgos, as Earls of Clanricarde, became, in great part, masters of Galway, Mayo, and other parts of the province of Connaught. Factions among the Celtic chiefs made their conquests easy. The Normans, wily as they were brave, fostered these feuds, and were particularly delighted when the formidable O'Neills and O'Donnells of Ulster wasted their strength in internecine strife. The politic foreigners occasionally allied themselves to either one of the contending septs, and generally succeeded in outwitting both contestants. Yet, as time wore on, the Norman warriors, forgetting their fathers' speech, shouted their battle cries in the Gaelic tongue, and, except for their armor, could hardly be distinguished from the Celts.

Henry III paid but small attention to Irish affairs. He ascended the English throne a minor, and his mature years were spent mainly in repeated civil wars with his barons, who finally compelled him to extend and confirm the Magna Charta of his father.   His son, Edward I, nicknamed "Long Shanks," the ablest king of the Plantagenet race, was almost constantly occupied, during his stirring reign, in wars of conquest against Wales and Scotland, and he succeeded in annexing the first-named country to the English crown.   His son and successor, Edward II, was the first English Prince of Wales.   This Edward inherited the Scotch war which his father had left unfinished, after great effusion of blood.   In 1314, his great English army, said to have numbered 100,000 knights, archers, and men-at-arms, was disastrously routed at Bannockburn ("Oaten-cake rivulet"), near Sterling, by King Robert Bruce, of Scotland, who had under his command not more than 30,000 men, horse and foot.   This great victory did not entirely end the Anglo-Scotch wars, which were always bitter and bloody down to the close of the sixteenth century, but it preserved the independence of Scotland for nearly four hundred years. That country ceased to be a separate nation in 1707. Many Irish clans of Ulster aided Bruce at Bannockburn, and some Connaught septs, under one of the O'Conors, fought on the English side, and were nearly exterminated, which "served them right."   As the Irish princes could not settle on one of their own number for High King, they, at the suggestion of the wise and generous Donald O'Neill, King of Ulster, agreed to elect Edward Bruce, brother of the Scotch monarch, king of all Ireland.   Their proffer of the Irish throne was accepted by the Bruces, and Edward was duly crowned in 1315. This provoked a destructive three years' war. Brave King Robert came to Ireland to aid his brother, and, in the field, they swept all before them, particularly in Munster. But the Norman-Irish fought them bitterly, notably the Geraldines, the Berminghams, and De Burgos. Felim O'Conor, the young and gallant king of Connaught, was forced into a repugnant alliance with De Burgo, who was powerful in the west. His heart, however, was with the Bruce, and he soon found an opportunity to break away from his repugnant Norman ally. Summoning all his fighting force, he marched upon the fortified town of Athunree, or Athenry, "the Ford of the Kings," in Galway, and came up with the Anglo-Norman army, arrayed outside the walls, on the morning of August 10, 1316. De Burgo and De Bermingham, two able veteran soldiers, headed the Anglo-Normans. The conflict was fierce and the slaughter appalling, particularly on the Irish side, because the heroic clansmen did not have, like their foes, the advantage of chain armor and long-bow archery. Night closed upon a terrible scene. The Irish refused to fly and died in heaps around the lifeless body of their chivalric young king, who, with twenty-eight princes of his house, proudly fell on that bloody field. Most of the Irish army perished—the loss being usually estimated at 10,000 men. The Anglo-Normans also suffered severely, but their armor proved the salvation of most of them. Connaught did not recover from this great disaster for many generations. Athenry proved fatal to the cause of Bruce, although, gallantly seconded by Donald O'Neill, he fought on for two years longer, but was at last killed in battle on Faughart Hill, in Louth,

A.D. 1318. With him disappeared, for that century at least, the hope of an independent Ireland.

After the battle of Athenry, the power of the De Burgo family, and of all the allies of their house, became predominant in Connaught, but all these Anglo-Norman chiefs became, also, much more Irish in manners and sympathy than they had ever been before. The desperate bravery displayed by O'Conor's clansmen had aroused the admiration of those born warriors, and they felt that to ally themselves in marriage with so martial a race was an honor, not a degradation, such as the English sought to make it appear. Ulster maintained its independence, and so also did much of Connaught and portions of Munster and Leinster, and there were periodical raids upon the Pale and carrying off of "Saxon" flocks and herds, followed by feasts and general jubilation. The Palesmen, whenever too weak to meet the Celts in the field, would resort to their time-honored strategy of shutting themselves up in their strongholds, and making, whenever opportunity offered, fierce retaliatory raids on the Irish territory. This kind of warfare was unfortunate for Ireland, because it kept the English feeling strong in the hearts of the Palesmen, who were constantly recruited by fresh swarms of adventurers from England. Outside of the Pale, however, the Old Irish and the Normans continued to affiliate and intermarry, as we have already said. Fosterage—a peculiarly Irish custom, which meant that the children of the king, prince, or chief should be nursed by the wives of the clansmen, instead of their own mothers—grew apace, and nearly every Norman lord had his heirs suckled by the women of the Celtic race, thus creating a bond of "kinship"—

if so it may be termed—in many instances stronger than even the brotherhood of blood.

Irish tradition abounds in examples of the devotion of foster-brethren to each other; and in all written history there is given but one instance of treachery in this connection, and that instance does not involve a man of Celtic, but of Latin, lineage. We refer to the betrayal of Lord Thomas Fitzgerald by Parez in the reign of Henry VIII, which will be dealt with in the proper place.

CHAPTER XIV

Prince Lionel Viceroy for Edward III—The Statute of Kilkenny

EDWARD III, that valiant, vigorous, and ambitious "English" king—he was almost a pure-blooded Frenchman and about the last Norman monarch who occupied the throne of England that did not speak with fluency the language of the people he governed—was so occupied with his unjust wars against France that he gave but small heed to Irish affairs and never visited the island at all. But he sent over his third son, Prince Lionel, ancestor of the royal house of York and Clarence, as viceroy. Lionel had with him a well-equipped army of native-born English, but he treated his Anglo-Irish allies so contemptuously that many fell away from him and joined the ranks of the Old Irish. His English army, unaccustomed to the Irish climate and mode of warfare, made but a poor figure in the field, and was everywhere beaten by the dauntless Irish clansmen. At last he was compelled to lower his imperious tone to the Anglo-Irish and these foolishly helped him out of his scrape. It is said that a more than doubtful campaign in the present county of Clare procured for him, from his flatterers, the title of Duke of Clarence—a title, by the way, which brought more or less misfortune to every English prince who has borne it, except William IV, from his day to our own.

Lionel was particularly jealous of the friendship which seemed to exist between old Anglo-Irish and the old Celtic-Irish, and his small mind conceived a method of putting an end to it. He summoned a parliament to meet at Kilkenny, and there it was enacted, among other things, "that all intermarriages, fosterings, gossipred, and buying or selling with the (Irish) enemy shall be accounted treason; that English names, fashions, and manners (most of these having disappeared) shall be resumed under penalty of confiscation of the delinquent's lands; that March laws (Norman) and Brehon laws (Irish) are illegal, and that there shall be no laws but English laws; that the Irish shall not pasture their cattle on English lands; that the English shall not entertain Irish rhymers, minstrels, or newsmen, and, moreover, that no 'mere Irishman' shall be admitted to any ecclesiastical benefice or religious house (England was then all Catholic) situated within the English district."

Other provisions of the Statute of Kilkenny, as this precious "law" is called in Irish history, forbade the wearing of long hair, mustaches, and cloaks, after the manner of the Irish, and the use of the Gaelic speech was also forbidden, under heavy penalties. With their usual subserviency to English demands, the Anglo-Irish barons of the Pale—the portion of Ireland held by the English settlers, as already explained—passed this barbarous enactment without opposition, although they themselves were the chief "offenders" against it, in the eyes of the tyrannical viceroy.

To the honor of the Anglo-Normans and Celtic-Irish be it remembered, the base statute became almost immediately inoperative, and the Norman lords and Irish ladies, and the Irish princes and the Norman ladies, intermarried more numerously than before—an example generally followed by their dependants. The gallant house of Fitzgerald, or Geraldine, as usual, set the example of disregard.

"These Geraldines! These Geraldines! Not long her air they
    breathed—
Not long they fed on venison in Irish water seethed—
Not often had their children been by Irish mothers nursed,
When from their full and genial hearts an Irish feeling burst!
The English monarch strove in vain, by law and force and bribe,
To win from Irish thoughts and ways this 'more than Irish' tribe;
For still they clung to fosterage—to Brehon, cloak, and bard—
No king dare say to Geraldine: 'Your Irish wife discard!'"

The immediate effect of the Statute of Kilkenny was to temporarily unite most of the Irish clans against the common enemy. They fell fiercely upon the Pale and again shut up the Normans in their fortresses. Prince Lionel returned to England grieved and humiliated. His viceroyalty had been a signal failure.

Throughout the viceroyalty of Clarence and his successor, William de Windsor, the desultory war between the Old Irish and the Anglo-Normans made many districts, in all the provinces, red with slaughter. The power of the De Burgos declined in Connaught after the death of the warlike Red Earl, who was the scourge of the O'Conors, and the latter family brought his descendants, who had assumed the name of MacWilliam, under their sway. The fierce tribes of Wicklow, Wexford, and Carlow harried the Pale, and were frequently joined by the O'Mores of Leix, and the Fitzpatricks of Ossory. In Ulster, Niel O'Neill, Prince of Tyrone, attacked and defeated the English armies and garrisons with so much success that he cleared Ulster of all foreigners, and won the title of Niel the Great. The Earl of Desmond met with a severe defeat at the hands of O'Brien, Prince of Thomond, who assailed him near the abbey of Adare in Limerick, and routed his army with terrible carnage. Desmond himself was mortally wounded and died upon the field. The Earl of Kildare, Desmond's kinsman, attempted to avenge his rout, but met with scant success, because the Irish had, by this time, grown used to the Norman method of warfare, and, in many cases, improved upon the tactics of their oppressors.

Edward III, just before his death in 1376, attempted to get the settlements of the Pale to send representatives to London to consult about the affairs of Ireland, but they demurred, saying that it was not their custom to deliberate outside of their own country. However, they sent delegates to explain matters to the king, who did not further insist on convening a Pale Parliament in the English capital. It is strange that so able a monarch as Edward was, even in his declining years, never thought of visiting Ireland. Of course, most of his reign was taken up with the wars in France, in which he proved so signally victorious, and he had but little time for other occupations. In truth, Edward III, although nominally English, was, in reality, a Frenchman in thought and speech, and his dearest dream was to rule over the

country of his Plantagenet ancestors, with England as a
kind of tributary province. Of course, the English people would never have acquiesced in this arrangement, for,
however willing to impose their yoke on other peoples,
they are unalterably opposed to having any foreign yoke
imposed upon themselves.

CHAPTER XV

Richard II's Invasions—Heroic Art MacMurrough

THE first half of the fourteenth century passed
away quietly enough in Ireland, except for occasional conflicts between the Anglo-Normans and the
Celtic tribes, or an odd encounter of the latter with one
another. Edward III had so many quarrels with Scotland and France that he could do nothing in Ireland,
even were he so inclined, and the sad experience of the
Duke of Clarence in that country warned succeeding
viceroys to let well enough alone. The Irish nation,
Celtic, Norman, and Saxon, was gradually fusing and
would soon have developed a composite strength nearly
equal to that of England herself. In the wars with
France, many Anglo-Irish septs fought under the orders
of Edward, and, probably, some of the Celtic septs also
joined his standard, rather as allies, through the bad
policy of their chiefs, than as mercenaries.

By the time that Edward completed, or nearly so, the
conquest of France, the English power in Ireland had
so shrunken as to be almost nominal. Dublin, Drogheda,
Kilkenny, and Waterford were the chief garrisons of the
English. The Lacys, Burkes, Fitzgeralds, and other

Norman-Irish houses and clans were scarcely to be distinguished from the Milesian families and septs. Such fighting as they indulged in between themselves was comparatively trivial. The island, blessed with partial peace, began to grow more populous and prosperous. Edward, the Black Prince, having crowned himself with glory in France, died before he could inherit the crown of England. Edward III, not so old as worn out by ceaseless warfare, died in 1377, and after him came to the English throne Richard, son of the Black Prince, a handsome boy of sixteen, who, at first, gave promise of great deeds, but who subsequently proved himself a weakling and voluptuary. In Ireland, Ulster, Connaught, and Munster remained tranquil for the most part, but, in Leinster, the royal house of MacMurrough—lineal descendants of the traitor of Strongbow's time—showed a determination to drive the remnant of the English garrison into the sea. They were as loyal to Ireland as their accursed ancestor had been faithless. King Art I, after a long series of successes and failures, died, and was succeeded on the Leinster throne by King Art II—one of the bravest, wisest, and truest characters in Irish history. He continued the war his father had begun. Richard II, like all of his race, was vain and greedy of military glory. As the war with France had closed for a period, he thought Ireland a good field in which to distinguish himself as a general. He had heard of "MacMore," as he called MacMurrough, and longed to measure swords with him. Accordingly, in the summer of 1394, he landed at Waterford with a large army. The historian McGee estimates it at 35,000 horse and foot, but we are inclined to think it was much less. That it was formidable, for those times, all historians who have dealt with the subject are agreed upon. He was accompanied, also, by a large retinue of nobility, among them Roger Mortimer, the young Earl of March, who, because of the childlessness of Richard, was heir to the British throne, through descent from the Duke of Clarence, in the female line. Richard did not wait long in Waterford, but proceeded on his march to Dublin, unfurling the banner of Edward the Confessor, for whom the Irish were supposed to have a deep veneration. MacMurrough, however, showed scant courtesy to the Confessor's ensign, not because it was the banner of a saint, but because, for the time, it represented the rapacity of England. Richard was met boldly at every point. His bowmen got tangled up in the woods. His horsemen floundered in the bogs. MacMurrough's army hovered in his front, on his flanks, and in rear. Not a single success did the English monarch gain. He summoned MacMurrough to a conference when he reached Dublin—having lost a third of his army while en route—and the Leinster king, having accepted the invitation, was ruthlessly thrown into prison. After a time, a treaty of some kind was patched up between King Richard and himself, and the Irish prince was allowed to go free. Richard then returned to England, leaving Roger Mortimer in command. Soon afterward, Mac-Murrough, objecting to the English encroachments in his territory, again rose in arms. He encountered Mortimer and the English army on the banks of the King's River at Kenlis or Kells in Westmeath, and utterly routed them. England's heir-apparent was among the slain. This circumstance had much to do with bringing about the bloody Wars of the Roses in the succeeding century.

About this time Art MacMurrough and his chief bard, who, as was then the Irish custom, accompanied his patron everywhere, were invited to a banquet by one of the Norman lords, who treacherously pretended friendship. The invitation was accepted. While seated at a window of the banquet-hall, the bard perceived a mustering of troops around the castle, and at once seized his harp and struck the chords to an ancient Irish air. The Gaelic words which accompanied the measure fell upon the ears of Art MacMurrough and warned him of his danger. His sword and buckler hung near by. On some trivial pretext, he arose and seized them, the bard having, meanwhile, armed himself. The two made a sudden onslaught and, surprising their foes, cut their way to the courtyard, where, fortunately, their horses still stood. They sprang upon them, and, before the astonished men-at-arms could rally, made good their escape. Art Mac-Murrough never again trusted the English, and remained their consistent foe to his latest hour.

But King Richard, maddened by the death of Mortimer, which he felt was dangerous to himself, raised another great army, and, in 1398, again invaded Ireland. He was accompanied by a younger son of his uncle, John of Gaunt, "time-honored Lancaster," and also by Prince Henry, eldest son of Henry of Hereford and afterward Henry V, the hero of Agincourt. The boy was only in his twelfth year, but well grown and brave as a lion. In the first encounter with the formidable MacMurrough, in the glens of Carlow, he so distinguished himself that Richard II knighted him on the field. This march from Waterford to Dublin proved, in the end, even more disastrous than the former one. MacMurrough kept up his harassing tactics, as usual. The rain poured down in torrents. The Irish drove all the cattle away from the English line of march, and destroyed the growing crops. Nearly all the baggage-animals of the invading force died for want of forage, and the army was in a state of famine and revolt, when it finally reached the seacoast near the present town of Arklow, where some English ships, laden with provisions, saved it from actual starvation. The remnant made its way to Dublin, where other disastrous news awaited King Richard. Henry of Hereford, eldest son of John of Gaunt, whom he had unjustly exiled, and whose lands he had seized, now, on the death of his father, having become Duke of Lancaster, came back from the continent, having heard of Richard's misfortunes in Ireland, and laid claim to the crown. Richard, after ordering young Prince Henry and his uncle to be imprisoned in the castle of Trim—still one of the finest Norman keeps in Ireland—set sail for England. Henry, who had by this time raised a large army, made him prisoner and sent him to Pontefract Castle, in Yorkshire, where, soon afterward, he was starved to death, or otherwise foully made away with. Prince Henry and his uncle were immediately released when the Duke of Lancaster ascended a usurped throne as Henry IV of England. And thus was laid the bloody foundation of the dreadful after wars between the rival royal houses of York and Lancaster, which ended in the extermination of the legitimate Plantagenets. An illegitimate branch, directly descended from John of Gaunt, still survives in the ducal house of Beaufort.

Art MacMurrough remained a conqueror to the end, and kept up the war with the Normans. In 1404, he defeated at Athcroe (Ford of Slaughter), near Dublin, Lord Thomas of Lancaster, brother of the king, putting most of the English to the sword, and desperately wounding the prince himself.   Only a few years ago, Irish laborers, excavating for a railroad at Athcroe, came upon nearly a thousand bent swords, some of them badly decomposed by rust, buried in the river bed.   They were the swords taken from the dead English, in 1404, and bent across the knees of the victorious Irish, according to their custom in those days.

MacMurrough's career of glory continued until 1417, when, having captured all the important towns of Leinster, except Dublin and Drogheda, he died at his capital of New Ross—then the second city in Ireland—as some say by poison, in the sixtieth year of his age and forty-fourth of his reign.   Taken for all in all, he was not alone the bravest, but the ablest, of Irish princes and warriors since the days of King Brian, and it was a sad day for Ireland when the word went through Leinster and rang around the island that King Art was dead.   Many a dark generation passed away before such another chief, or any one worthy to be mentioned as a rival of his fame, arose in that unfortunate land.

CHAPTER XVI

Ireland During the Wars of the Roses

AFTER the premature death of Henry IV, an able but unscrupulous sovereign, in 1413, the attention of England was again directed to the conquest of France by the chivalrous and skilful Henry V. His capture of Harfleur and marvelous victory of Agincourt, against overwhelming odds, in 1415, stamp him as one of the world's great military leaders. During the nine years of his reign, he succeeded in subduing France, and, finally, married Catherine, heiress of Charles VI, an almost imbecile king, and had himself declared regent and next in succession to the throne after his father-in-law. France was stupefied, but God, infinitely stronger than French arms, decreed Henry's early death. He died in the conquered country in 1422, leaving an only son, Henry VI, an infant of nine months, to succeed him, under the regency of his uncle, Humphrey, Duke of Gloucester, who, for a wonder, considering the history of the Plantagenets, remained faithful to his trust. John, Duke of Bedford, a younger brother of Henry, and a very brilliant soldier, became regent of France. This was the period of the inspired peasant-girl, Joan of Arc, whose story of victory and death belongs to the history of France, although, after having performed prodigies, she died at the stake to which the English, into whose hands she had fallen, condemned her. The Dauphin, as Charles VII, succeeded to his legitimate throne, and, about 1453, the

English were expelled from France, except the old town of Calais, which remained in their possession until 1558. In Ireland, meanwhile, the chief feuds were those between the Geraldines and the Butlers and the De Burgos and the Connaught chiefs. There were also minor feuds in different parts of the island, but, as a rule, the Irish people had things pretty much their own way, and might have thrown off the English yoke utterly, if they had had an Edward Bruce or Art MacMurrough to arouse and lead them to victory. Unfortunately they had not, and, as the English fetter was very light on Ireland during the Wars of the Roses, which began in 1455, they imagined, perhaps, that the old enemy, having plenty of fighting to do on their own account, might leave them alone for evermore—a vain hope if it were seriously entertained.

After an interval of six years, the Wars of the Roses —so-called because the red rose was the badge of the House of Lancaster and the white that of the House of York—broke out more violently than before, because Henry VI, who had been declared imbecile and unfit to reign, suddenly recovered his intellect, and Richard Plantagenet, Duke of York, who claimed a prior right to the throne, and had been appointed Regent, with the right of succession, refused to give up his authority. Henry had a son by his brave wife, Margaret of Anjou. He might be called a weakling, but she summoned the people to defend the rights of her son. York was defeated, captured, and beheaded at Wakefield, in 1461, but his son Edward, Earl of March, routed the queen's army immediately afterward and ascended the throne as Edward IV. Struggle succeeded struggle, but the House of

York achieved a crowning triumph at Tewkesbury and again at Barnet Heath, where Warwick, the King Maker, fell. The direct male line of the House of Lancaster perished at Tewkesbury, where, it is alleged, the gallant Prince Edward, son of Henry VI, was murdered, after having been made prisoner, by Edward IV and George, Duke of Clarence—the same afterward drowned in a butt of wine by order of his cruel brother. King Edward IV, after a reign of twenty-two years, marked by slaughter of his foes and some of his friends, notorious immorality, and swinish debauchery, died of a fever brought on by his excesses, in 1483, and his vile younger brother, the Duke of Gloucester, succeeded the boy king, Edward V, by process of murder, in the same year. The last battle of the Wars of the Roses was fought at Bosworth, near Leicester, August 22, 1485. Richard, last king of the Plantagenet family, fell and was succeeded by his rival, Henry Tudor, Earl of Richmond, descended, in the female line, from John of Gaunt, who ascended the throne as Henry VII.

Thus, you will see, Ireland was left pretty much to herself, during those thirty years of English civil war, in which twelve murderous pitched battles were fought. Most of the old nobility were killed in battle or executed, or otherwise destroyed, and more than one hundred thousand Englishmen of the middle and lower classes were immolated on the smoking altars of family pride and savage ambition. Every prince of the race of Plantagenet was exterminated when, in 1599, Henry VII ordered the beheading of the young Earl of Warwick, son of the Duke of Clarence. Many of the Anglo-Irish lords and their followings took part in the English wars, mainly on the side of the House of York, and the Geraldines, in particular, got sadly mixed up in them, for which they suffered amply in after days. No reigning king of England had set foot in Ireland since Richard II sailed to his death from Dublin, and Henry VII proved to be no exception to the rule. He, however, interfered in the quarrel between the Fitzgeralds and the Butlers—as bitter and prolonged as that between the Camerons and Campbells in Scotland—and made the Earl of Kildare viceroy. The Desmonds, the powerful southern branch of the Geraldines, were also eternally at variance with the Butlers. It is related that, on one occasion, the Earl of Desmond was wounded and made prisoner. While being borne on a litter to Butler's stronghold, one of the bearers insolently and brutally demanded, "Where is the great Earl of Desmond now?" To which the heroic captive immediately replied—"Where he ought to be" (alluding to the litter in which he was carried by his foes) : "still on the necks of the Butlers!"

The most memorable event of Henry VII's reign, as far as Ireland was concerned, was the coming over from England of Sir Edward Poynings, as Lord Deputy during the temporary retirement of Kildare. The English colonists of the Pale, almost from their first settlement of that district, possessed an independent parliament, modeled on that of England. It was, in general, oppressive toward the Celtic-Irish, but made good laws enough for the Palesmen. Poynings, soon after his arrival, called this parliament to assemble at Drogheda and there (1495) the Statute of Kilkenny was reaffirmed, except as regarded the prohibition of Gaelic, which had come into general use, even in the Pale itself. The main enactment—the first uttered in the English tongue in Ireland—was that known as 10 Henry VII, otherwise Poynings' Law, which provided that no legislation should be, thereafter, proceeded with in Ireland unless the bills were first submitted for approval or rejection to the monarch and privy council of England. In case of approval they were to be attested by the great seal of the English realm. It was, to be sure, a most unjust and insolent measure, and it seems almost incredible that even the Pales people—mere hybrids, neither English nor Irish —should have tamely submitted to its infamous provisions. It remained in force 287 years, or until 1782, when it was repealed under circumstances that will appear hereafter.

The close of this reign witnessed a bloody struggle between the Kildares and Clanricardes, in which many Celtic tribes also bore a part, and in which thousands of men lost their lives to no good purpose. In the two principal battles, those of Knockdoe and Monabraher (1507-10), artillery and musketry were first made use of on Irish soil.

As most of the Irish Palesmen, including the House of Kildare, were partisans of the House of York during the Wars of the Roses, the two pretenders—prepared by Margaret, Duchess of Burgundy, sister of Edward IV, to impersonate, respectively, Edward, Earl of Warwick, only son and heir of the late Duke of Clarence, and Richard, Duke of York, the second son of Edward IV, who was murdered in the Tower, by order, it is said, of his base uncle, Richard III, together with his brother, the boy-king, Edward V—found adherents when they landed on Irish soil. Indeed, Lambert Simnel, the

first of these pretenders, a handsome young Englishman, who resembled the princes of the House of York,
was crowned king, as "Edward VI," in Christ Church
Cathedral, Dublin. Many Pales Irish followed him to
England, where Henry VII defeated and made him prisoner. The real Warwick was taken from the Tower and
paraded through the streets—a sad spectacle of physical
comeliness marred, and intellect clouded, by long and
harsh confinement. Having been sufficiently exhibited
to satisfy the public of Simnel's imposture, the poor boy
was returned to his cell. Simnel, himself, was made a
"turnspit" in the royal kitchen, afterward raised to the
post of falconer, and ended his days in that humble position. The second pretender, Perkin Warbeck, a Belgian
by birth, had less support from Ireland than his predecessor, but involved some of the nobles of the Pale with
King Henry. But his adherents, remembering the imposition of the bogus Edward VI, soon fell away, and
Perkin went to Scotland, where James IV received him,
as if he were a genuine prince, and gave him his cousin,
the lovely Lady Catherine Gordon, in marriage. Peace
being concluded between James and Henry, Warbeck
and his beautiful bride went to Cornwall. There the
pretender, who was really a man of noble presence and
great ability, rallied 3,000 men to his standard. Successful at first, he proved himself a false Plantagenet
by basely deserting his confiding followers on the eve
of decisive battle. He shut himself up in the sanctuary
of Beaulieu, in the New Forest, but soon surrendered
himself, and was shown by the king to the populace of
London. He was well treated for a time, but his position was mortifying. He ran off to another sanctuary,

was again forced to give himself up, was placed in the public stocks, confessed he was an impostor, and was finally sent to the Tower, to keep company with the unhappy Warwick. This circumstance enabled the crafty Henry to get up a so-called plot, of which it was easy to convict two helpless prisoners. Warwick—last male of the Plantagenets—lost his head on Tower Hill, and Warbeck died by the rope at Tyburn. His charming widow became lady-in-waiting to the Queen.

Many abbeys and monasteries were built in Ireland during this comparatively tranquil period, and the passion for learning revived to a great extent among the native Irish nobility. Pilgrimages, as of old, were made to distant lands for the purpose of worshiping at famous shrines. Irish teachers and scholars began again to be numerous in Spain, Germany, and Italy. Henry VII, engaged in saving the wreck of England's almost extinguished nobility, and in hoarding money, for which he had a passion, took little account of Ireland and the Irish. But, already, low on the horizon, a blood-red cloud was forming, and it gradually thickened and extended until, at last, it broke in a crimson torrent on the fated Irish nation.

BOOK II

TREATING OF IRISH AFFAIRS FROM THE PERIOD OF
THE REFORMATION TO THE EXILE AND DEATH OF
THE ULSTER PRINCES IN THE REIGN OF JAMES I

CHAPTER I

The "Reformation"—New Cause of Discord in Ireland

THE bitterness of race hatred had almost died out when the Reformation, as the opponents of the Church of Rome called the great schism of the sixteenth century, began to shake Europe like an earthquake. Luther, and other dissenters from Catholic faith, carried most of the north of Europe with them. The Latin countries, South Germany, all of Ireland, and most of England, clung to the old faith, and Henry VIII, who succeeded his father at an early age, and was quite learned in theology, wrote a pamphlet defending the Catholic dogmas against Luther and the others. This work procured for him from the Pope the title of the "Defender of the Faith," which still, rather inappropriately, belongs to the sovereign of England. But Henry was a good Catholic only so long as religion did not interfere with his passions and ambitions. He had been married in early life to Catherine of Aragon, who had been the nominal wife of his elder brother, another Prince of Wales, who died uncrowned. After many years, Henry, who was a slave to his passions, tired of Catherine, and pretended to believe that it was sinful to live with his brother's widow, even though the latter relationship was but nominal. In truth, he had fallen in love with Anne Boleyn, one of Queen Catherine's maids-of-honor. The Pope was appealed to for a divorce and refused to grant it, after having carefully examined into the case. Then

Henry severed England's spiritual connection with Rome, and declared himself head of the English "Reformed" Church.   In this he was sustained by Wolsey, Cromwell, and other high churchmen, all of whom were either ambitious or afraid of their heads, for Henry never hesitated, like his grand-uncle, Richard III, at the use of the axe, when any subject, clerical or lay, opposed his will.   But the tyrant, while refusing allegiance to the Pope, still maintained the truth of Catholic dogma, and he murdered with studied impartiality those who gave their adhesion to the Holy See and those who denied its doctrines; no Englishman of note felt his head safe in those red days.   As for the common people, nobody of "rank" ever gave them a thought.   Henry now seized upon the Church property, and, therewith, bribed the great lords to take his side of the controversy.   The boors followed the lords, and so most of England followed Henry's schism and prepared to go farther.

Henry married Anne Boleyn when he had "divorced" Queen Catherine.   After the Princess Elizabeth was born, he tired of his new wife, had her tried for faithlessness and high treason and beheaded.   Scarcely was she dead when the inhuman brute married Lady Jane Seymour, of the great Somerset family.   She gave birth to Prince Edward and died.   Then he married Anne of Cleves, but, not liking her person, "divorced" her and sent her back to Germany.   For "imposing" her on him, he disgraced, and finally beheaded, the Lord Chancellor, Thomas Cromwell, who had been his great friend.   The monster next espoused Lady Catherine Howard, of the House of Surrey, but he had her beheaded, on charges almost similar to those urged against Anne Boleyn, within the year.   At last he married a widow of two experiences, Lady Catharine Parr, who, being a woman of tact and cleverness, managed to save her head, although frequently in danger, until the ferocious king, who must have been somewhat insane, finally fell a victim to his own unbridled vices.   "The plain truth," says Charles Dickens, in his "Child's History," "is that Henry VIII was a most intolerable ruffian, a disgrace to human nature, and a blot of blood and grease upon the history of England."

This was the crowned "fiend in human shape" who sought to effect his "Reformation in Ireland," where both the Old Irish and the Old English had united against his tyranny.   The weight of his wrath fell first upon the Leinster Geraldines, whom he dreaded.   He contrived to pick a quarrel with Gerald, ninth Earl of Kildare, who had been for many years his favorite viceroy in Ireland, and summoned him to London in hot haste, on flimsy, notoriously "trumped-up" charges of treason.   He flung him into a dungeon in the Tower of London.   Lord Thomas Fitzgerald, son of the Earl, called "Silken Thomas," because of the beauty of his person and the splendor of his apparel, was appointed deputy by his father, who thought his absence in England might be brief.   Lord Thomas was young, brave, and rash, and, in short, the very man to fall an easy victim to the wiles of his House's enemies.   Tradition says that the false news of Earl Gerald's execution, by order of King Henry, was spread in Dublin by one of the Butlers.   The privy council, over which he usually presided, was already in session at St. Mary's Abbey, when "Silken Thomas" heard the story.   He, at once, with a large escort, proceeded to the abbey, renounced his allegiance to the English monarch, and, seizing the sword of state from the sword-bearer, threw it, with violent gesture, on the council table, "the English Thanes among." Protests availed nothing. He rushed to arms, and for nearly two years held at bay Henry's power.   Had he but laid his plans with care and judgment, he would, no doubt, have ended the rule of England over Ireland, which, although not his primary, became his ultimate, object.   In the end, his stronghold of Maynooth Castle was betrayed into the hands of the English general, Sir William Skeffington, by Lord Thomas's foster-brother, Parez, for a sum in gold. General Skeffington paid the money on the surrender of the castle, and immediately hanged the traitor.   For this act of chivalric justice, the name of that stern English- man is still held in respect by all readers of Irish history. The loss of Maynooth depleted the strength of "Silken Thomas."   He struggled on for some time longer, but, at last, accepted the terms of Lord Deputy Gray, who offered him his life and guaranteed the safety of his five uncles —two, at least, of whom had had no hand in the outbreak. They were invited to a banquet by the Lord Deputy, and there, while drinking with their false hosts, were treach- erously seized, placed in irons, and sent to England in a ship called the *Cow*.   One of the uncles, hearing the name of the vessel, said: "We are lost!   I have dreamed that six of us, Geraldines, would be carried to England in the belly of a cow and there lose our heads!"   The augury was fulfilled.   Henry VIII, with his usual disre- gard of terms, had them beheaded immediately after their arrival in London, at Tyburn.   The old Earl of Kildare had not been executed after all, but died of a broken heart in the Tower on learning of the revolt and misfortunes of his son.   Only one heir-male of the noble House of Kildare now survived, and for him, although only twelve years old, Henry sought, through his agents, with the relentless ferocity of a Herod.   The boy was related to the great Celtic houses, for the Geraldines of that period preferred Irish wives, and his mother was a princess of the House of O'Neill of Ulster.   By her, and by other noble Irish ladies, he was concealed and protected until he was enabled to escape to France.   Thence he proceeded to Rome, where he was educated as befitted his rank and lineage.   This young Gerald was restored to his titles and estates by Queen Mary I, but he accepted Protestantism when Elizabeth came to the throne, because, otherwise, he could not have saved land and title—a most unworthy motive, but one very common in that violent and sanguinary era.   In his descendants the elder Geraldine branch still lives in Ireland—the present head of the family being Maurice Fitzgerald, "the boy-Duke" of Leinster.

"Bluff King Hal," as the English called their royal Bluebeard, never did anything by halves, if he could help it.   He did not think the title of "Lord of Ireland" sufficient for his dignity, and set about intriguing to be elected king.   Accordingly, he caused to be summoned a parliament, or rather what we of to-day would call a convention, composed of Anglo-Irish barons and Celto-Irish chiefs, to meet in Dublin, A.D. 1541.   This parliament or convention, at which the great Ulster princes, O'Neill and O'Donnell, did not attend, voted Henry the crown of Ireland—something the Irish chiefs, at least, had no power to do, as they held their titles by election of their clans and not by right of heredity. The outcome was, however, that Henry became King of Ireland—the first English monarch to achieve that distinction. In order to emphasize his power, he at once decreed that the old titles of the Irish princes should give way to English ones. Thus "The O'Brien" became "Earl of Thomond"; "The MacWilliam," "Earl of Clanricarde"; "The MacMurrough" became "Baron of Ballynun," and changed his family name to Kavanagh. Shameful to relate, O'Neill and O'Donnell, both old men, broken in health, "came in" and joined the titled serfs. The former became "Earl of Tyrone" and the latter "Earl of Tyrconnel."

When the news reached the Irish clansmen, there was a general revolt and new chiefs of the same families, with the old Irish designations unchanged, were elected. The English interest supported "the King's O'Donnell" and the others of his type, while the bulk of the Irish people stood for the newly chosen leaders. Thus was still another firebrand cast by English policy among the Irish people, and there was civil war, thenceforth, for generations in the clans themselves.

Nor was Henry satisfied with mere civil supremacy in Ireland. He also set himself up as head of the Irish Church. Many Anglo-Irish Catholic bishops basely acquiesced in his policy, but the Celtic bishops, almost to a man, spurned his propositions. The masses of the Irish nation, whether of Celtic, Norman, or Saxon origin, remained steadfastly Catholic, although, in the past, they had had little cause to be pleased with the political action of the Vatican, which had generally sided with the Catholic monarchs of England against Ireland's aspirations after independence. Now, however, the favored country had become Rome's most deadly enemy in Europe, while Ireland, inhabited by a highly spirited and stubborn people, who venerated the creed taught their fathers by St. Patrick, became the foremost European champion of the old faith.

We can not dwell at greater length on this lurid dawn of the Reformation in Ireland, because, fierce as was the persecution under Henry, it was trivial compared with what followed his reign, and made the distracted island a veritable den of outrage and slaughter.

CHAPTER II

The Reformation Period Continued—Edward VI, Mary I, Elizabeth, and "John the Proud"

WHEN Edward VI, another boy-king, came to the throne, in 1547, Ireland was pretty well distracted, owing to the seeds of discord sown by his ferocious father. The young monarch was under the absolute control of his maternal kinsmen, the Seymours, and all that was done to forward the Reformation in Ireland during his brief reign may be justly attributed to them. On his death, in 1553, Mary, daughter of Henry VIII and Catherine of Aragon, and wife of Philip II of Spain, succeeded. She was a bigoted Catholic and soon made things decidedly warm for the Protestants in England. Many of these fled for safety to Ireland, where the Catholic people—incapable of cruelty until demoralized by the ruthless tyranny of religious persecution—received and sheltered them—a noble page of Anglo-Irish history.

The Reformation, of course, came to a standstill in

Ireland, during this queen's reign, but the plunder and persecution of the Irish people did not, therefore, abate. There were raids and massacres and confiscations, as usual. Of course there were bloody reprisals on the part of the Irish, also—as was but natural. Some of the old Irish dictricts—particularly Leix and Offaly—were, under the sway of Mary, called the King's and Queen's Counties—the chief town of the one being named Philipstown, after the queen's Spanish husband, and the capital of the other Maryborough, after herself. The Irish Reformers "laid low," as was prudent in them, during Mary's period of power, because she had the unpleasant Tudor habit of putting to death, by divers violent modes of punishment, those who presumed to differ from her rather strong opinions. The English, who sincerely rejoiced when, after reigning about five years, she passed to her account, nicknamed her "Bloody Mary," although she was not a whit "bloodier" than her awful father, and had a very formidable rival for sanguinary "honors" in her younger half-sister, Elizabeth. Mary Tudor was the last *avowed* Catholic monarch who reigned in England, except the ill-fated James II. In this reign, the English law of primogeniture was first generally introduced into the Celtic districts annexed to the Pale, which had been divided into "shire-ground," and this was the cause of much internal disorder among the Irish tribes that clung to the old elective system of chieftaincy.

Elizabeth, called by her admiring English subjects "Good Queen Bess," on very insufficient grounds, ascended the throne in 1558. She had, apparently, "conformed" to Catholicity during the lively reign of her half-sister, fearing, no doubt, for her head in case of refusal.

Henry VIII's daughter, by Anne Boleyn, she inherited great energy of character, a masculine intellect, superabundant vanity, a passion for empire, and a genius for intrigue. Her morals were none of the best, according to many historians. She was, for that age, highly educated, could speak divers tongues, and possessed many of the polite accomplishments. Indeed, she was somewhat of a female pedant. In person, while yet young, she was not ill-favored, being well formed and of good stature. Her complexion was fair, her hair auburn, and her eyes small, but dark and sparkling. Her temper was irritable; she swore when angry, and, at times, her disposition was as ferocious as that of "Old Hal" himself. Like his, her loves were passing passions, and her friendship dangerous to those on whom she lavished it most freely. Flattery was the surest way by which to reach her consideration, but, in affairs of state, not even that could cloud her powerful understanding or balk her resolute will. She resolved to finish what her father and brother had begun, and finish it to the purpose—namely, the Reformation—in both England and Ireland. In the former country, her will soon became law, and Rome ceased to be considered, for generations, as a factor in English affairs. In Ireland, it was different. The people there refused, as a great majority, to conform to the new order of things. They obeyed the Pope, as their spiritual chief, and went to mass and received the sacraments as usual. In Ulster, particularly, the people, headed by John O'Neill, Prince of Tyrone, surnamed "The Proud," resisted all English encroachments, civil and religious. A bloody war resulted. The English generals and some of the Anglo-Irish lords were commissioned by Elizabeth to

force the new religion down the throats of the Irish people at the point of the sword. The Liturgy, she proclaimed, must be read in English, the mass abandoned,
and she herself be recognized as Pope in Ireland, as well
as in England. Accordingly, the English armies burned
the Catholic churches and chapels, assassinated the clergy,
and butchered the people wherever resistance was offered.
But John O'Neill was a great soldier and managed, for
many years, to defend his country with great success, defeating the best of the English captains in several fierce
conflicts. Elizabeth, struck with his bravery and ability,
invited him to visit her at her palace of Greenwich. The
invitation was sent through Gerald of Kildare, O'Neill's
cousin. The Irish prince accepted and proceeded to court
with a following of three hundred galloglasses, or heavy
infantry, clad in saffron-colored jackets, close-fitting pan-
taloons, heavy shoes, short cloaks, and with their hair
hanging down their backs, defiant of Poynings' Law, and
all other English enactments. They were gigantic warriors—all more than six feet tall—and with huge mustaches, the drooping ends of which touched their collar-
bones. They also carried truculent-looking daggers and
immense battle-axes, such as might have won the admiration of Richard Cœur de Lion himself. The English
courtiers—pigmies compared with the galloglasses—
might have been inclined to make fun of their costumes,
but those deadly appearing axes inspired awe, and no unpleasant incident occurred during the visit. "Shane the
Proud" made a deep impression on Elizabeth, for he was
physically magnificent and as fierce as her dreaded father.
"By what right do you oppose me in Ulster?" she asked.
"By very good right, madam," he answered. "You may

be queen here, but I am king in Ulster, and so have been the O'Neills for thousands of years!" Then she offered to make him Earl of Tyrone by letters patent. "Earl me no earls, madam," he replied. "The O'Neill is my title! By it I stand or fall!" There was nothing more to be said, so the queen made him rich presents, after asking him to be her "good friend," which, being a gallant, he promised, and then he went back to Ulster.

But Shane, although a good general and a great fighter, was a bad statesman, and by no means a conscientious character. He oppressed the neighboring Irish chiefs, being, indeed, half mad with pride, and made a most unjust and unnecessary attack on the Clan O'Donnell, next to the O'Neills the most powerful of Ulster tribes. He not alone ruined the O'Donnell, but also dishonored him, by carrying his wife away and making her his mistress, in mad disregard of Irish public opinion. He also quarreled with the old MacDonald colony of Antrim—said by some writers to be Irish, not Scotch, in their origin—and used them with extreme harshness. In the end, his misconduct produced a revolt even among his own followers. His enemies, including the injured O'Donnells, speedily multiplied, and he who had been fifty times victorious over the English, was, at last, signally defeated by his own justly indignant fellow-countrymen. In this extremity, he fled with his mistress and a few followers for refuge to the MacDonalds, who, at first, received the fugitives hospitably, but soon, instigated, it is said, by one Captain Piers, an Englishman, fell upon O'Neill at a banquet and stabbed him to death. Had he loved his own people as much as he hated the English, he might have lived and died a conqueror. The

MacDonalds did not respect the body of this dead lion. They severed the head from the trunk, pickled it, and sent the ghastly present to the English Lord Deputy in Dublin, who caused it to be spiked on the tower of Dublin Castle. O'Neill's death, in the very prime of his military genius, relieved Elizabeth of her most dangerous Irish enemy. But another scion of that warrior race was under the queen's "protection" in London, and was destined to raise the Bloody Hand, the cognizance of his house, to a prouder eminence than it had attained in Irish annals since the far-off days of Nial of the Hostages.

Treacherous massacres of Irish chieftains dangerous to England's supremacy in their country would appear to have been a special feature of Elizabeth's reign. Under the Lord Deputy Sydney's régime, A.D. 1577, Sir Francis Cosby, the English general commanding in the ancient territories of Leix and Offaly, unable to obtain the submission of the native chiefs by force of arms, invited several hundred of them to a banquet at the rath of Mullaghmast, in the present county of Kildare. The principal families represented were the O'Mores, O'Nolan's, O'Kelly's, and Lalors. The rath, or fort, was fitted up for the occasion, and, through the entrance, the unsuspecting Irish chieftains and their friends rode with happy hearts and smiling faces. But one of the Lalors who was rather belated, had his suspicions aroused by the dead silence which seemed to prevail in the rath, and by the peculiar circumstance that none of those who had entered came out to welcome the later arrivals. He bade the few friends who had accompanied him to remain outside, while he entered the fort to investigate. He took the precaution to draw his sword before

he went in.   Proceeding with caution, he was horrified
at stumbling over the dead bodies of some of his neighbors just beyond the entrance.   He retreated at once, but
was set upon by assassins placed there to murder him.
A powerful man, he wielded his blade with such good
effect that he cut his way out, mounted his horse, and
set off with his horrified associates at full gallop to his
home at Dysart.   More than four hundred confiding
Irish gentlemen had entered the rath that day, and of all
of them, only the sagacious Lalor escaped.   The tribe of
O'More alone lost nearly two hundred of its foremost
members, but was not entirely exterminated.   Rory Oge
O'More, son of the slaughtered head of the tribe, made
relentless war on the English Pale, and never desisted
until he had more than avenged his kindred slain in the
foul massacre of Mullaghmast.

CHAPTER III

The Geraldine War—Hugh O'Neill and "Red Hugh" O'Donnell

ULSTER was subdued, for a time, but, in Munster,
the younger branch of the Geraldines, known as
Earls of Desmond, rose against the edicts of Elizabeth
and precipitated that long, sanguinary, and dreary conflict known as the Geraldine War.   Most of the Irish
and Anglo-Irish chiefs of the southern province bore a
part in it, and it only terminated after a murderous struggle, stretching over nearly seven years.   The Desmonds
and their allies gained many successes, but lack of co-
hesion, as always, produced the inevitable result—final
defeat.   South Munster became a desert.   Elizabeth's

armies systematically destroyed the growing crops, and, at last, famine accomplished for England what the sword could not have done. The Munster Geraldines were mainly led by Sir James Fitzmaurice, a kinsman of the earl, who was a brave man and an accomplished soldier. The earl himself, and his brother, Sir John Fitzgerald, had been summoned to London by the queen, and were made prisoners and placed in the Tower, after the usual treacherous fashion. After a period of detention, they were transferred, as state prisoners, to Dublin Castle, but managed to effect their escape (doubtless by the connivance of friendly officials) on horseback and reached their own country in due time. The earl, foolishly, held aloof from Fitzmaurice until a dangerous crisis was reached, when he threw himself into the struggle and, in defence of his country and religion, lost all he possessed. The Pope and King of Spain, in the Catholic interest, sent men and money, but the Papal contingent, led by an English military adventurer, named Stukley, was diverted from its purpose, and never reached Ireland. The Spanish force—less than a thousand men—was brought to Ireland by Fitzmaurice himself. He had made a pilgrimage to Spain for that purpose. Smerwick Castle, on the Kerry coast, was their point of debarkation. With unaccountable timidity, Earl Desmond made no sign of an alliance, and Fitzmaurice was in search of other succor, when he fell, in a petty encounter with the De Burgos of Castle Connell. The Spaniards, who occupied Smerwick, were besieged by a large Anglo-Irish force, under the Earl of Ormond and other veteran chiefs. They made a gallant and desperate defence, but they were invested by land and sea, and were perfectly helpless against the shower of shot and shell rained upon them night and day by the English batteries. Seeing that further resistance was useless, the Spanish commander finally surrendered at discretion, but, disgraceful to relate, Lord Deputy De Grey refused quarter and the hapless Spaniards were butchered to the last man. It is not pleasant to have to state that among the fierce besiegers were the celebrated Sir Walter Raleigh, the great English poet Edmund Spenser, and Hugh O'Neill, then serving Elizabeth, "for policy's sake," in a subordinate capacity, but afterward destined to be the most formidable of all her Irish foes. The Munster Geraldines were exterminated, except for a few collateral families—the Knight of Kerry, the Knight of Glin, and some other chiefs whose titles still survive. But the great House of Desmond vanished forever from history, when Garret Fitzgerald, the last earl, after all his kinsmen had fallen in the struggle, was betrayed and murdered by a mercenary wretch, named Moriarty, in a peasant's hut in Kerry, not far from Castle Island. The assassin and his brutal confederates decapitated the remains and sent the poor old head to Elizabeth, in London, who caused it to be spiked over the "traitor's gate" of the Tower. So ended the Geraldine revolt, which raged in Munster from 1578 to 1584, until all that fair land was a desert and a sepulchre. The bravest battle fought during its continuance was that of Glendalough, in the summer of 1580. This was on the soil of Leinster, and the victory was won by the heroic Clan O'Byrne, of Wicklow, led by the redoubtable chief, Fiach MacHugh. The English, who were led by Lord De Grey in person, suffered a total rout, and the Lord Deputy, at the head of the few terrified survivors, fled in disgrace to Dublin, leaving behind him the dead bodies of four of his bravest and ablest captains—Audley, Cosby, Carew, and Moore.

"Carew and Audley deep had sworn the Irish foe to tame,
  But thundering on their dying ear his shout of victory came;
  And burns with shame De Grey's knit brow and throbs with rage his eye,
  To see his best, in wildest rout, from Erin's clansmen fly."

The defeat and death of "Shane the Proud" had left Ulster, temporarily, without a military chief competent to make head against the English, and, therefore, the Desmonds were left, practically, without help from the northern province. Notwithstanding, the new Lord Deputy, Perrott, kept his eyes fixed steadily on Ulster, the fighting qualities of whose sons he knew only too well. In Tyrconnel young Hugh Roe, or Red Hugh, O'Donnell, was growing fast to manhood, and his fame as an athlete, a hunter, and hater of the English, spread throughout Ireland. Hugh O'Neill, the son of Matthew, Baron of Dungannon, was enjoying himself at Elizabeth's court, where he made the acquaintance of Cecil, Essex, Bacon, Marshal Bagnal, Mountjoy, and numerous other celebrities, and basked in the sunshine of the royal favor, which he took particular pains to cultivate. He was a handsome young man, of middle size, rigidly trained to arms, and "shaped in proportion fair." The queen's object was to make him an instrument in her hands for the final subjugation of Ireland. He seemed to enter readily into her plans, which his quick intellect at once comprehended, and he met her wiles with a dissimulation as profound as her own. If any man ever outwitted Elizabeth, po-

litically, that man was Hugh O'Neill, whom she finally
created Earl of Tyrone—a title which, in his inmost
heart, he despised, much preferring his hereditary designation of "The O'Neill." But it was not Hugh's immediate purpose to quarrel with Elizabeth about titles, or, in
fact, anything else. He was graciously permitted to raise
a body-guard of his own clansmen, and to arm and drill
them at his pleasure. Nay, more, the queen allowed him
to send from England shiploads of lead wherewith to
put a new roof on his castle of Dungannon. And he
went to Ireland to look after his interests in person.
Soon, rumors reached Elizabeth that O'Neill, when he
had sufficiently drilled one batch of clansmen, substituted
another; and that enough lead had been shipped by him
from England to Tyrone to roof twenty castles. It was
further rumored that the clanswomen of Tyrone were
employed casting bullets at night, instead of spinning
and weaving. O'Neill, learning of these rumors from
English friends, repaired to London, and, at once, reassured the queen as to his "burning loyalty and devotion
to her person." So he was permitted to return to Dungannon unmolested. Unlike his fierce kinsman, John the
Proud, Hugh cultivated the friendship of all the Ulster
chiefs, within reach, and more particularly that of the
brave and handsome young Red Hugh O'Donnell. Nor
did he confine his friendly relations to the chiefs of Ulster. He also perfected good understandings with many
in the other three provinces, and managed to keep on good
terms with the English also. Indeed, he did not hesitate
to take the field occasionally "in the interest of the queen,"
and, on one occasion, during a skirmish in Munster, received a wound in the thigh. How could Elizabeth

doubt that one who shed his blood for her could be otherwise than devoted to her service? O'Neill, no doubt, liked the queen, but he loved Ireland and liberty much better. In his patriotic deceit he only followed the example set him at the English court. He kept "open house" at Dungannon Castle for all who might choose or chance to call. Among others, he received the wrecked survivors of the Spanish Armada cast away on the wild Ulster coast, and shipped them back to Spain, at his own expense, laden with presents for their king. A kinsman, Hugh of the Fetters—an illegitimate son of John the Proud by the wife of O'Donnell, already mentioned—betrayed his secret to the English Government. He explained his action to the satisfaction of the Lord Deputy, for he had a most persuasive tongue. Having done so, he exercised his hereditary privilege of the chief O'Neill, arrested Hugh of the Fetters, had him tried for treason, and, it is said, executed him with his own hand, because he could find no man in Tyrone willing to kill an O'Neill, even though proven a craven traitor.

Lord Deputy Perrott, in 1587, or thereabout, concocted a plan by which he got the young O'Donnell, whose rising fame he dreaded, into his power. A sailing-vessel, laden with wine and other merchandise, was sent around the coast of Ireland from Dublin and cast anchor in Lough Swilly, at a point opposite to Rathmullen. Red Hugh and his friends, young like himself, were engaged in hunting and fishing when the vessel appeared in the bay. The captain, in the friendliest manner, invited O'Donnell and his companions on board. They consented, and were plied with wine. By the time they were ready to return to shore, they found the hatches battened down and the ship under way for Dublin. And thus, meanly and most treacherously, was the kidnapping of this noble youth and his friends accomplished by, supposedly, an English gentleman.

O'Donnell, after a confinement of three years in Dublin Castle, managed to effect his escape, in company with some fellow captives. But they missed their way, and were overtaken and captured in the territory of O'Tuhill, at a place now called Powerscourt, in the county Wicklow. A second attempt, made two years later on, proved more successful, and the escaping party managed to reach the tribe-land of the O'Byrnes, whose brave chief, Fiach MacHugh, received and sheltered them. Art O'Neill, one of Red Hugh's companions, perished of cold and hunger—the season being winter—on the trip; and O'Donnell's feet were so badly frozen that he was partially disabled for life. This fact did not, however, interfere with his warlike activity. O'Byrne at once informed Hugh O'Neill of Red Hugh's escape and whereabouts, and the Ulster chief sent a guide, who brought him safely to Dungannon, where he was royally entertained and admitted to the knowledge of O'Neill's secret policy, which, as may have been surmised, aimed at the overthrow of English rule in Ireland.

After resting sufficiently, O'Donnell proceeded to Tyrconnel, where he was joyfully received by his people. His father, old and unenterprising, determined to abdicate the chieftaincy in his favor, and, accordingly, Red Hugh was proclaimed "The O'Donnell," with all the ancient forms. He proceeded with characteristic rigor to baptize his new honors in the blood of his foes. Old Turlough O'Neill had weakly permitted an English garrison to occupy his castle of Strabane. O'Donnell attacked it furiously and put all of the garrison to the sword. He followed up this warlike blow with many others, and soon struck terror into the hearts of all the "Englishry" and their much more despicable Irish allies, on the borders of Ulster and Connaught. His most active and efficient ally in these stirring operations was Hugh McGuire, Prince of Fermanagh—the best cavalry commander produced by either party during the long and devastating Elizabethan wars.

CHAPTER IV

Confiscation of Desmond's Domains—English Plantation of Munster

THERE had been, of course, a general "confiscation to the Crown"—that is, to the English "carpet-baggers"—of the broad domains of the defeated Desmonds, and their allies, and among the aliens who profited greatly thereby, for a time, at least, were the poetic Edmund Spenser, who obtained the castle and lands of Kilcolman, in Cork, and Sir Walter Raleigh, who fell in for extensive holdings in Youghal, at the mouth of the southern Blackwater, and its neighborhood. In the garden of Myrtle Grove House, Sir Walter's Youghal residence, potatoes, obtained from Virginia, were first planted in Ireland, and the first pipeful of tobacco was smoked. In connection with the latter event, a story is told that a servant-girl, about to scrub the floors, seeing smoke issuing from Sir Walter's nose and mouth, conceived him to be on fire, and emptied the contents of her pail over

him, in order, as she explained, "to put him out." Sir
Walter, we may be sure, did not relish her method of
fighting "the fire fiend."

The Desmond confiscation was by no means the first
case of the kind on record in Ireland. The original Geraldines took the lands by force from the Celtic tribes,
but they speedily amalgamated with the natives, and,
within a few generations, became full-fledged Irish in
every characteristic, except their family name. Neither
was this great confiscation the last, or greatest, as will be
seen in the progress of this narrative. The queen's ministers caused letters to be written to the officers of every
"shire" in England, "generously" offering Desmond's
plundered lands in fee simple—that is, practically, free of
cost—to all younger brothers, of good families, who
would undertake the plantation of Munster. Each of
these favored colonists was allowed to "plant" a certain
number of British, or Anglo-Irish, families, but it was
specifically provided that none of the native—that is, the
Celtic and Catholic and the Norman-Catholic—Irish were
to be admitted to the privilege. The country had been
made "a smoking desert" before this plantation of foreigners was begun. Most of the rightful owners had perished by famine and the sword, and those who still survived, "starvation being, in some instances, too slow,
crowds of men, women, and children were sometimes
driven into buildings, which were then set on fire" (Mitchel's "Life of Hugh O'Neill, page 68). "The soldiers
were particularly careful to destroy all Irish infants, 'for,
if they were suffered to grow up, they would become
Popish rebels.' " (*Ibid.* pp. 68, 69.) It is related by the
historian Lombard that "women were found hanging

upon trees, with their children strangled in the mother's hair."

And all this was done in the name of the "reformed religion." In good truth, although Elizabeth herself may have wished to make the Irish people Protestant in order that they might become more obedient to her spiritual and temporal sway, her agents in Ireland wished for nothing of the kind. They wished the Irish masses to remain Catholic. Otherwise, they would have had no good pretext for destroying them and usurping their lands. And this, too, satisfactorily explains why, for a very long period, the Irish national resistance to England was considered and described as a purely Catholic, sectarian movement. Protestantism, in the period of which we write, meant, to the average Irish mind, England's policy of conquest and spoliation in Ireland. It is hardly wonderful, therefore, that there grew up between the followers of the old and new creeds an animosity doubly bitter—the animosity of race supplemented by that of religion. In our own days, we have seen the same result in the Polish provinces of Russia and the Turkish principalities in the Danubian region of Europe. Well might the poet ask—

> "And wherefore can not kings be great,
>   And rule with man approving?
> And why should creeds enkindle hate
>   And all their precepts loving?"

CHAPTER V

Conditions in Ulster Before the Revolt of O'Neill

THE first jury "trial" in Ulster was that of Hugh Roe MacMahon, chieftain of Monaghan, who became entangled with Lord Deputy Fitzwilliam in some one-sided "alliance," and, failing in some slight particular to keep his side of the contract, was "tried" by twelve soldiers in Elizabeth's pay, condemned to death and shot at his own door. This and other brutal murders, attested by the English historian, Moryson, filled the north with rage, and the very name of English "law" became a menace and a terror throughout the length and breadth of Ulster. From that bloody period dates the hatred and distrust of English "justice" which still survives among the Irish people. Indeed, instances of judicial murder, almost rivaling that of MacMahon Roe, might be cited by living Irishmen as having occurred within their own experience. Elizabeth's deputy, Fitzwilliam, who was a consummate scoundrel and jobber in bribes, and would have made a champion modern "boodle alderman," succeeded in making the very name of "shire," or county, land detested in Ireland. When he informed McGuire, the bold chief of Fermanagh, that he was about to send a sheriff into his "county" to "empanel juries," the chief answered grimly, "Let him come; but, first, let me know his eric (price of his blood), so that, if my people should cut off his head, I may levy it on the country." This was the Irish method under the Brehon law. No sheriff appeared in Fermanagh for many a year after McGuire's significant statement.

Red Hugh O'Donnell continued to make things exceedingly lively for the English garrisons in Ulster and Connaught, and made them take to the cover of their strong places after nearly every encounter. Near Enniskillen, the gallant Hugh McGuire, aided by a small body of the clansmen of Tyrone, who came "on the quiet," under the command of O'Neill's brother, Cormac, met a large English escort, who were conveying supplies to the town, to which Red Hugh O'Donnell had laid siege, at a ford of the river Erne. The English suffered a total rout, and their bread-wagons having been lost in the current, or overturned in the shallows, the spot is known to this day as Bael-atha-an-Biscoid—in English "the Ford of Buscuits." Red Hugh, who had gone to Derry to meet a body of the Antrim Scots, who were coming to his aid, was necessarily absent when the battle was fought, and, on hearing of the victory, remarked he was "sorry he had not been in the fight, as he would have prevented the escape of so many of the English." The latter began to perceive, by this time, that they had to "strip for the combat" in earnest if they meant to retain their foothold on the borders of Ulster.

Rumors of O'Neill's disaffection had again reached the queen, and again he journeyed to London and reassured her of his "loyalty." He even made great show of accepting the English title of Earl of Tyrone, and returned to Dungannon encumbered with the gold chain symbolical of his new "rank." This did not please his clansmen, who could not see into his dissembling schemes, so he was obliged to placate them by consenting to be

installed as The O'Neill—a title he very much preferred
to his English one of Earl—at the rath of Tulloghoge
(Hill of the Youths), in his native Tyrone. Thomas
Davis, the poet of Young Ireland—a party of Irish
literary men and high-souled patriots who flourished from
1842 until 1848—in his fine ballad of the "True Irish
King," gives a vivid picture of the scene in the following lines:

> "Unsandaled he stands on the foot-dinted rock;
> Like a pillar-stone fixed against every shock.
> Round, round as the rath, on a far-seeing hill,
> Like his blemishless honor and vigilant will.
> The graybeards are telling how chiefs by the score
> Had been crowned on the rath of the kings heretofore:
> While crowded, yet ordered, within its green ring,
> Are the dynasts and priests round the True Irish King.

> "The chronicler read him the laws of the clan,
> And pledged him to bide by their blessing and ban.
> His skian and his sword are unbuckled to show
> That they only were meant for a foreigner foe;
> A white willow wand has been put in his hand—
> A type of pure, upright, and gentle command,
> While hierarchs are blessing, the slipper they fling
> And O'Cahan proclaims him a True Irish King.

> "Thrice looked he to heaven with thanks and with prayer,
> Thrice looked to his borders with sentinel stare—
> To the waves of Lough Neagh, to the heights of Strabane;
> And thrice to his allies, and thrice to his clan—
> One clash on their bucklers—one more—they are still—
> What means the deep pause on the crest of the hill?
> Why gaze they above him? A war eagle's wing!
> ''Tis an omen—hurrah for the True Irish King!'"

Those who may condemn the apparently tortuous policy of O'Neill must bear in mind that he was only practicing against the enemies of his country the double-

dealing and subtle acts they had themselves taught him, in order to make him a more facile instrument in their hands for that country's subjugation. The dark and crooked policy inculcated by Machiavelli was then in vogue at all the European courts, and at none was it practiced more thoroughly than at that of Elizabeth of England. It must be admitted that the English found in Hugh O'Neill a very apt pupil—a true case of "diamond cut diamond."

CHAPTER VI

O'Neill Draws the Sword—Victories of Clontibret and Armagh

MARSHAL SIR HENRY BAGNAL—one of Elizabeth's most potent military commanders—had never liked Hugh O'Neill, whom he had often met in London and Dublin, but this hatred of the Irish prince was not shared by the marshal's fair sister, the Lady Mabel Bagnal, who presided over his mansion at Newry, where were established the headquarters of the English army in Ulster. Lady Mabel was one of the most beautiful of women, and O'Neill, who had become a widower, grew desperately enamored of her. He managed to elude the vigilance of the hostile brother, and, assisted by a friendly "Saxon," succeeded in eloping with and making her his wife. The elopement filled Sir Henry with fury. He entered into a conspiracy against O'Neill with other Englishmen and Palesmen. A new Lord Deputy had come over from England in the person of Sir William Russell. Charges against O'Neill were laid before him. He communicated with the Court of London and commands soon came to arrest the Chief of Tyrone without delay. O'Neill, as usual, had means of secret information and soon knew all about the plot laid for his destruction. Instead of being dismayed, he hastened, at once, to Dublin and surprised his treacherous accusers in the midst of their deliberations. His old-time friend, the Earl of Ormond, stood by him and refused to be a party to the treachery planned by the new Lord Deputy. When a similar order had reached Ormond himself from Lord Burleigh—ancestor of the late Prime Minister of England—the earl replied scornfully in these words: "My lord, I will never use treachery to any man, for it would both touch her Highness's honor and my own credit too much; and whosoever gave the queen advice thus to write is fitter for such base service than I am. Saving my duty to her Majesty, I would I might have revenge by my sword of any man that thus persuadeth the queen to write to me." Noble words, gallant Ormond!

The earl, feeling convinced that Lord Russell, who was not much affected by honorable scruples, would obey the order from the queen and arrest O'Neill, advised the latter to fly from Dublin the very night of his arrival. The Ulster prince thought this very good advice and accepted Ormond's friendly offices. He managed to make his way in safety to Dungannon and at once set about perfecting his preparations for open warfare with the generals of Elizabeth. The latter were not idle either, for Russell surmised O'Neill's intention and sent Sir John Norreys (Norris), an experienced general, just returned from the wars in Flanders, to command against him. The remainder of the year 1594, as well as some of the succeeding year, was spent in useless negotiations, for both parties well knew that war was now inevitable. O'Donnell, McGuire, and some other chiefs kept up a fierce, but rather desultory, warfare, greatly annoying the English garrisons in the border strongholds. At last, in the early summer of 1595, O'Neill threw off the mask, unfurled the Red Hand of Ulster, and marched against the Castle of Monaghan, held by the enemy. In the midst of a siege but feebly carried on for lack of a battering train, he heard that Norreys, with a powerful force, was advancing northward to raise the siege. O'Neill at once decided to anticipate his movement and moved to Clontibret, about five miles off, and there took post. Norreys soon appeared, and, being a hot soldier, attacked at once. He was met with a veteran firmness that astonished him, and both he and his brother, Sir Thomas Norreys, were wounded in the main attack on the Irish battle-line. At the moment when all seemed lost for England, Colonel Segrave, an Anglo-Norman of Meath, charged the Irish home, with a body of horse, and, for a time, restored the battle. Segrave, himself, rushed madly on O'Neill and the two leaders fought hand to hand for some time, while both armies stood still to witness the result. Mr. Mitchel thus eloquently describes what followed: "Segrave again dashed his horse against the chief, flung his giant frame upon his enemy, and endeavored to unhorse him by the weight of his gauntleted hand. O'Neill grasped him in his arms, and the combatants rolled, in that fatal embrace, to the ground.

'Now, gallant Saxon! hold thine own—
No maiden's hand is round thee thrown!
That desperate grasp thy frame might feel
Through bars of brass and triple steel.'

"There was a moment's deadly wrestle and a death groan. The shortened sword of O'Neill was buried in the Englishman's groin beneath his mail. Then from the Irish ranks rose such a wild shout of triumph as those hills had never echoed before. The still thunder-cloud burst into a tempest; those equestrian statues became as winged demons, and with their battle-cry of Lamh-dearg-ahoo! ('The Red Hand to Victory'), and their long lances poised in eastern fashion above their heads, down swept the chivalry of Tyrone upon the astonished ranks of the Saxon. The banner of St. George wavered and went down before that furious charge. The English turned their bridle-reins and fled headlong over the stream (which they had crossed to attack the Irish), leaving the field covered with their dead, and, worse than all, leaving with the Irish that proud red-cross banner, the first of their disgraces in those Ulster wars. Norreys hastily retreated southward, and the castle of Monaghan was yielded to O'Neill."

About the same time, Red Hugh O'Donnell "prevailed mightily" in the west, "so that," says Mitchel, "at the close of the year 1595, the Irish power predominated both in Ulster and Connaught." O'Neill followed up his success by laying siege to Armagh, which he captured by an ingenious stratagem. Colonel Stafford had been appointed to the command of the English in the old city, and he proved himself equal to the occasion, so far as fighting bravely to hold it went. But provisions were running low, and it was known to Stafford that Norreys was sending to him, from Dundalk, a large convoy of provisions. O'Neill's scouts had the same information, so a body of Irish was detached to attack the convoy and capture the rations. The movement proved successful. About three hundred English soldiers were made prisoners. O'Neill ordered them to be stripped of their red surtouts, and bade the same number of his clansmen to put the garments on their own backs. Then he commanded the convoy to march toward Armagh as if nothing had happened. Meanwhile, he had caused his relative, Con O'Neill, to occupy an old ruined abbey near the main gate of the city. All this was accomplished under cover of the night. At sunrise, Stafford and his hungry soldiers, from the ramparts, gazed wistfully southward, and, to their great joy, beheld, as they imagined, the convoy marching rapidly to their relief. Almost on the instant, it was, seemingly, attacked by the Irish army. Volleys—blank cartridges being used—were exchanged, and many men appeared to fall on both sides. At last, the supposititious English seemed about to give way. Stafford and his famished men could stand the sight no longer. They rushed through the now open gate to the aid of their countrymen, as they thought. To their amazement, both red coats and saffron shirts fell upon them, and they perceived they had been tricked. A brave attempt was made by them to re-enter the town, but Con O'Neill and his party, rushing from the old ruin, seized the gate. All the English outside the walls were captured. Soon afterward, the city itself surrendered to the Irish leader. O'Neill made humane use of his victory. He disarmed and paroled the English prisoners and sent them, under safe escort, back to General Norreys. He was a man of strict honor, and, no doubt, the terms of the capitulation were properly observed. The Irish dismantled Armagh, as O'Neill had no need of for-

tresses, but, during his absence elsewhere, some English
made their way to the place and refortified it; only, however, to have it retaken by the Irish army.

CHAPTER VII

Ireland Still Victorious—Battles of Tyrrell's Pass and Drumfluich

THE year 1597 witnessed the recall of Lord Deputy
Russell from the government of Ireland, and the
substitution of Lord De Burgh. A temporary truce was
entered into by the belligerents, and neither side lost any
time in augmenting its strength. All Ulster was practically freed from English rule, but they had garrisons
shut up in the castles of Carrickfergus, Newry, Dundrum,
Carlingford, Greencastle, and Olderfleet—all on the coast.
When the truce came to an end, the Palesmen organized
a large force and prepared to send it northward, to aid
those garrisons, under young Barnewall, son of Lord
Trimleston. O'Neill detached a force of 400 men under the brave Captain Richard Tyrrell and his lieutenant,
O'Conor, to ambush and destroy it. Tyrrell moved
promptly to accomplish his mission, and rapidly penetrated to the present county of Westmeath. There, at a
defile now known as Tyrrell's Pass, not far from Mullingar, he awaited the coming of the Palesmen. In the
narrow pass, the latter could not deploy, so that the battle was fought by the heads of columns, which gave the
advantage to the Irish. Some of the latter managed to
get on the flanks of the Palesmen, and a terrible slaughter ensued. Of the thousand Palesmen, only Barnewall
himself and one soldier escaped the swords of the venge-

ful natives. The former was brought a prisoner to O'Neill, who held him as a hostage, and the soldier carried the dread news of the annihilation of the Meathian force to Mullingar.

But the Lord Deputy and the Earl of Kildare, with all the force they could muster, were in full march for Ulster. Sir Conyers Clifford, another veteran Englishman, attempted to join them from the side of Connaught, but was met by Red Hugh O'Donnell and compelled to go back the way he came, leaving many of his men behind him. At a place called Drumfluich, the Lord Deputy and Kildare, who were en route to recapture Portmore, which had fallen into the hands of O'Neill, encountered the Irish army. The latter was strongly posted on the banks of the northern Blackwater, but the English attacked with great resolution, drove its vanguard across the river and took possession of Portmore. O'Neill, however, held his main body well in hand, and while De Burgh was congratulating himself on his success, fiercely attacked the English who had crossed to the left bank of the river, and inflicted on them a most disastrous defeat. The Lord Deputy and the Earl of Kildare were both mortally wounded, and died within a few hours. The English army was practically destroyed. Red Hugh O'Donnell had arrived in the nick of time to complete the victory, and, with him, the Antrim MacDonalds, whose prowess received due honor. The historian of Hugh O'Neill says, succinctly: "That battlefield is called Drumfluich. It lies about two miles westward from Blackwater-town (built on the site of Portmore), and Battleford-bridge marks the spot where the English reddened the river in their flight."

But Captain Williams, a valiant "Saxon," held Portmore, in spite of O'Neill's great victory, and this fortress, in the heart of his country, proved a thorn in the side of Tyrone, who, as we have already mentioned, was destitute of battering appliances for many a day. The result at Drumfluich struck dismay into the hearts of the stoutest soldiers of the English interest, and the dreaded names of O'Neill and the Blackwater were on every trembling lip throughout the Pale. The queen, in London, grew very angry, and rated her ministers with unusual vehemence. It was fortunate for De Burgh and Lord Kildare that they died on the field of honor. Otherwise, they would have been disgraced, as was General Norreys for his defeat at Clontibret. He died of a broken heart soon after being deprived of his command in Ulster.

The English were also unfortunate in Connaught and Munster, and when the Earl of Ormond assumed the government of Ireland, by appointment, after the defeat and death of De Burgh, the English interest had fallen lower in the scale than it had been since the days of Richard II. The earl entered into a two months' armistice with O'Neill, and negotiations for a permanent peace were begun. O'Neill's conditions were: perfect freedom of religion not only in Ulster but throughout Ireland; reparation for the spoil and ravage done upon the Irish country by the garrisons of Newry and other places, and, finally, entire and undisturbed control by the Irish chiefs over their own territories and people. (Moryson, McGeoghegan, and Mitchel.)

Queen Elizabeth was enraged at these terms, when transmitted to her by Ormond, and sent a list of counterterms which O'Neill could not possibly entertain. He saw there was nothing for it but the edge of the sword, and grew impatient at the tardiness of King Philip of Spain in not sending him aid while he was prosecuting the war for civil and religious liberty so powerfully. The English Government, in order to discourage the Catholic powers and keep them from coming to the aid of Ireland, concealed or minimized O'Neill's splendid victories. Lombard, cited by McGeoghegan—a most conscientious historian—avers that an English agent was employed, at Brussels, "to publish pretended submissions, treaties, and pardons, so that the Spanish governor of Flanders might report to his master that the power of the Irish Catholics was broken and their cause completely lost." (Mitchel.) The same charge has been made against England in our own day—only in a different connection. Germany, France, and Russia have semi-officially declared that English agents at Berlin, Paris, and St. Petersburg have persistently misrepresented the attitude of those countries toward America during the recent Spanish War. Whatever may have been the truth regarding the Brussels agent, it is undeniable that King Philip abandoned Ireland to her fate until it was too late to hinder her ruin; and that, when Spanish troops landed at Kinsale, in 1601, they proved more of a hindrance than a help. O'Neill gave up all hope of assistance from Philip in the fall of 1597 and resolved to stake all on his genius as a commander, and on the tried valor of the glorious clansmen of Tyrone and Tyrconnel.

CHAPTER VIII

Irish Victory of the Yellow Ford, Called the Bannockburn of Ireland

WE dwell at greater length on the Elizabethan era in Ireland than, perhaps, on any other, because then began the really fatal turn in the fortunes of the Irish nation. Notwithstanding splendid triumphs in the field, cunning and treachery were fated to overcome patriotism and heroic courage. But, before this great cloud gloomed upon her, Ireland was still destined to witness many days of glory, and to win her most renowned victory.

The spring and early summer of 1598 saw Captain Williams still holding Portmore, on the Blackwater, stubbornly for England, but his rations were nearly exhausted and he managed to get word of his desperate condition to Marshal Bagnal, who, at the head of a splendidly appointed army of veteran troops, horse and foot, marched northward from Newry to his succor. His first operations were successful and he came very near to capturing O'Neill himself, at a place called Mullaghbane, not far from Armagh. Then Bagnal pushed on to raise the siege of Portmore, where Williams was living on his starved horses and suffering all the pangs of hunger.

O'Neill, having been fully informed of Marshal Bagnal's progress, summoned O'Donnell and his other allies to join him immediately, which they did. He left Portmore to the famine-stricken garrison, and turned his face southward fully resolved to give battle to his redoubted brother-in-law before he could reach the Blackwater. Thoroughly acquainted with the character of the country through which the English were to pass, he had no difficulty in choosing his ground. He took post, therefore, in the hilly, wooded, and marshy angle formed by the Callan and Blackwater Rivers, at a point where a sluggish rivulet runs from a large bog toward the main river, and which is called, in the Gaelic tongue, Beal-an-atha-buidhe, in English, "the Mouth of the Yellow Ford," destined to give title to the Irish Bannockburn. This field is about two and one-half miles N.W. from Armagh.

The superb English array, all glittering in steel armor and with their arms flashing back pencils of sunlight, Bagnal himself in the van, appeared at the opening of the wooded pass, which, all unknown to the marshal, was garrisoned by five hundred Irish kerns early on the sultry morning of August 10th—T. D. McGee says the 15th—1598. The head of the column was attacked immediately by the Celtic infantry, who, however, obedient to orders, soon fell back on the main body, which was drawn up behind a breastwork, in front of which was a long trench, dug pretty deep, and concealed by wattles (dry sticks) and fresh-cut sods—a stratagem borrowed by O'Neill from the tactics of Bruce, so successfully put in practice at Bannockburn, nearly three centuries before. Having finally cleared the pass, not without copious bloodshed, Bagnal debouched from it, and deployed his forces on the plain in face of the Irish army. His cavalry, under Generals Brooke, Montacute, and Fleming, shouting, "St. George for England!" charged fiercely up to the Irish trench, where the horses floundered in the covered trap set for them, and then the Irish foot, leaping over their breastwork, piked to death the unfortunate riders. Bagnal, in no wise daunted, pressed on with his chosen troops, animating them by shout and gesture. A part of the Irish works, battered by his cannon, was carried, and the English thought the battle won. They were preparing to follow up their success when, suddenly, O'Neill himself appeared, at the head of his main body, who had abandoned their slight defences, and came on to meet the English with flashing musketry and "push of pike." Bagnal's artillery, with which he was well provided, did much damage to O'Neill's men, but nothing could withstand the Irish charge that day. O'Donnell's dashing clan nobly seconded their kinsmen of Tyrone, and a most desperate conflict ensued. Bagnal and his soldiers deported themselves bravely, as became tried warriors, but, in the crisis of the fight, the marshel fell, a wagon-load of powder exploded in the English lines, their ranks became confused, and few of their regiments preserved their formation. The Irish cavalry destroyed utterly what remained of the English horse. "By this time," says Mitchel, "the cannon were all taken; the cries of 'St. George' had failed or were turned to death-shrieks, and once more, England's royal standard sank before the Red Hand of Tyrone." The English rout was appalling, and the chronicler of O'Donnell says: "They were pursued in couples, in threes, in scores, in thirties, and in hundreds." At a point where the carnage was greatest, the country people still show the traveler the Bloody Loaming (lane) which was choked with corpses on that day of slaughter. Two thousand five hundred English soldiers perished in the battle and flight; and among the fallen were the marshal, as already related, twenty-two other superior officers, and a large number of captains, lieutenants, and ensigns.   The immediate spoils of the victory were 12,000 gold pieces, thirty-four standards, all the musical instruments and cannon, and an immense booty in wagons, loaded with clothing and provisions. The Irish army lost 200 in killed and three times that number wounded.   By O'Neill's orders, the dead of both sides were piously buried.   (Irish annals cited by Curry and Mitchel.)

Sir Walter Scott, in his graphic poem of "Rokeby," which should be read by all students, as it deals with a stirring period of English history, thus refers to the battle of the Yellow Ford:

"Who has not heard, while Erin yet
Strove 'gainst the Saxon's iron bit,
Who has not heard how brave O'Neill
In English blood imbrued his steel;
Against St. George's cross blazed high
The banners of his tanistry—
To fiery Essex gave the foil
And reigned a prince on Ulster soil?
But chief arose his victor pride
When that brave marshal fought and died,
And Avonduff* to ocean bore
His billows red with Saxon gore."

The survivors of Bagnal's heroic, if defeated, army, fled to Armagh, which had again fallen into the possession of the English, and there took shelter.   O'Neill invested the place and, being now provided with artillery, captured from the enemy, speedily compelled its surrender.   The gallant Williams, starved out at Portmore, also capitulated.   O'Neill, with his customary magnanim-

---

* Blackwater.

ity, after depriving the prisoners of both places of their arms, took their parole and sent them in safety to the Pale, and, for a time, all English power whatever vanished from the soil of Ulster.

CHAPTER IX

How O'Neill Baffled Essex—O'Donnell's Victory of the Curlew Mountains

THE limits of this simple narrative of Irish history will not permit us to go into the details of the numerous "risings" of the Irish and encounters with the disheartened English in the other three provinces. O'Donnell swept through Connaught, like a very besom of destruction, drove the English generals into their castles, and other strong places, and carried Athenry by storm, "sword in hand." He also made a raid into Munster, and punished a degenerate O'Brien of Inchiquin for accepting an English title, and hugging his English chain as "Earl of Thomond." Then he returned to Connaught and finished up what English garrisons still remained there, with few exceptions. O'Neill himself also made a visit to Munster, said his prayers at the noble shrine of Holy Cross Abbey, on the winding Suir, and, the legitimate—according to English notions—Earl of Desmond being dead, set up an earl of his own. He "put heart into" the rather slow and cautious Catholic Anglo-Normans of this province, and caused them to join hands with their Celtic brothers in defence of country and creed. Under the new earl, they attacked the English with great spirit, and, although occasionally beaten, managed to hold the upper hand in most cases.

In Leinster, the O'Mores, the O'Byrnes, the O'Tuhills, and the Kavanaghs had also risen in arms, and never had Ireland presented so united a military front, since the first landing of the English on her shore. There was fighting everywhere, but, outside of O'Neill and O'Donnell, and, perhaps, the new Desmond, there would not seem to have been a concerted military plan—probably owing to the rather long distances between the respective bodies and the difficulty of communication.

Queen Elizabeth, when she heard of the Irish triumph at the Yellow Ford, was violently exasperated, and stormed against Ormond, her Lord Lieutenant, for remaining in Leinster, skirmishing with the O'Mores and other secondary forces, and leaving everything in the hands of O'Neill in Ulster. She was now an aged woman, but still vain and thirsty for admiration. Her reigning favorite was the brilliant Robert Devereux, Earl of Essex, who had made a reputation in the Spanish wars. In the middle of 1599, this favored warrior, accompanied by a picked force of at least 20,000 men, landed in Dublin and assumed chief command. Instead of at once moving with his fine army, reinforced by the Palesmen and the relics of Norreys' and Bagnal's troops, against O'Neill, he imitated the dilatory tactics of Ormond and wasted away his strength in petty encounters with the hostile tribes of Leinster and the Anglo-Irish of Munster, most of whom sided, because of common religious belief, with their Celtic neighbors. He also committed the grave fault of bestowing high command on favorites who possessed no capacity for such duties. While marching to besiege Cahir Castle, in the present county of Tipperary, he was obliged to pass through a

wooded defile in Leix (Queen's County), where his rearguard of cavalry was attacked by the fierce O'Mores and
cut to pieces. The Irish tore the white plumes from
the helmets of the fallen English troopers, as trophies,
and so great was their number that the gorge has been
called, ever since that tragical day, Bearna-na-cleite—in
English, the "Pass of Plumes." Essex, notwithstanding this disaster, which he made no immediate effort to
avenge, marched to Cahir and took the castle; but, in
subsequent encounters with the Munster Irish, he suffered severe reverses. Near Croom, in Limerick, he
was met by the Geraldines and their allies and badly
defeated. Sir Thomas Norreys, Lord President of
Munster—brother of the defeated English commander
at Clontibret—was among the slain. Thus baffled, the
haughty Essex made his way sadly back to Dublin, pursued for a whole week by the victorious Geraldines.
Smarting under his disgrace, he caused the decimation
of an English regiment that had fled from the O'Mores
—something he himself had also been in the habit of
doing. He had no heart to try conclusions with the
terrible O'Neill in his Ulster fastnesses, and sent many
letters of excuse to the queen, in which he dwelt on
the strength and courage of the Irish clansmen in war,
and asked for further reinforcements, before venturing
against O'Neill. These were sent him, to the number
of several thousand, and, at length, he seemed ready to
move. Sir Conyers Clifford, a very brave and skilful
officer, commanded for Elizabeth in Connaught. Essex
ordered him to march into Ulster and seize certain
strategic points that would open the way for the main
army when it should finally appear in the North. Clif-

ford obeyed his orders with veteran promptitude. He was soon at Boyle, in the present county of Roscommon, where he went into camp near the beautiful abbey, whose ruins are still the admiration of antiquarians. Thence, he marched northward through the passes of the Corslibh, or Curlew, Mountains, bent upon penetrating into Ulster. But, in a heavily timbered ravine, he was fallen upon by the fierce clansmen of Red Hugh O'Donnell, commanded by their fiery chief in person. When the English heard the terrible war-cry of "O'Donnell Aboo!" ("O'Donnell to Victory") echoing along the pass, they knew their hour had come. However, they met their fate like brave men, worthy of their gallant commander, and fought desperately, although in vain. They were soon totally broken and fell in heaps under the stalwart blows of the Clan-O'Donnell. General Clifford and his second in command, Sir Henry Ratcliffe, were killed, and their infantry, unable to stem the tide of battle, fled in disorder, carrying with them the cavalry, under General Jephson, a cool commander who displayed all the qualities of a good soldier although completely overmatched. Had he not gallantly covered the retreat, hardly a man of the English infantry would have reached Boyle in safety. But the valor of Jephson did not extend to all of his men, some of whom abandoned the field rather precipitately. The English historian, Moryson, excuses them on the ground that "their ammunition was all spent." Sligo, the key of North Connaught, fell to O'Donnell, as one result of this sharp engagement.

The defeat and death of Clifford would seem to have utterly demoralized Essex. He again hesitated to advance against O'Neill, and, instead of doing so, weakly

sought a parley with his able enemy. O'Neill agreed to
the proposal, and they met near Dundalk, on the banks
of a river and in presence of their chief officers. The
Irish general, with chivalrous courtesy, spurred his
charger half-way across the stream, but Essex remained
on the opposite bank. This, however, did not prevent
the two leaders from holding a protracted conversation,
in the course of which the wily O'Neill completely outwitted the English peer. They called five officers on both
sides into the conference, and O'Neill repeated the terms
he offered after the victory of Clontibret, in 1595. The
Englishman said he did not think them extravagant, but
his sincerity was never tested. Soon afterward, angered
by an epistolary outburst from the old queen, he threw
up his command, and returned to the London court, where
Elizabeth swore at him, ordered him under arrest, had
him tried for treason, and, finally, beheaded—the only
cruel act of her stormy life she ever repented of. The axe
that severed the head of Essex from his body left a scar
in Elizabeth's withered heart that never healed.

CHAPTER X

King Philip Sends Envoys to O'Neill—The Earl of Mountjoy Lord Deputy

PHILIP II of Spain died in September, 1598, and was
succeeded by his son Philip III, who, it would seem,
took more interest in the Irish struggle against Elizabeth's
temporal and spiritual power than did his father. Philip,
in all likelihood, cared very little about Ireland's national
aspirations, but, like all of his race, he was a zealous Catholic, and recognized the self-evident fact that the Irish

were, then, fighting not alone their own battle but also that of the Church, with heroic vigor. O'Neill began negotiations with the young monarch immediately after his accession, and Philip responded by sending two envoys to the Irish general—Don Martin de la Cerda and the Most Rev. Matthias de Oriedo, who had been appointed by the Pope Archibishop of Dublin—a purely titular office, seeing that the English were in full possession of that capital. The bishop presented O'Neill with "a Phœnix plume," blessed by his Holiness, and also with 22,000 pieces of gold—a generous contribution in that age, when money was much more valuable in proportion than it is now. (O'Sullivan, Moryson, and Mitchel.)

O'Neill, having sufficiently awed the English generals for a period, made a sort of "royal progress" through Munster and Leinster, visiting holy places, settling feuds, and inspecting military forces. He met with, practically, no opposition, but, near Cork, had the misfortune to lose his gallant cavalry commander, Hugh McGuire, chief of Fermanagh. The latter was leading a body of horse on a reconnoitring mission, when suddenly there appeared a force of English cavalry, bent on a similar errand, under Sir Warham St. Leger and Sir Henry Power, Queen's Commissioners, acting in place of Sir Thomas Norreys. St. Leger rode up to McGuire and discharged a horse pistol at close range. The heroic Irish chief reeled in his saddle from a mortal wound, but, before falling, struck St. Leger a crushing blow on the head with his truncheon, and killed him on the spot. McGuire, having avenged himself on his enemy, died on the instant. These were the only two who fell. The English retreated to Cork and kept within its walls until O'Neill had left the neighborhood. The Ulster prince turned back through Ormond and Westmeath and arrived in his own country, "without meeting an enemy, although there was then in Ireland a royal army amounting, after all the havoc made in it during the past year, to 14,400 foot and 1,230 horse" —this, too, exclusive of irregular forces. (Moryson.) This force was well provided with artillery and all military stores. (Mitchel.)

But O'Neill's days of almost unclouded triumph were drawing to a close. He was, at last, about to meet an English commander who, if not as able as himself, was infinitely more cunning and unscrupulous. This was Charles Blount, Earl of Mountjoy, a trained soldier, a veteran diplomat, a fierce Protestant theologian, and a ripe scholar. His motto, on assuming the duties of Lord Deputy in Ireland, would seem to have been "Divide and Conquer." Mountjoy saw, at once, that steel alone could not now subdue Ireland, and he was determined to resort to other methods, more potent but less manly. About the same time, there also came to Ireland two other famous English generals, Sir George Carew and Sir Henry Dowcra. The new deputy brought with him large reinforcements, so that the English army in Ireland was more powerful than it had ever been before; and Mountjoy's orders were, in effect, that Ulster, in particular, should be honeycombed with royal garrisons, especially along its coast-line. Although Mountjoy himself was checked, at the outset, by O'Neill's army, Sir Henry Dowcra, with a powerful force, transported by sea from Carrickfergus, occupied and fortified the hill of Derry, on the Foyle— the ground on which now stands the storied city of Londonderry. Other border garrisons were strengthened by the Lord Deputy, and everything was made ready for a vigorous prosecution of the war. The penal laws against the Irish Catholics were softened, so as, if possible, to detach the Anglo-Irish Catholics from the Celtic Catholic Irish, and also to impress the weak-kneed among the latter with "the friendly intentions of her Majesty's government"—very much like the court language in use to-day. The bait took, as might have been expected—for every good cause has its Iscariots—and we soon hear of jealous kinsmen of the patriot chiefs "coming over to" the queen's "interest" and doing their utmost—the heartless scoundrels—to divide and distract the strength of their country, engaged in a deadly struggle for her rights and liberty. These despicable wretches are foul blotches on the pages of Ireland's history. But for them, she could have finally shaken off the English yoke, which would have saved Ireland centuries of martyrdom and England centuries of shame. And so we find Sir Arthur O'Neill becoming "the queen's O'Neill"—his branch of the family had long been in the English interest; Connor Roe McGuire becoming "the queen's McGuire," and so on *ad nauseam*. These creatures had no love for England or Elizabeth, but simply hoped to further their own selfish ends by disloyalty to their chiefs and treason to their country. We confess that this is a chapter of Irish history from which we would gladly turn in pure disgust did not our duty, as a writer of history, compel us to dwell upon it yet a while longer. Dermot O'Connor, who held a command under O'Neill's Desmond in Munster, yielded to the seductions of Carew and turned upon his leader, in the interest of his brother-in-law, son of the "great earl," who was held as a hostage in London

Tower by Elizabeth, and was now used as a firebrand to stir up feud and faction among the Munster Irish. Mountjoy had not been many months in Ireland, when, to use the words of the historian Mitchel, "a network of English intrigue and perfidy covered the land, until the leaders of the (Irish) confederacy in Munster knew not whom to trust, or where they were safe from treason and assassination." Dermot O'Connor was willing to surrender Desmond, whom he had kidnapped, to Mountjoy, for a thousand pounds, but, before he could receive his blood-money, the "Suggawn (hay-rope) Earl," as he was called in derision by the English faction, was rescued by his kinsman, Pierce Lacy. But the White Knight—frightful misnomer—another relative of the earl —was more fortunate than O'Connor. He managed to receive the thousand pounds, delivered Desmond to Carew, and earned enduring infamy. The "Suggawn Earl" was sent to London and died a miserable prisoner in the Tower.

Thus, the policy of the Lord Deputy was doing its deadly work in Munster and also in Leinster, where the Irish were of mixed race, and where racial animosity could be more easily worked upon than in Ulster and Connaught, where most of the ancient clans still remained unbroken and uncontaminated by foreign influences. Yet Ulster and Connaught had their Benedict Arnolds, too, as we have shown in the cases of O'Neill and McGuire, and will show in other cases which yet remain to be mentioned. But in these provinces the war was national as well as religious, while in Munster it was almost entirely religious. Most of the Catholic Anglo-Irish would have fought with the English rather than the Celtic Irish, if their religion had been tolerated from the first. Among the Celtic Irish chiefs who went over to the English in Munster, were O'Sullivan More and McCarthy More (the Great). The latter had the cowardly excuse that his strong-minded wife had coerced him into treason, and refused to live with him until he came to terms with the enemy. Was there ever anything more disgraceful in the history of manhood and womanhood? They were, indeed, a couple entirely worthy of each other. The Lord Deputy, in the meantime, had ravaged the "rebellious" portions of Leinster, burning houses and crops, and doing other evil things common to the savage warfare of that period. His greatest piece of luck, however, was the killing of the brave O'More of Leix in a skirmish. (Mitchel.)

CHAPTER XI

Ireland's Fortunes Take a Bad Turn—Defeat of O'Neill and O'Donnell at Kinsale

THE English force in Ireland was now (1600-1601) overwhelming, and as the Irish had no fleet whatever, the English were enabled to plant garrisons, almost wherever they wished to, around the Ulster coast, and sometimes posts were also established in the interior of the country. Thus Derry, Dun-na-long, Lifford, and numerous other places held strong garrisons, and these sallied forth at will—the small Irish army being actively engaged elsewhere—and inflicted heavy damage on the harmless people of the surrounding districts. The process of crop-burning was in full blast again, and such Irish people as escaped the sword and the halter had the horrible vision of perishing by famine ever before their eyes. O'Neill and O'Donnell were aware of all this, and did the best they could, under such discouraging circumstances. They were almost at the end of their resources, and awaited anxiously for the aid, in men and money, solemnly promised them by the envoy of Philip of Spain. To add to their ever-growing embarrassment, Niall Garbh ("the Rough") O'Donnell, cousin of Red Hugh, and the fiercest warrior of Clan-Conal, revolted, because of some fancied slight, and also, no doubt, inflamed by unworthy ambition, against the chief, and went over to the enemy. Unfortunately, some of the clansmen, who did not look beyond personal attachment, followed his dishonored fortunes, but this was about the only serious case of clan defection. The great body of the Irish galloglasses and kerns—heavy and light infantry—remained true to their country and their God, and died fighting for both to the last.

Niall Garbh, after allying himself with the English, occupied the beautiful Franciscan monastery of Donegal, in which the Annals of the Four Masters, Ireland's chronological history, were compiled. Red Hugh, fiercely indignant, marched against the sacrilegious traitor and laid siege to him in the holy place. After three months' investment, it was taken by storm, and utterly destroyed by fire, except for a few walls which still remain. The traitor's brother, Conn O'Donnell, and several of the misguided clansmen were killed in the conflict, but, unfortunately, Niall Garbh himself escaped, to still further disgrace the heroic name of O'Donnell and injure the hapless country that gave birth to such a monster.

Mountjoy, after frequent indecisive skirmishes with

O'Neill, amused himself by offering a reward of £2,000 for that chieftain's head, and smaller amounts for those of his most important lieutenants. But no man was found among the faithful clansmen of Tyrone to murder his chief for the base bribe of the Lord Deputy. Yet Mountjoy continued to gain ground in Ulster, little by little, and he built more forts, commanding important passes, and garrisoned them in great force. He also caused most of the woods to be cut away, and thus laid the O'Neill territory wide open for a successful invasion. O'Neill was an admirable officer, and still, assisted by Hugh O'Donnell, presented a gallant front to Mountjoy, but he could do little that was effective against an enemy who had five times the number of soldiers that he had, and could thus man important posts, filled with all the munitions of war, without sensibly weakening his force in the field. Destitute of foundries and powder factories, he could make no progress in the matter of artillery, and such cannon as he had were destitute of proper ammunition. All this the Spaniards could have supplied, but their characteristic dilatoriness, in the end, ruined everything. Another circumstance also militated against the success of the brave O'Neill—the English and their allies were solidly unified for the destruction of the Irish, while the latter, as we have seen, were fatally divided by corruption, ambition, jealousy—fostered by their enemies—and endless English intrigue. No wonder that his broad brow grew gloomy and that his sword no longer struck the blows it dealt so fiercely at Clontibret and the Yellow Ford.

At last, however, out of the dark clouds that surrounded his fortunes, there flashed one sun-ray of hope and joy. News suddenly reached the north, as well as the Lord Deputy, that a Spanish fleet had landed in Kinsale Harbor, on the coast of Cork. It carried a small force—less than 6,000 men, mostly of poor quality—under the command of the arrogant and incompetent Don Juan de Aguila. He occupied Kinsale and the surrounding forts at once, but was disappointed when the Munster Irish—already all but crushed by Mountjoy—did not flock at once, and in great numbers, to his standard. Of all the Munster chiefs there responded only O'Sullivan Beare, O'Connor Kerry, and the brave O'Driscoll. They alone redeemed, in as far as they could, the apathy of South Munster, and were justified in resenting the Spanish taunt, bitterly uttered by Don Juan himself, that "Christ had never died for such people." The Spaniard did not, of course, take into consideration, because he did not know, the exhaustion of South Munster after the Geraldine war and the wars which succeeded it. Constant defeat is a poor tonic on which to build up a boldly aggressive patriotism.

The news of the landing at Kinsale reached Red Hugh O'Donnell while he was in the act of besieging his own castle of Donegal, surreptitiously seized by Niall Garbh, "the Queen's O'Donnell," while he was absent "at the front," with O'Neill. He instantly raised the siege, and, summoning all of his forces, marched southward without an hour's delay, as became his ardent and gallant nature. Neither did O'Neill hesitate to abandon "the line of the Blackwater," which guarded his own castle of Dungannon, to its fate, and at once marched his forces toward Kinsale. The Clan-Conal marched at "the route step," through Breffni and Hy-Many,

crossing the Shannon near where it narrows at the
east end of Lough Dearg. On through the Ormonds,
where "the heath-brown Slieve Bloom" mountains rise
in their beauty, they pressed, burning, at every footstep,
to reach Kinsale, join the Spaniards, and "have it out"
with Mountjoy and the English. O'Donnell, marching
in lighter order and by a different route, outstripped his
older confederate, but narrowly escaped being inter-
cepted in Tipperary by a superior English force, under
General Carew, detached by the Lord Deputy for that
purpose. As Red Hugh had no intention of giving battle until reinforced by O'Neill, or he had joined the Spaniards, he made a clever flank movement, by forced march,
over the Slieve Felim Hills, which interposed between
him and Limerick. But the rains had been heavy of late,
the mountain passes were boggy, and neither horses nor
carriages (wagons) could pass. Fortunately, it was the
beginning of winter, and, one night, there came a sharp
frost, which sufficiently hardened the ground, and the
Irish army, taking advantage of the kindness of Providence, marched ahead throughout the dark hours, and,
by morning, had left Carew and his army hopelessly in
rear. O'Donnell made thirty-two miles (Irish), about
forty-two English miles, in that movement and halted
at Croom, having accomplished the greatest march, with
baggage, recorded in those hard campaigns. (Pacata
Hibernia, cited by Mitchel.)

His coming among them, as well as the news of the
arrival of the Spaniards, put fresh life into the Irish of
West Munster, and, indeed, Red Hugh stood on scant
ceremony with such degenerate Irish as refused to fight
for their country, so that wherever he marched, fresh

patriots, eager to "save their bacon," in many cases, sprang up like crops of mushrooms. At Castlehaven he formed a junction with 700 newly arrived Spanish troops, and, together, they marched toward Kinsale, which Mountjoy and Carew were preparing to invest. O'Neill and his brave lieutenant, Richard Tyrrell, did not pursue the route taken by O'Donnell, but had to fight their way through Leinster and North Munster with considerable loss. At Bandon, in South Munster, they fell in with O'Donnell and the Spaniards, and all marched to form an immediate junction with De Aguila. Mitchel, quoting from O'Sullivan's narrative, gives the total strength of the force under O'Neill and O'Donnell at 6,000 foot and 500 horse. The Irish leader was opposed to risking a general engagement with so small a command, although O'Donnell, when he beheld Mountjoy's troops beleaguering the town, wanted to attack, which, judging by after events, might have been the better plan. O'Neill argued, however, that the inclement season would soon destroy a good part of the English soldiers and counseled delay. O'Donnell yielded reluctantly, and then the Irish, very badly provided, intrenched themselves and began "besieging the besiegers." Prudence, on this occasion, ruined the cause of Ireland—so often ruined by rashness, before and since; for, three days after O'Neill's policy had been acceded to, that is on Christmas eve, 1601, accident brought on an engagement, in the dark, which neither party seems to have anticipated. The tragedy is best related by Mitchel in his life of O'Neill, thus: "Before dawn, on the morning of the 24th (December), Sir Richard Graham, who commanded the night guard of horse, sent word to the deputy that the scouts had discovered the matches (matchlock muskets were used at this period) flashing in great numbers in the darkness, and that O'Neill must be approaching the camp in force. Instantly the troops were called to arms; messengers were despatched to the Earl of Thomond's quarter, with orders to draw out his men.   The deputy (Mountjoy) now advanced to meet the Irish, whom he supposed to be stealing on his camp, and seems to have effectually surprised them, while endeavoring to prevent a surprise upon himself.   The infantry of O'Neill's army retired slowly about a mile further from the town, and made a stand on the bank of a ford, where their position was strengthened by a bog in flank.   Wingfield, the marshal, thought he saw some confusion in their ranks, and entreated the deputy that he might be allowed to charge. The Earl of Clanricarde joined the marshal and the battle became general.   O'Neill's cavalry repeatedly drove back both Wingfield and Clanricarde, until Sir Henry Danvers, with Captains Taaffe and Fleming, came up to their assistance, when, at length, the Irish infantry fell into confusion and fled.   Another body of them, under Tyrrell, was still unbroken, and long maintained their ground on a hill, but at length, seeing their comrades routed, they also gave way and retreated in good order after their main body.   The northern cavalry covered the retreat, and O'Neill and O'Donnell, by amazing personal exertions, succeeded in preserving order and preventing it from becoming a total rout."

Such was the unfortunate battle of Kinsale—the most disastrous, perhaps, in Irish annals.   It was not even well fought, because the Irish troops, surprised in their sleep, owing to lack of vigilance on the part of the sentinels, had lost most of their effective arms, their baggage, and colors at the outset. Their camp, also, came into immediate possession of the enemy. Thus, they were discouraged—the Irish character being mercurial, like the French—if not badly demoralized, and they did not, in this ill-fated action, fight with a resolution worthy of the fame they had rightfully earned as soldiers of the first class, nor did they faithfully respond, as heretofore, to the military genius of their justly renowned leaders. They were mostly the troops of Ulster, far from home, and lacking the inspiration that comes to all men when conscious that they are fighting to defend their own hearths against the spoiler. Ulster, in that day, was almost alien to the southern province, although the soldiers of both were fighting in a common cause. Kinsale was, certainly, not a battle to which Ireland can look back with feelings of pride, but she may be thankful that there are few such gloomy failures recorded in her military annals. Yet the bitter fact remains that Kinsale clouded forever the glory achieved by the troops of O'Neill and O'Donnell on so many fields of victory. The Spaniards, who had joined O'Donnell on the march, refused to fly and were almost all destroyed. Their commander, Del Campo, two officers, and forty soldiers were all that survived out of seven hundred men, and they were made prisoners of war. (Mitchel.) In a note, this author, quoting Pacata Hibernia, says: "The most merciless of all Mountjoy's army that day was the Anglo-Irish and Catholic Earl of Clanricarde. He slew twenty of the Irish with his own hand, and cried aloud to 'spare no rebels.' Carew (the English general and writer) says that 'no man did bloody his sword more than his lordship that day.'" This episode shows how well

Mountjoy's policy of "Divide and Conquer" and temporary toleration of the Catholics worked for the English cause. Had the penal laws not been mitigated this Anglo-Irish and Catholic Earl of Clanricarde would have fought on the side of Ireland.

De Aguila, seeing that the Irish army was defeated, and that another effort on the part of O'Neill was rendered impossible by the loss of his munitions and the lateness of the season, proposed to capitulate. The Earl of Mountjoy offered him honorable terms, and De Aguila agreed to surrender to the English all the Irish castles on the coast to which Spanish garrisons had been admitted, "and shortly after," says Mitchel, "set sail for Spain, carrying with him all his artillery, treasure, and military stores." Some of the Irish chiefs, notably the O'Sullivan Beare, refused to ratify that part of De Aguila's capitulation which agreed to surrender their castles, occupied by Spanish troops, to the English. The fortresses had been thrown open to the Spaniards in good faith, and General de Aguila had no moral right to give them up. The most he could agree to do was to withdraw his men from the Irish castles and take them back with him to Spain. And this was the view taken by the Irish chiefs, with bloody, but glorious, result, as we shall see.

CHAPTER XII

Sad Death of O'Donnell in Spain—Heroic Defence of Dunboy

O'NEILL, when he perceived the hopelessness of the Irish situation in Munster, conducted what remained of his defeated army back to the north and cantoned it along the Blackwater for the winter months, where he felt quite sure the English, worn out by their exertions at the siege and battle of Kinsale, would not attack him. Red Hugh O'Donnell, exasperated beyond endurance at the disregard of his bold advice to attack the beleaguering English, in conjunction with the Spaniards, on the first arrival of the Irish army before Kinsale, gave up the command of his clan to his brother, Roderick, and, with a few followers, sailed for Spain, in search of further aid. He resolved to ask King Philip for an army, not a detachment. The chief landed at Coruna, and was received with high honors by the Spanish authorities. He finally reached the Spanish Court and placed the whole Irish situation clearly before Philip, who promised a powerful force and actually gave orders to prepare at once for a new expedition to Ireland. The sad sequel is well told in the eloquent words of Mitchel:

"But that armament never sailed, and poor O'Donnell never saw Ireland more; for news reached Spain, a few months after, that Dunboy Castle, the last stronghold in Munster that held out for King Philip, was taken, and Beare-haven, the last harbor in the South that was open to his ships, effectually guarded by the English; and the Spanish preparations were countermanded; and Red Hugh was once more on his journey to court to renew his almost hopeless suit, and had arrived at Samancas, two leagues from Valladolid, when he suddenly fell sick. His gallant heart was broken and he died there on the 10th of September, 1602. He was buried by order of the king with royal honors, as befitted a prince of the Kinel-Conal; and the stately city of Valladolid holds the bones of as noble a chief and as stout a warrior as ever bore the wand of chieftaincy or led a clan to battle."

While we do not believe in "painting the devil blacker than he is," we think it proper to state here that more recent researches would seem to have fixed the crime of assassination on the Earl of Mountjoy. In an account, quoted in several lectures by Frank Hugh O'Donnell, ex-member of the British Parliament, it is definitely stated that Red Hugh O'Donnell was poisoned at the inn in Samancas, where he died, by a hired murderer, named Blake, who acted for the English Lord Deputy. Such, if the statement is true, were the political ethics of the Elizabethan era.

Donal O'Sullivan Beare, the bravest of all the Munster leaders, wrested his castle of Dun-buidhe (Dunboy), in English, "Yellow Fort," from the Spaniards after De Aguila had agreed to surrender it to the English. He justified his conduct to the King of Spain in a pathetic letter in which he said: "Among other places that were neither yielded nor taken to the end that they might be delivered to the English, Don Juan tied himself up to deliver my castle and haven, the only key to mine inheritance, whereupon the living of many thousand persons doth rest, that live some twenty leagues upon the seacoast, into the hands of my cruel, cursed, misbelieving enemies."

The defence of this castle by the Irish garrison of one hundred and forty-three men, commanded by O'Sullivan's intrepid lieutenant, McGeoghegan, was one of the finest feats of arms recorded in history. Although only a square tower, with outworks, it held out against General Carew, the Lord President, for fifteen days. It was bombarded by the fleet from the haven, and battered by artillery from the land side. Indeed, Carew had an army of 4,000 veteran soldiers opposed to McGeoghegan's 143 heroes. A breach was finally effected in the castle, but the storming parties were repeatedly repulsed. The great hall was finally carried, and the little garrison, under the undaunted McGeoghegan, retreated to the vaults beneath it, where they sustained the unequal conflict for four-and-twenty hours, and, by the exertion of unexampled prowess, at last cleared the hall of the English. The latter replied with an overwhelming cannonade, and the walls of the castle crumbled about the ears of its heroic defenders. The latter made a desperate sortie with only forty men and all perished. The survivors in the castle continued the defence, but, in the end, their noble commander, McGeoghegan, was mortally wounded and they laid down their arms. While their wounded chief lay gasping in the agonies of approaching death, on the floor of the vault, he saw the English enter the place. The sight seemed to renew his life and energy. He sprang to his feet, seized a torch, and made a rush for an open barrel of powder, intending to blow assailants and assailed into the sky. But an English soldier was too quick for the dying hero. He seized him in his arms, and a comrade wrested the torch from the failing hand and extinguished it. Then they ran their swords through McGeoghegan's body, and his glorious deeds and great sufferings were at an end. It should have been stated that ten of the garrison, who were of the party that made the sortie, on the failure of their bold effort, attempted to reach the mainland by swimming across the haven. This movement was anticipated by the English commander. Soldiers were stationed in boats to intercept the swimmers, and all were stabbed or shot, as if they had been beasts of prey. The survivors of the band of Irish Spartans, who made Dunboy forever memorable in the annals of martial glory, were instantly hanged by order of Carew, so that not one of the heroic 143 was left. Ruthless as he was, the Lord President himself, in an official letter, bore this testimony to their valor: "Not one man escaped; all were slain, executed, or buried in the ruins, and so obstinate a defence hath not been seen within this kingdom." The defence of Dunboy Castle deserves to rank in history with Thermopylæ and the Alamo of Texas, and the butchery of its surviving defenders, in cold blood, was a disgrace to English manhood. How differently the gallant O'Neill treated the English prisoners taken at Armagh, Portmore, and other places in Ulster during the period of his amazing victories. It is cruelties of this character that made the English name abhorred in Ireland, not the prowess, or even the bloodthirstiness, of the English soldiery in the heat of battle. The massacre at Dunboy is an indelible stain on the memory of Lord President Carew.

CHAPTER XIII

Wane of Irish Resistance—O'Neill Surrenders to Mountjoy at Mellifont

WITH the fall of Dunboy, Ireland's heroic day was almost at an end for that generation. O'Sullivan and some other Munster chiefs still held out, but their efforts were only desultory. O'Neill, accompanied by Richard Tyrrell, the faithful Anglo-Irish leader, rallied the remnants of his clan and attempted to hold again the line of the Blackwater. But the English were now too many to be resisted by a handful of brave men. They closed upon him from every side, and advanced their posts through the country, so as to effectually cut him off from communication with Tyrconnel, whose chief on hearing of the death of his noble brother, Red Hugh, in Spain, made terms with the Lord Deputy. So, also, did many other Ulster chiefs, who conceived their cause to be hopeless. O'Neill, still hoping against hope, and thinking that a Spanish army might yet come to his aid, burned his castle of Dungannon to the ground, and retired to the wooded and mountainous portions of his ancient principality, where he held out doggedly. But the Lord Deputy resorted to his old policy of destroying the growing crops, and, very soon, Tyrone, throughout its fairest and most fertile regions, was a blackened waste. Still the Red Hand continued to float defiantly throughout the black winter of 1602-3; but, at length, despair began to shadow the once bright hopes of the brave O'Neill. His daring ally, Donal O'Sullivan Beare, having lost all he possessed in Munster, set out at this inclement season on a forced march from Glengariff, in Cork, to Breffni, in Leitrim, fighting his enemies all the way, crossing the Shannon in boats extemporized from willows and horsehides; routing an English force, under Colonel Malby, at the "pass of Aughrim," in Galway, destined to be more terribly memorable in another war for liberty; and, finally, reached O'Ruarc's castle, where he was hospitably welcomed, with only a small moiety of those who followed him from their homes,

> "—Marching
> Over Murkerry's moors and Ormond's plain,
> His currochs the waves of the Shannon o'erarching
> And pathway mile-marked with the slain."

Even the iron heart of Hugh O'Neill could not maintain its strength against conditions such as those thus described by Moryson, the Englishman, who can not be suspected of intensifying the horrid picture at the expense of his own country's reputation: "No spectacle," he says, "was more frequent in the ditches of towns, and especially of wasted countries, than to see multitudes of poor people dead, with their mouths all colored green, by eating nettles, docks, and all things they could rend up above ground." There were other spectacles still more terrible, as related by the English generals and chroniclers themselves, but we will spare the details. They are too horrible for the average civilized being of this day to contemplate, although the age is by no means lacking in examples of human savagery which go to prove that the wild beast in the nature of man has not yet been entirely bred out.

Baffled by gold, not by steel, by the torch rather than the sword, deprived of all his resources, deserted by his allies, and growing old and worn in ceaseless warfare, it can hardly be wondered at that O'Neill sent to the Lord Deputy, at the end of February, 1603, propositions of surrender. Mountjoy was glad to receive them—for the vision of a possible Spanish expedition, in great force, still disquieted him—and arranged to meet the discomfited Irish hero at Mellifont Abbey, in Louth, where died, centuries before, old, repentant, and despised, that faithless wife of O'Ruarc, Prince of Breffni, whose sin first caused the Normans to set foot in Ireland. So anxious was Mountjoy to conclude a peace, that nearly all of O'Neill's stipulations were concurred in, even to the free exercise of the Catholic religion in the subjugated country. He and his allies were allowed to retain, under English "letters patent," their original tribe-lands, with a few exceptions in favor of the traitors who had fought with the English against their own kindred. It was insisted, however, by the Deputy, that all Irish titles, including that of "The O'Neill," should be dropped, thenceforth and forever, and the English titles of "nobility" substituted. All the Irish territory was converted into "shire ground." The ancient Brehon Law was abolished, and, for evermore, the Irish clans were to be governed by English methods. Queen Elizabeth had died during the progress of the negotiations, and a secret knowledge of this fact no doubt influenced Mountjoy in hurrying the treaty to its conclusion, and granting such, comparatively, favorable conditions to Hugh O'Neill and the other "rebellious" Irish chiefs. Therefore, it was to the representative of King James I that Tyrone, at last, yielded his sword—not to the general of Elizabeth. It is said that in the bitter last moments of that sovereign, her almost constant inquiry was: "What news from Ireland and that rascally O'Neill?" The latter's most elaborate historian estimates that the long war "cost England many millions in treasure, and the blood of tens of thousands of her veteran soldiers, and, from the face of Ireland, it swept nearly one-half of the entire population." (Mitchel.) And, he continues: "From that day (March 30, 1603, when O'Neill surrendered at Mellifont), the distinction of 'Pale' and 'Irish country' was at an end; and the authority of the kings of England and their (Anglo) Irish parliaments became, for the first time, paramount over the whole island. The pride of ancient Erin—the haughty struggle of Irish nationhood

against foreign institutions and the detested spirit of
English imperialism, for that time, sunk in blood and
horror, but the Irish nation is an undying essence, and
that noble struggle paused for a season, only to recom-
mence in other forms and on wider ground—to be renewed, and again renewed, until—Ah! quousque, Dom-
ine, quousque?"

CHAPTER XIV

Treachery of James I to the Irish Chiefs—"The Flight of the Earls"

AT the outset of his reign, James I, of England, and
VI of Scotland, collateral descendant of that Edward Bruce who had been crowned King of the Irish
in the beginning of the fourteenth century, promised to
rule Ireland in a loving and paternal spirit. He had
received at his London court, with great urbanity, Hugh
O'Neill and Roderick O'Donnell, and had confirmed
them in their English titles of Earl of Tyrone and Earl
of Tyrconnel, respectively. They had accompanied
Mountjoy to England, to make their "submissions" in
due form before the king, and, while en route through
that country, were grossly insulted at many points by
the common people, who could not forget their relatives
lying dead in heaps in Irish soil, because of the prowess
of the chieftains who were now the guests of England.
It is most remarkable that the English people have always honored and hospitably entertained the distinguished "rebels" of all countries but Ireland. Refugees from Poland, from Austria, from Hungary, from
France, from Italy—many of them charged with using
assassin methods—have been warmly welcomed in London, and even protected by the courts of law, as in the

case of the Orsini-infernal-machine conspirators against
Napoleon III, in 1859; but no Irish "rebel" has ever
been honored, or sheltered, or defended by the English
people, or the English courts of law; although individual
Englishmen, like Lord Byron, Percy Shelley, and a few
others of their calibre, have written and spoken in assertion of Ireland's right to a separate existence. Of course,
the reason is that all the other "rebels" fought in "good
causes," and, according to English political ethics, no
cause can possibly be just in which the right of England
to govern any people whatever against their will is contested. America learned that bitter lesson nearly two
centuries after O'Neill and O'Donnell were hooted and
stoned by the English populace for having dared to defend the rights and the patrimony of their people.

The Catholic religion continued to be tolerated by
James until 1605, when, suddenly, a penal statute of
the time of Elizabeth was unearthed and put into operation with full force. Treaty obligations of England
with the Irish chiefs were also systematically violated.
The lands of Ulster were broad and fair, and the great
body of military adventurers who had come into Ireland
from England during the long wars of the preceding
reign, were greedy for spoil. These and the Irish traitors
—Art O'Neill, Niall Garbh O'Donnell, the false Mc-
Guire, and the rest—pestered the government and made
never-ending charges of plots and "treasons" against
"the earls," as the Irish leaders of the late war now came
to be called. The plotters were ably assisted by Robert
Cecil, Earl of Salisbury, ancestor of the late Marquis
of Salisbury, who was also his namesake. Another able
English conspirator against the Irish chiefs was Sir

Arthur Chichester, who became one of the chief benefi-
ciaries of the subsequent "confiscations," and whose
descendants still hold, as "titled nobility," a very comfortable slice of ancient Ulster. Some "Reformed" bishops also took great interest in getting the earls into hot
water with the government. Finally an alleged plot on
the part of O'Neill and O'Donnell to overthrow the
King of England's government in Ulster—an absurdity
on its face, considering their fallen and helpless condition—was made the pretext for summoning them to appear before the English courts established in Ireland, in
whose justice they had no confidence, remembering the
ghastly fate of MacMahon Roe. A hired perjurer,
named O'Cahan—the unworthy scion of a noble house
—was to be chief "witness" against O'Neill, and no
secret was made of the fact that others would be forthcoming, hired by Chichester, to finish the work begun
by the principal informer. Meanwhile the free exercise
of the Catholic religion—so solemnly guaranteed by
Mountjoy—was strictly prohibited, under the penal enactment of Elizabeth, known as the "Act of Uniformity," already referred to; and again began those horrid
religious persecutions, for politics' and plunder's sake,
which had no termination in Ireland, except for one
brief period, during nearly two centuries. Such Catholics as desired to practice their faith had to betake themselves to the mountain recesses, or the caves of the seacoast, where, before rude altars, Mass was celebrated by
priests on whose heads a penal price was set. Sheriffs
and judges, attended by large bands of soldiers, made
circuit of the new Ulster "counties" and succeeded in
completely terrifying the unfortunate Catholic inhabi-

tants. Education, as far as Catholics were concerned, was prohibited, and then began that exodus of Irish ecclesiastical students to the Continent of Europe, which continued down to the reign of William IV, notwithstanding the partial mitigation of the penal laws, in the reign of his father, and the passage of the Catholic Emancipation Bill during his brother's reign, A.D. 1829.

The persecuted earls clearly saw there was no hope of peace for them in Ireland, and that their presence only wrought further ill to their faithful clansmen, now reduced, for the first time, to the condition of "subjects" of the King of England. Lord Howth, a powerful Catholic noble of the Pale, was suspected of having given information to the Lord Deputy of a meeting held at Maynooth the previous Christmas at which the earls and several Anglo-Catholic noblemen were present. It was claimed that the enforcement of the Act of Uniformity was there discussed, and that another effort to overthrow the English power would be made by the parties to the meeting. This "plot," if there were any at all, was communicated to the Clerk of the Privy Council by an anonymous letter dropped at the Castle of Dublin in March, 1607. "O'Neill," says McGee, "was with Chichester, at Slane, in September when he received a letter from the McGuire—not the traitor of that title—who had been abroad, conveying some startling information upon which Tyrone seems to have acted at once. He took leave of the Lord Deputy, as if to prepare for a journey to London, whither he had been summoned on some false pretext; and, after spending a few days with his old friend, Sir Garrett Moore, at Mellifont, repaired to his

seat of Dungannon, where he, at once, assembled all of
his immediate family and all proceeded to the shores of
Lough Swilly, at Rathmullen, where they were joined by
Roderick O'Donnell and all of his household. They embarked immediately on the French ship which had conveyed McGuire to Ireland, and set sail for France, where,
on landing, they were warmly welcomed and royally entertained by the chivalric King Henry IV, who, as became
a stout soldier and able captain, greatly admired the
prowess displayed in the Ulster wars by Hugh O'Neill.
There sailed to France with the latter his last countess,
daughter of McGenniss of Iveagh; his three sons, Hugh,
John, and Brian; his nephew, Art O'Neill, son of Cormac,
and many of lesser note. With O'Donnell sailed his
brother Cathbar; his fair sister, Nuala, wife of Niall
Garbh, who had, in righteous indignation, forsaken the
traitor when he drew the sword against Ireland and
her noble brother, Red Hugh; the lady Rose O'Doherty,
wife of Cathbar, and, after his death, of Owen O'Neill;
McGuire, Owen MacWard, the chief bard of Tyrconnel,
and several others. It proved to be a fatal voyage, for
it exiled forever the best and bravest of the Irish chiefs.
Well might the Four Masters in their Annals of the succeeding generation say: "Woe to the heart that meditated, woe to the mind that conceived, woe to the council
that decided on the project of voyage, without knowing
whether they should to the end of their lives be able to
return to their ancient principalities and patrimonies."
And, adds the graphic Mitchel, "with gloomy looks and
sad forebodings, the clansmen of Tyrconnel gazed upon
that fatal ship, 'built in the eclipse and rigged with curses
dark,' as she dropped down Lough Swilly, and was hidden

behind the cliffs of Fanad Head. They never saw their chieftains more."

Everything was now settled in Ulster, for the English interest, except for the brief "rebellion" of Sir Cahir O'Doherty, the young chief of Inishowen, who fell out with Sir George Powlett of Derry, and flew at once to arms. He made a brave struggle of some months' duration, but, as no aid reached him from any outside quarter, he was speedily penned up in his own small territory, and, fighting to the last, died the death of a soldier—the noblest death he could have died, surrounded by the armies of Marshal Wingfield and Sir Oliver Lambert, on the rock of Doon, near Kilmacrenan, in August, 1608. Thus went out the last spark of Ulster valor for a generation.

King James, having used Niall Garbh O'Donnell for all he was worth to the English cause, grew tired of his importunities and had him conveyed to England, under guard, together with his two sons. All three were imprisoned in the Tower of London from which the traitor, at least, never emerged again. He met a fate he richly merited. Cormac O'Neill, the brave captor of Armagh, and the legitimate O'Cahan, both of whom had incurred the hatred of Chichester, also perished in the same gloomy prison.

And now all that remained to be done was to parcel out the lands of the conquered Ultonians and others of "the Meer Irish" between the captains of the new conquest. Chichester was given the whole of O'Doherty's country, the peninsula of Inishowen, and to this was added O'Neill's former borough of Dungannon, with 1,300 acres of valuable land in the neighborhood of the town. Wingfield was created Lord Powerscourt and

obtained the beautiful district of Ferçullen, near Dublin
—one of the most charming domains in all Europe.
Lambert became Earl of Cavan and had several rich estates, including that of Carrig, bestowed upon him in addition. All the counties of Ulster were declared forfeited
to the Crown of England. The primate and other Protestant prelates of Ulster claimed, and received, 43,000
acres. Trinity College, Dublin, received 30,000 acres, in
Tyrone, Derry, and Armagh, together with six advow-
sons, or Church beneficies, in each county. The various
guilds, or trades, of the city of London, England, obtained the gross amount of 209,800 acres, including the
city of Derry, to which the name of "London" was then
prefixed. Grants to individuals were divided into three
classes of 2,000, 1,500, and 1,000 acres each. Catholic
laborers were required to take the oath of supremacy—
acknowledging King James as spiritual head of the
Church—which they, notwithstanding all their misfortunes, nobly refused to do. In the end, seeing that the
fields would remain uncultivated for the most part, the
English and Scotch "undertakers," or settlers, for prudence' sake, rather than from liberal motives, practically
made this tyrannical requirement a dead letter. But the
Catholic tillers of the soil were driven from the fertile
plains and forced to cultivate miserable patches of land
in the bogs or on the mountains. When these became in
any degree valuable, an exorbitant "rent" was charged,
and the poor Catholics, utterly unable to pay it, were
again compelled to move to some even more unpromising
location, where the same procedure again and again produced the same wretched result.

It was thus that the ancient Irish clans, and families,

were actually robbed, in spite of solemn treaties and royal pledges, of their rightful inheritance, and that strangers and "soulless corporations" became lords of their soil. It was the beginning, in Ulster at least, of that system of "felonious landlordism" which is the curse of all Ireland, in spite of recent remedial measures, even in this day. So, too, began that English garrison in Ireland—pitting race against race and creed against creed—which has divided, distracted, and demoralized the Irish nation ever since. The "Plantation of Ulster" was the most fatal measure ever carried into effect by English policy in Ireland. Some of the Irish princes did not long survive their exile. From France they had proceeded to Rome and were very kindly received by the Pontiff, who placed residences commensurate with their rank and fame at their disposal. Roderick O'Donnell died in the Eternal City in July, 1608. McGuire died at Genoa, while en route to Spain in August, and, in September, Cathbar O'Donnell also passed away, and was laid in the same grave with his gallant brother, on St. Peter's Hill. (McGee.) O'Neill's fate was sadder still. The historian just quoted says of him: "He survived his comrades as he did his fortunes, and, like another Belisarius, blind and old, and a pensioner on the bounty of strangers, he lived on eight weary years in Rome." Death came to his relief, according to a historian of his own period, in 1616, when he must have been over seventy years of age. He sleeps his last sleep amid the consecrated dust of ages, beneath the flagstones of the convent of St. Isidore; and there, in the words of the Irish orator and American general, Meagher, "the fiery hand that rent the ensign of St. George on the plains of Ulster has mouldered into dust."

BOOK III

RECORDING THE DOINGS OF THE ENGLISH AND IRISH, IN IRELAND, FROM THE TIME OF JAMES I TO THE JACOBITE WARS IN THE DAYS OF JAMES II AND WILLIAM III

BOOK III

CHAPTER I

Confiscations and Penal Laws—The Iron Rule of Lord Strafford

THE first Anglo-Irish Parliament held within a period of twenty-seven years was summoned to meet in Dublin on May 18, 1613, and, notwithstanding the Act of Uniformity, it would appear that quite a large number of Catholics, styled in the language of the times "recusants," because of their opposition to the spiritual supremacy of the king, were elected to serve in that body. They would have had a majority but for the creation of some forty "boroughs," each entitled to a member, under the patronage of some Protestant peer. This was the beginning of that "rotten borough" system which finally led to the abolition of the sectarian Irish Parliament of after times. Scenes of great disorder occurred in this Parliament of 1613, chiefly occasioned by the intolerant, and even violent, proceedings of the anti-Catholic party, unreasonable bigots, having an eye to the main chance in the matter of confiscated property, to whom the presence of any "Papist" in that body was as gall and wormwood. This bitter prejudice led finally to the utter exclusion of all Catholics from the Anglo-Irish Parliament, and even the few Catholic commoners previously entitled to a vote were deprived of that privilege, or rather right, until the last decade of the eighteenth century. Still, the Catholic minority in the Parliament of 1613 succeeded in preventing ultra-tyrannical legislation, and, really, made the first stand for the constitutional rights of Ireland, from the colonial standpoint. It was finally adjourned in October, 1615, and no other Parliament was called to meet in Ireland until 1635, when Charles I had already been ten years on the throne. "Government," meanwhile, had been carried on arbitrarily, without constitutional restraint of any kind, as under the Tudor sovereigns—only with far less ability. The Tudors, at least—particularly Henry and Elizabeth —were intellectual tyrants, which their immediate successors were not. Never was so shameful a system of public spoliation carried out as in the reigns of James I, and his equally despotic, and still more unscrupulous, son Charles I. The viceroy was not responsible to any power whatever, except that of the English monarch. Chichester was succeeded by Lord Grandison, and under his régime the infamous "Commission for the Discovery of Defective Titles" was organized, of which the surveyor-general, Sir William Parsons, ancestor of the Earls of Rosse, was the head. This Commission, "aided by a horde of clerkly spies, employed under the name of Discoverers (McGee), ransacked Old Irish tenures in the archives of Dublin and London with such good effect, that in a very short time 66,000 acres in Wicklow and 385,000 acres in Leitrim, Longford, the Meaths, and Kings and Queens Counties were 'found by inquisition to be vested in the crown.' The means employed by the Commissioners in some cases to elicit such evidence as they required were of the most revolting description. In the Wicklow case, courts-martial were held, before which unwilling witnesses were tried on charge of treason, and some actually put to death. Archer, one of the number, had his flesh burned with red-hot iron, and was placed on a gridiron over a charcoal fire till he offered to testify anything that was necessary. Yet on evidence so obtained, whole counties and towns were declared forfeited to the crown." (*Ibid.*) Is it any wonder, therefore, that a people so scourged, plundered, and degraded should cherish in their hearts fierce thoughts of reprisal when opportunity offered? These wholesale land robberies were not confined to the Celtic Irish alone, but were practiced on all Irishmen, of whatever descent, who professed the Catholic faith. Add to these the bitter memories of the murder and persecution of many bishops and innumerable priests and communicants of that faith, and the only wonder is that the Irish Catholic people of the seventeenth, and most of the succeeding, century, retained any of the milder and nobler characteristics of the human family. They were stripped of their property, education, civil rights, and, in short, of all that makes life worth living, including freedom of conscience—that dearest privilege of a people naturally idealistic and devotional. The idea of religious toleration never seems to have entered into the minds of what may be called the "professional Protestant" ascendency, except, as we have seen, for purposes of diplomacy which tended to weaken and divide Irish national opposition to foreign rule. In addition to the grievances we have enumerated, the office of Master of Wards was bestowed upon Sir William Parsons, and thus "the minor heirs of all the Catholic proprietors were placed, both as to person and property, at the absolute disposal of one of the most intense anti-Catholic bigots that ever appeared on the scene of Irish affairs." (McGee.) This was one of the pernicious influences that, not for conscience' sake, but for sordid gain, changed the religion of so many of the ancient families of Ireland from the old to the new form of belief; and no English policy was more bitterly resented and vengefully remembered by the Irish Catholic masses. And because of this dishonest system of proselytizing, carried on by one process or another from the period of the Reformation to the reign of Victoria, the Irish Catholic peasant has associated "conversion" of any of his neighbors to the Protestant belief with personal degradation. The Irish Catholic peasant has no feeling but that of utter contempt and aversion for a "turn-coat" Catholic; but he is most liberal in his feelings toward all Protestants "to the manor born," as has been frequently and emphatically manifested by his choice of Protestant leaders, from Grattan to Parnell. Whatever of religious bigotry may linger in the warm heart of the Catholic peasant may be justly charged to outrageous misgovernment, not to his natural disposition, which, in the main, is both loving and charitable. The faults we can trace in the Irish character to-day are partially those of human nature, which averages much the same in all civilized peoples, but many of them, and the gravest, can be attributed, without undue prejudice, to the odious penal laws which were sufficient to distort the characteristics of angels, not to speak of mortal men.

Charles I, of England, was a thorough Stuart in despotic character, wavering policy, base ingratitude, and fatuous obstinacy. His reign was to furnish to Ireland one of the most consummate tyrants and highway robbers that ever cursed a country with his cruelty and greed. This moral monster was the infamous Thomas Wentworth, Earl of Strafford, whose "tiger jaws" closed

on the unfortunate country with the grip of a dragon.
This dishonorable "noble" counseled King Charles to
commit an act of moral delinquency which, in our day,
would be rightly, if coarsely, called "a confidence game."
The Irish Catholics, in convention assembled, had drawn
up a sort of Bill of Rights, which they urged the king
to confirm, and agreed to pay into the royal treasury
the sum of £100,000, which they could ill spare, to show
their "loyalty," and also, no doubt, to influence Charles,
who, like all of his family, dearly loved money, to grant
"the graces" prayed for.   Strafford advised the base king
to take the money, but to manage matters so that the
concessions he had solemnly promised should never go
into effect! And the ignominious Stuart actually acted
on the advice of this ignoble mentor. And so the poor
Irish Catholic "gentry" lost both their money and their
"concessions."   When we read this chapter of Irish
history, we are tempted to feel less sympathy for the
fate of Charles I, who was afterward sold to Cromwell
and the English Parliament by the Scottish mercenary
army of General Leslie, with which the king had taken
shelter, for back pay, amounting to £200,000 (see Sir
Walter Scott's "Tales of a Grandfather"). This miserable
monarch so far degraded himself, further, as to cause
writs for the election of a Parliament to grant the Catholic
claims issued in Ireland, but privately instructed Lord
Falkland to have the documents informally prepared, so
that the election might prove invalid; and, meanwhile,
his Lords Justices went on confiscating Catholic property in Ireland and persecuting prelates, priests, and
people almost as savagely as in the worst days of Mountjoy and Chichester. Strafford came to Ireland as Lord

Deputy in July, 1633, and entered at once on his "thorough" policy, as he called it; and, to prepare himself for the task he had set himself to perform, he through the "Lords Justices" extracted a "voluntary contribution" of £20,000 additional out of the terrorized Catholic "nobility and gentry" of the "sister" island, who, no doubt, wrung it, in turn, out of the sweat of the faces of their peasant retainers. But this was a mere bagatelle to what followed. He compelled Ireland to pay subsidies to the amount of £200,000 in 1634, and imposed £100,000 more in the succeeding year. He carried the war of wholesale confiscation into Connaught, and compelled grand juries, specially "packed" for the work, to give the King of England title to the three great counties of Mayo, Sligo, and Roscommon. The grand jury of Galway County refused to return such a verdict. They were summoned to the court of the Castle Chamber in Dublin, and sentenced to pay a fine of £4,000 each to the crown. The sheriff who empaneled them was fined £1,000. (McGee.) The very lawyers who pleaded for the actual proprietors were stripped of their gowns; "the sheriff died in prison and the work of spoliation proceeded." (*Ibid.*) Similar, if not quite so general, robberies went on in Kildare, Kilkenny, Cork, and other counties. It must be said, however, that Strafford was, in a manner, impartial, and robbed, his master granting full approval, without distinction of creed. We can not help feeling thankful that the London companies which swallowed, in the reign of King James, the lands of Tyrone and Tyrconnel, were compelled by "Black Tom," as the earl was nicknamed, to pay £70,000 "for the use of the king." Out of all this plunder, and much more beside, Strafford was enabled to maintain in Ireland 10,000 infantry and 1,000 excellently equipped horse, "for the service of his royal master." When this great robber visited London in 1639, fresh from his crimes in Ireland, the king, on whom so much ill-deserved sympathy has been wasted, assured him, in person, that his actions in Ireland had his (Charles') "most cordial approval" (McGee), and even urged the earl to "proceed fearlessly in the same course." To still further mark his approbation of Strafford's policy, the king promoted him to the rank of Viceroy of Ireland. Strafford took the king at his word and did proceed so fearlessly in Ireland that his name of terror has been overshadowed in that country by only one other—that of Oliver Cromwell. Every Parliament called to meet by the tyrant in the conquered country—for so the earl regarded Ireland —was used simply as an instrument wherewith to extort still more tribute from the impoverished Irish people. This terrible despot, having accomplished his deadly mission in Ireland, returned to England and there, as before, became chief adviser to the weak and wicked monarch. He counseled the latter to ignore, as far as he dared, the action of Parliament, and was imprudent enough to remark that he (Strafford) had an army in Ireland to support the royal will. He was, soon afterward, impeached by the House of Commons, led by stern John Pym, for treasonable acts in seeking to change the constitutional form of the English Government. This method of procedure was abandoned, however, and Parliament passed a bill of attainder, to which the "false, fleeting, perjured" Charles, frightened by popular clamor, which accused himself of being implicated in a plot to admit soldiers to the Tower for the rescue of Strafford, gave the "royal assent." The earl, on learning this, placed a hand upon his heart and exclaimed, "Put not your trust in Princes!" And thus the master he had but too faithfully served consigned Strafford to the block. He was beheaded on Tower Hill, May 12, 1641. When the hour of his similar doom approached, nearly eight years thereafter, Charles said that the only act of his reign he repented of was giving his assent to the bill which deprived his favorite minister of life.

Some Irish historians, McGee of the number, claim that, outside of his land robberies and tributary exactions, the Earl of Strafford made an able ruler of Ireland, and that trade and commerce flourished under his sway. While this may be, to a certain extent, true, nothing can palliate the crimes against justice and liberty of which he was guilty. He was only a degree less contemptible than the treacherous master who finally betrayed and abandoned him.

CHAPTER II

Irish Military Exiles—Rory O'More Organizes a Great Insurrection

SINCE Sir Cahir O'Doherty fell on the rock of Doon, in 1608, no Irish chief or clan had risen against the English interest throughout the length and breadth of the island. The masses of the Irish people had, apparently, sunk into a condition of political torpor, but the fires of former generations still smouldered amid the ashes of vanquished hopes, and needed but a breath of inspiration to fan them into fierce, rebellious flame. Most of the ancient Celtic and many of the Anglo-Norman

families of Catholic persuasion had military representatives in nearly all the camps of Europe.   One Irish
legion served in the army of Philip III of Spain, and was
commanded successively by two of the sons of Hugh
O'Neill, victor of the Yellow Ford—Henry and John.   In
it also served the hero's gallant nephew, Owen Roe
O'Neill, who rose to the rank of lieutenant-colonel and
made a brilliant defence of Arras in France, besieged by
Marshal de Meilleroye, in 1640.   Of this able soldier we
shall hear more in the future.   The English Government
never lost sight of those Irish exiles, and, about this time,
one of its emissaries on the Continent reported that there
were in the Spanish Netherlands alone "twenty Irish
officers fit to be colonels and a hundred fit to be captains."
The same agent reported, further, that the Irish military
throughout Europe had long been procuring arms for an
attempt upon Ireland, and had 6,000 stand laid up in
Antwerp for that design, and that these had been bought
out of the deduction of their "monthly pay."   At the defence of Louvain against the French, the Irish legion,
1,000 strong, commanded by Colonel Preston, of a distinguished Anglo-Irish family, received honorable mention, and again at the capture of Breda.   These are only
a few of the stirring events abroad which raised the martial reputation of the Irish people in the eyes of all Europe, and the fame of those exploits, reaching Ireland
by means of adventurous recruiting officers or courageous
priests, who defied the penal laws and all their terrors,
found a responsive echo in many a humble home, where
the hope of one day throwing off the foreign yoke was
fondly cherished.   The exiled priesthood, many of whose
members became prelates of high rank abroad, aided the

sentiment of the military at the Catholic courts, and thus was prepared the way for the breaking out of the great insurrection of 1641, which, but for the foolish over-confidence of an Irish chief and the dastardly treason of an obscure drunkard, might have been gloriously successful.

The moving spirit in the new project was Roger, or Rory O'More, of the ancient family of Leix, who had been educated in Spain and was, virtually, brought up at the Spanish court, in company with the sons of Hugh O'Neill, of Tyrone. O'More would seem to have been a born organizer, and a man of consummate tact and dis-cretion. It is a pity that but little is known of his early career, and, indeed, the precise time of his return to Ire-land remains an unsettled question, but it is certain that he returned quietly there, and took up his residence, with-out parade, on his estate of Ballynagh in Leinster. He never appeared in Dublin, or any other populous centre, unless on some public occasion, that would be sure to at-tract the attendance of the principal men of the country. Thus, during the Parliamentary session of 1640, we are told by McGee and other Irish annalists, he took lodg-ings in Dublin, and succeeded in drawing into his plan for a general insurrection, Connor McGuire, MacMahon, Philip O'Reilly, Turlough O'Neill, and other prominent gentlemen of Ulster. He made a habit, also, of visit-ing the different towns in which courts of assize were being held, and there becoming acquainted with influ-ential men, to whom, after due sounding, he outlined his plans for the final overthrow of the English government in Ireland, and the restoration to the Irish people of the lands and rights of which they had been robbed. On

one of these tours, we are told, he made the acquaintance
of Sir Phelim O'Neill, of Kinnaird, in Tyrone—head of
the branch of that great family still tolerated by the ascendency — Sir Connor McGennis of Down, Colonel
Hugh MacMahon of Monaghan, and the Right Rev.
Heber MacMahon, Administrator of Clogher, by connivance or toleration, for, during the penal laws, there
was no "legal" recognition of a Catholic prelacy, although, under Charles I, especially about this period,
there was no very rigid enforcement of the Act of Uniformity, probably because the king and government had
enough trouble on their hands in vainly trying to force
Protestant episcopacy on the Scotch covenanters.

O'More did not confine his operations exclusively to
Ulster. He also made a tour of Connaught, with his
usual success; for he was a man of fine person, handsome countenance, and courtly manners. Tradition still
preserves his memory green among the Irish people of all
classes. He was equally courteous to the lord and to
the peasant. In the castles and mansions of the aristocracy he was ever the favored guest, and he charmed all
his entertainers with the brilliancy of his conversational
powers and the versatility of his knowledge. Among
the poor, he was looked upon as "some glorious guardian
angel," who had come as a messenger from the God of
Freedom to rid them of their galling chains. It is a
singular fact that, although he must have taken thousands, high and low, into his confidence, not a man seems
to have betrayed him to the Castle Government, which
remained in profound ignorance of his plot until the very
eve of insurrection. Robert Emmet, in after times, practiced the methods of O'More, but with far less wisdom,

although influenced by the same lofty principles of patriotism.

The records of the times in which he lived do not show that O'More went extensively into Munster, but he did excellent missionary work among the Anglo-Catholic nobles of his own native province of Leinster. He found them, as a majority, very lukewarm toward his project, influenced, no doubt, by fears of the consequences to themselves should the contemplated revolution prove abortive. Although not a trained soldier, O'More had keen military foresight. The army raised by Strafford in Ireland was mainly made up of Catholics—for he does not seem to have discriminated very much in the matter of creed—and these troops were, in consequence, regarded with distrust, and even intense hatred, by the people of England, to whom the very name of Catholic was, in those days, odious. The vacillating king, influenced by the prejudices of his English subjects, resolved to get rid of his Irish army, and gave such of the regiments as might so elect permission to enter the service of Spain. Some did volunteer, but O'More prevailed on many of the officers to keep their battalions together, and thus secured the nucleus of a well-trained military force at the very outset of hostilities. Among the influential Irish officers who acted on O'More's suggestion were Colonel Plunket, Colonel Sir James Dillon, Colonel Byrne, and Captain Fox. These, with O'More, constituted the first Directory of the Irish Confederates of Leinster. Meanwhile active communication was kept up with their friends on the Continent, and emissaries were coming and going all the time between the two organizations. The head of the movement abroad appears to have been John

O'Neill, Earl of Tyrone, who, however, died suddenly—
some writers aver by the hand of a poisoner—early in
1641; and the military exiles immediately transferred
their allegiance to his cousin, Colonel Owen Roe O'Neill,
with whom we have already made acquaintance. It was
agreed among the allies that the uprising for Irish liberty should occur about the 1st of November, and October 23, 1641, was finally decided upon as the fateful
day. The date was made known to only the most trusted
chiefs of the projected insurrection.

Everything appeared to prosper with the plans of the
patriots until the actual eve of the rising. On that night
(October 22), as fate would have it, there dined with
Colonel Hugh MacMahon—to whom was intrusted the
command of 200 picked men who were to surprise the
Castle—several Irish officers concerned in the conspiracy.
Among the guests was one Owen O'Connolly, an unworthy creature for whom MacMahon would appear to
have entertained an unaccountable friendship. According to tradition, O'Connolly remained with Colonel Mac-
Mahon after the other guests had gone to their several
abodes, and, in a moment of inexcusable weakness, the
unhappy host, who must have been rendered reckless
by wine, confided to his traitor-guest the secret so momentous to Ireland. O'Connolly was more than half
intoxicated, but, unknown to MacMahon, he was in the
service of a strong government supporter, named Sir
John Clotworthy, and the danger which menaced his
patron made the fellow sober enough to outwit his foolish informant. In order to divert suspicion, he pretended, after a time, that he wished to retire, and left
his sword in MacMahon's room. He managed to reach

the rear door of the lodgings, and made his way over all kinds of obstacles, in the dark, to the castle, where, after much trouble, he succeeded in getting audience of Sir William Parsons, to whom he related what Colonel MacMahon had revealed to him.   Parsons, observing that O'Connolly was still under the influence of strong drink, at first refused to believe him, and was on the point of turning him out of doors, when something in the rascal's earnestness made him pause and consider. As a result of his musing, he sent for his colleague, Sir John Borlaise, Master of the Ordnance; the latter immediately advised the summoning of the council.   Several members of that body soon appeared, and the deposition of the informer was formally taken.   A squad of soldiers surrounded MacMahon's lodgings and captured him.   Lord McGuire was also taken, but Colonels Plunket and O'Byrne, Rory O'Moore, and Captain Fox, who were also in the city, succeeded in making good their escape.   MacMahon, on being arraigned before the Privy Council in the Castle, at daylight on the memorable 23d, defiantly acknowledged his share in the plot, and declared that it was then too late for the power of man to prevent the revolution.   He showed great courage, as did also his colleague, Lord McGuire, but MacMahon's bravery could have been much better spared than his discretion, the want of which sent himself and his companion in misfortune to the scaffold, and, undoubtedly, lost to Ireland the best chance she had ever had of severing the connection with Great Britain.   This unhappy result teaches a harsh, but useful, political lesson: Never to confide a secret that concerns a great cause to a dubious "hanger-on," and to avoid the cup that inebriates when one is the possessor of such a secret, or whether one is or not. O'Connolly's treachery was rewarded by a grant of lands from "the crown," and he was afterward a colonel in Cromwell's army. His ultimate fate is involved in obscurity. But his name is embalmed in the annals of enduring infamy.

The Lords Justices of England, in Dublin, once made aware of the situation, lost no time in putting the Castle and city at large in a posture of defence. The guards were doubled and reinforcements were summoned, by special messengers, from neighboring garrisons. Two tried soldiers were invested with the military power— Sir John Willoughby, who had been Governor of Galway, assumed command of the Castle; and Sir Charles Coote—one of the blackest names in Irish annals—was made military governor of the city. The Earl of Ormond—afterward Duke—was summoned from Carrick-on-Suir to assume chief command of the royal army. Thus, the Irish capital was again preserved, through folly and treason, to the English interest.

MacMahon made no vain boast before the Privy Council, when he declared that the rising was beyond the power of man to prevent. Ulster did its full duty, and, on the morning of October 23, the forts of Mountjoy and Charlemont and the town and castle of Dungannon were in the hands of Sir Phelim O'Neill or his chief officers. Sir Connor MacGennis captured Newry; the MacMahons took Carrickmacross and Castleblaney, the O'Hanlon's, Tandragee, while O'Reilly and McGuire— a relative of the lord of that name—"raised" Cavan and Femanagh. (McGee.) Rory O'More supplemented a brief address of the northern chiefs, wherein they declared they bore no hostility to the king, or to his English or Scotch subjects, "but only for the defence and liberty of themselves and the native Irish of the kingdom," with one more elaborate, in which he ably showed that a common danger threatened the Protestants of the Episcopal Church with Roman Catholics. In all the manifestos of the time, there was entirely too much profession of "loyalty" to a king who was constitutionally incapacitated for keeping faith with any body of men whatsoever. Never was the adage that "Politics makes strange bedfellows" more forcibly illustrated than during this period of Irish history. The manliest of all the declarations issued was that of Sir Connor MacGennis, from "Newry's captured towers." "We are in arms," wrote he, "for our lives and liberties. We desire no blood to be shed, but if you (the English and their allies) mean to shed our blood, be sure we shall be as ready as you for that purpose."

CHAPTER III

Horrors of Civil War in Ulster—Battle of Kilrush—Rory O'More
Disappears from History

AT first the civil war in Ulster—for in the main it was the Old Irish against the Anglo-Irish settlers of the Elizabethan régime, or their immediate descendants— was carried on without ferocity, but the Scottish garrison of Carrickfergus, in the winter of 1641, raided Island Magee, in the neighborhood, and put to the sword or drove over the cliffs, to perish in the breakers beneath them, or be dashed to pieces on the rocks, 3,000 of the Celtic-Catholic inhabitants, without regard to age or sex. Protestant historians claim that acts of cruelty had been committed on the Anglo-Irish settlers by the Celtic Irish before this terrible massacre was accomplished. There may have been some isolated cases of murder and rapine—for bad and cruel men are to be found in all armies—but nothing that called for the wholesale slaughter at Island Magee by fanatical Scottish Covenanters, who made up a majority of the Carrickfergus garrison. Christians, not to mention Mohammedans and savage heathens, have shed oceans of blood in fierce persecution of each other, as if they were serving a furious devil, rather than a merciful God. They forget, in their unreasoning hatred, that the gentle Messiah, whose teachings they profess to follow, never made the sword the ally of the Cross. The man made mad by religious bigotry is a wild beast, no matter what creed he may profess. Let us, as Americans, be thankful that we live under a government which recognizes the equal rights of all the creeds, and permits every citizen to worship God in peace, after his own fashion. May the day never come when it shall be different in this Republic!

The frightful event we have chronicled naturally aroused the worst passions of the angered Catholic population of Ulster, and some cruel reprisals resulted. We are sorry to be obliged to state that credible history ascribes most of the violence committed on the Irish side to Sir Phelim O'Neill; but no charge of the kind is made against O'More, MacGennis, McGuire, Plunket, O'Byrne, or any of the other noted chiefs of the period. It is impossible to arrive at any accurate statement of the number of those who perished on both sides, outside of the numerous battlefields of the long struggle; but it is certain they have been grossly exaggerated, particularly by English writers, who took for granted every wild statement made at the period. But, even granting that all the charges made were true, which, of course, we do not admit, the fact would not stamp the charge of cruelty on the Irish nation. It was an age of cruelty—the age of the Thirty Years' War in Germany, which gave to the world the horrors of the sack of Magdeburgh; the age of the wars of the Fronde in France, and almost that of the Spanish atrocities in the Netherlands. And Cromwell was soon to appear upon the scene in Ireland, to leave behind him a name more terrible than that of Tilly in Germany or of Alva in the Low Countries. In fact, in the seventeenth century, Europe, from east to west, was just emerging from Middle-Age barbarism, and Ireland, most likely, was neither better nor worse than most of her sister states. We love and respect the Irish race, but we do not believe in painting it whiter than it is. The nation, plundered and outraged, was goaded to madness, and whatever crimes were committed under such circumstances may well be attributed to the workings of temporary insanity. It is, however, regrettable that around the history of the Irish insurrection of 1641 there should linger blood-red clouds, which even the lapse of two and a half centuries has not been able to dissipate.

On the Anglo-Irish side of the conflict, the name of Sir Charles Coote stands out in bloody pre-eminence. Like Sir Phelim, he had the grand virtue of physical courage—he feared nothing in mortal shape—but in all else he was a demon-brute, and his memory is still execrated throughout the length and breadth of the land he scourged with scorpions. His soldiers are accused of having impaled Irish infants on their pikes—their mothers having been dishonored and butchered—without rebuke from their inhuman commander. On the contrary, McGee, a very painstaking and impartial historian, quotes Sir Charles Coote as saying that "he liked such frolics." (McGee's "History of Ireland," Volume I, p. 502.) It is not unpleasant to note that, after a career of the most aggressive cruelty, he was finally killed by a musket-shot during a petty skirmish in the County Meath, and it is popular belief that the shot was fired by one of his own band of uniformed assassins.

The war proceeded in a rather desultory manner, chiefly because of lack of skill in the Irish generals—only a few of whom had seen service—and the promised Irish military leaders had not yet sailed from the Continent. Sir Phelim O'Neill made an unsuccessful attack on Drogheda, and was also repulsed at other fortified places, owing to the lack of a suitable battering train. English reinforcements kept pouring into Dublin by the shipload, until a fine army of not less than 25,000 men, with a numerous and well-served artillery, was in the field. The Irish army amounted, nominally, to 30,000 men, but only a third of it was armed and properly trained.

The excesses of the English army in the peaceful Anglo-Catholic districts of Leinster aroused the resentment of the hitherto apathetic nobility and "gentry" of that fine province. They appointed Sir John Read to bear a protest to the king, but, while en route, he was arrested, confined in Dublin Castle and put to the rack by the Parliamentary Government. Even this outrage did not drive the aristocrats of Leinster into immediate warfare. Other outrages followed in quick succession. Finally, Lord Gormanstown called a meeting of the Catholic peers and gentlemen to assemble at the hill of Crofty, in the County Meath. They met there accordingly, headed by the caller of the gathering. Other distinguished Palesmen present were the Earl of Fingal, Lords Dunsany, Louth, Slane, Trimleston, and Netterville; Sir Christopher Bellew, Sir Patrick Barnewall, Nicholas Darcy, Gerald Aylmer, and many others. While these personages were still deliberating, they observed a group of horsemen, bearing arms, approaching at a rapid pace. They were attended by a guard of musketeers, and proved to be the insurgent chiefs of Roger O'More, Philip O'Reilly, Costello MacMahon, Captains Byrne and Fox, and other leaders of the people. The party on the hill immediately galloped on horseback to meet them, and Lord Gormanstown, in loud and stern tones, asked: "Who are you, and why come you armed into the Pale?" To this question O'More replied: "We represent the persecuted people of the Catholic faith, and we come here for the assertion of the liberty of conscience, the maintenance of the royal prerogative, which we understand to be abridged, and the making of the subjects in this Kingdom of Ireland as free as those of England." "Then," replied Gormanstown, "seeing that these be your true end and object, we will likewise join with you!" The leaders on both sides then joined hands, amid the applause of their followers. A more formal meeting was arranged for at the hill of Tara, and at that gathering, held the next month, the alliance was formally concluded.

The faulty training of the Irish army was painfully illustrated soon afterward, when the forces of the newly made allies encountered those of Lord Ormond at a place called Kilrush, near the town of Athy, in Kildare, April

13, 1642. The numbers were about equal — perhaps 7,000 men each. The Irish were commanded by a brave but inexperienced officer, Lord Mountgarret, and with him were Lords Dunboyne and Ikerrin, Rory O'More, Colonel Hugh O'Byrne, and Sir Morgan Kavanagh. Mountgarret failed to occupy in time a difficult pass through which Ormond must march on his way to Dublin, and this failure compelled him to rearrange his plan of battle. Confusion—as is always the case when this experiment is tried with raw soldiers—resulted. The Irish fought bravely for a time, but were soon outmanœuvred and outflanked. The Anglo-Irish cavalry took them in reverse. Colonel Kavanagh, fighting desperately at the head of his regiment, met a hero's death. His fall discouraged his troops, who broke and fled to a neighboring bog, whither the hostile cavalry could not safely pursue them. The other Irish troops, surrounded on all sides, made a rush for the morass also, broke through the enemy's ranks and joined their vanquished comrades. On the Irish side, 700 officers and men fell in this untoward affair. The loss of the Anglo-Irish was much smaller, and Ormond was enabled to proceed in a species of triumph to Dublin, where the news of his victory preceded his arrival.

It is passing strange that, after the battle of Kilrush, the great organizer of the insurrection, Roger O'More, is heard of never more in his country's troubled annals. All accounts agree that, during the combat, he acted his part like a true soldier, but he failed to reappear in the Irish ranks during subsequent conflicts. His was certainly a mysterious and unaccountable disappearance.

The late Rev. C. P. Meehan, author of "The Confederation of Kilkenny," who gave more attention to that period of his country's story than any other writer, says, on page 26 of his interesting work: "After the battle of Kilrush, one bright name disappears [he mentions O'More in a foot-note]; the last time the inspiriting war-shout of his followers fell on his ear was on that hillside. What reasons there may have been for the retirement of the gallant chief, whose name was linked with that of God and Our Lady, are not apparent; but it is said, upon authority, that he proceeded to Ferns, and devoted the rest of his days to peaceful pursuits in the bosom of his family." The historian Coote says that he died at Kilkenny. This was, surely, a "lame and impotent conclusion" to such a career. The defeat of his countrymen may have destroyed his hopes, or he may have had reason to doubt the loyalty of his allies of the Pale. We are inclined to believe an old Leinster tradition, which says that he died of a broken heart immediately after the lost battle, on which he had built such high hopes. Such a spirit as his could not have remained inactive during the nine long years of the struggle, inaugurated by himself, which followed the disaster at Kilrush.

We can not dismiss this extraordinary man from our pages without quoting the following introduction to a ballad dealing with his career in Edward Hayes's remarkable collection of poetry, called "The Ballads of Ireland," vol. I, page 173:

"Roger, or Rory, O'More, is one of the most honored and stainless names in Irish annals. Writers who concur in nothing else agree in representing him as a man of the loftiest motives and the most passionate patriotism. In 1640, when Ireland was weakened by defeat and confiscation, and guarded with a jealous care, constantly increasing in strictness and severity, O'More, then a private gentleman with no resources beyond his intellect and courage, conceived the vast design of rescuing her from England, and accomplished it. In three years England did not retain a city in the island but Dublin and Drogheda. For eight years her power was merely nominal, the land was possessed and the supreme authority exercised by the Confederation created by O'More. History contains no stricter instance of the influence of an individual mind. Before the insurrection broke out the people had learned to know and expect their Deliverer, and it became a popular proverb, and the burden of national songs, that the hope of Ireland was in 'God, the Virgin, and Rory O'More.' It is remarkable that O'More, in whose courage and resources the great insurrection had its birth, was a descendant of the chieftains of Leix, massacred by English troops at Mullaghmast a century before. But if he took a great revenge, it was a magnanimous one. None of the excesses which stained the first rising in Ulster is charged upon him. On the contrary, when he joined the northern army, the excesses ceased, and strict discipline was established, as far as it was possible, among men unaccustomed to control, and wild with wrongs and sufferings." Says De Vere, in his sadly beautiful dirge, which assumes that the great leader died in 1642, as the people of Leinster have been taught to believe—

"'Twas no dream, Mother Land! 'Twas no dream, Innisfail!
    Hope dreams but grief dreams not—the grief of the Gael!
    From Leix and Ikerrin to Donegal's shore,
    Rolls the dirge of thy last and thy bravest O'More!"

CHAPTER IV

Proceedings of the Confederation of Kilkenny—Arrival of Owen
Roe O'Neill and Rinuccini

OUT of the chaos of a popular uprising, and a number of minor councils, which could decide only for localities, there sprang into existence the National Synod, composed of clerics and laymen of the Catholic persuasion, because, at this period, few, if any of the Irish Protestants were in sympathy with the insurrection, or revolution, which is a more fitting term. The "oath of association" was formulated by the venerable Bishop Rothe, and, somewhat unnecessarily, seeing that the King of England was using all the forces at his disposal to crush "the rebellion," pledged true faith and allegiance to Charles I and his lawful successors. The fundamental laws of Ireland and the "free exercise of the Roman Catholic faith and religion" were to be maintained. Then came the second, and most important, part of the solemn and, as some thought, stringent obligation, which bound all Confederate Catholics never to accept or submit to any peace without the consent and approbation of their own general assembly.

A constitution was framed which declared the war just and constitutional, condemned racial distinctions such as "New" and "Old" Irish, ordained an elective council for each of the four provinces, and a national council for the whole kingdom, condemned, as excommunicate, all who might violate the oath of association, or who should be guilty of murder, assault, cruelty, or plunder under cover of the war.

The bishops and priests, very wisely, decided that a layman should be elected president of the National Council, and Lord Mountgarret was so chosen, with Richard Belling, lawyer and litterateur, as secretary. Both were men of moderate opinion and free from any taint of prejudice.

It was decided that the Supreme, or National, Council should hold its first session in the city of Kilkenny on October 23, 1642, the anniversary of the rising; and "the choice of such a date," says McGee, "by men of Mountgarret's and Belling's moderation and judgment, six months after the date of the alleged 'massacre,' would form another proof, if any were now needed, that none of the alleged atrocities (of 1641) were yet associated with that particular day."

Between the adjournment of the National Synod, in May, and the meeting of the Council in October, many stirring events occurred. The confederate general in Munster, the aged Barry, made an unsuccessful attempt to capture Cork, but had better success at Limerick, which surrendered to the Irish army on June 21. Soon afterward the Anglo-Irish leader, General St. Ledger, died at Cork, and the command devolved upon Murrough O'Brien, Baron of Inchiquin, who had been brought up from an early age as one of Parsons' chancery wards, and had, therefore, become a Protestant. Furthermore, he had grown to be an anti-Irish Irishman of the blackest and bloodiest type. In Irish history, he is known as "Black Murrough the Burner," because the torch, under his brutal sway, kept steady company with the sword, and both were rarely idle. He served the king as long as the royal policy suited his views, but, when it did not, his services were at the disposal of the opposition. Murrough had served his military apprenticeship under Sir Charles Coote and was a past master in all the cruelties practiced by his infamous instructor. The curse of the renegade was strong upon him, for he hated his own kin more bitterly than if he were an alien and a Briton. Of the ancient royal houses of Ireland, those of MacMurrough and O'Brien present the strongest contrasts of good and evil.

The Irish forces succeeded in taking the castles of Loughgar and Askeaton, but Inchiquin inflicted a severe defeat upon them at Liscarroll, where the loss was nearly a thousand men on the side of Ireland, whereas the victor boasted that there fell only a score on his side. There were also some skirmishes in Connaught, where the peculiar inactivity of Lord Clanricarde produced discontent, and led to a popular outbreak in the town of Galway which General Willoughby speedily suppressed, with every circumstance of savage brutality. Affairs in Leinster continued rather tranquil. Ormond was raised by the king to the dignity of marquis, but does not seem to have been trusted by the Puritan Lords Justices, Parsons and Borlaise. The fall of the year was signalized, however, by the landing in Ireland of three able generals, all of whom fought on the national side—Right Hon. James Touchet, Earl of Castlehaven, who had been imprisoned as a suspect in Dublin Castle, but managed to effect his escape; Colonel Thomas Preston, the heroic defender of Louvain, who debarked at Wexford, bringing with him 500 officers of experience, several siege guns, a few light field-pieces, and a limited quantity of small arms; and last, but most welcome to Ireland, arrived from Spain

Colonel Owen Roe O'Neill, who made a landing on the Donegal coast with 100 officers, a company of Irish veterans, and a quantity of muskets and ammunition. He immediately proceeded to the fort of Charlemont, held by his fierce kinsman, Sir Phelim O'Neill, who, with commendable patriotic self-sacrifice, resigned to him, unsolicited, the command of the Irish army of the North, and became, instead of generalissimo, "President of Ulster."

Simultaneously with the arrival of Owen Roe, General Lord Leven came into Ireland from Scotland with 10,000 Puritan soldiers. He had met O'Neill in the foreign wars and expressed publicly his surprise that he should be "engaged in so bad a cause"—to which Owen replied that he had a much better right to come to the rescue of Ireland, his native country, than Lord Leven had to march into England against his acknowledged monarch. Leven did not remain long in Ireland, and the command of his troops fell to General Monroe—a brave but slow man, on whom the advice of his predecessor to act with vigor was thrown away. Monroe's dilatory tactics enabled O'Neill, who had wonderful talent for military organization, to recruit, drill, and equip a formidable force, mainly made up of the men of Tyrone and Donegal—as fine a body of troops as Ireland had ever summoned to her defence. The valorous clansmen were speedily molded into a military machine by their redoubted chief, who set the example of activity to all of his command.

When the Supreme Council of the Irish Confederation met in Kilkenny, according to agreement, one of its most important acts was the appointing of generals to command in the several provinces. It named Owen

O'Neill commander-in-chief in Ulster, General Sir
Thomas Preston in Leinster, General Barry in Munster,
and General Sir John Burke in Connaught.   Fighting
was resumed with vigor.   Preston met with alternate
successes and reverses in his province, but, on the whole,
came out victorious.   Barry and his lieutenants did brilliant work in Munster, and routed both Vavassour and
Inchiquin.   O'Neill played a Fabian game in Ulster,
training his army in partial engagements with the enemy
and husbanding his resources for some great occasion,
which, he saw, would surely come.   But the brightest
laurels of the campaign were gathered by General Sir
John Burke, who, after other brilliant exploits, compelled
General Willoughby to surrender the city of Galway to
the Irish forces on June 20, 1643; and the national flag
waved from the tower of its citadel until the last shot of
the war was fired nine years thereafter.   Clanricarde,
who could have had the command-in-chief, paltered with
time, and thus lost the opportunity of linking his name
with a glorious exploit.

All the Irish armies, and particularly that under
O'Neill, occupied excellent strategic positions, and the
hopes of the military chiefs and the nation rose high
when, suddenly, there came a blight upon those hopes in
the shape of a cessation of hostilities—in other words, a
prolonged armistice—agreed to between the Anglo-Catholic majority in the National Council on the one side,
and the Marquis of Ormond, representing the King of
England, on the other.   The Anglo-Catholics were again
duped by pretences of liberality toward their religion, as
their fathers had been in the days of Elizabeth; and this
ill-considered truce wrested from Ireland all the advan-

tages won in the war—which had already lasted two years—by the ability of her generals and the courage of her troops.   Vain was the protest of O'Neill, of Preston, of Burke, of Barry, of the Papal Nuncio, of the majority of the Irish nation.   Charles was in straits in England, fighting the Parliamentary forces arrayed against his acts of despotism, and Ormond promised everything in order to end the war in Ireland, temporarily at least, and so be enabled to send needed succor to a sovereign whom he loved and served much better than he did God and country.   With incredible fatuity, the Anglo-Catholic majority in the National Council listened to the voice of Ormond, and voted men and money to support the cause of the bad king who had let Strafford loose upon Ireland!   We are glad to be able to say that the "Old Irish" element, represented by the brave and able O'Neill, was in nowise responsible for this act of weakness and folly. O'Neill saw into futurity, and frightful must have been that vision to the patriot-hero, for it included the horrors of Drogheda and Wexford, where the thirsty sword of Cromwell bitterly avenged on Ireland the foolish and fatal "truce of Castlemartin"; another lesson to nations, if indeed another were needed, to avoid mixing up in the quarrels of their neighbors.   Ireland invited ruin on that dark day when she voted to draw the sword for the ungrateful Charles Stuart against the Parliament of England.   The temporary concession of Catholic privileges —designed to be withdrawn when victory perched on the royal banner—was poor compensation for the loss of advantages gained at the price of the blood of brave men, and the sowing of a wind of vengeance which produced the Cromwellian whirlwind.   If King Charles had ever done a fair or manly act by Ireland—even by the Anglo-Catholics of Ireland—the folly of that country might be, in a measure, excusable, but his whole policy had been, on the contrary, cold-blooded, double-faced, and thoroughly ungrateful. In this instance, the Anglo-Irish Catholics brought all their subsequent misfortunes on themselves. As if to emphasize its imbecility, the National Council placed Lord Castlehaven, an English Catholic, in supreme command over O'Neill in Ulster. Owen Roe was, of course, disgusted, but was also too good a soldier and too zealous a patriot to resign his command and go back to Spain, as a man of less noble nature might have done. Meanwhile, Monroe and his army of 10,000 Lowland Scotch and Ulster "Undertakers" kept gathering like a thundercloud in the north. In Scotland a body of 3,000 Antrim Irish, under Alister MacDonald, called Cal-Kitto, or "the Left-handed," were covering themselves with glory, fighting under the great Marquis of Montrose in the unworthy royal cause. And we read that the Irish Confederate treasury, about this time, is somewhat replenished by funds sent from Spain and Rome. Even the great Cardinal Richelieu, of France, to show his sympathy with Ireland, invited Con, the last surviving son of the great O'Neill, to the French court, and permitted the shipment of much needed cannon to Ireland. But all of those good foreign friends of the Irish cause were sickened and discouraged by the miserable policy of armistice, so blindly consented to by the lukewarm "Marchmen of the Pale" who had assembled in Kilkenny.

Many Irish Protestants, particularly the High Church element, were ardent royalists and refused to take the oath of the Covenanters prescribed in Ulster by General Monroe. They were driven with violence from their homes, and many fled for succor to their Catholic brethren, who treated them with hospitable consideration. In Munster, the ferocious Inchiquin, and still more savage Lord Broghill, son of Boyle, first Earl of Cork, foiled in their ambitious schemes by some royal refusal, broke out most violently, pretending the armistice was violated, and seized upon three leading Southern towns—Cork, Kinsale, and Youghal, where their excesses were too horrible for narration—murder and arson being among the lightest of their crimes. Ormond, in his peculiarly adroit way, succeeded in still further prolonging the truce, and stated that he had power from the king to come to a permanent agreement with the Confederates. The cause of Ireland about this time lost a true and ardent friend and champion in the death of the good Pope Urban VIII, who was succeeded by Innocent X—a Pontiff whose noble generosity is still gratefully remembered by the Irish nation. It was to one of their worthy predecessors, in the time of the Elizabethan wars, O'Donnell's bard referred, when addressing Ireland, in allegorical fashion, he sang:

> "O! my dark Rosaleen!
>   Do not sigh, do not weep—
> The priests are on the ocean green—
>   They march along the deep!
> There's wine from the Royal Pope,
>   Upon the ocean green,
> And Spanish ale to give you hope,
>   My dark Rosaleen!"

Nathless the truce, those two bad Irishmen, Inchiquin and Broghill, continued to do base work in the South,

where their cold-blooded atrocities struck terror into the
wretched people of Munster. They even corrupted old
Lord Esmond, commandant of Duncannon fort, which
partly commanded the important harbor of Waterford
from the Wexford side. Esmond was blind and almost
senile, and, perhaps, too, was terrorized by the brutal
threats of Inchiquin. But Lord Castlehaven and the
Confederate Irish immediately laid siege to the place,
and, after ten weeks of beleaguerment, succeeded in retaking it. The traitorous commandant perished in the
assault, and thus escaped an ignominious death, which
his crime had richly merited. Several other Munster
towns, held by Inchiquin and his officers, were success-
sively attacked and taken by the Confederates. In Connaught, however, the latter met with serious reverses.
The town of Sligo was captured by Sir Charles Coote,
Jr.—a worse scourge than even his infamous father—
and, in an attempt to recover it, several gallant Irishmen
perished. Archbishop O'Healy, of Tuam, fell into the
hands of Coote and was barbarously tortured to death,
Sunday, October 26, 1645. It must be remembered that
these hostilities were the work of the Parliamentary
forces, which were opposed by the "Old Irish" party.
The royal troops had been sent to England to assist
Charles, or else lay supine in their garrisons, as did
also the Anglo-Irish, waiting for further developments.

The king sent the Earl of Glamorgan, an English
Catholic, who had intermarried with the O'Brien family,
to Ireland to negotiate a new treaty with the Confederates. He succeeded in having a preliminary document
drawn up, signed by himself for Charles, and by Lord
Mountgarret and Muskerry on behalf of the Confed-

erates. Ormond, with his customary dilatoriness, haggled over the provisions regarding toleration of the Catholic Church in the kingdom, and thus frittered away much valuable time, which the Parliamentary forces made good use of. Ormond caused the treaty to be greatly modified, and while the negotiators were working on it at Kilkenny, there arrived in Ireland a new Papal Nuncio, in the person of the famous John Baptist Rinuccini, Archbishop of Ferns, and, afterward, Cardinal. He came to represent Pope Innocent X, who sent also substantial aid. The Irish in exile and their friends sent, through Father Luke Wadding, a further contribution of $36,000. The Nuncio complained that he had been unreasonably detained in France—it was greatly suspected by the intrigues of Cardinal Mazarin, who had succeeded Richelieu, Ireland's true friend. In spite of this trickery, however, he managed to purchase, with Pope Innocent's funds, a 26-gun frigate, which he called the *San Pietro,* 2,000 muskets, 2,000 cartridge boxes, 4,000 swords, 2,000 pike-heads, 800 horse pistols, 20,000 pounds of powder, and other much needed supplies. (McGee.) A ludicrous cause of one of his delays in France was the obstinacy of the wife of Charles I, Henrietta Maria, daughter of Henry of Navarre, who insisted that she would not receive the Papal Nuncio unless he uncovered in her presence. Rinuccini was proud and fiery, and, as representing the Pope, declined to remove his biretta, which so angered the queen that, after six weeks' parleying on this point of etiquette, the pair separated without coming to an interview. Such is the farcical folly of "royal minds."

CHAPTER V

Treason of Ormond to the Catholic Cause—Owen Roe O'Neill,
Aided by the Nuncio, Prepares to Fight

THE Papal Nuncio, although only in the prime of life, was in feeble health, and had to be borne on a litter by relays of able-bodied men, from his landing-place, at Kenmare in Kerry, to the city of Limerick, where he was received with all the ceremony due to his high rank, noble character, and chivalrous mission. From Limerick he proceeded by the same mode of conveyance to Kilkenny, the Confederate capital, where honors almost regal in their splendor awaited him. Lord Mountgarret, President of the National Council—a veteran soldier who had participated in the wars of Hugh O'Neill against Elizabeth—met the Papal dignitary, surrounded by a guard of honor, composed of the youthful chivalry of the Confederation, in the picture gallery of the Castle of Kilkenny—the palatial residence of the Duke of Ormond, the most politic nobleman of the age. The so-called Glamorgan treaty proceeded smoothly enough until certain demands of the exiled English Catholics, made through the Nuncio, were included in its provisions. Armed with the amended parchment, Glamorgan and the representatives of the Confederates returned to Dublin and laid the matter before Ormond. The latter acted in so strange a manner as to take the Confederate delegates completely by surprise. He had Glamorgan arrested while at dinner, on charge of having exceeded his instructions, and threw him into prison. The Confederate envoys were sent back to Kilkenny, charged to inform the President and Council that the clauses concerning the English Catholics were inadmissible and never could be entertained by the English people who supported the cause of Charles.   Lord Mountgarret and his associates broke off all negotiations with Ormond pending the release of Glamorgan, which they firmly demanded.   Ormond required bail to the amount of £40,000, and the bond was furnished by the Earls of Kildare and Clanricarde.   When Glamorgan was enlarged, he proceeded to Kilkenny, where, to the amazement of the Confederates and the Nuncio he defended, rather than censured, Ormond's course toward himself.   On which McGee grimly remarks: "To most observers it appeared that these noblemen understood each other only too well."

Frequent bickerings occurred at Kilkenny between Mountgarret's followers, or the Anglo-Irish, and the Nuncio's followers, the "Old Irish," who were in the minority.   Rinuccini's heart was with the latter, for, by instinct as well as observation, he recognized that they were the only real national party among the Irish factions.   The rest he put down, with good reason, as timeservers and provincialists—ever ready to go back to their gilded cages the moment the English power filled their cups with Catholic concessions.   With a little more knowledge of Ireland and her people; the Nuncio would have been a marvelous leader.   As it was, he did the very best he could for Ireland—according to his lights—and he was one of the very few foreigners who, on coming in close contact with the situation—remained true to the Irish cause through good and evil report.   He was, of course, a devoted Catholic, but in no sense a bigot.   Irishmen should always hold his name in high honor. Any mistakes the Nuncio committed were due to lack of familiarity with surrounding conditions, very excusable in an alien.

But the Glamorgan treaty would appear to have been taken up at Rome, where Sir Kenelm Digby and the pontifical ministers concluded a truce favorable to the interests of both Irish and English Catholics. The king needed the 10,000 Irish troops which he knew the Confederates could place at his disposal. In March, 1646, a modified Glamorgan treaty was finally signed by Ormond for King Charles, and by Lord Muskerry and other Confederate leaders for their party. "These thirty articles," comments McGee, "conceded, in fact, all the most essential claims of the Irish; they secured them equal rights as to property, the army, the universities, and the bar. They gave them seats in both Houses and on the bench. They authorized a special commission of Oyer and Terminer, composed wholly of Confederates. They declared that 'the independency of the Parliament of Ireland on that of England' should be decided by declaration of both Houses, agreeably to the laws of the Kingdom of Ireland. In short, the final form of Glamorgan's treaty gave the Irish Catholics, in 1646, all that was subsequently obtained, either for the Church or the country, in 1782, 1793, and 1829. Though some conditions were omitted, to which the Nuncio and a majority of the prelates attached importance, Glamorgan's treaty was, upon the whole, a charter upon which a free church and a free people might well have stood, as the fundamental law of their religious and civil liberties."

These concessions proved to be a new "delusion, mockery, and snare." Ormond tricked the Confederates, and the poltroon king, just before his fatal flight to the camp of the mercenary Scots' army of General Lord Leven, which promptly sold him to the English Parliament, for the amount of its back pay, disclaimed the Glamorgan treaty in toto—a policy entirely in keeping with his unmanly, vacillating nature.

Owen Roe O'Neill, notwithstanding many and grievous vexations, chiefly arising from the absurd jealousy of General Preston, had his army well in hand on the borders of Leinster and Ulster, prepared to strike a blow at the enemy wherever it might be most needed. He was in free communication with the Nuncio, who, according to all the historians of the period, supplied him with the necessary means for making an aggressive movement. The Anglo-Scotch army of General Monroe presented the fairest mark for O'Neill's prowess, and against that force his movements were, accordingly, directed.

CHAPTER VI

The Famous Irish Victory of Benburb—Cruel Murder of the Catholic Bishop of Ross

THE forces of the belligerents were not large, according to our more modern standards. In his comprehensive "History of Ireland," the Rev. Abbe McGeoghegan credits Owen Roe with only 5,000 infantry and 500 horse, while he calls Monroe's force 6,000 foot and 800 cavalry. The objective of both generals was the ancient city of Armagh, and the grand-nephew of the great Hugh O'Neill was destined to win one of Ireland's proudest victories in the immediate neighborhood of his grand-uncle's most famous battlefield—the Yellow Ford. Marching northward from the borders of Leinster, Owen Roe crossed the historic Blackwater and took position at a place called Benburb, in the present county of Tyrone. Monroe advanced to attack him, and ordered his younger brother, George Monroe, who commanded a strong detachment, to join forces with the main body without delay. O'Neill, apprised by his scouts of this movement, sent two regiments, under Colonels MacMahon and Mac-Nenay, to intercept young Monroe at a pass through which he would be compelled to defile his troops in order to form a junction with his brother. The two colonels obeyed their orders so strictly that George Monroe's force was so utterly broken and routed that it was unable to render any service to the Puritan general during the remainder of the campaign. The victors immediately rejoined O'Neill, who, in the interim, had detached Colonel Ricard O'Ferrall to obstruct the elder Monroe's march from Kinaird to Caledon, where he had crossed the Blackwater. The Scotchman's cannon proved too much for O'Ferrall, who could only reply with musketry, but he retired in admirable order, although closely pressed by Monroe's stronger vanguard. The battle of Benburb began on the morning of June 16th, new style, 1646. O'Neill's post was near the river, his flanks protected by two small hills, and his rear by a wood—all held by chosen troops. Throughout most of the day, the Scots, who had both sun and wind at their backs, seemed to have the advantage, in so far as partial demonstrations could determine the question. O'Neill, in expectation of a reinforcement from the direction of Coleraine, "amused" the Scotch general until the sun had shifted position and no longer shone full and dazzlingly in the faces of the Irish soldiers. Almost at this propitious moment, the expected auxiliary force reached the field, and took up position in O'Neill's line of battle. Rev. C. P. Meehan, historian of the "Confederation of Kilkenny," who quotes Monroe's despatch, Rinuccini's letters, and other contemporaneous authorities, says: "It was the decisive moment. The Irish general, throwing himself into the midst of his men, and, pointing out to them that retreat must be fatal to the enemy, ordered them to charge and pursue vigorously. A far resounding cheer rose from the Irish ranks. 'Myself,' said he, 'with the aid of Heaven, will lead the way. Let those who fail to follow me remember that they abandon their general.' This address was received with one unanimous shout by the army. The Irish colonels threw themselves from their horses, to cut themselves off from every chance of retreat, and charged with incredible impetuosity." Some musketry was used, but the victory was decided in Ireland's favor by her ancient and favorite weapon, the deadly pike, which may be called the parent of the bayonet. Monroe's cavalry charged boldly that bristling front of spears, but was overthrown in an instant and all but annihilated. Vain, then, became the fire of the vaunted cannon of the Scotch commander and the crashing volleys of his small arms. Vainly he himself and his chosen officers, sword in hand, set an example of courage to their men. With the shout of "Lamh Dearg Aboo!" which, fifty years before, had sounded the death-knell of Bagnal, Kildare, and De Burgh, on the banks of the same historic river, the Irish clansmen rushed upon their foes. The struggle was brief and bitter. Lord Blaney's English regi-

ment perished almost to the last man, fighting heroically
to the end.   The Scottish cavalry was utterly broken and
fled pell-mell, leaving the infantry to their fate.   Lord
Montgomery's regiment alone retired in good order, although with considerable loss, but Montgomery himself,
fifty other officers, and some two hundred soldiers, were
made prisoners.   Monroe fled, without hat or wig, and
tradition says he lost his sword in swimming his horse
across the Blackwater.   Of the Anglo-Scotch army, there
died upon the field 3,243 officers and men, and many
more perished during the vengeful pursuit of the victors,
who do not appear to have been in a forgiving mood.
O'Neill acknowledged a loss of seventy men killed and
several hundred wounded.   The Scottish army lost all
of its baggage, tents, cannon, small arms, military chest,
and, besides, thirty-two stand of battle-flags.   Fifteen
hundred draught horses and enough food supplies to last
the Irish army for many months also fell into the hands
of the vanquishers.   Monroe's army was, virtually, destroyed, and he sullied a previously honorable record by
plundering and burning many villages and isolated houses
to gratify his spite against the people whose soldiers had
so grievously humiliated him.

O'Neill's fine military instinct impelled him to follow
up his success by giving Monroe no rest until he had
driven him from Ulster, but, unfortunately, there came
at this crisis a request, which really meant an order, from
the Nuncio, to march the Ulster army into Leinster in
order that it might support those who were opposed in
the Council at Kilkenny to entering into further peace
negotiations with the bigoted Ormond and the now impotent king.   O'Neill could hardly decline this misdi-

rected mission, but it proved to be, in the end, a fatal act of obedience. From that hour the Irish cause began to decline. General Preston, O'Neill's fierce Anglo-Irish rival, and fanatically devoted to the cause of Charles, engaged in battle with the Parliamentary general, Michael Jones, at Dungan Hill in Meath, and was totally routed, with immense loss. It is only proper to remark here, that the "Old" Irish did the best fighting during this war, because their hearts were in the struggle, while the Anglo-Irish, who mainly composed the armies under Preston and Lord Taaffe—the latter of whom was ignominiously defeated at Knockinoss, near Mallow in Cork—were only half-hearted in their efforts. Taaffe's defeat was aggravated by the cruel murder of the brave "Left-handed" MacDonnell of Antrim, who, after having been made prisoner, was barbarously put to death by order of the murderous renegade, "Murrough the Burner," who commanded the victors. This bloody-minded wretch further signalized his cruelty by storming the city of Cashel and sacking the grand cathedral, founded by one of his own princely ancestors, in the twelfth century. Hundreds of non-combatants of all ages and both sexes, who had taken refuge in the holy place, were ruthlessly massacred, and twenty priests were dragged from under the high altar and wantonly butchered. Lord Broghill emphasized his brutality in Cork County by hanging before the walls of Macroom Castle the saintly Bishop MacEagan of Ross, who refused to counsel the Irish garrison to surrender. Dr. Madden, a gifted poet, summed up the noble refusal and its tragical consequences in the following lines:

"The orders are given, the prisoner is led
   To the castle, and round him are menacing hordes:
Undaunted, approaching the walls, at the head
   Of the troopers of Cromwell, he utters these words:

" 'Beware of the cockatrice—trust not the wiles
   Of the serpent, for perfidy skulks in its folds!
Beware of Lord Broghill the day that he smiles!
   His mercy is murder!—his word never holds!

" 'Remember, 'tis writ in our annals of blood,
   Our countrymen never relied on the faith
Of truce, or of treaty, but treason ensued—
   And the issue of every delusion was death!'

"He died on the scaffold in front of those walls,
   Where the blackness of ruin is seen from afar,
And the gloom of their desolate aspect recalls
   The blackest of Broghill's achievements in war."

CHAPTER VII

Ormond's Treacherous Surrender of Dublin—Ireland's Choice of Two Evils

ORMOND would seem to have been the evil genius of the Irish nation at this period of its history. He was suspected by the Confederates and distrusted by the Parliamentarians. The former, convinced that he meant to betray Dublin, which was poorly fortified, to the latter, ordered O'Neill and Preston to unite their forces and take it from Ormond. Preston, who was, to all appearance, more of a royalist Palesman than an Irishman, threw obstacles in the way of the intended assault, and proposed to parley with Ormond before assuming the aggressive. Owing to this dilatoriness, and because of a false alarm, the combined Irish forces retired from before the city without accomplishing anything. There was mutual distrust between the unwilling allies, and, as usual, Ireland was the sufferer. Preston's jealousy of O'Neill amounted to a frenzy, and, before an accommodation could be arrived at, Ormond surrendered the city to the Parliamentary forces, under General Jones, and fled to France, where, unaccountably, considering his suspicious conduct, he was favorably received. After a year's absence, he returned to Ireland, and, finding the royal cause desperate, concluded a peace between the king's supporters, the Confederates, and the National party, headed by Owen O'Neill. This treaty was, virtually, a revival of that submitted by Glamorgan, and fully recognized, when all too late, the justice of the Catholic claims to liberty of conscience. Had the original instrument been adopted, Charles could have held Ireland against the Parliament. But his days were now numbered, and he died on the scaffold, in front of his own palace of Whitehall, on January 30, 1649.

The Royalist party at once recognized his heir as Charles II. They were reinforced by many Parliamentarian Protestants who were shocked and horrified by the decapitation of the king; and so Old Irish and New Irish, Confederates and Ormondists, made common cause against the Parliament, which was defended in Dublin by the redoubtable General Jones, and in Derry by the ferocious younger Coote. Even the sanguinary Inchiquin again became a Royalist and captured several towns of strength and importance from his recent allies. Ormond massed his army and, aided by Major-General Purcell, made an attempt to storm Dublin. But Michael Jones made a night sortie from the city and scattered Ormond and Purcell and their followers to the winds of heaven. The

Irish generals mutually blamed each other and there was much bitter crimination and recrimination, but all this could not remedy the disaster that incapacity and over-confidence had brought about. Owen O'Neill kept his army, which fronted Coote, near Derry, intact, but lost his best friend when the impetuous Nuncio, who had spared neither denunciation nor excommunication in dealing with the trimming Anglo-Catholic leaders, disgusted with the whole wretched business, suddenly departed for the port of Galway and sailed in his own ship for Rome. Had this good man had to deal with leaders like Owen O'Neill, faithful, sensible, and unselfish, Ireland would have been an independent nation ere he returned to the Eternal City. His retirement placed O'Neill and the "Old Irish" in great perplexity as regarded a military policy. Ormond, the treacherous, was, nominally at least, commander-in-chief of the royal army, and his trusted lieutenants, Preston and Inchiquin, were O'Neill's bitter foes.

Under such disadvantages, we are not surprised to learn that O'Neill adopted a policy of his own, at once bold and original. He temporized with the Parliamentarians, and actually entered into a three months' truce with General George Monck, who had succeeded to the unlucky Monroe's command in the North. The distrust and hatred of Ormond, whose military power waned immediately after his crushing defeat by General Jones, already mentioned, were so great that both Galway and Limerick refused to admit his garrisons. He and his wretched ally, Inchiquin, became utterly discredited with the Old Irish party, and soon fled the kingdom their infamies had cursed. Ormond re-

turned to England after the Restoration and was one of
Charles II's intimates. It can hardly be wondered at,
therefore, that, to use McGee's language, "the singular
spectacle was exhibited of Monck forwarding supplies
to O'Neill to be used against Ormond and Inchiquin,
and O'Neill coming to the rescue of Coote and raising
for him the siege of Derry." It was unfortunate that
all of the Parliamentary generals were not possessed of
the chivalric qualities of Monck and that hard fortune
again compelled Owen Roe to draw the sword for the
cause of the ingrate Stuarts. As for the Anglo-Irish,
whether of the Church of Rome or the Church of England, they clung to the fortunes, or rather the misfortunes, of Charles II as faithfully and vehemently as to
those of his infatuated father. This was all the more
noteworthy, as the younger Charles had even less to
recommend him to public estimation than his sire. He
lived to be a disgrace to even the throne of England,
which has been filled too often by monarchs of degraded
and dissolute character. The second Charles of England
was destitute of every virtue, except physical courage.
He had, in a high degree, that superficial good nature
which distinguished his race, but he was a libertine, an
ingrate, and a despicable time-server. But Ireland did
not learn these truths about his character until long after
the period of his checkered career here dealt with. It
must be borne in mind, however, that in the middle of
the seventeenth century the divinity which is alleged to
hedge a king was much more apparent to the masses of
the people than it is in our own generation, when the
microscopic eye of an educated public opinion is turned
upon the throne and detects the slightest flaw, in the

"fierce light" which beats upon it. The Old Irish party cared little for Charles, but when it came to a choice between him and Cromwell, there was nothing left them but to throw their swords into the scale for the youthful monarch, who was not nearly as "merry" then as he became in after days, when he quite forgot the friends of his adversity.

CHAPTER VIII

"The Curse of Cromwell"—Massacres of Drogheda and Wexford —Death of Sir Phelim O'Neill

THEIR adherence to the cause of the young Stuart brought upon the Irish nation the blighting "curse of Cromwell," so terribly remembered down to the present hour in every nook of Ireland visited by his formidable and remorseless legions. The English Parliament well knew that a general of the first class was needed to crush the Irish army in field and fort, and so Oliver Cromwell, commander of the famous "Ironsides," or Parliamentary cuirassiers, the greatest and most relentless soldier of that age, was sent to Ireland, commissioned to work his will upon her. He landed in Dublin with an army of 4,000 cavalry and 9,000 infantry, augmented by the forces already in the island, on August 14, 1649. Plentifully supplied with money and military stores, he at once made ready for a vigorous campaign. His second in command was General Ireton, a son-in-law and pupil, who is remembered in Ireland only a degree less bitterly than the great regicide himself. The latter marched his formidable army, after a very brief rest, from Dublin to Drogheda, which was held for Charles II by a garrison of about 3,000 men, burdened with many helpless non-combatants, under the orders of Sir Arthur Aston, a brave and experienced officer, who had suffered the loss of a leg in the Continental wars. He spurned Cromwell's insolent summons to surrender, and successfully repulsed two furious assaults, led by the English general in person. A third attack, made September 10, 1649, was successful. General Aston fell, and the Puritan soldiers quarreled over his artificial leg, which was said to be made of gold. Examination proved it to be of wood—a much less costly and tempting material. The garrison, seeing their leader fall, laid down their arms, believing that quarter would be extended. But Cromwell, by his own admission (see his letters compiled by Thomas Carlyle), refused this accommodation, on the flimsy pretext that Drogheda did not, at once, surrender on summons; and the Puritan army was let loose upon the doomed city. For five dreadful days and nights there ensued a carnival of rapine and slaughter. The affrighted people fled to cellars, many sought refuge in churches, and some climbed even to the belfries in the vain hope of escaping the general massacre. But they were relentlessly pursued, sabred, suffocated, or burned to death in the places in which they hoped to obtain shelter. The few miserable survivors—less than one hundred—were spared, only to be shipped as slaves to the Barbadoes. (See Cromwell's Letters, per Carlyle.)

Cromwell, in his despatch to the speaker of the English Parliament, called this brutal achievement "an exceeding great mercy," and, blasphemously, gave all the praise of the universal slaughter to the most High God! There is absolutely no excuse for the regicide's outrageous conduct at Drogheda, although Froude, Carlyle, and other

British historians have vainly sought to make apology for his inhuman actions. Many of the garrison were English and Protestant, so that race and creed did not entirely influence him, as the same considerations undoubtedly did at other places in Ireland. His cold-blooded idea was to "strike terror" into Ireland at the outset of the campaign; and in this he certainly succeeded only too well. It made his subsequent task of subjugation much easier than it would, otherwise, have been. Having accomplished his work in the fated city, and left it a smoking ruin, he counter-marched to Dublin, rested there for some days, and then marched toward Wexford, capturing several small towns, which offered but feeble resistance, on his way. His lieutenants had, meanwhile, added Dundalk, Carlingford, and Newry to his conquests in the North. Wexford prepared for a brave defence, but was basely betrayed by Captain James Stafford, an officer of English ancestry, who surrendered the outer defences, without the knowledge of his chief, Colonel David Sennott. Quarter was refused, as at Drogheda, and three hundred maids and matrons, many of the latter with infants in their arms, who fled to the market square, and took refuge, as they thought, under the sacred shadow of the gigantic cross which stood there, were butchered, notwithstanding their pleadings for mercy. Nearly all of these people were Catholic in creed, if not all of Celtic race, so that Cromwell manifested what may be called an impartial spirit of cruelty on both bloody occasions. His hatred for the English Protestant royalists was as hot, to all appearance, as that which he entertained toward the Irish Catholics, who had embraced the Stuart cause. But his remorseless policy of general confiscation of the lands of the vanquished, and the sending into banishment, as veritable slaves, of the unhappy survivors, have left a deeper scar on the heart of Ireland than all the blood he so cruelly, and needlessly, shed on her soil.

The tidings from Drogheda and Wexford soon spread throughout the country, and the faint-hearted governors of many strong towns surrendered without attempting to make an honorable defence. Kilkenny proved an exception. There a brave stand was made, and garrison and inhabitants received favorable terms of surrender. But Cromwell's most difficult task was in front of "rare Clonmel," in Tipperary, which was garrisoned by a few regiments of the aboriginal Ulster Irish—among the bravest men that ever trod a battlefield or manned a breach—under the command of Major-General Hugh Duff (Black) O'Neill, nephew and pupil of the glorious Owen Roe. This brave and skilful officer repulsed, with much carnage, several of Cromwell's fiercest assaults, and the siege would, undoubtedly, have been raised only for failure of ammunition in the Irish army. O'Neill, having satisfied himself that this was the unfortunate fact, evacuated the city on a dark midnight of May, 1649, and retreated to Limerick. Cromwell, ignorant of this movement, demanded the surrender of Clonmel next morning. Favorable terms were requested and granted. There was no massacre, and Cromwell's sardonic nature made him rather enjoy the masterly trick played upon him by young O'Neill. Some years afterward, when the latter, after a most noble defence of Limerick, fell into the hands of Ireton and was condemned to death, we are informed that Cromwell, then virtually Lord Protector, caused his sentence to be commuted and allowed him to return to the Continent.   Such is the effect true courage produces on even the most brutal natures.

Owen Roe O'Neill, who, of all the Irish generals, was alone fitted, both by nature and experience, to combat the able Cromwell, died soon after that tyrant's arrival in Ireland, as some say by poison.   He was on the march to attack the English army, when he surrendered to death at Clough Oughter Castle, in Cavan, bitterly mourned by all who had dreamed of an independent Ireland.   How beautifully Thomas Davis laments him:

"We thought you would not die—we were sure you would not go,
And leave us in our utmost need to Cromwell's cruel blow!
Sheep without a shepherd, when the snow shuts out the sky,
Oh, why did you leave us, Owen, why did you die?

"Soft as woman's was your voice, O'Neill! bright was your eye,
O! why did you leave us, Owen? why did you die?
Your troubles are all over, you're at rest with God on high;
But we're slaves and we're orphans, Owen! why did you die?"

Immediately after the capitulation of Clonmel, Cromwell, summoned by Parliament to operate against the royalists of Scotland, set sail for England, leaving behind him Ireton and Ludlow to continue his bloody work.   By Oliver's direction, confiscation followed confiscation, and, when he became Protector of the English Commonwealth, many thousands of innocent boys and girls were shipped from Ireland to the West Indies and other colonies of England, where most of them perished miserably.   Ireton died in Limerick, which yielded to his arms, after a desperate resistance, in 1651.   Tradition says that he rotted from the plague, and that his last hours were horrible to himself and to all who surrounded his repulsive deathbed.   He had caused to be killed in the city a bishop, many priests, and a multitude of other non-combatants; and these atrocities appalled his craven soul at the moment of dissolution.   Ludlow, an equally ferocious soldier, concluded the work of conquest in Ireland, and, in 1652, the whole island was again rendered "tranquil." "Order reigned in Warsaw," but it was not the order that succeeds dissolution.   Ireland, as subsequent events proved, was not dead, but sleeping.   The close of "the great rebellion," which had lasted eleven years, was signalized by the ruthless executions of Bishop Heber MacMahon—the warrior prelate who led Owen Roe's army after that hero's death—and Sir Phelim O'Neill, who was offered his life on the steps of the scaffold, if he consented to implicate the late King Charles I in the promotion of the Irish revolt. This, the English historians inform us, he "stoutly refused to do," and died, in consequence, like a soldier and a gentleman. He had his faults—this fierce Sir Phelim. He was by no means a saint, or even an exemplary Christian—but he acted, "according to his lights," for the best interests of his native country, and lost everything, including life, in striving to make her free. A gifted Irish poet (T. D. McGee) sings of him as "In Felix Felix," thus:

> "He rose the first—he looms the morning star
> Of that long, glorious unsuccessful war;
> England abhors him! has she not abhorr'd
> All who for Ireland ventured life or word?
> What memory would she not have cast away
> That Ireland keeps in her heart's heart to-day?

> "If even his hand and hilt were so distained,
> If he was guilty as he has been blamed,
> His death redeemed his life—he chose to die
> Rather than get his freedom with a lie.
> Plant o'er his gallant heart a laurel tree,
> So may his head within the shadow be!

"I mourn for thee, O hero of the North—
    God judge thee gentler than we do on earth!
    I mourn for thee and for our land, because
    She dare not own the martyrs in her cause;
    But they, our poets, they who justify—
    They will not let thy memory rot or die!"

CHAPTER IX

Sad Fate of the Vanquished—Cruel Executions and Wholesale Confiscations

THE subsequent fate of other chief actors in this great political and military drama is summed up by a learned historian thus: "Mountgarret and Bishop Rothe died before Galway (the last Irish stronghold of this war) fell. Bishop MacMahon, of Clogher, surrendered to Sir Charles Coote, and was executed like a felon by one he had saved from destruction a year before at Derry. Coote, after the Restoration, became Earl of Mountrath, and Broghill, Earl of Orrery. Clanricarde died unnoticed on his English estate, under the Protectorate. Inchiquin, after many adventures in foreign lands, turned Catholic in his old age; and this burner of churches bequeathed an annual alms for masses for his soul. A Roman patrician did the honors of sepulture for Father Luke Wadding. Hugh Duff O'Neill, the heroic defender of Clonmel and Limerick, and the gallant though vacillating Preston, were cordially received in France, while the consistent (English) Republican, General Ludlow, took refuge as a fugitive (after the Restoration) in Switzerland.

The same accomplished authority (T. D. McGee) informs us that under Oliver Cromwell's Protectorate, "A new survey of the whole island was ordered, under the direction of Sir William Petty, the fortunate economist who founded the House of Lansdowne. By him the surface of the kingdom was estimated at ten and a half million plantation acres, three millions of which were deducted for waste and water. Of the remainder, above 5,000,000 acres were in Catholic hands in 1641; 300,000 acres were college lands, and 2,000,000 acres were in possession of the Protestant settlers of the reigns of James I and Elizabeth. Under the Cromwellian Protectorate, 5,000,000 acres were confiscated. This enormous spoil, two-thirds of the whole island (as then computed), went to the soldiers and adventurers who had served against the Irish or had contributed to the military chest since 1641—except 700,000 acres given in 'exchange' to the banished in Clare and Connaught, and 1,200,000 confirmed to 'innocent Papists' who had taken no part in the warfare for their country's liberty. And," continues our authority already quoted, "Cromwell anticipated the union of the kingdoms by a hundred and fifty years, when he summoned, in 1653, that assembly over which 'Praise-God Bare-bones' presided. Members for Ireland and Scotland sat on the same benches with the Commons of England. Oliver's first deputy in the government of Ireland was his son-in-law, Fleetwood, who had married the widow of Ireton, but his real representative was his fourth son, Henry Cromwell, commander-in-chief of the army. In 1657, the title of Lord Deputy was transferred from Fleetwood to Henry, who united the supreme civil and military authority in his own person, until the eve of the Restoration, of which he became an active partisan. We may thus embrace the five years of the Protectorate as the period of Henry Cromwell's administration." High Courts of Justice were appointed for dealing with those who had been actively in arms, and many cruel executions resulted. Commissions were also appointed for the expatriation of the people, particularly the young. "Children under age, of both sexes, were captured by the thousands, and sold as slaves to the tobacco planters of Virginia and the West Indies. Secretary Thurloe informs Henry Cromwell that 'the Council have authorized 1,000 girls, and as many youths, to be taken up for that purpose.' Sir William Petty mentions 6,000 Irish boys and girls shipped to the West Indies. Some contemporary accounts make the total number of children and adults, so transported, 100,000 souls. To this decimation we may add 34,000 men of fighting age, who had permission to enter the armies of foreign powers at peace with the Commonwealth."

As there was no Irish Parliament called under Cromwell's régime, the "government" of Ireland consisted, during that period, of the deputy, the commander-in-chief, and four commissioners—the Puritan leaders, Ludlow, Corbett, Jones, and Weaver—all of whom looked upon the Celtic-Catholic Irish, and, in fact, all classes of the Irish people, with bigoted hatred and insolent disdain. And these men had, until the Restoration, absolute dominion over the lives and liberty, the rights and properties of the nation they hated!

The Act of Uniformity, which played such a terrible part in the reigns of Elizabeth and James, was put into relentless force. The Catholics were crushed, as it were, into the earth, and Ireland again became a veritable counterpart of the infernal regions. Priests, of all ranks, were hunted like wild beasts, and many fell victims to their heroic devotion to their flocks. Catholic lawyers were rigidly disbarred and Catholic school-teachers were subjected to deadly penalties. "Three bishops and three hundred ecclesiastics" perished violently during the Protectorate. "Under the superintendence of the commissioners," says McGee, "the distribution made of the soil among the Puritans 'was nearly as complete as that of Canaan by the Israelites.' Such Irish gentlemen as had obtained pardons were obliged to wear a distinctive mark on their dress under pain of death. Those of inferior rank were obliged to wear a round black spot on the right cheek, under pain of the branding iron and the gallows. If a Puritan lost his life in any district inhabited by Catholics, the whole population were held subject to military execution. For the rest, whenever 'Tory' (nickname for an Irish royalist) or recusant fell into the hands of these military colonists, or the garrisons which knitted them together, they were assailed with the war-cry of the Jews—'That thy feet may be dipped in the blood of thy enemies, and that the tongues of thy dogs may be red with the same.' Thus, penned in (according to the Cromwellian penal regulation) between 'the mile line' of the Shannon and the 'four-mile line' of the sea, the remnant of the Irish nation passed seven years of a bondage unequaled in severity by anything which can be found in the annals of Christendom."

When the news of Oliver Cromwell's death, which occurred on September 3, 1658, reached Ireland, a sigh of intense relief was heaved by the persecuted nation. Many a prayer of thankfulness went up to the throne of God from outraged Irish fathers and mothers, whose children were sweltering as slaves under tropical suns.

Cromwell himself had passed away, but the "curse of Cromwell" remained with Ireland for many a black and bitter day thereafter.

What followed after his death until the Restoration belongs to English history. Under his son Richard, and his associates, or advisers, the Protectorate proved a failure. Then followed the negotiations with General Monck, and the restoration of the monarchy under Charles II, who landed on English soil, at Dover, May 22, 1660, proceeded to London, where he was cordially welcomed, and renewed his interrupted reign over a country which, at heart, despised and distrusted him and all of his fated house.

CHAPTER X

Ireland Further Scourged Under Charles II—Murder of Archbishop Plunket—Accession of James II

THE Irish Catholics had built high hopes on the restoration of Charles, but were not very jubilant when they learned that he had appointed as Lords Justices, in Dublin, their ancient foes and persecutors, Coote and Broghill, the latter now called the Earl of Orrery. In the Irish (provincial) Parliament, the "Undertaking" element was in the ascendant, and the Protestants, barely one-fifth of the nation, had, in the House of Lords, 72 peers of their faith to 21 Catholics. In the Commons the same disparity existed, there being 198 Protestant to 64 Catholic members. In England, the defenders of the crown, who had fought against Cromwell, were, in most cases, treated with justice, and many had their possessions restored to them. In Ireland, the Royalists, of all creeds and classes, were treated by the king and his advisers with shameful ingratitude. Most of the confiscations of the Cromwell period were confirmed, but the Catholic religion was tolerated, to a certain extent, and the lives of priests and schoolmasters were not placed in jeopardy as much as formerly. The Catholics made a good fight for the restoration of their property, and were faithfully aided by the Earl of Kildare in Ireland and by Colonel Richard Talbot—afterward Earl of Tyrconnel—in England. But the Cromwellian settlers maintained the advantage in property they had gained. In 1775, they still held 4,500,-000 acres against 2,250,000 acres held by the original proprietors. The figures, according to the most reliable authorities, were almost exactly the reverse before the Cromwellian settlement. An attempt on the part of the Catholics, to be allowed greater privileges than they possessed, was met in a most unfriendly spirit in England. One of their delegates, Sir Nicholas Plunkett, was mobbed by the Londoners and forbidden the royal presence by the order of the Council, while Colonel Talbot, because of his bold championship of the Catholic cause, was sent for a period to the Tower. The Irish Catholics were, finally, forbidden to make any further address in opposition to the Bill of Settlement—as the act confirming the confiscations was called — and the perfidious Charles signed it without compunction, although he well knew he was beggaring his own and his father's friends. An English tribunal, appointed to sit in Dublin and hear the Irish claims, declared in favor of the plundered native proprietors, but as it was met immediately by the intrigues of the ruthless Ormond, who again became Lord Lieutenant of Ireland, the duration of this honest

English tribunal was limited to a certain day, when only about 800 out of 3,000 cases had been heard. A measure called "An Act of Explanation" was then passed (1665), by which it was decreed that "no Papist who had not been adjudged innocent under the former act could be so adjudged thereafter, or entitled to claim any lands or settlements." "Thus," remarks a historian, "even the inheritance of hope, and the reversion of expectation, were extinguished forever for the sons and daughters of the ancient gentry of the kingdom."

An attempt made by the titled Catholic laity and the prelates and priests of that faith to establish their true position in regard to their spiritual and secular allegiance was also met in a hostile manner by Ormond, who so managed as to excite a bitter controversy in regard to a document called "The Remonstrance," which was supposed to embody the Catholic idea of the period. The viceroy succeeded to the top of his bent. Dissension prevailed at a meeting of the surviving prelates of the Church, and the superiors of regular orders, held in Dublin, and Ormond made the failure of the gathering an excuse for persecuting the prelates and priests, whom he bitterly hated as a body he could not use, with penal severities, which the selfish and sensual king, who was himself a Catholic in secret, allowed to pass without interference.

In this same year (1666) the importation of Irish cattle into England was declared, by Parliamentary enactment, "a nuisance," for the reason that when the Londoners were starving, at the time of the Great Fire, Ireland contributed for their relief 15,000 fat steers. Instead of being grateful for the generous gift, the English lawmakers pretended to believe it a scheme to preserve the trade in cattle between the two kingdoms. The Navigation Act—invented by Cromwell—which put fetters on Irish commerce, was also enforced, and these two grievances united, for a time, the Puritans and the Old Irish, as both suffered equally from the restrictions placed upon industry. Ormond showed favor to the discontented Puritans, and was recalled in consequence. His retirement lasted nine years, and during that period he became a patron of Irish manufactures, especially in the county of Kilkenny. A bogus "Popish plot"—an offshoot of that manufactured in England, during this reign, by that arch-impostor and perjurer, Titus Oates—was trumped up in Ireland for purposes of religious and political terrorism. The attempt to fasten it upon the masses of the people happily failed, but, without even the shadow of proof, the aged and venerated archbishop of Armagh, Oliver Plunkett, was accused of complicity in it, arrested and confined, without form of trial, for ten months in an Irish prison. Finally he was removed to London and placed on trial. One of his "judges" was the notorious Jeffreys—the English Norbury—a man destitute of a heart. Even one of the paid perjurers, called a crown agent, stung by remorse, offered to testify in behalf of the unfortunate archbishop. All was in vain, however. The judges charged the jury against the accused, violating every legal form, and the hapless prelate was found guilty. He was sentenced to be "hanged, drawn, and quartered" on July 1, 1681. This sentence was carried out in all its brutal details. When the Earl of Essex appealed to the king to save the illustrious martyr, Charles replied: "I can not pardon him, because I dare not. His blood be upon your conscience. You could have saved him if you pleased!" And this craven king, a few years afterward, on his deathbed, called for the ministrations of a priest of the Church outraged by the murder of an innocent prelate! The slaughter of Oliver Plunkett was the most atrocious political assassination in English history, which reeks with such crimes. The shooting of Duc d'Enghien by Napoleon did not approach it in cold-blooded infamy. The king, the minister, the court, the jury—everybody—believed the archbishop innocent, and yet he was sacrificed that his blood might satisfy the rampant bigotry of the times.

The Catholics were ferociously pursued in Ireland after this shameful tragedy. Proclamations were issued against them by Ormond, who had yet again become Lord Lieutenant. They were forbidden to enter fortresses or to hold fairs, markets, or gatherings within the walls of corporate towns. They were also forbidden the use of arms—an old English expedient in Ireland—and they were commanded to kill or capture any "Tory" or "outlaw" relative within fourteen days from the date of proclamation, under penalty of being arrested and banished from Ireland. This was the setting of brother against brother with a vengeance. Few of the Irish people were found base enough to comply with the unnatural order, but Count Redmond O'Hanlon, one of the few Irish chiefs of ancient family who still held out against English penal law in Ireland, was assassinated in a cowardly manner by one of Ormond's ruthless tools. The blood stains from the heart of the brave O'Hanlon will sully forever the escutcheon of the Irish Butlers.

Just as the spirit of persecution of Catholics began to subside both in England and Ireland, Charles II, who

had been much worried by the political contentions in
his English kingdom, which resulted in the banishment
of Monmouth and the execution of Lord William Russell and Algernon Sidney, had a stroke of apoplexy,
which resulted in his death on February 6, 1685. In
his last moments he was attended by the Rev. Father
Huddlestone, who received him into the Catholic Church,
which he had betrayed so foully. He was immediately
succeeded by his Catholic brother, the Duke of York,
who ascended the throne under the title of James II.
James was a man of resolute purpose, good intentions, no
doubt, but had a narrow intellect and sadly lacked dis-
cretion—at least in the moral sense. His physical courage has been questioned, although the famous Marshal
Turenne certified to it, when he, in his fiery youth, served
in the French armies. He was destined, as we shall see,
to ruin his friends, exalt his enemies, and wreck the ancient Stuart dynasty.

CHAPTER XI

Well Meant but Imprudent Policy of King James—England In-
vites William of Orange to Assume the Throne

ALTHOUGH the final outcome of his policy was disastrous to Ireland, we feel justified in saying that
James II meant well by all his subjects. He was a
friend of religious equality—an idea hateful to the English and a large portion of the Scottish nation at that
period. In Ireland, too, the Protestant minority resented
it, because, to their minds, it meant Catholic ascendency
and the restoration of stolen estates. But James went
about his reforms so awkwardly, and imprudently, that
he brought on himself almost immediately the all but

unanimous ill-will of his English subjects. He dared to profess his Catholic faith openly—an unforgivable offence in England at that time. He sought to equalize the holding of office by the abolition of the Test Act, aimed against Catholics, so that English, Scotch, and Irish Catholics should have the same rights and privileges in that respect as their Protestant brethren. This, also, was an idea hateful to the English mind of the period. The king undertook to regulate the judiciary, the privy council, the army, the civil list—every public appointment—according to his own notions. This meant recognition of the Catholics and produced an uproar in England. He recalled Ormond from the viceroyalty of Ireland and sent Lord Clarendon to take his place. Finally, Clarendon resigned and Richard Talbot, who had been created Duke of Tyrconnel, was made Lord Lieutenant of Ireland. This appointment alarmed the Irish Protestants, who, as usual, feared that the Catholics would get back their lands under a friendly executive, such as Tyrconnel—whose former exertions in regard to the Catholic claims were not forgotten—was well known to be. He was injudicious enough, at the outset, to dismiss many Protestant officers from the Irish military establishment and place Catholics in their positions. Although this was done by proportion, Protestant jealousy was aroused and the seeds of revolt were deeply planted.

In England, popular feeling against the king was at fever heat. His illegitimate Protestant nephew—putative son of Charles II—the Duke of Monmouth, who had been exiled, returned to England and organized a rebellion against him. This ill-starred movement culminated at Sedgemoor, in Somersetshire, in the summer of 1685.

A battle was fought there between the unorganized English peasants, under "King Monmouth," as they called him, and the royal army, under the Earl of Feversham. The rebels fought with commendable courage, but were badly commanded and suffered an overwhelming defeat. Monmouth escaped from the field, but was captured soon afterward, tried, found guilty, and beheaded on Tower Hill, of bloody memory, July 15, 1685. He had appealed in vain to James for mercy, and appealed in a manner so craven and undignified that he aroused the disgust of his stern uncle. But the blood of the vanquished did not cease to flow when Monmouth died. The "Bloody Assizes," conducted by Jeffreys, the "great crimson toad," as Dickens describes him, and four assistant judges, spread death and terror throughout the English districts recently in revolt. This period of English history bore a striking resemblance to the 1798 period in Ireland, when other "great crimson toads" hanged the hapless peasantry, and some of higher rank, by the hundred and thousand. All this butchery made James unpopular with a vast majority of the English people, but, as he had no male heir, the nation hesitated to rise against him, especially as Monmouth himself had been the aggressor. But James, while Duke of York, had married a young wife, the Princess Mary, sister of the Duke of Modena, who bore him a son—afterward called by the Hanoverian faction the Pretender—in June, 1688. This altered the whole aspect of affairs and a revolution became imminent immediately. Mary of Modena, although an intelligent and amiable woman, was of a haughty and somewhat punctilious disposition at times. This made her almost as unpopular with the English people as was her husband. Sir

Walter Scott relates that, while Duchess of York, she accompanied her husband to Scotland, whither he went at the behest of his brother, King Charles. James got along very well with the Scotch, particularly the Highlanders, who adored him, and whose loyalty to his family remained unshaken until after Culloden. He invited an old Continental veteran, Sir Thomas Dalzell, to dine with him. The duchess had the bad taste to object to the company of a commoner. "Make yourself easy on that head, madam," remarked Sir Thomas; "I have sat at a table where your father might have stood behind my chair!" He alluded to a dinner given him and others by the Emperor of Austria, who was the suzerain of the Duke of Modena. The latter, if called upon by the emperor, would have had to act in the capacity of an honorary waiter. All students of history are, doubtless, familiar with the romantic chivalry displayed by Edward the Black Prince, when he waited upon his captive, King John of France, whom he had vanquished at Poitiers. Mary of Modena was, we may be sure, not formed by nature to make friends for her husband, as the brave Margaret of Anjou did for the physically and mentally degenerate Plantagenet, Henry VI. Had Mary been a Margaret, William of Orange might never have occupied the throne of "the Three Kingdoms." The climax of King James's political imprudences—they can not, in the light of modern ideas of religious equality, be called errors—was reached when he issued his famous declaration against test oaths and penal laws, and decreed that it should be read from the altars of the Protestant, as well as the Catholic, churches throughout England. Six Protestant prelates, headed by the Archbishop of Canterbury, made protest by petition and even visited the king in his bedchamber to dissuade him from his purpose. But he persisted, as was usual with him.

On the Sunday following the bishops' call, out of 10,000 English clergymen only 200 complied with the royal decree. Of course we, Americans, who have equal laws for all creeds and classes, can not consistently condemn King James for advocating what we ourselves practice, but we can afford to lament the fatuity which led him to dare Protestant resentment by seeking to make Protestant pulpits the mediums of his radical policy. It was playing with fire. Had he stopped short at this point, James might have still held his crown, but, with incurable obstinacy, he insisted on prosecuting the recalcitrant bishops before the Court of King's Bench, and they were finally committed by the Privy Council to the Tower of London. All England was now ablaze with fierce resentment. At the Tower the right reverend prisoners were treated more like royal personages than captives. The officers and soldiers of the army—excepting the Irish regiments raised by Tyrconnel for James, and sent to do garrison duty in England—openly drank to their speedy release. When they came to trial in the King's Bench, the jury, after being out on the case all night, found the six prelates not guilty on the charge of censuring the king's government and defying the king's mandate, and they were immediately released amid popular acclamation.

The "loyal" Protestant majority had succeeded in placing the Catholic minority, their own fellow-countrymen, in a position of political nonentity, simply because they worshiped God according to their belief. Who could,

then, have imagined that the England which refused
equality in the holding of office to Catholic subjects would,
about two hundred years later, have a Catholic for Lord
Chief Justice and an Irish Catholic (Lord Russell of Kill-
owen) at that? Five generations have done much toward
a change of sentiment in England. But King James, we
are told, on hearing the shouts of the people when the
acquittal was announced, asked of Lord Feversham, who
happened to be with him: "What do they shout for?"
And Feversham replied, carelessly: "Oh, nothing—only
the acquittal of the bishops!" "And you call that nothing?" cried the king. "So much the worse for them,"
meaning the people. These latter were excited by the
Protestant lords and gentry, who much feared a Catholic
succession, now that the king had an heir-male to the
throne. Both of his daughters—Mary, married to William, Prince of Orange, the king's nephew, and Anne,
who became the wife of the Prince of Denmark—were
Protestants, their mother having brought them up in
that belief. William, half a Stuart and half a Dutchman,
brave, resolute, and wise withal, seemed to the English
malcontents to be the "heaven-appointed" man to supplant
his own uncle and father-in-law. William was nothing
loth, and Mary, who was to share the throne with him,
made no objection to this most unfilial proceeding.
Neither did Anne, who, like the unnatural creature she
was, fled from her father's palace, guided and guarded
by the Protestant Bishop of London, as soon as she heard
of William's almost unobstructed march on the capital.
That personage had landed at Torbay, in Devonshire, on
November 5—the anniversary of the Gunpowder Plot
of the days of James I—convoyed by an immense fleet,

which carried to the shores of England a picked veteran army of 15,000 men. This army was commanded, under William, by the Marshal Duke of Schomberg, Count Solmes, General De Ginkel, and other officers of European renown. The principal plotters who invited William to seize the crown of England were the Earls of Danby, Shrewsbury, Devonshire, the Bishop of London, Lord Lumley, Admiral Russell, and Colonel Sidney. Just a little while before the coming of William, James took the alarm and attempted to make concessions to the Protestants. He also decreed the strengthening of the army, and the enlistment of Irish Catholics and Scotch Highlanders, most of whom had retained the old faith, was encouraged.

At the news of William's arrival in Exeter, whither he had marched from Torbay, the English aristocracy became wildly excited and hastened to join his standard. The faculty of the University of Oxford sent him word that, if he needed money to carry out his enterprise, the plate of that institution would be melted down to furnish him with a revenue. An agreement of the nobility and gentry was drawn up and signed, and in it they promised to stand by William of Orange and each other, "in defence of the laws and liberties of the three kingdoms and the Protestant religion." Thus, it will be noticed, Protestant interests was the cry of the majority in England, opposed to James, who, as we have said, aimed at equality of all creeds before the law, while in Ireland, where the old faith "prevailed mightily," Catholic interests, or civil and religious liberty, became, also, the war-cry of the majority. In England the Catholic minority remained mostly supine during this period and until long afterward. In Scotland the Catholics and many Episcopalians rallied for James under the leadership of the implacable and brilliant Claverhouse, afterward created Viscount Dundee. They took the field for "James VII of Scotland," as they called the exiled king, at the first tap of the war drum. The Catholic majority in Ireland naturally recognized in the unfortunate monarch a friend who offered them religious and political liberty, and so they resolved to place their "lives, fortunes, and sacred honor" at his disposal.

The Irish Catholics can not be justly blamed for their devotion to the cause of James, who, whatever his motives, was the first King of England who ever attempted to do them even ordinary justice. Tyrconnel, like Strafford in a preceding reign, although with a very different intention, began the organization of a formidable Irish army, which was designed to be composed of twenty regiments of horse, fifty of foot, and artillery in the usual proportion. There were men for the mere asking, but arms, ammunition, and equipments were sadly lacking. The weakest arm of the military branch of the public service was the artillery, and this continued to be the fact throughout all of the subsequent war. As William drew nearer to London, the bulk of the native English army, following the example of the highest officers—including Colonel John Churchill, afterward the great Duke of Marlborough—went over to him. This determined James to abandon his capital, yet his friends induced him to return for a period. But the still nearer approach of "the Deliverer," as the English called William of Orange, again induced him to fly from London. He had previously provided for the safety of the queen and the infant heir to the now forfeited crown, who had taken refuge in France. The date of his final departure from Whitehall Palace was December 11. After not a few perilous adventures, he reached the court of his cousin, Louis XIV, at Versailles, on Christmas Day, 1688. He was most honorably and hospitably received, and Louis placed at his disposal the royal palace of St. Germain, in the neighborhood of Paris. When James heard of the desertion of his youngest daughter, Anne, to his enemies, the wretched parent, who has been called "the modern Lear," exclaimed in the anguish of his soul: "God help me! My very children have deserted me!"

CHAPTER XII

Irish Soldiers Ill-Treated in England—Policy of Tyrconnel—King James Chosen by the Irish Nation

SUCH Irish soldiers as had remained in England after the flight of James were mobbed, insulted, and even murdered by the unthinking multitude, so easily excited to deeds of cruelty. These men had done the English people no wrong—they had shed no English blood, and they even wore the English uniform. Many fell in savage combats with the furious mobs, but the majority fought their way to the seaports, where they, by some means, obtained shipment to Ireland, carrying with them many a bitter memory of England and her people. Many of these persecuted troops were well-trained cavalry, who afterward manifested splendid prowess at the Boyne and in other engagements. Their colonels were all members of the ancient Irish nobility, Celtic or Norman, and they were quite incapable of the crimes the credulous English mobs were taught to believe they were ready to commit at the earliest opportunity. Although the English people, in their normal condition, are a steady and courageous race, they are, when unduly excited, capable of entertaining sentiments and performing acts discreditable to them as a nation. A people so ready to resent any imposition, real or fancied, on themselves, should be a little less quick to punish others for following their example. It is not too much to say that the English, as a majority, have been made the victims of more religious and political hoaxes—imposed upon them by evil-minded knaves—than any other civilized nation. It was of the English, rather than ourselves, the great American showman, Barnum, should have said: "These people love to be humbugged!"

From the French court, which entirely sympathized with him, James entered into correspondence with his faithful subject and friend, Tyrconnel, in Ireland. The viceroy sent him comforting intelligence, for all the Catholics of fighting age were willing to bear arms in his defence. James sent Tyrconnel about 10,000 good muskets, with the requisite ammunition, to be used by the new levies. These were obtained from the bounty of the King of France. As Tyrconnel was convinced that Ireland, of herself, could hardly make headway against William of Orange, backed as he was by most of Great Britain and half of Europe, he conceived the idea of placing her, temporarily at least, under a French protectorate, in the shape of an alliance defensive and offensive, if necessary. He had the tact to keep King James in ignorance of this agreement, because he did not wish him to jeopardize his chance of regaining the British crown, which a consenting to the French protectorate would have utterly forfeited. Tyrconnel's policy, under the circumstances in which Ireland was placed, may have been a wise one, although, in general, any dependency of one country upon another is fatal to the liberty of the dependent nation. Ireland, contrary to general belief, is large enough to stand alone, if she had control of her own resources. To illustrate briefly, she is within a few thousand square miles of being as large as Portugal, and is much more fertile; while she is almost a third greater in area than Holland and Belgium combined. Her extensive coast line, numerous safe harbors, and exceeding productiveness amply compensate for the comparative smallness of her area.

In February, 1689, the national conventions of England and Scotland, by vast majorities, declared that King James had abdicated and offered the crown to William and Mary, who, as might have been expected, accepted it with thanks. Ireland had nothing to say in the matter, except by the voices of a few malcontents who had fled to Britain. Nevertheless, the new sovereigns finally assumed the rather illogical title of "William and Mary, 'by the grace of God,' King and Queen of England, Scotland, France, and Ireland." In France they held not a foot of ground; and in Ireland four-fifths of the people acknowledged King James. James Graham, of Claverhouse (Viscount Dundee), expressed his dissent from the majority in the convention of Scotland. Sir Walter Scott has immortalized the event in the stirring lyric which begins thus:

"To the Lords of Convention 'twas Claverhouse spoke,
  'Ere the king's crown shall fall, there are crowns to be broke,
  So let each cavalier, who loves honor and me,
  Come follow the bonnet of Bonnie Dundee!"

James had some strong partisans in England also—mostly among the Roman Catholic and Episcopalian High Church elements, but they were powerless to stem the overwhelming tide of public opinion against him. Ireland was with him vehemently, except the small Protestant minority, chiefly resident in Ulster, which was enthusiastic for William and Mary. Representatives of this active element had closed the gates of Derry in the face of the Earl of Antrim, when he demanded the town's surrender, in the name of the deposed king, in December, 1688. This incident proved that the Irish Protestants, with the usual rule-proving exceptions, meant "war to the knife" against the Catholic Stuart dynasty. Thus civil war, intensified by foreign intervention, became inevitable.

The towns of Inniskillen, Sligo, Coleraine, and the fort of Culmore, on the Foyle, either followed the example of Derry, or were seized without ceremony by the partisans of William and Mary in Ulster and Connaught. These partisans, headed by Lord Blaney, Sir Arthur Rawdon, and other Anglo-Irishmen, invited William to come into the country, "for the maintenance of the Protestant religion and the dependency of Ireland upon England." Thus, again, was the Protestant religion made the pretext of provincializing Ireland, and because of this identification of it with British supremacy the new creed has remained undeniably unpopular with the masses of the Irish people. The latter are very ardent Catholics, as their long and bloody wars in defence of their faith have amply proven, but while this statement is undeniable, it can not be denied either that had the so-called Reformation not been identified with

English political supremacy, it might have made much greater inroads among the Irish population than it has succeeded in doing. Ireland was treated not a whit better under the Catholic rulers of England, from 1169 to the period of Mary I—Henry VIII was a schismatic rather than a Protestant—than under her Protestant rulers, until James II appeared upon the scene, and his clemency toward the Irish was based upon religious rather than national grounds. Even in our own day, the English Catholics are among the strongest opponents of Irish legislative independence, and in the category of such opponents may be classed the late Cardinal Vaughan and the present Duke of Norfolk.

King James, at the call of the Irish majority, left his French retreat, and sailed from Brest with a fleet provided by King Louis, which saw him in safety to memorable Kinsale, where he landed on March 12, old style, 1689. He was accompanied by about 1,200 veteran troops, French and Irish, with a sprinkling of royalists, Scotch and English, and several officers of high rank, including Lieutenant-General De Rosen, Lieutenant-General Maumont, Major-General De Lery, Major-General Pusignan, Colonel Patrick Sarsfield, afterward the renowned Earl of Lucan, and the king's two natural sons, the Duke of Berwick and Grand Prior Fitzjames. There came with him also fifteen Catholic chaplains, most of whom could speak the Gaelic tongue, and these gentlemen were very useful to him on a mission such as he had undertaken. The progress of the ill-fated monarch through Ireland, from Kinsale to Dublin was, in every sense, a royal one. The Irish masses, ever grateful to any one who makes sacrifices, or who even appears to

make them, in their behalf, turned out in all their
strength. A brilliant cavalcade, headed by the dashing
Duke of Tyrconnel, escorted the king from town to
town. His collateral descent from King Edward Bruce,
freely chosen by Ireland early in the fourteenth century,
was remembered. James was, therefore, really welcomed as King of Ireland. The Irish cared nothing for
his British title. If the choice of the majority of a
nation makes regal title binding, then James II was as
truly elected King of Ireland, in 1689, as Edward Bruce
was in 1315. And we make this statement thus plainly,
because it will enable non-Irish and non-Catholic readers
to understand why Catholic Ireland fought so fiercely
and devotedly for an English ruler who had lost his
crown in the assertion of Catholic rights and privileges.
There was still another cause for this devotion of the
majority of the Irish people to King James. He had
consented to the summoning of a national Irish parliament, in which Protestants as well as Catholics were to
be represented in due proportion, and this decision on
his part made many of the Episcopalian Irish either neu-
tral in the civil conflict or active on his side. The number of such persons as were comprised in the latter class
was comparatively insignificant—just enough to mitigate
the curse of absolute sectarianism in the contest. The
Dissenting or non-conforming Irish were, almost to a
unit, hostile to the Jacobite cause.

BOOK IV

CHRONICLING IMPORTANT EVENTS IN IRELAND FROM
THE ARRIVAL OF JAMES II IN THAT COUNTRY UNTIL
THE DEPARTURE OF THE DUKE OF BERWICK TO
FRANCE AFTER THE FIRST SIEGE OF LIMERICK, IN 1690

CHAPTER I

King James in Ireland—Enthusiastic Reception of Him by the Irish
People—Military Operations

NOTHING could exceed the enthusiasm with which
the Irish people welcomed King James. In the
cities and towns, flowers were strewn in his path, corporation officials turned out in their robes of state, and
speeches of welcome were delivered in English or read
in Latin. The entry into Dublin was a magnificent spectacle. The whole city was in gala dress, and the different trades paraded before him. Harpers played at the
triumphal arches under which he passed. Beautiful young
girls, costumed in pure white, and coroneted with wreaths,
danced the ancient Irish national dance, known as the
Rinka, in the progress of which flowers were profusely
scattered by the fair performers. The religious orders
were out in force, a great cross being borne at their
head. The viceroy, lord mayor, and members of the
corporation, on horseback or in carriages, made up an
imposing part of the procession. When he reached the
Castle, the sword of state was presented to him by the
Lord Lieutenant, and the Recorder handed him, according to an old custom, the keys of the city. "Te Deum"
was sung in the Chapel Royal, one of the architectural
creations of the Duke of Tyrconnel. From the flagstaff
on the tower of the Castle itself, floated an Irish national flag, with a golden harp upon its folds; and on
this broad ensign were inscribed the inspiring and sadly

prophetic words, "Now or Never! Now and Forever!"
Wherever the king appeared in public, he was greeted
with enthusiastic shouts, in Gaelic, of "Righ Seamus!—
Righ Seamus, Go Bragh"! ("King James—King James,
Forever!")

The military situation of King James's adherents in
Ireland could not be called encouraging when he took up
his residence in Dublin. As usual, arms and ammunition were scarce. Some 30,000 men had volunteered to
fight for Ireland, and there were not more than 20,000
stand of arms, all told, to place in their hands. And
of this small supply, fully three-fourths were antiquated
and worthless. While there were, nominally, fifty regiments of infantry enrolled, the only serviceable regiments
of horse were those of Galmoy, Tyrconnel, and Russell.
There was one regiment of dragoons, and of cannon
only eight field pieces had been collected. The two best-
equipped bodies of Irish troops were the command of
General Richard Hamilton, in Ulster—about 3,000 men;
and that of General Justin McCarthy, Lord Mountcashel,
in Munster—slightly more numerous. Derry and Inniskillen held out for William of Orange, and notwithstanding some successes of General Hamilton in the
North, there seemed no immediate prospect of reducing
them. The stubborn attitude of Inniskillen delayed the
junction of Mountcashel's and Hamilton's forces, which
had been ordered by the Duke of Tyrconnel, commander-
in-chief of the Irish army, with General De Rosen as
his second in command. The smaller places occupied
by the Williamite forces were abandoned as being untenable, and the little garrisons fell back on Londonderry, which had now become the main objective of the

Jacobite army. The military governor, Lundy, was suspected of being, at heart, a Stuart sympathizer, but he was soon virtually superseded, first by Governor Baker and afterward by the celebrated Rev. George Walker, rector of the living of Donoughmore, to whom history awards the glory of the long, desperate, brilliant, and successful defence of Derry against the armies of King James. It is a pity that the ability and bravery displayed by Dr. Walker have been made causes of political and religious irritation in the north of Ireland for upward of two centuries. Lundy, when his authority was defied, escaped from the city at night, in the disguise of a laborer, and cut no further figure in Irish history. Before his flight, King James's flatterers in Dublin had persuaded him to advance against Derry in person and demand its surrender. Tyrconnel opposed the idea in vain. He well knew that Lundy was in correspondence with Hamilton and De Rosen for the surrender of the city. It is quite probable that Derry would have finally surrendered, on honorable terms, had James taken Tyrconnel's advice; but, with his usual fatuity, the obstinate king took the advice of the shallow courtiers, and did actually present himself before the walls of Derry and demand its unconditional surrender! The reply was a cannon shot, which killed an officer at James's side. The king retired with precipitation, and the citizens sent after him the "Prentice Boys'" shout of "No surrender!" Mortified by his rather ignominious failure, James retired to Dublin, and summoned Parliament to meet on the lines already indicated.

CHAPTER II

Jacobites Foiled at Londonderry—Mountcashel Defeated at Newtown Butler—King James's Irish Parliament

THE siege of Derry was continued under the super-
vision of Maumont and Hamilton, who had quite a
large force at their disposal.   It is regrettable to have to
state that the Protestant population of Ulster was further
inflamed against the Stuart cause by the needless excesses
of Galmoy and the barbaric severity of De Rosen, who
placed a crowd of helpless women and children between
two fires under the ramparts of Derry, in the hope of
compelling the garrison to surrender.   The brilliant victories obtained over the Williamites at Coleraine and
Cladysford, by General Hamilton, in the earlier part of
the campaign, were more than offset by the overwhelming defeat inflicted by General Wolseley, at Newtown
Butler, on the Jacobite army under Mountcashel.   It was
Irish against Irish, but the Inniskilleners, who made up
the bulk of Wolseley's force, were seasoned soldiers, well
armed and well directed.   Mountcashel's men were
chiefly green levies, and the battle was really lost through
their faulty manœuvring.   One brigade mistook an order to change front, so as to form a new line against a
flank attack of the enemy, for an order to retreat, and so
spread a panic that proved fatal.   Mountcashel himself
was dangerously wounded and made prisoner.   He lost
2,000 men in killed and wounded, and 400 fugitives, completely surrounded, surrendered at some distance from
the field.   This battle was fought on July 31, 1689, and,

on the same day, Derry was relieved by an English fleet, which succeeded in breaking the boom that had been constructed by the Jacobite engineers across the mouth of the harbor.

It will be remembered that the gates of the city were closed against Lord Antrim on December 7, 1688. Hamilton's bombardment of the place began on the 17th of April, 1689, and lasted for three months. There was a total blockade for three weeks, and provisions became so scarce that the defenders actually devoured dogs, cats, rats, mice—anything, however revolting, that might satisfy the cravings of absolute hunger. The besiegers also suffered from bad weather and the shots from the hostile batteries. A rough computation places the total loss of the defenders at about 4,000 men, and that of the assailants at 6,000—the latter loss chiefly by disease. The relief of Derry was a mortal blow to the cause of King James, and soon afterward he lost every important post in Ulster, except Carrickfergus and Charlemont. Yet, as an Irish writer has well remarked, Ulster was bestowed by the king's grandfather "upon the ancestors of those who now unanimously rejected and resisted him." His cause also received a fatal stroke in Scotland by the death of the brave Dundee, who fell, vainly victorious, over the Williamite general, Mackay, at the battle of Killecrankie, fought July 26, 1689. Duke Schomberg arrived in Belfast Lough with a large fleet and army on August 13th. Count Solmes was his second in command. He laid siege to Carrickfergus, which capitulated on fair terms after eight days' bombardment. Charlemont, defended by the brave and eccentric Colonel Teague O'Reagan, held out till the following May,

when it surrendered with the honors of war. It is said
that King William, on his arrival in Ireland, knighted
O'Reagan in recognition of the brilliancy of his defence.
The young Duke of Berwick made a gallant stand in the
neighborhood, but was finally compelled to yield ground
to the superior forces of Schomberg. Critics of the latter's strategy hold that he committed a grave military
error in failing to march on the Irish capital, which was
not in a good posture of defence, immediately after landing in Ulster. Had he done so, King James must have
had to evacuate Dublin and fall back on the defensive
line of the Shannon, as Tyrconnel and Sarsfield did at a
later period. Then Schomberg, it is claimed, would not
have lost more than half of his army, by dysentery, at his
marshy camp near Dundalk, where King James, in the
autumn, bearded and defied him to risk battle with the
stronger and healthier Jacobite forces. There would
have been no occasion for the Battle of the Boyne, the
memory of which has divided and distracted Irishmen
for more than two centuries, had the challenge been
accepted.

The Parliament summoned by James met in the Inn's
Court, Dublin, in the summer of 1689. It was composed
of 46 peers and 228 commoners. Of the former body,
several were High Church Protestants, but, in the Lower
House, there were comparatively few members of the
"reformed religion." This, however, was not the fault
of the king or his advisers, as they were sincere in their
desire to have a full Protestant representation in that
Parliament. But, perhaps naturally, the Protestants were
suspicious of the king's good intentions, and so the majority held aloof from the Parliamentary proceedings.

The most important acts passed by that Parliament were one establishing liberty of conscience, which provided, among other things, that Catholics should not be compelled to pay tithes to Protestant clergymen, and *vice versa;* another act established the judicial independence of Ireland, by abolishing writs of error and appeal to England. The Act of Settlement was repealed, under protest by the Protestant peers, who did not, for obvious reasons, wish the question of land titles obtained by fraud and force opened up. An act of attainder, directed against persons in arms against their sovereign in Ireland, was added to the list of measures. Heedless of the advice of his wisest friends, James vetoed the bill for the repeal of the infamous Poynings' Law, which made the Irish Parliament dependent upon that of England; and also declined to approve a measure establishing Inns of Court for the education of Irish law students. In the first-mentioned case, James acted from a belief that his own prerogative of vetoing Irish measures in council was attacked, but his hostility to the measure for legal education has never been satisfactorily explained. Taken as a whole, however, King James's Irish Parliament was a legislative success; and it enabled the Protestant patriot and orator, Henry Grattan, when advocating Catholic claims in the Irish Parliament a hundred years afterward, to say: "Although Papists, the Irish Catholics were not slaves. They wrung a Constitution from King James before they accompanied him to the field."

CHAPTER III

King James's Imprudent Acts—Witty Retort of a Protestant Peer
—Architectural Features of Dublin

OUR last chapter showed that Ireland, although her population was overwhelmingly Catholic, began her struggle for civil liberty by a non-sectarian enactment, which left the exercise of religion free. Yet, strange to say, this wise and liberal policy did not win her the sympathy of Europe, Protestant or Catholic, outside of France, whose king had personal reasons for his friendliness. Louis XIV was both hated and feared by the sovereigns of continental, as well as insular, Europe. A combination, called the League of Augsburg, was formed against him, and of this League the Emperor of Germany was the head and William of Orange an active member. Spain, Savoy, and other Catholic states were as zealous against Louis as the Protestant states of Sweden and North Germany. Even the Pope was on the side of the French king's foes. In fact, when Duke Schomberg landed, the war had resolved itself into a conflict between the rest of Europe, except Muscovy and Turkey and their dependencies, and France and Ireland. It was a most unequal struggle, but most gallantly maintained, with varying fortune, on Irish soil chiefly, for two long and bloody years.

King James made enemies among his warmest supporters by increasing the subsidy voted him by Parliament to twice the original amount, payable monthly. He also debased the currency, by issuing "brass money," which led to the demoralization of trade, and Tyrconnel, after James's departure from Ireland, was compelled to withdraw the whole fraudulent issue in order to stop the popular clamor. Some Protestant writers, notably Dr. Cooke Taylor, have warmly commended the king's judicial appointments in Ireland, with few exceptions. In short, to sum up this portion of his career, James II acted in Ireland the part of despot benevolently inclined, who thought he was doing a wise thing in giving the people a paternal form of government. But the Irish people can not long endure one-man rule, unless convinced that the one man is much wiser than the whole mass of the nation, which is not often the case. It certainly was not in the case of King James. His establishment of a bank by proclamation and his decree of a bank restriction act annoyed and angered the commercial classes, whose prices for goods he also sought to regulate. But his crowning act of unwisdom was interference with the government of that time-honored educational institution, Trinity College, Dublin, on which, notwithstanding its statutes, he sought to force officers of his own choosing. He also wished to make fellowships and scholarships open to Catholics—a just principle, indeed, but a rash policy, considering that every act of the kind only multiplied his enemies among the Protestants of Ireland, who were already sufficiently hostile. Had King James proceeded slowly in his chosen course, he might have come down to posterity as a successful royal reformer. Unfortunately for his fame, posterity in general regards him as a conspicuous political as well as military failure.

Among King James's chosen intimates and advisers during his residence in Dublin, the most distinguished were the Duke of Tyrconnel, the Earl of Melfort, Secretary of State; Count D'Avaux, the French Ambassador; Lord Mountcashel, Colonel Sarsfield, afterward so famous; Most Rev. Dr. McGuire, Primate of Ireland, and Chief Justice Lord Nugent. He generally attended Mass every morning in the Chapel Royal, and, on Sundays, assisted at solemn High Mass. One Sunday, he was attended to the entrance of the chapel by a loyal Protestant lord, whose father had been a Catholic, as James's had been a Protestant. As he was taking his leave, the king remarked, rather dryly: "My lord, your father would have gone farther." "Very true, sire," responded the witty nobleman, "but your Majesty's father would not have gone so far!"

The Dublin of that time was not, in any sense, the attractive city it is to-day. Beyond the great cathedrals and the ancient Castle, there was little to attract the eye, except the beauty of the surroundings, which are still the admiration of all visitors. A century after the reign of King James, Dublin, from an architectural standpoint, became one of the most classical of European capitals; and the Houses of Parliament, the Four Courts, the Custom House, and other public buildings, became the pride of the populace. These monuments of Irish genius still exist, although shorn of their former glory; but they serve, at least, to attest what Ireland could accomplish under native rule. There is not a penny of English money in any of these magnificent structures. All the credit of their construction belongs to the Irish Parliaments of the eighteenth century.

CHAPTER IV

Composition of the Hostile Armies—King William Arrives in Ireland—Narrowly Escapes Death on Eve of Battle

DURING the spring and early summer of 1690, the war clouds began to mass themselves heavily in the northeastern portion of the island, where Duke Schomberg, his depleted army somewhat recruited, still held his ground at Dundalk, with small garrisons posted throughout Ulster. But it was soon known that William of Orange, in person, was to command in chief in this fateful campaign. Several engagements, with varying fortune, had occurred between the rival armies in different parts of the north country, where the Duke of Berwick waged a vigorous campaign against the Williamites. James, dissatisfied with the French Ambassador, D'Avaux, and Lieutenant-General De Rosen, demanded, and obtained, their recall by King Louis. By an arrangement between the two monarchs, Mountcashel's command of 6,000 men was exchanged for 6,000 French troops, under Lieutenant-General De Lauzun, who eventually proved to be even a greater marplot and blunderer than the odious De Rosen. Mountcashel's force formed the Old Irish Brigade, of immortal memory, in the French service, and almost immediately after its arrival in France was sent to operate under the famous Lieutenant-General St. Ruth in Savoy. It also served in several campaigns under the great Marshal Catinat, "Father Thoughtful," as he was fondly called by the French army. The exchange proved a bad bargain for Ireland, as will be seen in the course of this narration. James hoped much from the skill and daring of the French contingent, but was doomed to bitter disappointment. "His troops," says McGee, "were chiefly Celtic and Catholic. There were four regiments commanded by O'Neills, two by O'Briens, one each by McCarthy More, Maguire, O'More, O'Donnell, McMahon, and Magennis, chiefly recruited among their own clansmen. There were also the regiments of Sarsfield, Nugent, De Courcy, Fitzgerald, Grace, and Burke, chiefly Celts in the rank and file. On the other hand, Schomberg led into the field the famous Blue and White Dutch regiments; the Huguenot regiments of Schomberg (the Younger), La Millinier, Du Cambon, and La Caillemotte; the English regiments of Lords Devonshire, Delamere, Lovelace, Sir John Lanier, Colonels Langston, Villiers, and others; the Anglo-Irish regiments of Lords Meath, Roscommon, Kingston, and Drogheda, with the Ulstermen under Brigadier Wolseley and Colonels Gustavus Hamilton, Mitchellburn, Lloyd, White, St. John, and Tiffany."

The absence of a fleet, the entire navy having gone over to William, placed James at a great disadvantage, and explains why there were no sea fights of importance in British and Irish waters during this war. Isolated French squadrons could not be expected to make headway against the united navies of Britain and Holland. William, on the contrary, had the seas wide open to him, and, on June 14, 1690, he landed at Carrickfergus with reinforcements and supplies for his army in Ireland, and accompanied by the Prince of Hesse-Darmstadt, Prince George of Denmark, the Duke of Ormond, the Earls of Portland, Manchester, Oxford, and Scarborough; General Mackay, General Douglas, and many other warriors well known

to British and Continental fame. He established headquarters at Belfast and caused a muster of all his forces,
which showed him to be at the head of about 40,000 men,
mostly veterans, and made up of contingents from Scandinavia, Holland, Switzerland, Brandenburg, England,
Scotland, Ulster, together with the exiled Huguenot regiments of France and the Anglo-Irish battalions of the
Pale. Allowing for detachments, William had under him
an army of, at least, 36,000 effective men, officered by the
best military talent of the period.

James, according to all Irish and some British authorities, commanded a force of 17,000 Irish, of whom alone
the cavalry, numbering, probably, from five to six thousand men, were considered thoroughly trained. In addition, he had 6,000 well-appointed French infantry, under
De Lauzun, which brought his total up to some 23,000
men, with only twelve pieces of cannon. William, on the
other hand, possessed a powerful and well-appointed artillery. Once again, James was advised not to oppose his
comparatively weak and ill-disciplined army to an encounter with the veteran host of William, and again the
advantages of the defensive line of the Shannon were
pointed out to him. But he would not listen to the voice
of prudence, and marched northward to meet his rival, almost immediately after learning of his debarkation at
Carrickfergus. The Stuart army reached Dundalk about
June 22, when William was reported to be at Newry. His
scouts were soon seen on the neighboring heights, and the
Franco-Irish forces fell back on the river Boyne, and took
post on the southern bank, within a few miles of Drogheda. The Irish camp was pitched immediately below the
hill of Donore and near the small village of Oldbridge, in

the obtuse salient, pointing northwestward, formed by the second bend in the river in its course from Slane—about six miles from Oldbridge—to the sea. In the chart of the battle, published by the Rev. George Story, King William's chaplain, in 1693, three strong batteries are shown in front of the right of the Irish army, on the south bank of the Boyne, and one protecting its left opposite to the point where the Mattock rivulet falls into the main river. But no Irish account mentions these batteries. Some critics have thought it strange that the Williamites, instead of making a long and tedious movement by Slane, did not endeavor to attack both sides of the river salient at once, and thus place the Irish army between two fires. The water, apparently, was no deeper above than below the rivulet, but even were it deeper, William had with him a well-appointed bridge train, and the feeble battery, if any existed at all, would be insufficient to check the ardor of his chosen veterans. On the summit of Donore Hill, which slopes backward for more than a mile from the river, stood a little church, with a graveyard and some huts beside it. Even in 1690, it was an insignificant ruin, but it is noted in Anglo-Irish history as marking the headquarters of King James during the operations on the Boyne.

The right wing of the Irish army extended itself toward that smaller part of Drogheda which is situated on the south bank of the river, in the County Meath. The centre faced the fords in front of Oldbridge, where several small shoals, or islands, as marked in Story's map, rendered the passage of an attacking force comparatively easy of accomplishment. The left wing stretched in the direction of Slane, where there was a bridge, and, nearer to the Irish army, a ford practicable for cavalry. James was urged to strengthen this wing of his army, sure to be attacked, the day before the battle, but he could only be induced to send out some cavalry patrols to observe the ground. When the tide, which backs the water up from below Drogheda, is out, many points on the river in front of the Irish position are easily fordable, and there has been little or no change in the volume of the current during the last two centuries. Therefore, the Boyne presented no such formidable obstacle to a successful crossing as some imaginative historians have sought to make out. Neither did nature, in other respects, particularly favor the Irish in the choice of their ground. Their army occupied a fairly good defensive position, if its advantages had been properly utilized. King James interfered with the plans of his generals, as it was his habit to interfere in every department of his government, not at all to the advantage of the public service. An able general, such as William or Schomberg was, might have made the Irish ground secure; that is, with sufficient cannon to answer the formidable park brought into action by the enemy. The Irish army was in position on June 29, and on the following day, King William, accompanied by his staff and escort, appeared on the opposite heights. His main army was concealed behind the hills in the depression now known as King William's Glen. With his customary daring activity, the astute Hollander immediately proceeded to reconnoitre the Jacobite position, of which he obtained a good view, though some of the regiments were screened by the irregularities of the ground. Although within easy range of the Irish lines, he was not molested for some time. Having concluded his observations, William, with his officers, dismounted. Lunch was spread on the grass by the attendants, and the party proceeded to regale themselves. They were allowed to finish in peace, but when they remounted and turned toward their camp, the report of a field-piece came from the Irish side. A round shot ricochetted and killed a member of the escort. A second ball caught the king upon the shoulder, tore his coat and broke the skin beneath it. He fell forward on his horse, but immediately recovered himself, and the entire party rode rapidly out of range. The Irish officers, who had observed the confusion caused by the second shot, imagined that William had been killed. The news was circulated in the camp, speedily traveled to Dublin, and soon found its way to Great Britain and the Continent. But William was not dead. After the surgeons had dressed his wound, he insisted on again mounting his horse, and, like Napoleon when he was wounded in front of Ratisbon, in 1809, showed himself to the army, whose shouts of joy speedily informed the Irish troops that their able enemy was still in the saddle. A brisk cannonade, which did but little damage, was then exchanged between the two armies. It was the noisy prelude of a much more eventful drama. On the morrow was to be decided the fate not alone of the ancient Stuart dynasty, but also of Ireland, with all Europe for witnesses. Night put an end to the artillery duel, and the hostile hosts, except the sentinels, disposed themselves to sleep. History fails to record the watchward of King James's army, but Chaplain Story is authority for the statement that the word in William's camp was "Westminster." The soldiers on both sides, to use the military phrase, "slept upon their arms."

CHAPTER V

Battle of the Boyne—Death of Marshal Schomberg—Valor of Irish
Cavalry—Inexcusable Flight of King James

TUESDAY morning, July 1, old style, dawned beautifully on the river Boyne. Both of the royal hosts were drawn out in all their bravery, and the early sun glittered on their burnished arms. We have no good account of their uniforms, but, judging by prints of the period, the British, in general, wore scarlet and the Continental allies blue. Some of the French regiments allied to the Irish army wore white and others blue coats, which were the favorite colors of the Bourbon kings. The Irish army must surely have worn scarlet—the livery of the House of Stuart—because, we are informed by George Story and other historians, they bore white badges in their hats, to distinguish themselves from the Williamites, who wore green boughs in theirs. The white cockade, or rosette, was the emblem of the Dukes of York—a title borne by James, as will be remembered, before his accession. The irony of fate, surely, was made manifest by the circumstance of William's soldiers wearing Ireland's national color, as now generally recognized, on the occasion of her most fateful, although not bloodiest, defeat.

At 6 o'clock A.M., William took the initiative by ordering above 10,000 horse and foot, under General Douglas, Schomberg, Jr., and Lords Portland and Overkirk, to march along the river bank toward Slane, cross at, or near, that point, and so turn the left flank of the Irish

army. This manœuvre was plainly seen and understood
by James and his lieutenants. Sir Neal O'Neill, at the
head of his dragoons, was detached to check the movement. The brave leader was in time to charge the enemy's cavalry, which had crossed nearer to Oldbridge
than was originally designed, as they had found a practicable ford. The main body crossed higher up, at
Slane. O'Neill, according to all accounts of the engagement on this flank of the Jacobite army, must have made
a most gallant fight, because it was well on toward 9
o'clock before the enemy was able to secure a footing
on the Irish bank of the Boyne, and then only after the
brave O'Neill had been mortally wounded, and his surviving soldiers discouraged by his fall. Notwithstanding, the Irish dragoons drew off the field in excellent
order, bearing their dying general along with them.
With his latest breath, O'Neill sent word to King James
of how matters stood on his left wing, to which Douglas's
whole imposing force had now formed itself perpen-
dicularly, that is, at right angles, threatening not alone
the left of the Irish line of battle, but also the rear, or
line of retreat, on the pass of Duleek, which was the
gateway to Dublin. James, observing this, became demoralized. Instead of using the French veterans at
Oldbridge ford, where he must have seen the main attack
was to be delivered, he placed in the hedges, and other
defences which covered it, untried Irish levies, badly
weaponed, brave enough, it is true, but at absolute disadvantage when placed in opposition to the splendid armament and perfect discipline of William's veterans, many
of whom had been in a score of pitched battles. Lauzun
and his French were sent toward the Irish left, accom-

panied by Sarsfield, with a weak squadron of horse. But Douglas had formed his troops in such strong array that Lauzun, in spite of the direct orders of King James, declined to attack him, or receive his attack. Instead, he manœuvred so as to place a morass between his troops and the enemy, and then began falling back on the pass of Duleek, fearing to be outflanked and cut off by young Schomberg's powerful cavalry. Sarsfield, according to his custom, charged the hostile horse boldly, but his men were too few, and he was reluctantly compelled to follow the retrograde movement of the French. In this operation he lost one cannon, which got stuck in the mud of a bog that intervened between the river and Donore. At the latter point he rejoined the king. James seemed to think only of his line of retreat. Had he thought of his line of advance, everything might still have been rectified. His army remained unshaken, except by his own wretched fears. The dread of being made a prisoner was his bane. He had sent most of the baggage and half the cannon toward Dublin at the first news of the reverse at Slane—a remarkable way by which to raise the spirits of an army already sadly conscious of the incompetency of its royal commander, and its own inferiority to the Williamite host in everything but ardent zeal and knightly courage.

William, on learning of the success of his right wing, immediately ordered Marshal Schomberg, at the head of the formidable Dutch guards, two regiments of Huguenots, two of Inniskilleners, Sir John Hammer's regiment, and several others on that front, including the Danes, to ford the Boyne in hot haste. They plunged in bravely, opposite to Oldbridge, and so dense were

their columns, according to Chaplain Story, that the
water rose perceptibly.   Still it could not have risen
much above the knees of the shortest soldier, for the
historian, Haverty—a scrupulous writer—says, in his
admirable work, that the water did not reach to the
drums of the bands that accompanied the attack. The
unseasoned Irish dragoons and infantry, armed with
old fusils and half-pikes, received the enemy with a hasty
and ill-directed fire, which did little damage. William's
troops replied with overpowering volleys, and his batteries threw balls into the defences. It would seem that
little was done at this point to rally the defenders, for
they soon broke and abandoned the hedges, but formed
again in the lanes of Oldbridge and the fields in its vicinity.   The shout of triumph from Schomberg's men was
answered by a roar of anger that seemed to come from
the battle-clouds above the river.   There was a sound
as of many waters, a terrific crashing of hoofs, a flashing
of sabres, dying groans—Richard Hamilton, at the head
of the superb Irish cavalry, was among the Williamite
regiments, dealing death-strokes right and left. Even
the Dutch Blues reeled before the shock—the Danes and
Huguenots were broken and driven back across the
stream. Old Duke Schomberg, in trying to restore order,
was killed near the Irish side of the river, and there, too,
fell Caillemotte, the Huguenot hero, and Bishop Walker,
the defender of Derry. It was a splendid charge, and,
had it been sustained by the whole Irish army, might
have saved the day. But King James's eyes were not
turned toward Oldbridge ford, but to the pass of Duleek.
Fresh bodies of hostile infantry continued to cross the
stream, and were charged and driven back several times

by the Irish horse. This part of the battle began about 10.15 o'clock and continued until nearly noon.

King William now took a hand in the fight, and crossed with most of his cavalry nearer to Drogheda. It is said that the tide had risen so high, he was obliged to swim his horse, which, also, got "bogged" on the Irish bank, and was extricated with difficulty. When the animal was freed, William remounted, and, although his shoulder was still stiff and sore from contact with the cannon-ball on the previous day, he drew his sword and placed himself at the head of such of his horse as had crossed with him. He also rallied some foot-soldiers who had been scattered by Hamilton's furious charges. Nor were these yet over. Hardly had William placed his men in order, when Hamilton came down again, with a whirlwind rush, and Chaplain Story says, with great simplicity: "Our horse were forced to give ground, although the king was with them!" William, on recovering his breath, observed the Inniskillen regiment of cavalry at a short distance, rode up in front of them and said, in his blunt fashion: "What will *you* do for me?" They answered with a cheer, and rode to meet the Irish cavalry, who were again coming on at a fierce gallop, urged by Hamilton. The shock was terrible, but again the presence and the leadership of the warlike William proved unavailing, and the Inniskilleners, sadly cut up, followed the routed Williamite ruck down the hill toward the river. Cool in the moment of danger, William of Orange retired slowly and managed to rally some foot and horse to his assistance. By this time more of his cavalry had crossed, under Ruvigny and Ginkel. The former captured some colors, according to Story, but Ginkel's force was routed and he, himself, did not conceal his vexation at their want of firmness. He kept in their rear, in order to prevent them from bolting at sight of the Irish horse.

King James was urged by all of those about him who had regard for his honor, including the brave General Sheldon and the ever gallant Sarsfield, to place himself at the head of his reserve of cavalry and charge full upon William as he ascended toward Donore. The unfortunate man, more of a moral than a physical coward, seemed unable to collect his faculties; and, instead of doing what became him, yielded to the advice of the timid, and, even while the battle raged hotly below him, turned his horse, and, accompanied by his disgusted officers and astonished troopers, rode toward the pass of Duleek, held by the French and some of the Irish, who repulsed every effort of General Douglas to force it. Hamilton's cavalry still continued to charge the Williamite advance, and thus enabled the Irish infantry to retire slowly on Donore, where the bold Duke of Berwick rallied them and presented an unbroken front to King William. Then, in turn, they retired toward Duleek. Hamilton made a final furious charge, in which his horse was killed and fell upon him. He was also wounded in the head and made prisoner. He was taken before William, who said: "Well, sir, is this business over with, or will your horse show more fight?" Hamilton responded: "Upon my honor, sir, I think they will." The king, who was incensed against the general for having sided with James and Tyrconnel against himself, looked askance at the gallant prisoner and muttered: "Your honor! Your honor!" And this was all that passed between them.

Chaplain Story, from whose book we have taken many

of our facts, was a most graphic and interesting writer, but a sad hater of the Irish, against whom he seems to have borne a grudge, perhaps because they killed his brother, an English officer, in action. He never said a good word for them if he could avoid doing so. Yet, in spite of this failing, the truth would escape him occasionally. Many English writers leave the impression that the Irish army was defeated at the Boyne within an hour or so after the engagement began. We have seen that the first movement was made about daylight, and that the battle near Slane opened about 8 o'clock. In front of Oldbridge the attack was made at 10:15, and continued hotly until nearly noon, when King William himself took command, crossed the river with his left wing and was bravely checked by Hamilton. Duleek is not more than three miles from the fords of Oldbridge. Therefore, the Irish must have fought very obstinately when Chaplain Story makes the following admission on page 23 of his "Continuation of the Wars of Ireland": "Our army then pressed hard upon them, but meeting with a great many difficulties in the ground, and being obliged to pursue in order, our horse had only the opportunity of cutting down some of their foot, and most of the rest got over the pass at Duleek; then night coming on* prevented us from making so entire a victory of it as could have been wished for." Thus, on the testimony of this Williamite partisan and eye-witness, the battle of the Boyne, counting from its inception to its close, lasted about fifteen hours. Evidently the overpowered Irish army did not retreat very fast.

---

* In Ireland, at that season, there is a strong twilight until nearly 9 o'clock.—*Author.*

We have already mentioned the principal men who fell on the Williamite side. On the Jacobite side there fell Lords Dungan and Carlingford, Sir Neal O'Neill and some other officers of note, together with some 1,200 rank and file killed or wounded. Few prisoners were taken. Mr. Story, as usual, underestimates William's loss, when he places it at "nigh four hundred." More candid English estimates place it at nearer a thousand, and this was, probably, the true figure. The Chaplain, in dwelling on the casualties, says plaintively: "The loss of Duke Schomberg, who was killed soon after the first of our forces passed the river near Oldbridge, was much more considerable than all that fell that day on both sides."

Drogheda, occupied by an Irish garrison of 1,500 men, surrendered, on summons, the day after the battle. Had their commander made a spirited sortie on William's left wing, as it was crossing the river, good might have resulted for the cause of James. It would seem that, like himself, many of his officers lacked the daring enterprise that can alone win the smiles of Bellona.

King James, shamefully for himself, deserted the battlefield, or, rather, the outer edge of it, before the fight at the fords was over. An Irish Protestant poet, the late Dr. W. R. Wilde, of Dublin, says of the incident:

> "But where is James? What! urged to fly,
> Ere quailed his brave defenders!
> Their dead in Oldbridge crowded lie,
> But not a sword surrenders!"

He reached Dublin at 9 o'clock that evening, while still the Irish army exchanged shots with William's troops across the Nannywater at the pass of Duleek! Tradition says that, meeting Lady Tyrconnel at the Castle, he exclaimed: "Your countrymen run well, madam!" The spirited Irishwoman at once replied: "I congratulate your Majesty on having won the race!"

English historians, in general, taking their cue from Story, are ungenerous to the Irish in connection with the Boyne. English troops had comparatively little hand in obtaining the victory. The French writers, also, in order to screen the misconduct, and possibly treason, of De Lauzun, seek to throw all the blame for the loss of the battle on their Irish allies. Not so, many of the Irish Protestant writers, whose coreligionists bore a great deal of the brunt of the fighting on William's side, and were thus enabled to know the truth. Among those writers may be mentioned Colonel William Blacker, poet-laureate of the Orange Order in Ireland, who wrote at the beginning of the last century, and, in his poem, "The Battle of the Boyne," gives full credit to his Catholic fellow-countrymen for their valor, thus:

"In vain the sword Green Erin draws and life away doth fling—
Oh! worthy of a better cause and of a braver king!
In vain thy bearing bold is shown upon that blood-stained ground;
Thy towering hopes are overthrown—thy choicest fall around.

"Hurrah! hurrah! the victor shout is heard on high Donore!
Down Plottin's Vale, in hurried rout, thy shattered masses pour.
But many a gallant spirit there retreats across the plain,
Who 'change but kings' would gladly dare that battlefield again!"

The expression, in regard to exchanging monarchs, alluded to in the ballad, is founded on a saying attributed to Sarsfield, who, on being taunted by a British officer at the Duleek outposts the night of the engagement, exclaimed: "Change kings with us, and we will fight the battle over again with you!"

James, after his defeat, remained but one day in Dublin. He summoned the State Council and the Lord Mayor, bade them farewell, and left the government of the kingdom and the command of the army in the hands of Tyrconnel. Then, accompanied by a small staff, he rode to Bray and thence by easy stages to Waterford, where he embarked for France and reached that kingdom in safety. He was generously received by King Louis. In justice to a monarch who is alleged to have spoken harshly and unjustly of his Irish troops and subjects after the battle of the Boyne, we must state that his published Memoirs, as also those of his son, the heroic Duke of Berwick, bear the very highest testimony to the bravery and devotion of the Irish army, particularly in dealing with the closing campaign in Ireland, when it crowned itself with glory. Remembering this, we may join with the poet in saying—

"Well, honored be the graves that close
    O'er every brave and true heart,
And sorrows sanctified repose
    Thy dust, discrownèd Stuart!"

CHAPTER VI

Irish Army Retires on "The Line of the Shannon"—Douglas Repulsed at Athlone—King William Begins Siege of Limerick —Sarsfield's Exploit

TYRCONNEL, Sarsfield, Berwick, De Lauzun, and their forces immediately evacuated Dublin and its neighborhood, and, practically, gave up all of Leinster to the enemy, while they retired on the Shannon and heavily garrisoned Athlone, Limerick, and Galway—the latter a most important seaport at that time. The flight of James demoralized Tyrconnel, who was aging fast, and further discontented Lauzun, but Sarsfield and Berwick remained steadfast, and were determined not to give up Ireland without a bitter and bloody struggle. Most of the officers agreed with them. If they had lost a king, their country still remained, and they would defend it to the last.

William's first attempt was made against Athlone, which is the most central fortified place in Ireland, situated masterfully on the river Shannon, the commerce of which it commands for many miles. The garrison was commanded by an aged veteran of the Confederate war, Colonel Richard Grace, to whom fear was unknown. General Douglas, with 12,000 men and a fine battering train, including several mortars, was detached from the Williamite army at Dublin to attack the town. He appeared before it on July 17, and sent an offensive message for immediate surrender to the governor. Colonel Grace discharged a pistol over the head of the startled envoy, and said: "That is my answer!" The siege began when the messenger returned. Athlone, divided by the Shannon, is partly in Westmeath and partly in Roscommon. The latter portion alone was defensible. Colonel Grace abandoned the Leinster side, called "Englishtown," after leveling the works. He also destroyed the bridge, thus confining himself to "Irishtown," where still stands the strong castle. Douglas bombarded it furiously. Grace responded fiercely and honors were about even, when news arrived in the English camp that Sarsfield, at the head of a powerful Irish force, was en route from Limerick to raise the siege. For seven days the English general rained balls and bombshells on Athlone, but, on the seventh day, the indomitable Grace hung out a red flag on the castle, to indicate that the fight was to be to a finish, and that quarter would be neither taken nor given. The English doubled their efforts to subdue the place, but made no impression. Finally Douglas, in abject fear of Sarsfield, raised the siege and left the town amid the cheers of the defenders of the Connaught side. The garrison and people gave Governor Grace an ovation, which, indeed, no warrior, young or old, better deserved.

King William reserved for himself, as he thought, the honor and pleasure of capturing Limerick, which, in the days of Ireton, had won celebrity by the obstinacy of its defence. Toward the end of July, 1690, he marched from the capital, at the head of his main army, toward that fortress. He was joined by the defeated Douglas, with his depleted division, at Caherconlish, within a short distance of Limerick, on the 8th of August. This junction brought his force up to 38,000 men, not to speak of a siege train and other warlike appliances. The Irish force consisted of 10,000 infantry within the city, and 4,000 horse, encamped on the Clare side of the Shannon. There was, as at Athlone, an Irishtown and Englishtown —the former situated on the Limerick side of the stream, and the latter on an island, called King's Island, formed by the two branches of the great river. In addition to an infantry force, some regiments of Irish dragoons, intended to fight either on foot or horseback, occupied Englishtown. The defences were in a wretched condition. Lauzun, who seems to have been the wet blanket of the period, declared that "King Louis could take them with roasted apples." Tyrconnel and he were for surrender-

ing the city "on terms," but Sarsfield, ably seconded by
the brave and youthful Duke of Berwick—the best of the
Stuarts—made fierce protest. De Boisseleau, a French
officer of engineers, who sympathized with the Irish people, became their ally, and agreed to reconstruct the
works, with the aid of the soldiery and the citizens. De
Lauzun, eager to return to the delights of Paris, abandoned the city and marched with his French contingent
to Galway. It would appear, from contemporaneous accounts, that his troops were not all native Frenchmen.
Many were Swiss and German—a kind of Foreign Legion in the French service. Louvois, the elder, at that
time Louis's Minister of War, detested Lauzun—King
James's appointee—and would not give him a corps of
choice troops. The Swiss and Germans were courageous soldiers, but their hearts were not in the cause they
were engaged in, and many of them deserted to the
Williamites after the battle of the Boyne. Lauzun remained in Galway until he heard of King William's unsuccessful attempt on Limerick, when he and his forces
sailed for France, the old Duke of Tyrconnel accompany-
ing them. The Duke, on reaching Paris, made charges
of insubordination and general misconduct against Lauzun, who, thereby, lost the favor of the French monarch.
His downfall followed, and, in after years, he was one
of the unfortunates doomed to captivity in the Bastile.
He deserves no sympathy, as his whole conduct in Ireland made him more than suspected of having been a
traitor.

John C. O'Callaghan, the noted historian of the Williamite wars, in his "Green Book," written in refutation
of Voltaire, Lord Macaulay, and other libelers of the

Irish nation, says that the Louvois, father and son, who held in succession the portfolio of war in France, during the time when James was struggling to regain his crown, were inimical to his cause, and did all they could to thwart the friendly efforts of King Louis in his behalf. Louvois, Sr., it is explained, wished the command of the French troops sent to Ireland conferred upon his son; but James preferred Lauzun. Thus originated the feud which, no doubt, led to the utter ruin of the Stuart dynasty. The hostility of the Louvois also explains the miserable quality of the arms, equipments, and clothing sent by the French Government to Ireland. How fatal a choice James made in preferring Lauzun has already appeared. By universal consent, De Boisseleau was made military governor of Limerick. Berwick, in the absence of Tyrconnel, was recognized as commander-in-chief, mainly because of his kinship with the king, while the able and trusty Sarsfield was second in command, and, as will be seen, did the lion's share of the fighting. King William, with his formidable army, arrived within sight of Limerick and "sat down before it" on August 9, confining his attentions mostly to the southern defences of Irishtown, which appeared to offer the most favorable point of assault. Although he had with him a powerful artillery, he did not hope to reduce the city without a further supply of heavy ordnance. Before leaving the Irish capital, he had ordered a great siege train to be put in readiness, so that it might reach him about the time he would be ready to begin the investment of Limerick. He knew, therefore, that it was near at hand. But another soldier, even bolder than himself, knew also of the close approach of the siege train from Dublin, and that it was escorted by a strong cavalry force. This was Sarsfield, who, at the head of five hundred chosen horse, left the camp on the Clare side of the river on Sunday night, August 10, rode along the right bank toward Killaloe, and, near that town, crossed into the County Tipperary by a deep and dangerous ford, seldom used and never guarded. He chose it in preference to the bridge at Killaloe, because the utmost secrecy had to be preserved, so that the Williamites might have no information of his design to intercept the train. His guide was a captain of irregular horse—called Rapparees—and he bore the sobriquet of "Galloping O'Hogan." Dawn found the adventurous force in the neighborhood of the picturesque village of Silvermines, at the foot of the Keeper Mountain. In the deep glen, which runs along its eastern base, Sarsfield concealed his party all day of the 11th; but sent his scouts, under O'Hogan, southward toward the County Limerick border, to locate the siege train. The peasantry of the locality still point out the exact spot where the Irish general awaited impatiently, and anxiously, news from the scouts. The horses were kept saddled up, ready for immediate action, and, while they grazed, the men held their bridle-reins. Pickets were posted behind the crests of every vantage point, to prevent surprise, because the patrols of King William's army were ceaseless in their vigilance and might come upon the bold raiders at any moment. The scouts returned at nightfall and reported that the siege train and its escort had gone into camp near the castle of Ballyneety, about two miles from the village of Cullen, in the County Limerick, and twelve miles, by English measurement, in rear of the Williamite army. Sarsfield immediately put his troops in motion, and, after a laborious journey, reached the neighborhood of the rock and ruined castle of Ballyneety some hours before daybreak. The convoy, thinking itself secure, kept a careless lookout, and, besides, Sarsfield, in some mysterious manner, secured the password, which happened to be his own name. Tradition of the neighborhood says that, as he approached the camp, the noise of the horses' hoofs startled one of the English sentinels, who, immediately, leveled his piece at the Irish leader, and demanded the password. "Sarsfield is the word!" replied the general, "and Sarsfield is the man!" Before the sentry could fire off his musket, he was cloven down, and, at a fierce gallop, the Irish horse fell upon the sleeping escort, nearly all of whom were sabred on the spot. The captured cannon, charged with powder to their full extent, were placed, muzzle downward, over a mine filled with the same explosive, and the tin boats of a pontoon train, which was also bound for William's camp, were piled up near them. The Irish force, humanely taking the English wounded with them, drew away to witness the result of the coming explosion with greater security. Soon all was ready; the train was ignited, and cannon and pontoons were blown into the sky. The report was heard and the shock felt for twenty miles around, and startled even the phlegmatic King William in his tent. He divined at once, with military sagacity, what had taken place. There was no mistaking it. Already, on the information of an Irish Williamite, named Manus O'Brien, who had accidentally encountered Sarsfield's cavalcade on the Clare side, the king had sent Sir John Lanier, with five hundred dragoons, to the rescue. Sarsfield eluded the latter and got back to his camp, recrossing the Shannon much higher up than Killaloe, without the loss of a man. When the news was confirmed to King William, by General Lanier, he said, simply, "It was a bold movement. I did not think Sarsfield capable of it." Some authors affirm that Sarsfield himself said to a wounded English officer, whom he had captured, "If this enterprise had failed, I should have gone to France." He was destined to do other stout service for Ireland before he finally shed his life-blood for the French lilies on a Belgian battlefield.

CHAPTER VII

William's Assault on Limerick Repulsed with Slaughter—Heroism
of the Irish Women—Irish Humanity to the English Wounded

WILLIAM was not discouraged by the loss of his siege material. He found that two of the cannon captured by Sarsfield had failed to explode. Some heavy pieces, with mortars, also reached him, within a few days, from Waterford, and these, with the ordnance he had brought with him from Dublin, made a formidable array of breach-producing engines. The siege, accordingly, was vigorously pressed, as against the Irishtown and King's Island, but hardly any demonstration was made against the Clare section, connected with Limerick by Thomond bridge, probably because of the loss of the pontoon train.

The Irish soldiery and the citizens of Limerick, encouraged by De Boisseleau, Berwick, and Sarsfield, had made considerable improvement in the defences of Limerick before William came up, and, even after his arrival, continued to repair the breaches made in the walls by his cannon. Their batteries vigorously replied to those of the enemy, although much inferior in number and weight of metal, and the Williamites suffered quite heavy losses in officers and rank and file. The Irish leaders had sent many non-combatants to the safer side of the Shannon, but most of the women refused to leave and worked at the earthworks like the men. Many of them were killed by the English fire while so occupied.

At last, on the morning of August 27, the Williamite

engineers declared the breach in the neighborhood of St.
John's Gate and the Black Battery on the south side of
the town practicable. Some authorities say it was twelve
yards wide, and others, including Thomas Davis, one of
Ireland's most accurate writers, six perches, which would
make quite a difference. Five hundred British grenadiers, drawn from the right flank companies of the line
regiments, as was then and for long afterward the custom, constituted the forlorn hope. Their immediate reserves were a battalion of the Blue Dutch Guards—the
heroes of the Boyne—and the regiments of Douglas, Stuart, Meath, Lisburn, and Brandenburg. The whole
army stood ready to support these picked troops. The
signal, three cannon shots, was given from Cromwell's
Fort, where William witnessed the operation, at 3.30 P.M.
Story tells us the day was torrid. The orders to the
stormers were to seize the Irish counterscarp—the exte-
rior slope of the ditch—and maintain it. The assault was
delivered with great spirit, the grenadiers leaping out of
their trenches, advancing at a run, firing their pieces and
throwing their hand grenades among the Irish in the
works. The attack was fierce and sudden—almost in the
nature of a surprise—but the Irish met it boldly, for,
says Chaplain Story, in his thrilling narrative of the
event, "they had their guns all ready and discharged great
and small shot on us as fast as 'twas possible. Our men
were not behind them in either, so that, in less than two
minutes, the noise was so terrible that one would have
thought the very skies ready to rent in sunder. This was
seconded with dust, smoke, and all the terrors the art of
man could invent to ruin and undo one another; and, to
make it more uneasie, the day itself was so excessive hot

to the bystanders, and much more, sure, in all respects to those upon action.   Captain Carlile, of my Lord
Drogheda's regiment, ran on with his grenadiers to the
counterscarp, and tho' he received two wounds between
that and the trenches, yet he went forward and commanded his men to throw in their grenades, but in the
leaping into the dry ditch below the counterscarp an
Irishman below shot him dead.   Lieutenant Barton, however, encouraged the men and they got upon the counterscarp, and all the rest of the grenadiers were as ready
as they."

It would seem that, at this point of the attack,
some of the Irish soldiers began to draw off and
made for the breach, which the Williamites entered
with them.   Half of the Drogheda regiment and
some others actually got into the town.   The city
seemed nearly won, as the supports came up promptly to
the assistance of their comrades.   But the Irish troops
rallied immediately and fell vehemently on their pursuers.   These, in their turn, retreated from the breach,
"but some were shot, some were taken, and some came
out again, but very few without being wounded."   The
Williamite chaplain thus describes the outcome, still preserving his tone of contemptuous hatred of the brave
Irish soldiery: "The Irish then ventured (*sic*) upon the
breach again, and from the walls and every place so
pestered us upon the counterscarp, that after nigh three
hours resisting bullets, stones (broken bottles from the
very women, who boldly stood in the breach and were
nearer our men than their own), and whatever ways
could be thought on to destroy us, our ammunition being
spent, it was judged safest to return to our trenches!

When the work was at the hottest, the Brandenburg
regiment (who behaved themselves very well) were got
upon the Black Battery, where the enemies' powder happened to take fire and blew up a great many of them, the
men, fagots, stones, and what not flying into the air with
a most terrible noise . . . From half an hour after
three, until after seven, there was one continued fire of
both great and small shot, without any intermission; in
so much that the smoke that went from the town reached
in one continued cloud to the top of a mountain [Keeper
Hill, most likely] at least six miles off. When our men
drew off, some were brought up dead, and some without
a leg; others wanted arms, and some were blind with
powder; especially a great many of the poor Branden-
burgers looked like furies, with the misfortune of gunpowder . . . The king [William] stood nigh Cromwell's Fort all the time, and the business being over, he
went to his camp very much concerned, as, indeed, was
the whole army; for you might have seen a mixture of
anger and sorrow in every bodie's countenance. The
Irish had two small field-pieces planted in the King's Isl-
and, which flankt their own counterscarp, and in our attack did us no small damage, as did, also, two guns more
that they had planted within the town, opposite to the
breach and charged with cartridge shot.

"We lost, at least, five hundred on the spot, and had
a thousand more wounded, as I understood by the surgeons of our hospitals, who are the properest judges.
The Irish lost a great many by our cannon and other
ways, but it can not be supposed that their loss should
be equal to ours, since it is a much easier thing to defend
walls than 'tis by plain strength to force people from

them, and one man within has the advantage of four without."

Mr. Story acknowledges fifty-nine officers of the English regiments engaged killed and wounded. Fifteen died upon the ground and several afterward of their injuries. "The Grenadiers are not here included," continues the English annalist, "and they had the hottest service; nor are there any of the foreigners, who lost full as many as the English."

We have quoted this English authority, prejudiced though he was, because the testimony of an eye-witness is much more valuable than the allegations of writers who give their information at second hand. We may add, however, that all Irish historians have declared that the Black Battery was mined for such an emergency as destroyed the Brandenburg regiment, and some of them assert that Sarsfield, in person, fired the mine. As he was the Ajax of the campaign, on the Irish side, it seems quite natural that every extraordinary feat of skill or valor should have been credited to him. His own merits made him the idol of his people, and he was farther endeared to them, as being the son of Anna O'More, daughter of the famous organizer of the Irish insurrection of 1641. On the paternal side, he was of Norman stock. His father had been a member of the Irish House of Commons, and was proscribed and exiled because he had sided with the patriots in the Parliamentary wars. General Sarsfield—the rank he held at the first siege of Limerick—had seen hot service on the Continent, during the early part of his career, and commanded a regiment of the royal cavalry at the battle of Sedgemoor, where the unfortunate Duke of Monmouth

met with his fatal defeat at the hands of Lord Feversham.   In stature, he was tall—considerably over six
feet—fair and strikingly handsome.   His flowing wig—
in the queer fashion of the period—fell in massive ring-
lets over the corselet of a cuirassier, and, in the rush of
battle, he must have been the counterpart of Murat, Napoleon's "Emperor of Dragoons."   Irish poets have called
him "headlong Sarsfield."   "Long-headed Sarsfield" would
have been a better sobriquet, for, had his advice been
taken by his royal master and the generals sent by the
latter to command over him, Ireland would never have
bowed her head to the yoke of William.   Even the most
envenomed of English historians against the adherents
of King James—including Lord Macaulay—do ample
justice to the courage, talents, and virtues of Patrick
Sarsfield.

The heroic women of Limerick, who fought and bled
in the breach, are complimented by Chaplain Story, as
we have seen, at the expense of their countrymen, but
the glorious military record of the Irish race in the wars
of Europe and of this continent, since that period, would
make any defence of the conduct of the heroes of Lim-
erick-breach superfluous.   The women, too, deserve immortal honor; because, in defence of their country and
hearthstones, they dared the storm of war, and "stalked
with Minerva's step where Mars might quake to tread."

The Irish loss in killed and wounded was about four
hundred.   Many lives, on both sides, were lost by sickness—dysentery and enteric fever chiefly—during this
siege.   A conservative estimate places William's loss,
by wounds and sickness, at 5,000, and the Irish at 3,000.

The day after his bloody repulse, King William sent a

flag of truce to De Boisseleau asking the privilege of burying his dead. After consultation with Berwick and Sarsfield, the French governor refused the request, as he suspected a ruse of some kind behind it. All the dead were buried by the Irish as quickly as possible, because the heat was intense, and, aside from feelings of humanity, they dreaded a plague from the decomposition of the corpses left above ground. We are informed by the late Mr. A. M. Sullivan, M.P., in his admirable "Story of Ireland," that, during the pursuit by the Irish of King William's men from the breach to their trenches, the temporary hospital established by the king for his wounded caught fire. The Irish troops immediately paused in their fierce pursuit, and devoted themselves to saving their helpless foes in the hospital, who, otherwise, must have perished miserably in the flames.

King William, after carefully considering the situation, and taking counsel with his chief officers, decided that there was no hope of capturing Limerick that year. Therefore, he declared the siege raised—that is, abandoned—and, on August 30th, the entire Williamite army drew off from before Limerick, posting strong rearguards at points of vantage, so as to baffle pursuit. The king, leaving Baron De Ginkel in command, retired to Waterford. There he embarked for England, bidding Ireland what proved to be an eternal farewell. Although this gloomy monarch was not quite as ferocious as some of his contemporaries, and was a marked improvement on Cromwell, Ireton, and Ludlow in Ireland, he is charged by careful Irish historians—like McGee, O'Callaghan, and Sullivan—with having, like his lieutenant, General Douglas, permitted many outrages on the people, both in person and property, on his march from Dublin to Limerick. Making due allowance for the difficulty of restraining a mercenary army, filled with hatred of the people they moved among, from committing excesses, it is regrettable that the martial renown of William of Orange is sullied by this charge of cruelty in Ireland, as, afterward, in connection with the foul massacre of the Macdonalds of Glencoe in Scotland. Brave men are rarely cruel, but we fear, in these instances, William was an exception to the rule.

The story of the first defence of Limerick, in the Williamite war, reads like a chapter from a military romance, and yet it was, indeed, a stern and bloody reality. It was, in truth, a magnificent defence against a powerful foe, not surpassed even by that of Saragossa against the French. Limerick, like Saragossa, was defended by the citizens, men and women, quite as much as by the soldiery. All took equal risks, as in the case of Londonderry. The latter was also a brilliant defence—more, however, in the matter of splendid endurance than in hand-to-hand conflict. Londonderry wears the crown for fortitude and tenacity—Limerick and Saragossa for heroic prowess and matchless courage.

CHAPTER VIII

Fall of Cork and Kinsale—Lauzun, the French General, Accused by
Irish Writers—Sarsfield's Popularity—Tyrconnel Returns
to Ireland—Berwick Departs

THE successful defence of Limerick by the Irish was
somewhat offset in the following month of September by the victorious expedition from England, against
Cork and Kinsale, led by John Churchill, afterward
Duke of Marlborough, the greatest general of that age.
Cork, under the military governor, McEligott, defended
itself vigorously during a siege of five days, but the defences and garrison were both weak, and, eventually, the
city capitulated on honorable conditions. These were
subsequently violated by some soldiers and camp-followers of the English army, but Marlborough suppressed, in
as far as he could, the disorders as soon as he heard of
them. The English lost the Duke of Grafton—natural
son of Charles II—and many other officers and private
men during the siege. Marlborough, with characteristic
promptitude, moved at once on Kinsale. The old town
and fort, not being defensible, were, after some show of
resistance, abandoned by the Irish troops, who took post
in the new fort, commanding the harbor, which they held
with creditable tenacity, during fourteen days. They,
at last, capitulated, their ammunition having run low,
and were allowed, in recognition of their valor, to retire
to Limerick, the garrison in that city being thus augmented by 1,200 tried warriors. Marlborough accomplished his task within five weeks, and returned to Eng-

land a popular idol. The loss of Cork and Kinsale, particularly the latter, was a severe blow to the Irish army, as it was, thereby, deprived of the most favorable seaports by which supplies from France could reach it. It should have been stated that Marlborough, in the capture of those towns, was materially assisted by the English fleet. His army was a very formidable one, consisting of 9,000 picked men from England, and a detachment, nearly equal in numbers, which joined him, under the Duke of Wurtemburg and General Scravenmore. The latter body consisted of troops who had fought at the Boyne and Limerick. Wurtemburg, on account of his connection with royalty, claimed the command in chief. Marlborough, who was as great a diplomat as he was a general, agreed to command alternately, but he was, all through the operations, the real commander. Students of history will remember that, in after wars on the Continent, Marlborough and Prince Eugene of Savoy commanded on alternate days. But there was a great difference in this case, Eugene having been regarded as nearly as good a general as Marlborough himself.

O'Callaghan attributes the failure of the main Irish army to succor the Cork and Kinsale garrisons to the misconduct of Lauzun in deserting Ireland, with his remaining 5,000 French troops, at this critical period. He quotes King James's and Berwick's memoirs, the Rawdon papers, and other authorities, to show that the Duke of Berwick had advanced with 7,000 men as far as Kilmallock, in Limerick County, to raise the siege of Cork, when he found himself destitute of cannon, which had been carried off by the French general, and could not expose his inferior force, destitute of artillery, to the formidable force under his uncle, Marlborough. He was, therefore, most reluctantly compelled to abandon the enterprise. Lauzun, it is further claimed, carried off most of the powder stored in Limerick, and, had it not been for Sarsfield's exploit at Ballyneety, that city must have fallen if a second assault had been delivered by William, as only fifty barrels of powder remained after the fight of August 27th.

The autumn and winter of 1690-91 were marked by constant bloody skirmishes between the cavalry and infantry outposts of the two armies. Hardly a day passed without bloodshed. Considerable ferocity was exhibited by both parties, and neither seemed to have much the advantage of the other. Story's narrative of this period is one unbroken tale of disorder and strife. His narration, if taken without a grain of salt, would lead us to believe that nearly all the able-bodied Celtic-Irish were put to the sword, at sight, by his formidable countrymen and their allies, although he does admit, occasionally, that the Irish succeeded in killing a few, at least, of their enemies. The most considerable of these lesser engagements occurred between Sarsfield and the Duke of Berwick on the Irish side and General Douglas and Sir John Lanier on the side of the Williamites. The Irish leaders made an attack on Birr Castle in September, and were engaged in battering it, when the English, under Lanier, Douglas, and Kirk, marched to relieve it. They were too many for Berwick and Sarsfield, who retired on Banagher, where there is a bridge over the Shannon. The English pursued and made a resolute attempt to take the bridge, but the Irish defended it so steadily, and with such loss to the enemy, that the latter

abandoned the attempt at capture and retired to Birr.
Sarsfield possessed one great advantage over all the
higher officers of King James's army. He could speak
the Irish (Gaelic) language fluently, having learned it
from the lips of his mother, Anna O'More. This gave
him vast control over the Celtic peasantry, who fully
trusted him, as he did them, and they kept him informed
of all that was passing in their several localities. The
winter was exceptionally severe—so much so that, at
some points, the deep and rapid Shannon was all but
frozen across. Besides, there were several bridges that,
if carelessly guarded, could be easily surprised and taken
by the invaders. Sarsfield's Celtic scouts, in December,
observed several parties of British cavalry moving along
the banks of the river. Their suspicions were excited,
and they, at once, communicated with their general.
The latter had no sooner taken the alarm than one English force, under Douglas, showed itself at Jamestown,
and another, under Kirk and Lanier, at Jonesboro. The
English commanders were astonished at finding the Irish
army prepared to receive them warmly at both points.
After severe skirmishing, they withdrew. The cold had
become so severe that foreign troops were almost useless,
while the Irish became, if possible, more alert. Sarsfield,
at the head of his formidable cavalry, harassed the retreat of the Williamites to their winter quarters.

The Duke of Tyrconnel, who had, according to O'Callaghan, and other annalists, sailed from Galway with
Lauzun, and, according to other authorities from Limerick, with De Boisseleau, after William's repulse, returned from France, in February, accompanied by three
men-of-war well laden with provisions. They carried

but few arms and no reinforcements, but the aged duke, who seeemed to be in good spirits, said that the latter would speedily follow. The amount of money he brought with him was comparatively insignificant—only 14,000 louis d'or—which he devoted to clothing for the army, as most of the men were nearly in rags, and had received no pay in many months. He had deposited 10,000 louis, additional, at Brest for the food supply of the troops.

He found unholy discord raging in the Irish ranks. Sarsfield had discovered that some members of the Senate, or Council, appointed by Tyrconnel before he left for France, had been in treasonable correspondence with the enemy, and that this treachery had led to the attempt at the passage of the Shannon made by the English in December. The Council consisted of sixteen members, four from each province, and was supposed to have supreme direction of affairs. Through the influence of Sarsfield, Lord Riverston and his brother, both of whom were strongly suspected of treason, were dismissed from that body, and Judge Daly, another member, whose honesty was doubted, was placed under arrest in the city of Galway. A difference had also arisen between Sarsfield and Berwick, although they were generally on good terms, because the former did not always treat the latter with the deference due an officer higher in rank. Berwick was an admirable soldier, but he lacked Sarsfield's experience, and, naturally, did not understand the Irish people quite as well as the native leader did. In fact, Sarsfield was the hero of the time in the eyes of his countrymen, and, had he been unduly ambitious, might have deposed Berwick, or even Tyrconnel, and made himself dictator. But he was too good a patriot and true a soldier to even harbor such a thought. After all his splendid services, he was ungratefully treated. He deserved the chief command, but it was never given him, and he received, instead, the barren title of Earl of Lucan, the patent of which had been brought over from James by Tyrconnel. But it was gall and wormwood for Sarsfield to learn from the duke that a French commander-in-chief, Lieutenant-General the Marquis de St. Ruth, had been chosen by Louis and James to take charge of military matters in Ireland forthwith. Already he ranked below Tyrconnel and Berwick, although having much more ability than the two combined, as he had proven on many occasions.

General St. Ruth, if we are to believe Lord Macaulay and other Williamite partisans, was more distinguished for fierce persecution of the French Protestants, called Huguenots, than anything else in his career. He had served in the French army, in all its campaigns, under Turenne, Catinat, and other celebrated soldiers, since 1667, and, while yet in vigorous middle life, had won the rank of lieutenant-general. He had married the widow of old Marshal De Meilleraye, whose page he had been in his boyhood, and, according to St. Simon's gossipy memoirs, the couple led a sort of cat-and-dog existence, the king having been often compelled to interfere between them. Of St. Ruth's person, St. Simon says: "He was tall and well-formed, but, as everybody knew, extremely ugly." The same authority says the general was "of a brutal temper," and used to baton his wife whenever she annoyed him. It is well known that St. Simon was a venomous detractor of those who had incurred his resentment, or that of his friends, and this may account for his uncomplimentary references to St. Ruth. Irish tradition says that the latter was hard-featured, but of commanding person, with a piercing glance and a voice like a trumpet. It is certain that he had an imperious disposition and was quick to fly into a rage. When appointed to the command in Ireland, he had just returned from a successful campaign in Savoy, where Mountcashel's Irish Brigade, as already stated, had formed a portion of his victorious forces. He had learned to appreciate Irish courage and constancy during that campaign, and was, on that account as much as any other, deemed the fit man to lead the Irish soldiers on their own soil to victory.

Tyrconnel had accepted St. Ruth from Louis and James, because he could not help himself, and, also, because he was jealous of Sarsfield. The viceroy was no longer popular in Ireland. He was aged, infirm, and incompetent, and it would seem his temper had grown so bad that he could not get along peaceably with anybody. One faction from the Irish camp had sent representatives to James in the palace of St. Germain, begging that Tyrconnel be recalled and the command placed in the hands of Sarsfield. But Tyrconnel, because of old association, was all-powerful with the exiled king, and his cause, therefore, prevailed. Soon afterward the gallant Duke of Berwick, who subsequently won the battle of Almanza and placed Philip V—King Louis's grandson —on the throne of Spain, unable to agree with either Tyrconnel or Sarsfield, was relieved of command in Ireland and joined his father in France. This was an additional misfortune for Ireland. Berwick, the nephew of the great Duke of Marlborough, was, both by nature and

training, a thorough soldier. He was the very soul of
bravery, and could put enthusiasm into an Irish army by
his dashing feats of arms. He was missed in the subsequent battles and sieges of that war. His career in the
French army was long and brilliant. After rising to the
rank of marshal, he was killed by a cannon shot while
superintending the siege of Philipsburgh, in 1734. The
aristocratic French family of Fitzjames is lineally descended from the Duke of Berwick, and that house, although of illegitimate origin, represents the male Stuart
line, just as the House of Beaufort, in England, represents, with the bend sinister shadowing its escutcheon,
the male line of the Plantagenets. Strange to say, the
Duke of Berwick's great qualities as a general were not
even suspected by his associates, either French, English,
or Irish, in Ireland. When Tyrconnel left him in command, leading officers of the Irish army declared that they
would not serve, unless he consented to be governed by
a council more national in composition than that nominated by Tyrconnel. After some strong protests, Berwick yielded the point, but never afterward made any
attempt at bona-fide command. He felt that he was but
a figurehead, and was glad when Tyrconnel's return led
to his recall from a position at once irksome and humiliating. Had he been King James's legitimate son, the
House of Stuart would probably have found in him a
restorer. He inherited the Churchill genius from his
mother, Arabella, who was King James's mistress when
that monarch was Duke of York. She was not handsome
of feature, but her figure was perfect, and the deposed
king, to judge by his selections, must have had a penchant
for plain women. O'Callaghan, in his "History of the

Irish Brigades," says of the Duke of Berwick: "He was one of those commanders of whom it is the highest eulogium to say that to such, in periods of adversity, it is safest to intrust the defence of a state. Of the great military leaders of whose parentage England can boast, he may be ranked with his uncle, Marlborough, among the first. But to his uncle, as to most public characters, he was very superior as a man of principle. The Regent Duke of Orleans, whose extensive acquaintance with human nature attaches a suitable value to his opinion, observed: 'If there ever was a perfectly honest man in the world, that man was the Marshal Duke of Berwick.'" We have also the testimony of his French and other contemporaries that he was a man of majestic appearance—much more "royal" in that respect than any other scion of his race.

BOOK V

RECORDING IMPORTANT EVENTS FROM THE ARRIVAL
OF GENERAL ST. RUTH IN LIMERICK TO HIS GLORIOUS
DEATH AT THE BATTLE OF AUGHRIM, IN JULY, 1691

CHAPTER I

General St. Ruth Arrives at Limerick to Command the Irish Army
—His Marvelous Activity—Brave and Able, but Vain
and Obstinate

THE garrison of Limerick was beginning to despair
of any farther succor from France, and murmurs
against the viceroy became loud and deep, when runners
arrived from the southwestern coast, announcing that a
French fleet had been sighted off the Kerry coast, and
that it was, probably, steering for the estuary of the
Shannon. This was in the first week of May, and, on
the 8th of that month, the French men-of-war cast anchor
in the harbor of Limerick. On board was Lieutenant-
General St. Ruth, with Major-General D'Usson, Major-
General De Tesse, and other officers. He brought with
him, in the ships, provisions, a supply of indifferent clothing, and a quantity of ammunition, but no reinforcements of any kind. The general, however, had a large
personal staff and a retinue of servants and orderlies.
He was received, on landing, by Tyrconnel, Sarsfield,
Sheldon, and other army leaders. He and his officers
attended pontifical High Mass at St. Mary's Cathedral,
where Te Deum was chanted. Macaulay, a somewhat
imaginative authority, informs us that St. Ruth was
disappointed, if not disgusted, by the conditions then
existing in Limerick. He had been accustomed to command troops perfectly uniformed and equipped. The
Irish army was poorly dressed and indifferently armed.

He had seen the splendid legions of Mountcashel in Savoy, dressed scrupulously and bearing the best arms of that day, and he was quite unprepared to behold the undeniable poverty of the brave defenders of Athlone and Limerick. But he was a practical soldier, and at once set about what an American general would call "licking his army into shape." Dissatisfied with the cavalry mounts, he resorted to a ruse to supply the deficiency. The "gentry" of the surrounding districts were summoned to King's Island to deliberate on the question of national defence. They came in large numbers— every man, as was the custom of the times, mounted on a strong and spirited horse. When all had assembled, St. Ruth, through an interpreter, addressed them in spirited words. One of the chief needs of the hour was cavalry horses. The gentlemen were invited to dismount and turn over their horses to the public service. This most of them did cheerfully, while others were chagrined. However, St. Ruth gained his point, and the Irish troopers were as well mounted as any in the world.

The new French general, although much given to pleasure, was a man of extraordinary energy. He gave balls to honor the country gentlemen and their families, and the French uniform became very familiar in all the aristocratic Catholic circles of Munster and Connaught. St. Ruth participated in the dancing and feasting, but was always "up betimes," and away on horseback, attended by his staff and interpreters, to inspect the posts held by the Irish along the Shannon and Suck. It was during one of those rides, tradition says, he noticed the hill of Kilcommodan, rising above the little hamlet of Aughrim, near Ballinasloe, and, casting a glance at the position, exclaimed to his officers, in French, "That is the choicest battleground in all Europe!" We shall hear more about Aughrim, and what there befell Monsieur St. Ruth and the Irish army.

That brave army, at Limerick, Athlone, and Galway, was put through a course of drilling, such as it had never received before, under the orders of the ardent and indefatigable Frenchman. He repressed disorder with an iron hand, and made such examples, under martial law, as seemed necessary. It is said he was severe to his officers and contemptuous to the rank and file of his army, but these assertions come mainly from Chaplain Story and chroniclers of his class. The haughty Irish aristocrats would have run St. Ruth through the body with their swords if he had dared to be insulting toward them. He was necessarily strict, no doubt, and this strictness bore glorious fruit when the reorganized army again took the field. One of the chief embarrassments of the time was lack of money. Lauzun, while in Ireland, had played into the hands of the English by crying down King James "brass money," as it was called, issued on the national security. The poor devoted Irish soldiers took it readily enough, but the trading and commercial classes, always sensitive and conservative where their interests are affected, were slow to take the tokens in exchange for their goods. King Louis had promised a large supply of "good money," but, somehow, it was not forthcoming, except in small parcels, which did little good. We may be sure, however, that St. Ruth, accustomed to Continental forced loans, did not stand on ceremony, and, under his vigorous régime, the Irish army was better armed, better fed, and better clad than it had

been since the outbreak of the war. Old Tyrconnel ruled
Ireland nominally. The real ruler, after he had, by repeated representations and solicitations, obtained unre-
stricted military command, was St. Ruth himself. Unhappily for Ireland, he slighted Tyrconnel, who was a
very proud man, and did not get along smoothly with
Sarsfield, whose sage advice, had he taken it, would have
saved him from a fatal disaster.

Baron De Ginkel, commander-in-chief for William,
marched with an army computed at 19,000 men from Dublin to open the campaign against the Irish on the line of
the Shannon, on May 30, 1691. On June 7, he reached the
fort of Ballymore, held by a small Irish force under Lieutenant-Colonel Ulick Burke, and summoned it to surrender. Burke answered defiantly, and Ginkel immediately
opened upon his works. A detached post, held by a sergeant and a few men, was defended desperately and caused
the Williamites serious loss. It was finally captured, and
De Ginkel, with inexcusable cruelty, hanged the brave
sergeant, for doing his duty, as O'Callaghan says, on the
shallow pretext that he had defended an untenable position. Colonel Burke, nothing daunted, continued his
defence of Ballymore, although Ginkel threatened him
with the unfortunate sergeant's fate. The fire of eighteen
well-served pieces of heavy artillery speedily reduced the
fort to a ruin. The Irish engineer officer, Lieutenant-
Colonel Burton, was killed, and many men had also fallen.
Burke hung out a flag of truce and demanded the honors
of war if he were to surrender the place. Ginkel refused
and called for immediate submission. The utmost time
he would grant was two hours, and he agreed to allow
the women and children to depart within that period.

Once he proceeded to storm the position, he said, the garrison need expect no quarter. Colonel Burke declined to be intimidated and the work of destruction began anew —the women and children still remaining in the beleaguered fort. The latter was situated near the town of the same name, in the County Westmeath, on a peninsula which jutted into a small loch, or lake, and was too far from support to make a successful defence. It stood about midway between Mullingar and Athlone on the road from Dublin. Finally, Ginkel managed to assail it on the water front, breaches were made, and further resistance was useless. Therefore, Governor Burke finally surrendered. He and his command were made prisoners of war, and, in the sinister words of Story, the four hundred women and children, destitute of food, shelter, and protection, were "set at liberty." What subsequently became of them is not stated. Colonel Burke was exchanged and fell in battle, at Aughrim, soon afterward. Seven days were occupied by De Ginkel in again putting Ballymore into a state of defence. He then resumed his march on Athlone, and, on June 18, was joined at Ballyburn Pass by the Duke of Wurtemburg and Count Nassau, at the head of 7,000 foreign mercenaries, and these, according to O'Callaghan, the most painstaking of historical statisticians, brought his force up to "between 26,000 and 27,000 men of all arms."

CHAPTER II

De Ginkel Besieges Athlone—Memorable Resistance of the Irish
Garrison—The Battle at the Bridge—St. Ruth's Fatuous
Obstinacy—Town Taken by Surprise

ST. RUTH had been advised by the Irish officers of
his staff not to attempt the defence of the "Englishtown" of Athlone, on the Leinster bank of the Shannon;
but, rather, to confine himself to the defence of the Connaught side, as Governor Grace had done so successfully
in the preceding year. He paid no attention to their
counsel, considering, after reflection, that the Williamite
army should be met and beaten back from the Englishtown, and believing that the bridge, which, in the event
of abandonment, must be destroyed, might prove useful
in future military operations. Accordingly, Colonel
John Fitzgerald was appointed governor of this portion
of Athlone, and, with a very insufficient force, prepared
to do his duty. Ginkel, his well-fed ranks, according
to Macaulay, "one blaze of scarlet," and provided with
the finest artillery train ever seen in Ireland, appeared
before Athlone on the morning of June 19th. His advance was most gallantly disputed and retarded by a detachment of Irish grenadiers, selected by Governor Fitzgerald, for that important duty. He took command of
them in person, and they fought so bravely and obstinately, that the enemy were delayed in their progress for
several hours, so that the Irish garrison was well prepared to receive them, when they finally appeared within
gunshot of the walls. The attack on Englishtown began
immediately, Ginkel planting such of his cannon as had

already come up with great judgment; and Fitzgerald replied to his fire with the few and inefficient pieces he possessed. But his Irish soldiers performed prodigies of heroism. Their deeds of unsurpassed valor are thus summed up by Mr. O'Callaghan in an epitaph which he suggested, in his "Green Book," should be engraved on a memorial stone in the locality of the action to be revered by the Irish people of all creeds and parties:

"Be it remembered that, on the 19th and 20th of June, 1691, a little band, of between three hundred and four hundred Irishmen, under Colonel Fitzgerald, contested against an English army of about 26,000 men, under Lieutenant-General Ginkel, the passes leading to, and the English town of, Athlone. And though the place had but a slender wall, in which the enemy's well-appointed and superior artillery soon made a large breach, and though its few defenders were worn down by forty-eight hours' continual exertion, they held out till the evening of the second day, when, the breach being assaulted by a fresh body of 4,000 Dutch, Danish, and English troops, selected from above 26,000 men, who fought in successive detachments, against but three hundred or four hundred, with no fresh troops to relieve them, these gallant few did not abandon the breach before above two hundred of their number were killed or disabled. Then, in spite of the enemy, the brave survivors made their way to the bridge over the Shannon, maintained themselves in front of it till they demolished two arches behind them, and finally retired across the river by a drawbridge into the Irish town, which was preserved by their heroism till the coming up, soon after, of the Irish main army under Lieutenant-General St. Ruth."

Having at last attained possession of Englishtown, Baron De Ginkel proceeded without delay to bombard the Connaught, and stronger, section of Athlone. His cannonade knocked a portion of the grim old castle to pieces, and did considerable other damage, but produced no depressing effect on the resolute Irish garrison, commanded by two such heroes as Colonel John Fitzgerald and the veteran Colonel Grace, who acted as a volunteer. The experienced Dutch general, fearing the appearance on the scene of St. Ruth, with a relieving army, became a prey to anxiety. Impressed by the spirit displayed by the Irish troops, he knew there was little chance of forcing the mutilated bridge by a direct assault, and he looked for some means of flanking the place, either by a ford or a bridge of boats. He did not have, at first, sufficient material for the latter, so he "demonstrated" with detachments of horse, toward Lanesborough, east of Athlone, and Banagher west of it. The vigilance of the Irish patrols at both points baffled his design.

Meanwhile, St. Ruth, who had been on the march from Limerick for some days, at the head of 15,000 men, if we are to believe King James's Memoirs, appeared beyond the Shannon and went into camp on a rising ground about a mile and a half from the town. He was soon made aware of the condition of affairs, and strengthened the castle garrison. He also had an earthen rampart constructed to protect the bridge and ford. The latter was practicable at low water only, and the summer of 1691 was exceptionally dry. The river had never been known to be so shallow within the memory of living man. This fact alone should have warned the French general to be exceptionally vigilant. He retired the brave Fitzgerald from the governorship, to which he appointed General Wauchop—a good soldier, but not an Irishman—and the French officers, Generals D'Usson and De Tesse, were made joint commandants in the town. The apologists for St. Ruth's mistakes in front of Athlone claim that the ill-fated chief gave orders to the French commandants to level all the useless old walls near the bridge, but that his orders were neglected. As is usual in such cases, disobedience led to tragical results. Foiled in his attempt at flank operations, Ginkel determined to assault the partially destroyed bridge across the Shannon, which, under cover of a tremendous cannon fire, he did. But it was defended with Spartan tenacity. Attack after attack failed. Movable covered galleries were tried, and these contained planks wherewith to restore the broken arches. Not less than nine English batteries, armed with heavy guns, rained death on the Irish army, but still it stood unmoved, although losing heavily. Under cover of the fire of nearly fifty great guns, the English pontoniers, protected also by their galleries, succeeded in laying planks across the broken arches. They accounted their work done, when suddenly out of the Irish trenches leaped eleven men clad in armor, led by Sergeant Custume, or Costy, who, according to Sullivan, called on them "to die with him for Ireland." They rushed upon the bridge and proceeded to tear away the planks. Instantly, all the English cannon and muskets sent balls and bullets crashing upon them. The whole eleven fell dead—shattered by that dreadful fire. Some planks still remained upon the arches. Eleven more Irish soldiers leaped from their works, and, following the example of their fallen comrades, gained the bridge and sought to throw the planks

into the river. Nine of these heroes were killed before
their work was accomplished. But the planks were floating down the Shannon, and two heroic survivors of
twenty-two Homeric heroes regained the Irish lines!
Pity it is that their names have not come down to us.
Aubrey de Vere, in his fine poem, commemorating the exploit, tells us that St. Ruth, who, with Sarsfield, witnessed
the glorious deed, rose in his stirrups and swore he had
never seen such valor displayed in the Continental wars.
Chaplain Story, with incredible meanness, tries to steal
the glory of this deed from the Irish army by saying that
the heroes were "bold Scots of Maxwell's regiment."
The slander has been sufficiently refuted by O'Callaghan,
Boyle, and other writers. Maxwell was a Scotchman, but
he commanded Irish troops exclusively, and there was not
a single Scotch battalion in the service of King James in
Ireland from first to last. For further information on
this point, the reader can consult O'Callaghan's "Green
Book" and "History of the Irish Brigades," and also Dal-
ton's "King James's Irish Army List," which gives the
roster of the field, line, and staff officers of each Irish regiment, including Maxwell's. The defence of the bridge
occurred on the evening of June 28. On the morning of
the 29th another attempt was to have been made, but,
owing to some miscalculation, was deferred for some
hours. St. Ruth was ready for it when it came, and, after
another murderous struggle at the bridge, where the English and their allies were led by the Scottish General
Mackay, the assailants were again beaten off, their covered gallery destroyed, and their bridge of boats, which
they bravely attempted to construct in face of the Irish
fire, broken up. St. Ruth commanded the Irish army in

person and displayed all the qualities of a good general. Success, however, would seem to have rendered him over-confident. The conflict over, he led his main body back to camp, and is said to have given a ball and banquet at his quarters—a country house now in a neglected condition and popularly known as "St. Ruth's Castle." The Roscommon peasants still speak of it as "the owld house in which the French general danced the night before he lost Athlone."

By some unaccountable fatality, St. Ruth, instead of leaving some veteran troops to occupy the works near the bridge, committed them to new and untrained regiments, which were placed under the command of Acting Brigadier Maxwell. The latter, who has been—unjustly, perhaps—accused of treason by Irish writers, would seem to have shared the fatal over-confidence of St. Ruth. Therefore, no extraordinary precautions were adopted to prevent a surprise—something always to be anticipated when a baffled enemy grows desperate. Colonel Cormac O'Neill, of the great Ulster family of that ilk, happened to be on duty at the defences of the river front during the night and morning of June 29-30, and noticed suspicious movements among the English troops occupying the other side of the Shannon. Becoming alarmed, he immediately communicated his suspicions to Maxwell, observing, at the same time, that he would like a supply of ammunition for his men. Maxwell sneered and asked, "Do your men wish to shoot lavrocks (larks)?" However, O'Neill's earnest manner impressed him somewhat, and, in the gray of the morning, he visited the outer lines, and, from what he saw, at once concluded that De Ginkel had some serious movement in contemplation.

He sent immediately to St. Ruth for a regiment of veteran infantry, at the same time giving his reasons for the request. St. Ruth, it is said, sent back a taunting reply, which reflected on Maxwell's courage. We are told that Sarsfield remonstrated with St. Ruth, who declared he did not believe Ginkel would make an attempt to surprise the town, while he was so near with an army to relieve it. English historians say that, upon this, Sarsfield apostrophized British valor and remarked that there was no enterprise too perilous for it to attempt. The discussion—if, indeed, it ever took place—was cut short by the ringing of bells and firing of cannon in the town. "Athlone is surprised and taken!" Sarsfield is credited with having said, as he observed the untrained fugitives running from the Irish trenches. "Impossible!" St. Ruth is represented to have replied, "Ginkel's master should hang him if he attempts the capture of the place, and mine should hang me if I were to lose it!" But the uproar from the city soon showed the Frenchman that something terrible had occurred. When too late, he gave orders to rectify his mistake. The English were already in the works and could not be dislodged. Maxwell's men had fled in disorder, most of them being surprised in their sleep, and the general and some of his officers became prisoners of war. It was the most complete and successful surprise recorded in military annals, except, perhaps, that of Mannheim by General, afterward Marshal, Ney, in 1799. It would seem that Ginkel, by the advice of Mackay, and other officers, looked for a ford, and found it by the aid of three Danish soldiers who were under sentence of death, and were offered their lives if they succeeded. They found the ford, and the

Irish, seeing them approach the bank of the river fearlessly, concluded they were deserters and refrained from firing. After them plunged in sixty armored English grenadiers, led by Captain Sandys, a noted military daredevil, and these were followed by the main body under Mackay, another experienced commander. The hour was six in the morning of June 30, and, after one of the bravest defences of which we have record, Athlone, through the infatuation of St. Ruth, was in English hands before noon on that eventful day. And so it came to pass, that after a conflict of more than a year, the defensive line of the Shannon was, at last, broken. It is estimated by most historians that Ginkel's total loss amounted to 1,200 men and that of St. Ruth was somewhat greater, owing to the surprise. Among those killed in St. Ruth's army were two colonels, named McGinness, Colonel MacMahon, Colonel O'Gara, Colonel Richard Grace, who fell in defence of the bridge on the 29th, and the French adjutant-general. Few officers of note fell on the English side. Ginkel, during the siege, "expended 50 tons of gunpowder, 12,000 cannon balls, 600 bombshells, and innumerable tons of stone, hurled from the mortars, when the shells were exhausted." After the capture, the English found only a mass of ruins, and it took De Ginkel several days to put the place in some kind of repair.

CHAPTER III

The Irish Army Falls Back and Takes Post at Aughrim—Description of the Field—Disposition of the Irish Forces—Baal Dearg O'Donnell's Apathy

BOTH history and tradition affirm that St. Ruth and Sarsfield almost came to swords' points over the loss of Athlone, and it is still believed, in that section of Ireland, that the Irish general, indignant at the criminal blunder that had been committed by his superior, took all of his cavalry from under the Frenchman's command and marched to Limerick. But this tradition is more than doubtful. It is, however, certain that the two leaders, who should have been so united in council, had a bitter altercation over the disaster, and were hardly on speaking terms during the few momentous days they were destined to serve together. St. Ruth was filled with rage and mortification. He felt that he had committed a grievous error, and dreaded the anger of King Louis, who was a severe judge of those who served him ill. He declared his determination to hazard all on a pitched battle. Against this resolve, Tyrconnel, who had come to the camp from Limerick, and others, protested, but in vain. St. Ruth was in no humor to be balked. Tyrconnel left the camp in dudgeon and retired once more to Limerick, which he was destined never to leave again. Having made up his mind to fight, St. Ruth at once broke camp and moved by Milton Pass, where he halted for a night, toward Ballinasloe, which stands on the river Suck and in the county of Galway. The cavalry covered the retreat, but no attempt whatever was made at pursuit.

The army took post along the fords of the Suck, as if it intended to fight in front of Ballinasloe, which was considered quite defensible, but St. Ruth's previous knowledge of the country would appear to have determined him to retire about three and a half miles south by west of his first position, as soon as reinforcements, drawn from the abandoned, or reduced, posts along the Shannon, had joined him. In his retreat from Athlone, some of the Connaught troops, disgusted by the loss of that town and doubtful of the general's motives, deserted, and these had to be replaced by the soldiers of the Irish garrisons broken up or depleted. About July 9, old style, St. Ruth decamped from Ballinasloe, and a few hours afterward his devoted army, which, according to our best information, consisted of about 15,000 foot and 5,000 horse and dragoons, with only nine field-pieces, defiled by the causeways of Urachree and Aughrim to the slopes of Kilcommodan Hill, where the new camp was established, on the eastern side of the eminence, facing toward Garbally and Ballinasloe. Kilcommodan, at that period, was almost surrounded by red bog, and, on the front by which De Ginkel must approach, ran a small stream, with several branches, which made the morass impracticable for horse and difficult for infantry. In our day, this morass has become meadow-land, but it is about the only natural feature that has undergone considerable change since the period of the battle. From north to south, the hill is estimated to be a little more than a mile in length, and its mean elevation is about 350 feet. The bog lay closer up to Aughrim, where stand the ruins of an old castle which commanded the narrow and difficult pass, than to Urachree, where there is another pass not par-

ticularly formidable to a determined assailant. The
road through the pass of Aughrim ran then, and still
runs, by Kilconnell Abbey and village—after which the
French have named the battle—to Athenry, Loughrea,
and Galway. The road through the pass of Urachree
connects Ballinasloe with Lawrencetown, Eyrecourt, and
Banagher Bridge, and also, by a branch route, with Por-
tumna; and these were the natural lines of retreat for the
Irish army in the event of disaster. Near the crest of
Kilcommodan Hill are the remains of two so-called Danish raths, circular in shape, and in the one nearest to
'Aughrim Castle St. Ruth is said to have pitched his tent.

Most of the elevation was then a wild common, but at
its base, on the Irish front, were many fields under tillage,
and these small inclosures were divided from each other
by thick, "quickset" hedges, or, rather, fences, such as
are still common in Ireland—formidable against the encroachments of cattle, but still more formidable when
applied to military purposes. The French general had
found his intrenchments ready-made, and proceeded to
use them to the best possible advantage. Weak points
in them were strengthened, and passageways connecting
one with the other, from front to rear and from right to
left, were constructed. The design was to enable the
formidable Irish cavalry to aid the infantry when a crisis
should arrive. In the direction of Urachree, St. Ruth
caused the construction of regular breastworks, conceiving that his point of danger lay to the right, and having,
as a military writer has well observed, "a fatal confidence in the strength of his left flank," resting as it did
on an old castle and "a narrow, boggy trench through
which two horsemen could hardly ride abreast." All

his arrangements were completed by the 10th of July, and, according to Boyle, the author of "The Battlefields of Ireland," his line of battle, which contemporaneous accounts say covered a front of about two miles, had its right resting on Urachree and its left upon Aughrim. The London "Gazette" of July, 1691, says that this wing of the Irish army "extended toward the Abbey of Kilconnell," which was considerably to the left and almost in rear of Kilcommodan Hill. The Irish centre rested on the mid slope of the elevation, "between its camp and the hedgerows." Each division consisted of two front and two rear lines; the former of infantry and the latter of cavalry. Of St. Ruth's nine brass pieces, two were devoted to the defence of Aughrim Castle; a battery of three pieces was constructed on the northeastern slope of Kilcommodan, so as to rake the castle pass, a part of the morass, and the firmer ground beyond it, and thus prevent any hostile troops from deploying there and so threaten his left. His other battery, of four pieces, was planted on his right and swept the pass leading to Urachree. It is said that a strong reserve of horse, under Sarsfield, was posted on the west side of the hill, out of view of the approaching enemy, but that Sarsfield had been particularly enjoined by St. Ruth to make no movement whatever without a direct order from himself. Story, who ought to know, says that Sarsfield was second in command, but neither to him nor to any other of his subordinate generals did St. Ruth communicate his plan of battle, so that, if he were doomed to fall, the conflict could still be waged as he had from the first ordained it. This was St. Ruth's most fatal error, as it placed the fate of Ireland on the life or death of a single man.　He had no cannon with which to arm a battery on his centre, nor does he seem to have wanted any for that purpose—his apparent plan being to let the English infantry cross at that point, where he felt confident the Irish foot and dragoons would soon make an end of them.　Although King James's memoirs aver that St. Ruth had "a mean [*i.e.* poor] opinion" of the Irish infantry, until it developed its prowess in the battle, his disposition of this arm at Aughrim would not convey that opinion to the observing mind.　Most of the Irish foot lacked discipline, in the strict sense of the term, but no general who had seen them fight, as St. Ruth did, at the bridge of Athlone, could doubt their courage.　His expectation that the English troops sent against his centre would be roughly handled was not doomed to disappointment.

Owing to many untoward causes, a full and correct list of the Irish regiments that fought at Aughrim is not to be obtained, but Boyle holds that Colonel Walter Bourke and his brother, Colonel David Bourke, held the position in and around the castle of Aughrim; that Lord Bophin, Brigadier Henry Luttrell, and Colonels Simon Luttrell and Ulick Bourke commanded on the left; that Major-General Dorrington, Major-General H. M. J. O'Neill, Brigadier Gordon O'Neill, Colonel Felix O'Neill, and Colonel Anthony Hamilton held the centre; and that Lords Kilmallock, Galmoy, Galway, Clare, and Colonel James Talbot commanded on the right, toward Urachree. Thus it may be inferred, says the historian, that the Munster troops were on the right, the Leinster and Ulster contingents in the centre, and the soldiers of Connaught were posted on the left.　The general in command of the entire infantry was William Mansfield Barker, and Major-General John Hamilton was in chief command of the horse. The discord among the chief officers in the Irish camp must have been something unusual, when to none of the distinguished commanders enumerated did the French commander-in-chief reveal his order of battle. But the historian recently quoted says, in reviewing the character of the unfortunate Frenchman: "Whatever were the foibles of St. Ruth, from his advent in the country to his retreat from Athlone, we have now to look on an entirely different character. He had learned, though at a fearful cost, that his name had no fears for his potent adversary; that deeds alone were to be the test of high emprise, and that his folly had narrowed down the campaign, and in fact the whole war, to the last resource of fallen heroes—death or victory. With this feeling, all that was vainglorious in his character at once disappeared; the mist was removed from his mind, and it shone out to the end of his short career as that of a true hero in adversity. Unlike his French predecessors, he scorned to hide his faults behind the shield of calumny; he candidly acknowledged his error and bitterly lamented it. He became courteous to his officers, affable to his soldiers, changed at once from the despot to the patriarch, and, touched by his sorrows, as much as by their own calamity, they again rallied round him and determined on a final throw for religion and liberty."

A proclamation issued by the English Lords Justices, in the name of William and Mary, immediately after the fall of Athlone, offered inducements, in the shape of promotion and money, to such officers and soldiers of the Irish army as would desert their colors and accept service with

De Ginkel. Very few traitors availed themselves of the offer, but many of those who were indignant with St. Ruth abandoned the camp and joined the irregular forces of the military Hiberno-Spanish adventurer, Baal Dearg O'Donnell, who claimed to be of the noble House of Tyrconnel, and had lately come from Spain, apparently without a settled purpose or principle. Instead of uniting his 7,000 irregulars with the regular Irish army under St. Ruth, who had no French troops whatever with him, O'Donnell assumed the airs of a hereditary Irish prince, affected to despise James as well as William, and established his camp and court in the country between Tuam and Athenry, within two short marches, if made even in ordinary time, of the Irish encampment on Kilcommodan Hill. St. Ruth summoned him to his aid, but the adventurer, whose selfish conduct some Irish writers, notably Mr. Haverty, have sought to explain and excuse, made no reply, and, to this day, he is remembered in Ireland with detestation not unmingled with contempt. His duty, when within sound of the cannon of Aughrim, was to hasten to the field and spare the fate of his gallant countrymen.

CHAPTER IV

De Ginkel Marches After St. Ruth—The Latter Prepares to "Conquer or Die"—His Speech to the Irish Army on the Eve of Fighting

REINFORCEMENTS continued to reach De Ginkel's camp near Athlone, where he lingered much longer than he originally intended, owing to the utter ruin which the bombardment had wrought. Another cause of his delay was his anxiety to obtain fresh supplies of ammunition, and he judged correctly that St. Ruth, rendered desperate by his late misfortune, would give him decisive battle at the very first opportunity. But, about July 10, all was in readiness, and leaving in Athlone a powerful garrison, the Dutch general and his fine army set out in pursuit of St. Ruth, who had now so many days "the start" of his enemy. The English halted that night at Kilcashel, on the road to Ballinasloe. On the 11th they reached the fords of the Suck, and the scouts reported the Irish pickets in full view on the heights of Garbally—now the domain of the Earl of Clancarty, whose ancestor distinguished himself as an artillerist on the English side at Aughrim. De Ginkel, taking with him a formidable force of cavalry, crossed the river by the ford and rode forward to reconnoitre St. Ruth's position. The Irish pickets fell back as he advanced, and, reaching the crest of the heights, he beheld, through his field-glass, on an opposite elevation, about a mile and a half distant, the Irish army drawn up in "battle's magnificently stern array," matches lighted at the batteries, and their colors advanced, challenging to combat. He rode forward farther still, to get a closer view, and St. Ruth allowed him to gratify his curiosity unmolested, although he came within less than half a mile of the Irish lines. What he saw made De Ginkel thoughtful. His military glance showed him the strength of the Irish position, and St. Ruth's reputation as a competent general stood high in all the camps of Europe. He rode back to his camp and called a council of his officers, Mackay, Ruvigny, Talmash, and the rest. Having explained the situation, he asked for their opinion. Some were for trying a flank movement, which would draw St. Ruth from his chosen ground, but the bolder spirits said they had gone too far to turn aside without loss of honor, and a forward movement was decided on. The camp, guarded by two regiments, was left undisturbed. All superfluous clothing was laid aside, and, in light marching order, De Ginkel's army crossed the Suck, the movement being visible to St. Ruth from Kilcommodan Hill, "the foot," as Story has it, "over the bridge; the English and French [Huguenot] horse over the ford above, and the Dutch and Danes over two fords below." It was six o'clock in the morning of Sunday, July 12, 1691 (July 23, new style), while the early church bells were ringing in Ballinasloe, when they prepared to march on Aughrim. English annalists, intending, perhaps, to minimize the prowess of the Irish army, place De Ginkel's strength at 18,000 men of all arms, but the roster of his regiments, as given by Story and other contemporaneous writers, shows conclusively that his force could not have been less than from 25,000 to 30,000 men, nearly all seasoned veterans. The Williamite chaplain's map of Ginkel's order of battle shows over seventy (70) regimental organizations, not including Lord Portland's horse, which joined after the line was formed. Some of the bodies shown as regiments may have been battalions or squadrons, but, making due allowance for these, and counting 400 men as the average of seventy distinct formations, which is an almost absurdly low estimate, the Williamite army could not, possibly, have been less than 28,000 men. Its artillery was formidable, and the cavalry—British, Dutch, Danish, German, and Huguenot—was accounted the best in Europe. As this fine force advanced toward its objective, the scared rural folk fled before it, remembering, no doubt, the excesses committed by the armies of William and Douglas in Leinster and Munster during the preceding year. The writer lived for some years almost within sight of Kilcommodan Hill, and heard from the simple, but intelligent, peasantry, whose great-grandfathers had spoken with soldiers of King James's army, how De Ginkel's troops defiled in four great, glittering columns of scarlet and blue and steel, horse, foot, and cannoneers, over the Suck and took up their positions on the Galway side of the river. Their brass field-pieces shone like burnished gold in the morning sun. They halted where the road from Ballinasloe, running west by south, branches around the north side of Kilcommodan, toward Kilconnell, Athenry, and Galway, and around the south end of that elevation toward Kiltormer, Lawrencetown, and Clonfert. The Irish pickets fell back before them, firing as they retired, from the heights of Knockdunloe, Garbally, and Liscappel. De Ginkel marshaled his army into two lines of battle, corresponding almost exactly to the Irish formation, the infantry in the front line, and strongest, finally, toward the centre, and the cavalry on the flanks, supported by the cannon.

Up to about 7.30 o'clock, tradition says, the morning remained beautifully clear, and the Irish camp, on the rising ground, was plainly visible to the enemy. St. Ruth's army, except the officers and men on duty and the few non-Catholic Jacobites who followed its fortunes, was observed to be assisting at mass—altars having been erected by the chaplains at the head of every regiment. It was, according to the imposing French custom, which St. Ruth closely followed, military High Mass, during which, at the elevation of the Host, there was rolling of the drums and blare of trumpets, instead of the pealing of cathedral bells. The horses of the Irish cavalry were "on herd" along the grassy hillside, under guard; but, when the English advance was sighted, the bugles sounded "To Horse," and there was "mounting in hot haste" of Sarsfield's and Galmoy's and Kilmallock's bronzed and bearded troopers—the paladins of the Boyne and Ballyneety. Divine service over, the Irish army at once occupied the positions assigned to the several corps by their general on the preceding day. Story and some other English writers claim that, on that day, also, St. Ruth addressed to his army a pompous, vainglorious, and rather insulting speech, which he caused to be translated into English and Irish, by his interpreters, for the benefit of those to whom it was directed. But Irish chroniclers aver that he spoke to the troops with paternal consideration, reminded them of their country's sufferings, and their own duty, and called upon them, in words of nervous eloquence, in the name of honor, religion, and liberty, and for Ireland's military glory, to conquer or die.

CHAPTER V

Decisive Battle of Aughrim—It Opens Favorably for the Irish—Desperate Fighting in the Centre and at Urachree—Fortune or Treason Favors De Ginkel

BUT the fog, "arising from the moist valley of the Suck," had, meanwhile, gathered so densely that the rival armies, for a time, lost sight of each other, and De Ginkel's forward movement was suspended; but his soldiers rested in the positions previously determined on, although the formation had to be somewhat modified later in the day. It was about noon when the fog finally rolled away, and Ginkel's line of battle moved slowly onward, until, at last, to use the graphic words of Lord Macaulay, the rival armies "confronted each other, with nothing but the bog and the breastwork between them." The Irish historian, John Boyle, states, in his fine account of the conflict at Aughrim, that, at sight of the Williamite array, on the other side of the morass, the Irish army broke into loud shouts of defiance, which were vigorously responded to by their foes. There was a mutual mortal hatred expressed in those cheers. It meant "war to the knife," and, as at our own Buena Vista,

"Who heard the thunder of the fray
Break o'er the field beneath,
Well knew the watchword of that day
Was 'Victory or death!'"

Observing the strength of the Irish left at Aughrim Castle, De Ginkel resolved to manœuvre toward Urachree, where his horse had a better chance, and, about one o'clock, began the battle with a cavalry advance in the direction of the latter point. The first charge was made by a Danish troop on an Irish picket. The latter met the shock so fiercely that the Danes, although superior in numbers, by the admission of Story, fled in great haste. Another party was sent forward, and still another—the Irish responding with fresh bodies of their own, until, at last, Cunningham's dragoons, Eppinger's cavalry, and Lord Portland's horse—all under the veteran General Holztapfel—were drawn in on the English side. They charged furiously, and, for a moment, the Irish cavalry gave ground, drawing their opponents after them. The

English, carried away by apparent success, rode at a gallop past the house of Urachree and were immediately charged in flank by the brave Lord Galmoy. A murderous conflict followed, but, as at the Boyne, the Irish horsemen showed their superiority, and their gallant enemies were forced to fall back in terrible disorder, leaving hundreds of their comrades dead or dying on the ensanguined field. Many of the Irish troopers fell also, and, on both sides, every man was killed or wounded by the sabre. The English left their heroic commander, General Holztapfel, among their dead. When De Ginkel saw his chosen cavalry repelled with slaughter from Urachree, he became profoundly anxious. There had been, up to this time, only a few partial demonstrations by the Anglo-Dutch infantry which had produced no impression whatever on St. Ruth's sturdy foot, who lay quietly in their works, waiting for their foes to advance to closer quarters.

De Ginkel, in deep distress of mind, summoned a council of war, which debated whether it were better to defer the battle until next day or renew the attack immediately. At one time, during the discussion, it was determined upon to send back to Ballinasloe for the tents, and encamp for the night where the army stood. This decision was afterward set aside, and, says Chaplain Story, "it was agreed to prosecute the battel on the enemies' right, by that means proposing to draw part of their strength from Aghrim [so he spells it] Castle, nigh which their main body was posted, that so our right might have the easier passage over to attack their left, and then our whole army might have opportunity to engage. This, I am told, was the advice of Major-General Mackay, a

man of great judgment and long experience, and it had
its desired success."

We will take the Williamite chaplain's account of the
movement against the Irish right wing, which immediately followed the council of war: "About half an hour
past four in the afternoon, a part of our left wing moved
toward the enemy, and, at five o'clock, the battel began
afresh. A party of our foot marched up to their ditches,
all strongly guarded with musketiers, and their horse
posted advantageously to sustain them: here we fired one
upon the other for a considerable time, and the Irish behaved themselves like men of another nation [mark the
ungracious sneer], defending their ditches stoutly; for
they would maintain one side till our men put their
pieces over at the other, and then, having lines of communication from one ditch to another, they would presently post themselves again, and flank us. This occasioned
great firing on both sides, which continued on the left
nigh an hour and a half, ere the right of our army or the
centre engaged, except with their cannon, which played
on both sides. All this time, our men were coming up in
as good order as the inconveniency of the ground would
allow, and now General Mackay and the rest, seeing the
enemy draw off several bodies of horse and foot from the
left, and move toward their right, when our men pressed
them very hard; they [the English generals] laid hold
on that advantage, and ordered the foot to march over
the bogg, which fronted the enemies' main battel. Colonel
Earl, Colonel Herbert, Colonel Creighton, and Colonel
Brewer's regiments went over at the narrowest place,
where the hedges on the enemies' side run farthest into
the bogg. These four regiments were ordered to march

to the lowest ditches, adjoining to the side of the bogg, and there to post themselves till our horse could come about by Aghrim Castle and sustain them, and till the other foot marched over the bogg below, where it was broader, and were sustained by Colonel Foulk's and Brigadier Stewart's [forces]. Colonel Earl advanced with his regiment, and the rest after him, over the bogg, and a rivulet that ran through it, being most of them up to their middles in mudd and water. The Irish at their near approach to the ditches fired upon them, but our men contemning all disadvantages, advanced immediately to the lowest hedges, and beat the Irish from thence. The enemy, however, did not retreat far, but posted themselves in the next ditches before us, which our men seeing and disdaining [sic] to suffer their lodging so near us, they would needs beat them from thence also, and so from one hedge to another, till they got very nigh the enemies' main battel. But the Irish had so ordered the matter as to make an easy passage for their horse amongst all those hedges and ditches, by which means they poured in great numbers both of horse and foot upon us: which Colonel Earl seeing, encouraged his men by advancing before them, and saying: 'There is no way to come off but to be brave!' As great an example of true courage and generosity as any man this day living [1693]. But, being flanked and fronted, as also exposed to the enemies' shot from the adjacent ditches, our men were forced to quit their ground, and betake themselves to the bogg again, whither they were followed, or rather drove [sic] down by main strength of horse and foot, and a great many killed. Colonel Earl and Colonel Herbert were here taken prisoners; the former, after twice taking and retaking, got free at last, tho' not without being wounded.

"While this was doing here, Colonel St. John, Colonel Tiffin, Lord George Hambleton, the French [Huguenots] and other regiments were marching below on the same bogg. The Irish, in the meantime, laid so close in their ditches that several were doubtful whether they had any men at that place or not; but they were convinced of it at last; for no sooner were the French and the rest got within twenty yards, or less, of the ditches, but the Irish fired most furiously upon them, which our men as bravely sustained, and pressed forwards, tho' they could scarce see one another for the smoak [sic]. And now the thing seemed so doubtful, for some time, that the by-standers would rather have given it on the Irish side, for they had driven our foot in the centre so far back that they were got almost in a line with some of our great guns, planted near the bogg, which we had not the benefit of at that juncture, because of the mixture of our men and theirs.

"Major-General Ruvigny's French horse and Sir John Lanier's, being both posted on the right, were afterward drawn to the left, where they did very good service. And the right wing of our horse, in the meantime, were making what haste they could to succor our foot; for, seeing the danger, and, in fact, that all was in hazard by reason of the difficulty of the pass, they did more than men, in pressing and tumbling over a very dangerous place, and that amongst showers of bullets, from a regiment of dragoons and two regiments of foot, posted conveniently under cover by the enemy, to obstruct our passage. Our horse at this place were sustained by Major-General Kirke and Colonel Gustavus Hambleton's foot, who, after we had received the enemies' fire for a considerable time, marched under the walls of the castle, and lodged themselves in a dry ditch, in the throng of the enemies' shot [globular buttons cut from their jackets, when their ammunition failed], and some other old walls and ditches adjoining."

Commenting on the foregoing account of the Williamite chaplain, Mr. O'Callaghan, in his "Green Book," page 224, says: "He [Story] has the same fraudulent coloring I have previously exposed respecting this [the Huguenot] portion of the English left having 'kept their ground.' The Huguenot narrative [of the battle] is only wrong in the supposition that La Forest [Huguenot general] on the English left was successful with the French [Huguenot] infantry, before Ruvigny [Huguenot general], with his horse, had conquered in the centre; the first progress of the English having been on their right opposite Aughrim . . . where Sir Francis Compton with the van and Mackay with the rest of the English horse succeeded in forcing a passage; secondly, on the centre, where Talmash next to Mackay, and Ruvigny next to Talmash advanced; and, thirdly, on the left, where La Forest first, and then the Danish horse and foot were enabled to cross."

CHAPTER VI

Battle of Aughrim Continued—Its Crisis—The English Turn Irish
Left—St. Ruth Killed by Cannon Ball—Confusion and
Final Defeat of Irish Army

THE lodgment made by the English, or, rather, Ulster regiment of Gustavus Hamilton in the dry ditch, as described by Chaplain Story, together with another lodgment made in front of the Irish left centre by some of the infantry who escaped the slaughter when they were so gallantly repulsed at that point shortly before, however effected, threw the chances of victory, for the first time that day, heavily on the side of De Ginkel. St. Ruth, whose sharp attention was, doubtless, mainly drawn off toward his centre and right, where the battle had raged fiercely and continuously for nearly two hours, soon became aware of the movement inaugurated by the enemy's cavalry at the castle pass. He seemed astonished, conceiving that the point was strongly garrisoned, and asked of his officers: "What do they mean?" The reply was: "They mean to pass there and flank our left!" St. Ruth observed them for a moment, laughed incredulously, having still "that fatal confidence in the strength of his left flank," and exclaimed in his impetuous fashion: "Pardieu! but they are brave! What a pity they should be so exposed!" A few minutes previously, exhilarated by the splendid prowess of the Irish infantry, in the centre and at Urachree, he threw his plumed hat in the air and shouted: "Well done, my children! The day is ours! Now we will beat them back even to the gates of Dublin!"

The unlooked-for passage of the English horse on the Irish left has been variously explained, or, rather, sought to be explained. Almost every Irish writer, the careful O'Callaghan included, attributes the disaster to a lack of proper ammunition on the part of Colonel Walter Bourke's regiment, to which was committed the defence of the castle. Having exhausted their original supply, the soldiers opened the barrels in reserve and found that the bullets were cast for the calibre of the English guns which they had used earlier in the war, and were too large

for the bore of the French muskets, which they carried
at Aughrim.   Other authors aver that when the Irish left
was weakened, to strengthen the right, the front instead of the rear line of the covering brigade (Henry
Luttrell's) was withdrawn, thus enabling the infantry
that accompanied Sir Francis Compton's horse—who
were twice repulsed, but, being heavily reinforced, again
advanced—to post themselves in "the dry ditch" referred
to by Chaplain Story; while General Talmash made a
corresponding lodgment, with his rallied foot, on the
right centre.   Gross carelessness, deliberate treason, or
both combined, contributed to the Irish disaster.   St.
Ruth himself, however, would not seem to have been
much concerned by the apparition of the English cavalry forming toward his left flank, in the small area of
firm ground, just across from the old castle.   On the
contrary, like Napoleon before the final charge at Waterloo, "the flash of victory passed into his eyes," and, as
he observed the enemy forming with some difficulty in
that narrow space, while the single infantry regiment in
the dry ditch cowering under the rain of Irish bullets,
cried out to his staff, "We have won the battle, gentlemen!   They are beaten.   Now let us beat them to the
purpose!"   His bodyguard was formed in rear of the
staff and he had already ordered his cavalry reserve to
report to him.   Therefore, these formidable squadrons
came up at a trot that shook the ground over the hill
behind him.   We are not informed of the name of the
officer who led them—fortunately for his fame, for he
must have been either a dastard or a traitor.   Instead of
committing the command to a subordinate general, as he
should have done, St. Ruth prepared to lead the attack in

person, and the mass of horsemen, proud and confident, began to move slowly down the slope in the direction of the disheartened but still determined enemy. The general, dismounting, halted for a brief space at the battery which defended that flank of the army, addressed some remarks to the officer in command, and, it is said, directed the fire of one of the cannon, with his own hand, toward a particular point of the causeway leading to the castle. Then he remounted his superb gray charger—the third he had ridden that fatal day—and, dressed as he was in full uniform, made a conspicuous mark for the English gunners. He drew his sword, his hard features, according to tradition, kindling with enthusiasm, and was about to utter the command to charge Compton's and Levinson's cavalry—a charge that must have given the victory to Ireland, because, according to Macaulay, De Ginkel already meditated a retreat—when, right before the eyes of his horrified followers, his head was dashed from his shoulders by a cannon shot, fired from the English battery at the other side of the bog! His sword remained firmly gripped in his right hand, but his affrighted horse galloped down the hill, the body of the rider remaining erect in the saddle, until it was knocked off by the overhanging branches of a tree whose remnants are still pointed out to the traveler. A general paralysis of the Irish left wing, chiefly among the horse, would seem to have immediately followed the sudden and ghastly death of St. Ruth. The French attendants at once threw a cloak over the headless trunk, with the well-meant, but, as it turned out, ill-considered object of concealing the general's unlooked-for fall from the all but victorious Irish army.

St. Ruth's bodyguard halted the moment he fell, and, when the servants bore the body over the hill toward the rear, they acted as escort. The Irish horse, through the timidity or treachery of their chief, halted also, and, unaccountably, followed the movement in retreat of the bodyguard. The single word "Charge!" uttered by any general officer, before the cavalry retired, would have saved the day; but it was never uttered. The stubborn Mackay and his lieutenants, from their position near the castle below, divined, from the confusion they observed on the near hillside, that something fatal had occurred. They took fresh heart. More of their cavalry, strongly supported by infantry, came up. All these reheartened troops began to push forward beyond the pass, and even on their beaten centre and left the long-baffled British and their allies again assumed the offensive. No orders reached the Irish troops— mainly foot—still in position on the right and centre and even on a portion of the left—for the order of battle had perished with St. Ruth. Was it possible that, impressed by repeated dissensions, he doubted the fidelity of his chiefs and feared to take any of them into his confidence? He must have misjudged most of them sorely if this was the case. Mere selfishness or vanity can not explain his fateful omission. The English cavalry, now practically unopposed, poured through the pass, penetrated to the firm ground on the north slope of the hill, and, finally, appeared in rear of the infantry of the Irish left wing. Their foot, too, had succeeded in making firm lodgment in the lowest ditches. The Irish still continued to fight bravely, "but without order or direction." At the sight of the repeatedly routed British infantry crossing the bog in the centre, and the cavalry threatening their left and rear, it is averred by Boyle that a cry of "Treason!" rang through the ranks of the regiments so placed as to be able to observe the hostile movements.

The enemy now vigorously attacked the Irish right and centre, but were as vigorously met, and again and again repulsed. For a long time, on the right particularly, they were unable to advance, and it would appear that the Irish soldiers in their front were totally ignorant of what had occurred in other parts of the field. The Irish infantry on the left, destitute of ammunition and having expended even their buttons and ramrods for projectiles, retired within the castle, where nearly all of them were finally slaughtered; or else broke off to the left, toward Kilconnell, and made for the large, red bog, which almost surrounded that flank, where many of them found refuge from the sabres of the pursuing cavalry. But even still the devoted centre and right, although furiously assaulted, refused to give way. At last, the uproar toward Aughrim, and the bullets of the outflanking enemy in the left rear, taking them in reverse, warned these brave troops that their position had become desperate. Twilight had already set in—it was more than an hour after the fall of St. Ruth—when the English horse and foot appeared almost behind them, toward the northwest; while the Dutch, Danish, and Huguenot cavalry, so long repelled at Urachree, supported by the foot that had, at long run, crossed the morass, began to hem them in on all sides. Their bravest leaders had fallen, but this admirable infantry retired slowly from inclosure to inclosure, fighting the fight of despair, until they reached their camp, where the tents were still standing in the order in which they were pitched. Here they made their last heroic stand, but were, at length, broken and fled toward the red bog already mentioned. The English leveled the tents, so as to render pursuit more open, and then a dreadful slaughter of the broken Irish foot followed. Few of these brave men, worthy of a better fate, escaped the swords of the hostile horse. "Our foreigners, and especially the Danes, make excellent pursuers," writes Chaplain Story grimly. Irish historians say that two of the Irish regiments, disdaining to fly, took position in a ravine, and there waited "till morning's sun should rise and give them light to die." They were discovered by the enemy next morning and perished to a man! The spot where they died is still pointed out and is called by the peasantry "the glen of slaughter."

We have, unhappily, no better authority than tradition for stating that, toward the end of the battle, a part of the Irish cavalry, led by Sarsfield, covered the retreat of the survivors of the Irish foot on Loughrea and Limerick. In fact there seems to be a complete mystery about the action of the Irish cavalry after the death of the French general. Certain it is that this force did not act with the vigor it showed in the early part of the combat on the right or with the spirit it displayed at the Boyne; and this fact deepens the doubt as to whether Sarsfield was in the fight or not. Had it not been, as we are informed by the learned Abbé McGeoghegan, in his able "History of Ireland," for one O'Reilly, the almoner of a regiment, who caused the charge to be sounded as the fugitives passed through a boggy defile on the line of retreat, the entire Irish infantry might have been destroyed. They were also aided by darkness, caused by "a thick misty rain," brought on, no doubt, by the detonations of the firearms, acting on a humid atmosphere. Numbers of small arms and other munitions were abandoned in the flight; all the cannon, most of the colors, and the whole camp material fell into the hands of the enemy. Aughrim was to Ireland what Culloden was to Scotland and Waterloo to France—an irretrievable military disaster, redeemed only by the desperate valor of the defeated army. Even the most bitter and partisan of the English annalists admit, although with manifest reluctance, that the Irish army fought heroically in this murderous battle. Its losses are placed by Story, who witnessed the conflict throughout, at 7,000 killed on the spot and 500, including officers, made prisoners. This statement of his shows conclusively that almost all of the Irish wounded were put to the sword. Other writers, including King James himself, make the Irish loss somewhat less, but we are inclined to think that Story, in this case, came pretty near to the truth. He says in his interesting narrative, "looking amongst the dead three days after, when all of ours and some of theirs were buried, I reckoned in some small inclosures 150, in others 120, etc., lying most of them in the ditches where they were shot, and the rest from the top of the hill, where their camp had been, looked like a great flock of sheep, scattered up and down the country for almost four miles round." The bodies had been stripped by the camp followers, which accounts for the white appearance to which Story makes allusion. Most of these corpses were inhumanly left above ground, to be the prey of birds and beasts, by the conquerors, and thus Aughrim is known to the Irish people as the "Field of our Unburied Dead." It was customary a generation

ago, and may be so in our day, for the Catholic peasantry passing along the roads that wind around Kilcommodan, to uncover their heads reverently and offer up
prayers for the souls of the heroes of their race who
died there for faith, land, and liberty.

Story says he never could find out what became of St.
Ruth's corpse, "some say that it was left stripped amongst
the other dead when our men pursued beyond the hill,
and others that it was thrown into a bog." In the neighborhood of Aughrim it was long believed that while still
the left of the Irish army remained in position, the
French staff officers laid the remains to rest under the
chancel floor of the adjacent Abbey of Kilconnell. Other
traditions are to the effect that they were buried in Loughrea Abbey, or beside those of Lord Galway, who fell in
the same battle, in the ruined church of Athenry. Boyle,
after mentioning the two last-named probabilities, says:
"There is, however, reason to doubt both, and the writer
is aware that the people of the locality where the battle
was fought, directed by tradition, point to a few stunted
white thorns, to the west of the hill toward Loughrea,
beneath which, they say, rest the ashes of that great but
unfortunate general."

CHAPTER VII

Mortality Among Officers of Rank on Both Sides—Acknowledged
English Loss at Aughrim—English and Irish Comments
on Conduct of Battle

BESIDES St. Ruth, the chief officers killed on the
Irish side were, according to Story's account, Gen-
eral Lord Kilmallock, General Lord Galway, Brigadier-
General Connel (O'Connell), Brigadier-General W.

Mansfield Barker, Brigadier-General Henry M. J. O'Neill, Colonel Charles Moore, his lieutenant-colonel and major; Colonel David Bourke, Colonel Ulick Bourke, Colonel Connor McGuire, Colonel James Talbot, Colonel Arthur, Colonel Mahony, Colonel Morgan, Major Purcell, Major O'Donnell, Major Sir John Everard, with several others of superior rank, "besides, at least, five hundred captains and subordinate officers." This latter statement has been challenged by Irish historians, who claim that non-commissioned officers were included in the list. Story omitted from the number of superior officers slain the name of Colonel Felix O'Neill, Judge-Advocate-General of the Irish army, whose body was found on the field. Of the less than five hundred Irish prisoners taken, twenty-six were general or field officers, including General Lord Duleek, General Lord Slane, General Lord Bophin, General Lord Kilmaine, General Dorrington, General John Hambleton (Hamilton), Brigadier-General Tuite, Colonel Walter Bourke, Colonel Gordon O'Neill, Colonel Butler, Colonel O'Connell (ancestor of Daniel O'Connell), Colonel Edmund Madden, Lieutenant-Colonel John Chappel, Lieutenant-Colonel John Butler, Lieutenant-Colonel Baggot, Lieutenant-Colonel John Border, Lieutenant-Colonel McGinness, Lieutenant-Colonel Rossiter, Lieutenant-Colonel McGuire, Major Patrick Lawless, Major Kelly, Major Grace, Major William Bourke, Major Edmund Butler, Major Edmund Broghill, Major John Hewson, "with 30 captains, 25 lieutenants, 23 ensigns, 5 cornets, 4 quartermasters, and an adjutant."

Chaplain Story, to whom, with all his faults, we are much indebted for the details of this momentous battle—

one of the few "decisive battles" of the world—says:
"We [the English and their allies] lost 73 officers, who
were killed in this action, with 111 wounded, as appears
by the inserted lists [*vide* his History of the "Wars in
Ireland"] of both horse and foot, given in two days
after by the general's command, and sent to the king."
The lists referred to acknowledged, also, 600 soldiers
killed and 906 wounded. The allied losses were, no
doubt, underestimated for political effect in England,
which had been taught that one Englishman could kill
any number of Irishmen without much fear of a fatal
result to himself. And this superstition was useful, we
believe, to the morale of the British soldiers of the period, whose stomachs failed them so notably when they
were "up against" the defences of Limerick, as will be
seen hereafter. Captain Taylor, a Williamite writer,
who was present at the battle and published a graphic account of it, says that the loss of the allies (British, Dutch,
Danes, Germans, and Huguenots) was little less than
that of the Irish, most of the latter having fallen in the
retreat after the death of General St. Ruth. Of the
Anglo-Dutch troopers, there were killed by the Irish cavalry at the pass of Urachree, in the early part of the
fight, 202, and wounded 125, thus showing the superior
strength, reach of arm, and dexterity of the Irish horsemen. In hand-to-hand conflicts, whether mounted or
on foot, the Irish soldiery, in whatever service, ever excelled, with sword or battle-axe, pike or bayonet. Clontibret and the Yellow Ford, Benburb and Fontenoy, Almanza and Albuera, Inkerman and Antietam bear witness
to the truth of this assertion. As a charging warrior,
the Irishman has never been surpassed, and, no matter

how bloodily repulsed, an Irish regiment or an Irish army is ever willing to try again. There may be soldiers as brave as they, but none are braver, even when they fight in causes with which they have no natural sympathy. It may be set down as a military axiom that the Irish soldier is, by force of untoward circumstances, frequently a mercenary, but rarely, or never, a coward.

The principal officers who fell on the English side, at Aughrim, were Major-General Holztapfel, who commanded Lord Portland's horse at Urachree; Colonel Herbert, killed in the main attack on the Irish centre; Colonel Mongatts, who died among the Irish ditches while trying to rally his routed command; Major Devonish, Major Cornwall, Major Cox, and Major Colt. Many other officers of note died of their wounds at the field hospital established on the neighboring heights of Garbally—now converted into one of the most delightful demesnes in Europe; and some who survived the field hospital died in the military hospitals of Athlone and Dublin. Those who fell in the battle were buried on the field, with the usual military honors.

Captain Parker, who fought in the English army in this battle, and who has left a narrative, frequently quoted by O'Callaghan, Haverty, Boyle, and other historians, says: "Our loss was about 3,000 men in killed and wounded," and, as he was in the thick of the fight and came out unwounded, he had full opportunity, after the battle closed, to verify his figures. He certainly could have no object in exaggerating the English loss, for the tendency of all officers is to underrate the casualties in their army. And Captain Parker says, further: "Had it not been that St. Ruth fell, it were hard to say how matters would have ended, for, to do him justice, notwithstanding his oversight at Athlone, he was certainly a gallant, brave man, and a good officer, as appeared by the disposition he made of his army this day . . . . His centre and right wing [after his fall] still held their ground, and had he lived to order Sarsfield down to sustain his left wing, it would have given a turn to affairs on that side"—"or," O'Callaghan says in comment, "in other words, have given the victory to the Irish."

Lord Macaulay—anti-Irish as all his writings prove him to have been—says in his "History of England": "Those [the Irish] works were defended with a resolution such as extorted some words of ungracious eulogy even from men who entertained the strongest prejudices against the Celtic race." He then quotes Baurnett, Story, and, finally, the London "Gazette," of July, 1691, which said: "The Irish were never known to fight with more resolution."

In his interesting, but partial, "Life of William III," published in the beginning of the seventeenth century, Mr. Harris, a fierce anti-Jacobite, says: "It must, in justice, be confessed that the Irish fought this sharp battle with great resolution, which demonstrates that the many defeats before this sustained by them can not be imputed to a national cowardice with which some, without reason, impeached them; but to a defect in military discipline and the use of arms, or to a want of skill and experience in their commanders. And now, had not St. Ruth been taken off, it would have been hard to say what the consequence of this day would have been."

Now we will give a few comments of the Irish historians upon this Hastings of their country: O'Halloran, who was born about the time the battle was fought, and who, as a native of Limerick, must have been, at least, as familiar with soldiers who fought in the Williamite wars as we are with the Union and Confederate veterans, in Vol. 1, page 106, of his "History of Ireland," replying to some slurs cast by the Frenchman, Voltaire, on the Irish people, says: "He should have recollected that, at the battle of Aughrim, 15,000 Irish, ill paid and worse clothed, fought with 25,000 men highly appointed and the flower of all Europe, composed of English, Dutch, Flemings, and Danes, vieing with each other. That, after a most bloody fight of some hours, these began to shrink on all sides, and would have received a most complete overthrow but for the treachery of the commander of the Irish horse, and the death of their general [St. Ruth] killed by a random shot."

On pages 532-533 of the same work, the historian says: "Sir John Dalrymple tells us that [at Aughrim] the priests ran up and down amongst the ranks, swearing some on the sacrament, encouraging others, and promising eternity to all who should gallantly acquit themselves to their country that day. Does he mean this by way of apology for the intrepidity of the Irish, or to lessen the applause they were so well entitled to on that day? Have they required more persuasions to fight the battles of foreign princes than the native troops, or are they the only soldiers who require spiritual comfort on the day of trial? I never thought piety was a reproach to soldiers, and it was, perhaps, the enthusiasm of Oliver's troops that made them so victorious. This battle was, certainly, a bloody and decisive one. The stake was great, the Irish knew the value of it, and, though very inferior to

their enemies in numbers and appointments, and chagrined by repeated losses, yet it must be owned they fought
it well.   Accidents which human wisdom could not fore-
see, more than the superior courage of their flushed enemies, snatched from them that victory, which already
began to declare in their favor.   Their bones yet (1744)
lie scattered over the plains of Aughrim, but let that
justice be done to their memories which a brave and
generous enemy never refuses."

Abbé McGeoghegan, who wrote about 1745, and was
chaplain of the Franco-Irish Brigade, says in his "History of Ireland," page 603: "The battle began at one
o'clock, with equal fury on both sides, and lasted till
night.   James's infantry performed prodigies of valor,
driving the enemy three times back to their cannon."

Rev. Thomas Leland, an Irish Protestant divine, who
published a history of Ireland about 1763, after describ-
ing the catastrophe which befell St. Ruth, says: "His
[St. R.'s] cavalry halted, and, as they had no orders,
returned to their former station.   The Irish beheld this
retreat with dismay; they were confounded and disordered.   Sarsfield, upon whom the command devolved,
had been neglected by the proud Frenchman ever since
their altercation at Athlone.   As the order of battle had
not been imparted to him, he could not support the dis-
positions of the late general.   The English, in the meantime, pressed forward, drove the enemy to their camp,
pursued the advantage until the Irish, after an engagement supported with the fairest prospect of success,
while they had a general to direct their valor, fled
precipitately."

The Right Rev. Dr. Fitzgerald, Episcopalian bishop,

in his "History of Limerick," published some sixty years ago, says: "It [Aughrim] was the bravest battle ever fought on Irish soil." The bishop, evidently, had not read the lives of Art MacMurrough, Hugh O'Neill, Hugh O'Donnell, and Owen Roe O'Neill, when he penned the words.

"Such," writes O'Callaghan, at the conclusion of his account of it, in the "Green Book," page 230, "was the battle of Aughrim, or Kilconnell, as the French called it, from the old abbey to the left of the Irish position; a battle unsuccessful, indeed, on the side of the Irish, but a Chæronea, or a Waterloo, fought with heroism and lost without dishonor."

A. M. Sullivan, in his fascinating "Story of Ireland" (American edition, page 458), says, or rather, quotes from a Williamite authority: "The Irish infantry were so hotly engaged that they were not aware either of the death of St. Ruth or of the flight of the cavalry, until they themselves were almost surrounded. A panic and confused flight were the result. The cavalry of the right wing, who were the first in action that day, were the last to quit the ground. . . . St. Ruth fell about sunset [8.10], and about 9, after three hours' [nearer four hours'] hard fighting, the last of the Irish army [who were not killed, wounded, or captured] had left the field."

John Boyle, in his "Battlefields of Ireland," quotes Taylor, an English military author who fought at Aughrim, as saying: "Those [the Irish dead] were nearly all killed after the death of St. Ruth, for, up to that, the Irish had lost scarcely a man;" and, says he, further, "large numbers were murdered, after surrender and promise of quarter, by order of General Ginkel, and among those, so murdered, in cold blood, were Colonel O'Moore and that most loyal gentleman and chivalrous soldier, Lord Galway." This same able writer, in concluding his graphic story of the famous battle, remarks, with indignant eloquence: "It is painful to speculate on the cause that left the Irish army without direction after the death of St. Ruth. Many have endeavored to explain it, but all—as well those who doubt Sarsfield's presence on the field as those who maintain the contrary—are lost in conjecture, and none who participated in the battle, and survived it, has placed the matter beyond speculation. So leaving that point as time has left it, what appears most strange in the connection is the absence of all command at such a conjuncture. The disposition of the Irish troops, though dexterous, was simple. The day was all but won. The foiling of Talmash (Mackay) would have been the completion of victory. A force sufficient was on his front; a reserve more than ample to overwhelm him was on its way to the ground—nay, drawn up and even ready for the word. The few British troops that held a lodgment in the hedges, at the base of the hill, were completely at the mercy of those above them. It required no omniscient eye to see this, nor a voice from the clouds to impel them forward, and, surely, no military etiquette weighed a feather in opposition to the fate of a nation. Any officer of note could have directed the movement, and many of experience and approved courage witnessed the crisis. Yet, in this emergency, all the hardwon laurels of the day were tarnished, and land and liberty were lost by default! Nor can the rashness of St. Ruth, his reticence as to his plans, his misunderstanding with Sarsfield, nor the absence of the latter, justify the want of intrepid action among those present. This stands unexplained and inexplicable, nor will the flippant appeal to Providence, whose ways are too frequently offered as an excuse for human misconduct, answer here. The want of ammunition at such a moment was, no doubt, of some import, but the concurrence of events too plainly indicates that Aughrim was won by the skill of St. Ruth and the gallantry of his troops, and that it was lost through want of decision in his general officers, at a moment the most critical in the nation's history."

De Ginkel's army remained in the neighborhood of the field of battle long enough to give it an opportunity of burying all of the Irish dead, were it so disposed. The country-people remained away, in terror of their lives and poor belongings—particularly cattle—until decomposition had so far advanced as to make the task of sepulture particularly revolting. And thus it came to pass that nearly all the Irish slain were left above ground, "exposed to the birds of the air and the beasts of the field; many dogs frequenting the place afterward, and growing so fierce by feeding upon man's flesh that it became dangerous for any single man to pass that way. And," continues Story in his narrative so frequently quoted, "there is a true and remarkable story of a greyhound [meaning the large, rapacious, and ferocious, Irish Wolf Dog that existed in those days, although extinct since the last century] belonging to an Irish officer: the gentleman was killed and stripped in the battle, whose body the dog remained by night and day, and tho' he fed on other corps [es] with the rest of the dogs, yet he would not allow them, or anything else, to touch that of his master. When all the corps [es] were consumed, the other dogs departed, but he used to go in the night to the adjacent villages for food, and presently to return again to the place where his master's bones were only then left; and thus he continued till January following, when one of Colonel Foulk's soldiers, being quartered nigh hand, and going that way by chance, the dog, fearing he came to disturb his master's bones, flew upon the soldier, who, being surprised at the suddenness of the thing, unslung his piece, then upon his back, and killed the poor dog."

Ireland's national poet, Thomas Moore, in the beautiful words, set to that weirdly mournful air: "The Lamentation of Aughrim," thus pours out in deathless melody the heart of his unfortunate country:

"Forget not the field where they perished,—
The truest; the last of the brave—
All gone and the bright hopes we cherished
Gone with them and sunk in the grave.

"Oh, could we from death but recover
Those hearts as they bounded before,
In the face of high heaven to fight over
That combat for freedom once more.

"Could the chain for a moment be riven
Which Tyranny flung round us then—
No, 'tis not in man, nor in heaven,
To let Tyranny bind it again!

"But 'tis past; and tho' blazoned in story
The name of our victor may be;
Accurst is the march of that glory
Which treads on the hearts of the free!

"Far dearer the grave, or the prison,
Illumed by one patriot name,
Than the trophies of all who have risen
On liberty's ruin to fame!"

BOOK VI

TREATING OF THE PERIOD FROM THE SECOND SIEGE
OF LIMERICK, IN 1691, TO THE DISSOLUTION OF THE
EXILED FRANCO-IRISH BRIGADE A CENTURY LATER

CHAPTER I

Second Siege of Limerick—Terrific Bombardment—The English,
Aided by Treachery, Cross the Shannon—Massacre of
Thomond Bridge

THE decisive battle having been lost by Ireland, what followed in this campaign became almost inevitable. Louis XIV and his ministers were criminally culpable in encouraging the Irish people to resistance when they did not mean to give them effective aid. Ireland had proved, in breach and field, that she needed no foreign troops to do her fighting, but she badly needed arms, ammunition, quartermaster's supplies, and a money-chest. Perhaps the egotism of the French monarch and his advisers led them to underrate the importance of Ireland as a factor in the affairs of Europe, and the slanders of the perfidious Lauzun and his lieutenants had poisoned the mind of the ruler of France in regard to Irish valor. James, in his panic flight, had also carried with him to the French court a most unfavorable impression, and some Irish writers— among them Mr. Boyle—aver that Louis bitterly reproached the fallen king for his ignominious abandonment of Ireland after the affair of the Boyne. James, however, managed to conciliate his haughty cousin, and the latter made him still more promises of effective assistance.

De Ginkel, whose immediate objective, as before the great battle, was Galway, broke up his camp at Aughrim and marched to Loughrea, on July 16. He reached Athenry the following day, and Oranmore on the 18th. At this point he learned that Lord Dillon was Governor of

Galway town, and that the French general, D'Usson, commanded the garrison. Baal Dearg O'Donnell, with what remained of his irregular force, hovered about the city, but failed to throw himself into it. It has been stated, on seemingly good authority, that the Irish officials within the town distrusted him, as, indeed, was not unreasonable, seeing that Chaplain Story tells us that "his [O'Donnell's] design was to keep amongst the mountains till he could make terms for himself, upon which account he writ [wrote] the general, De Ginkel, before our army removed from Galway." He followed up this treason in a practical manner, and, some months later on, as the Chaplain circumstantially informs us, the adventurer entered the service of William in the Continental wars, and also received a pension of £500 per annum, for life, from the English treasury. The same consideration was subsequently given to Brigadier Henry Luttrell, on whom popular Irish tradition has fixed the odium of having "sold the pass at Aughrim." It is certain that twenty-six years afterward, A.D. 1717, this treacherous "general of the Irish horse" was shot to death in a sedan chair, while being carried through the streets of Dublin. No doubt remains among the Irish people that the deed was done in reprisal for Luttrell's villanous conduct in the campaign of 1691, and some have gone so far as to charge him with having been the officer who ordered the Irish cavalry off the field immediately after the death of St. Ruth on Kilcommodan Hill.

Galway, before which De Ginkel appeared on the 19th, after a respectable show of resistance, surrendered with the honors of war, and sundry liberal civil provisions, on the 22d. On the 26th it was evacuated by the Irish garrison, which marched to Limerick. This capitulation virtually ended Irish resistance in Connaught, except for the town of Sligo, which was stubbornly held by the gallant Sir Teague O'Regan, the hero of Charlemont, against a strong detachment of the English army, under Lord Granard, until the following September 16, when he, too, having done all that a brave commander might, yielded his post with honor, and was allowed to join the main Irish army in Limerick town. The adventurer, O'Donnell, assisted the English against Sligo. De Ginkel, after garrisoning Galway, moved toward Limerick by way of Athenry, Loughrea, Eyrecourt, Banagher Bridge, Birr, Nenagh, and Caherconlish, meeting but feeble resistance on his route. He halted at the last-mentioned place to refresh and reinforce his army, and to provide himself with a stronger siege train. This he finally brought up to the number of sixty "great guns," none of them less than a twelve-pounder, and about a score of mortars for the throwing of large shells. About this time, he issued several proclamations, and continued to do so throughout the subsequent operations, with the design of seducing the Irish officers and soldiers from their allegiance to a desperate cause. In this effort he was by no means successful, but several clever Irish spies passed themselves off as deserters, and gave him plenty of misinformation regarding the condition of affairs at Limerick. While in this camp at Caherconlish, the Dutch general's attention was called to the cupidity of the sutlers and other camp-followers, who appear to have been as greedy and conscienceless as their successor of our own times. The gossipy Chaplain informs us, in this connection, that General Ginkel "sent out an order that all ale from Dublin and Wicklow should be sold at 6 pence [12 cents] per quart; all other ale, coming above forty miles, at 5 pence, and all under forty miles at 4 pence; white bread to be sold at 3 pence per pound; brown bread at 2 pence; claret at 2 shillings and 6 pence, and Rhenish at 3 shillings [per quart]; brandy at 12 shillings [$2.88] per gallon, etc.; and that no person should presume to exceed these rates on the penalty of forfeiting all his goods, and suffering a month's imprisonment. But they promptly found out a trick for this," continues Mr. Story in disgust, "and called *all* drink that came to the camp Dublin or Wicklow ale!" This "touch of nature" shows how little mankind has changed in principle and practice after a lapse of more than six generations.

De Ginkel appeared in front of Limerick on August 25, and the city was immediately invested on the south, east, and north. The Clare side, connected by Thomond Bridge with Englishtown, or King's Island, still remained unattacked, as no English force had passed the river. The Irish horse and dragoons were all quartered on that side, while the infantry garrisoned the threatened portions of the city.

Notwithstanding the imposing array of Ginkel's superb army and powerful siege equipment as they approached the walls of their city, neither the people nor the garrison of Limerick seem to have been much concerned by the spectacle. The walls were much stronger than they had been in the previous siege, and the soldiers were seasoned to hardship and peril. D'Usson, the French lieutenant-general, was in chief command, with his fellow-countryman, general, the Chevalier De Tessé, second, and Sarsfield, it appears from the order of signature in the subsequent treaty, was third in rank, with the Scotch general, Wauchop, fourth. The Duke of Tyrconnel had died of apoplexy— Story hints at poison administered in wine—after dining heartily with the French generals and other officers on August 14. The misfortunes of his country, in the opinion of many writers, had more to do with hastening the end than any other cause. His remains lie under a nameless flagstone in the aisle of St. Mauchin's church in Limerick, but we are informed not even Irish tradition, usually so minute, can point out the exact place of sepulture. The powerful English batteries, raking the town on three sides, poured in torrents of bombs and red-hot cannon balls, day and night, and the place caught fire at several points. Most of the women and children had to be removed to the cavalry camp on the Clare bank, and the casualties among the defenders were numerous. The Irish replied spiritedly, but they were very deficient in weight of metal, and, also, because of the comparative shortness of supply, had to be sparing of their ammunition, whereas the English were always sure of a fresh supply both from the interior and their men-of-war on the adjacent coasts. The Chaplain, under date of September 8, 1691, relates how the "new batteries were all ready—one to the left with ten field-pieces to shoot red-hot ball; another to the right of 25 guns, all 24 and 18-pounders; and in the centre were placed 8 mortars, from 18¾ to 10½ inches in diameter; these stood all together on the northeast of the town, nigh the island: then there were 8 guns of 12-pound ball each, planted at Mackay's fort, and some also toward the river on the southwest, where the Danes were posted. These fell to work all the time and put the Irish into such a fright [more partisan venom] that a great many of them wished themselves at another place, having never heard such a noise before, nor I hope never shall in that kingdom."

Three days later the reverend chronicler tells us that

"the breach was widened at least forty paces, and, floats being prepared, there were great debates amongst the chief officers whether it should be attempted by storm. . . . Though indeed we could not do the enemy a greater pleasure, nor ourselves a greater prejudice, in all probability, than in seeking to carry the town by a breach, before those within [the Irish, to wit] were more humbled, either by sword or sickness." No finer tribute than this, coming from such a source, could be paid to Irish constancy and courage, after such treasons and disasters as marked the capture of Athlone and the loss of Aughrim.

Thoroughly convinced that he could not hope to carry Limerick by direct assault, De Ginkel now resolved to test the never-failing weapon of treachery and surprise on this stubborn foe. He had information that there was a strong peace-at-any-price party within the town, and that, could he but land a strong force on the Clare bank of the Shannon, the city would speedily capitulate. He, therefore, determined to construct, in all secrecy, a pontoon bridge across the river above St. Thomas Island, near a place called Annaghbeg, where Brigadier Robert Clifford commanded a strong body of Irish dragoons and infantry, quite sufficient, if only properly directed, to foil any hostile movement. On the night of the 15th of September, the bridge was laid—the most favorable point having been revealed by some fishermen, who, the historian O'Callaghan relates, were bribed to betray their country. It is much more probable, however, that they were forced to turn traitors under threat of death. However, on the morning of the 16th the bridge was completed and a formidable English force of horse and foot, under Generals Talmash and Scravenmore, succeeded in crossing. Apparently taken by surprise—although distinctly charged with treason by numerous Irish historians—General Clifford, at this important juncture, displayed neither zeal, courage, nor capacity. He brought his men up in a state of unreadiness and in detachments, instead of in a solid formation, and, of course, was easily put to rout. To show the criminal carelessness, to say no worse, of this commander, his cavalry horses were "out at grass" two miles from his camp, when the English attack was made! Such "generalship" would have demoralized an army of Spartans, and the Irish rank and file can hardly be blamed if, on this occasion, they did not manifest their customary intrepidity. Europe never beheld in the field a braver body of men than King James's Irish army, and the world never furnished a more incompetent staff of general officers, whether French or Irish, than that which commanded and, finally, wrecked it. We wish to except St. Ruth and Sarsfield and Boisseleau, who were able and gallant soldiers, thoroughly devoted to the cause in which they had embarked. De Ginkel's bold movement resulted in the partial turning of Thomond Bridge—the key to King's Island—and the capture of St. Thomas Island, another important Irish post above the city. He, therefore, felt justified in issuing, that same day, a proclamation inviting the garrison of Limerick to surrender on honorable conditions, but the Irish, although now under a veritable rain of fire and iron from every point of the compass, paid no heed to it, whereat the phlegmatic, but skilful, Dutch strategist greatly marveled.

But, although the river had been successfully passed, Ginkel was so discouraged by the firm countenance of the Irish garrison that he called a Council of War on the 17th, when it was, at first, decided to cross the whole English army into Clare, destroy the Irish resources of food and forage in that county, and then convert the siege into a blockade that might last indefinitely. Reflection, however, changed this decision. Winter was approaching, and the wet Irish winter meant wholesale death to the soft and pampered English and their foreign allies. Ginkel, then, resolved to again try his favorite manœuvre—a turning movement. Accordingly, on September 22, at the head of the greater portion of the allied army, he crossed the pontoon bridge and, commanding in person, made a sudden and tremendous attack on the small fort which commanded Thomond Bridge, and was garrisoned by about 800 Irish soldiers. The English cannon soon covered this fort with red-hot projectiles. Everything inflammable in the soldiers' quarters caught fire, and the desperate garrison made a sortie with the object of crossing into King's Island by Thomond Bridge. The connection was by means of a draw. A little over a hundred of the Irish had crossed in safety, when the French major in command at the drawbridge, fearing, it is said, that the English might enter the town with the fugitives, caused it suddenly to be raised. The men behind were not able to see what had happened, and the foremost ranks that stood on the western abutment were forced over the gulf and nearly all perished in the river. The others put up white handkerchiefs in token of surrender, but the savage victors showed no mercy. Story, who saw the whole sickening butchery, paints the scene in ghastly fashion thus: "Before the killing was over, they [the Irish] were laid in heaps upon the bridge, higher than the ledges of it." Out of 800 men, only the five score and odd that gained the drawbridge in time, and the few strong ones who swam the river, escaped. It, on a smaller scale, re-

sembled the disaster at Leipsic, in 1813, when the French
Major of Engineers, Montfort, caused the bridge over the
Elster to be blown up, while yet the corps of MacDonald
and Poniatowski, which formed Napoleon's rearguard, were
on the hostile bank of the river. Thus, through the stu-
pidity, or panic, of a subordinate officer, the emperor lost
the Polish marshal, who was one of his best generals,
and 20,000 of his choicest troops. A fool or coward commanding at a bridge over which an army is compelled to
retreat, is more deadly to his friends than all the bullets
and sabres of the enemy.

CHAPTER II

Capitulation of Limerick—Terms of the Famous "Violated Treaty" —Cork Harbor Tragedy

THE Irish cavalry, which would seem to have been
inefficiently commanded by General Sheldon during
the late operations, and now completely outnumbered, fell
back to Six-Mile-Bridge in Clare, dejected and almost hopeless. The men had lost faith in their commanders, and
that meant a speedy end of effective resistance. When it
became known in Limerick that the enemy had been
successful beyond the river, the peace party began again
to clamor loudly for a capitulation. A party eager for surrender within a beleaguered city is the very best ally a besieging force can have. In this case, their treason or pusil-
lanimity proved the destruction of their country. De Ginkel
had positive information that a great French fleet, under
a renowned admiral, Count Chateau-Renaud, was fitting out
at Brest for the relief of Limerick. Therefore he was ready
to promise almost anything in order to gain the timely sur-

render of the place, for he knew that if the French once landed in force, all the fruits of his recent victories would be irretrievably spoiled. The buoyant Irish would rally again more numerously than ever, better drilled, equipped, and thoroughly inured to war. His good opinion of their fighting qualities was unequivocally shown in his eagerness to enlist them as soldiers under the banner of King William. He felt morally certain that Sarsfield and the other chief Irish officers were entirely ignorant of the preparations going on in France. They imagined themselves absolutely deserted by that power. Irish tradition credits General Sarsfield with a disposition to hold out to the last, while it is believed, on the same rather unreliable authority, that the French generals, D'Usson and De Tessé, favored an honorable and immediate surrender. It is certain that most of the Anglo-Irish officers were tired of the war and desired to have an end of it on any reasonable terms. Ginkel was still over the river in Clare, when, on the evening of September 23, the Irish drums, from several points in the town, beat a parley. The siege had lasted almost a month, and the English officers were delighted at the near prospect of peace. They received Sarsfield, Wauchop, and their escort, under a flag of truce, with military courtesy, and directed them where to find the general-in-chief. The Irish officers crossed the Shannon in a rowboat, and found Ginkel in his camp by Thomond Bridge. He received them favorably, and a temporary cessation of hostilities was agreed upon. Next morning, it was decided to extend it three days. Then it was determined that the Irish officers and commands separated from the Limerick garrison should be communicated with, and that all, if terms were agreed upon, would surrender simultaneously. Meanwhile the English and Irish officers exchanged courtesies and frequently dined together, although the French generals held aloof, for some reason that has never been satisfactorily explained.

But now the ultra peace party having, in a measure, the upper hand, sought to commit the Irish army to a dishonorable and ungrateful policy—the abandonment of France, which, with all its faults, was Ireland's sole ally. Hostages were exchanged by the two armies, those for England being Lord Cutts, Sir David Collier, Colonel Tiffin, and Colonel Piper; and for Ireland Lords Westmeath, Iveagh (whose entire regiment afterward passed over to William), Trimelstown, and Louth. Following the arrival of the latter in the English camp came the peace party's proposals, which stipulated for the freedom of Catholic worship and the maintenance of civil rights, and then basely proposed that "the Irish army be kept on foot, paid, et cetera, the same as the rest of their majesties' forces, in case they were willing to serve their majesties against France or any other enemy."

The Irish army, nobly chivalrous and patriotic, with the usual base exceptions to be found in every considerable body of men, was not willing "to serve their majesties" as intimated, as will be seen further along. Ginkel, who was thoroughly coached by the "royal commissioners" from Dublin, who were rarely absent from his camp, rejected the Palesmen's propositions, chiefly because of the Catholic claims put forward in them. There is no evidence whatever that Sarsfield countenanced the policy attempted to be carried out by this contemptible faction.

On the 28th all the parties in Limerick town came to an agreement in regard to what they would propose to and accept from De Ginkel. The latter, who was quite a diplomatic as well as military "bluffer," began openly to prepare his batteries for a renewal of the bombardment—the three days' cessation having nearly come to an end. But, on the day stated, there came to him, from out of Limerick, Generals Sarsfield (Lord Lucan), Wauchop, the Catholic Primate, Baron Purcell, the Archbishop of Cashel, Sir Garret Dillon, Sir Theobald ("Toby") Butler, and Colonel Brown, "the three last counselors-at-law, with several other officers and commissioners." Baron De Ginkel summoned all of his chief generals to meet them, and "after a long debate, articles were agreed on, not only for the town of Limerick, but for all the other forts and castles in the kingdom, then in the enemies' possession." In compliance with the wish of the Irish delegation, De Ginkel agreed to summon the Lords Justices from Dublin to ratify the treaty. These functionaries, authoritatively representing King William and Queen Mary, soon arrived at the camp and signed the instrument in due form. The French generals, although they did not accompany the Irish commissioners on their visit to Ginkel, signed the terms of capitulation with the rest, the names appearing in the following order: D'Usson, Le Chevelier de Tessé, Latour Monfort, Mark Talbot, Lucan (Sarsfield), Jo Wauchop, Galmoy, M. Purcell. For England there signed Lords Justices Charles Porter and Thomas Conyngsby, Baron De Ginkel, and Generals Scravenmore, Mackay, and Talmash.

The Treaty of Limerick was thus consummated on October 3, 1691, with all the required forms and ceremonies, so that no loophole of informality was left for either party to this international compact. In the treaty there were 29 military and 13 civil articles. As they were quite lengthy, we will confine ourselves to a general summary, thus:

All the adherents of King James in Ireland were given permission to go beyond the seas to any country they might choose to live in, except England and Scotland. Volunteers and rapparees were included in this provision, as well as the officers and soldiers of the Irish regular army. These voluntary exiles were allowed to depart from Ireland in "whole bodies, companies, or parties; and it was provided that, if plundered by the way, the English Government would grant compensation for such losses as they might sustain. It was agreed that fifty ships of 200 tons burden each should be provided for their transportation, and twenty of the same tonnage in addition, if it should be found necessary, and that "said ships should be furnished with forage for horses and all necessary provisions to subsist the officers, troopers, dragoons, and [foot] soldiers, and all other persons [meaning families and followers] that are shipped to be transported into France." In addition, two men-of-war were placed at the disposal of the principal officers for the voyage, and suitable provision was made for the safe return of all vessels when their mission of transportation was accomplished. The thrifty De Ginkel further stipulated that the provisions supplied to the military exiles should be paid for by their government as soon as the Irish troops were landed on French soil. Article XXV provided: "That it shall be lawful for the said garrison [of Limerick] to march out at once, or at different times, as they can be embarked, with arms, baggage, drums beating, match lighted at both ends, bullet in mouth, colors flying, six brass guns, such as the besieged shall choose, two mortar pieces, and half the ammunition that is now in the magazines of the said place." This provision, which, as can be seen, included the full "honors of war," was also extended to the other capitulated Irish garri-

sons. Another significant provision was that all Irish officers and soldiers who so desired could join the army of
King William, retaining the rank and pay they enjoyed in
the service of King James.

Of the civil articles, the first read as follows: "The Roman Catholics of this kingdom shall enjoy such privileges
in the exercise of their religion as are consistent with the
laws of Ireland, or as they did enjoy in the reign of King
Charles II; and their Majesties, as soon as their affairs
will permit them to summon a Parliament in this kingdom,
will endeavor to procure the said Roman Catholics such
further security in that particular as may preserve them from
disturbance upon the account of their said religion."

The second article guaranteed protection in the possession
of their estates and the free pursuit of their several professions, trades, and callings to all who had served King James,
the same as under his own régime, on the taking of the
subjoined oath of allegiance prescribed by statute: "I ——
do solemnly promise and swear that I will be faithful and
bear true allegiance to their Majesties, King William and
Queen Mary: so help me God." A subsequent article provided that "the oath to be administered to such Roman
Catholics as submit to their Majesties' government shall be
the oath aforesaid and no other"—thus doing away, as the
Irish honestly supposed, with the odious penal "Test oaths,"
which were an outrage on Catholic belief and a glaring insult
to the Catholics of the whole world.

The third article extended the benefit of the first and
second articles to Irish merchants "beyond the seas" who
had not borne arms since the proclamation issued by William and Mary in the preceding February, but they were
required to return to Ireland within eight months.

Article IV granted like immunity to Irish officers in foreign lands, absent in pursuance of their military duties, and naming, specially, Colonel Simon Luttrell (the loyal brother of the traitor, Henry), Colonel Rowland White, Colonel Maurice Eustace, of Gormanstown, and Major Cheviers (Chevers) of Maystown, "commonly called Mount Leinster."

Article V provided that all persons comprised in the second and third articles should have general pardon for all "attainders, outlawries, treasons (?), misprisions of treasons, præmunires, felonies, trespasses, and other crimes and misdemeanors whatsoever, committed by them, or any of them since the beginning of the reign of James II; and if any of them are attainted by Parliament, the Lords Justices and the General will use their best endeavors to get the same repealed by Parliament, and the outlawries to be reversed gratis, all but writing-clerk's fees."

Article VI provided general immunity to both parties for debts or disturbances arising out of the late war. This provision applied also to rates and rents.

Article VII provided that "every nobleman and gentleman comprised in the second and third articles shall have liberty to ride with a sword and case of pistols, if they [sic] think fit, and keep a gun in their houses for the defence of the same, or for fowling."

The eighth article granted leave to the inhabitants, or residents, of Limerick, and other Irish garrisons, to remove their goods and chattels, if so disposed, without interference, search, or the payment of duties, and they were privileged to remain in their lodgings for six weeks.

The tenth article declared that "no person, or persons, who shall at any time hereafter break these articles, or any of them, shall thereby make or cause any other person or persons to forfeit or lose the benefit of the same."

Article XII read thus: "The Lords Justices and the General do undertake that their Majesties will ratify these articles within the space of three months, or sooner, and use their utmost endeavors that the same shall be ratified and confirmed in the Parliament."

The thirteenth, and final, article made provision for the protection from financial loss of Colonel John Browne, commissary-general of the Irish army, who, during the war, had seized the property of certain Williamites for the public use, charging the debt, pro rata, on the Catholic estates secured to their owners under the treaty; and requiring General (Lord Lucan) to certify the account with Colonel Browne within 21 days.

It will be remembered, in examining the religious provisions of the Treaty of Limerick, that Catholic worship in the reign of Charles II was permitted by connivance rather than by law. Many of the worst of the penal laws, although in abeyance, might be revived at any time by law officers tyrannically disposed toward the Catholics. The latter were once again to discover that it is one thing to obtain a favorable treaty from a formidable enemy, while they have arms in their hands and a still inviolate fortress at their backs, but quite a different matter to make the foe live up to the provisions of the treaty when the favorable conditions for the capitulators have passed away. But of this hereafter.

Not many days subsequent to the surrender of Limerick, Count Chateau-Renaud, with a powerful French fleet, having on board arms, cannon, and all kinds of military supplies, together with a veteran contingent of 3,000 men and

200 officers, cast anchor in Dingle Bay, on the southern coast, without once coming in contact with the naval might of England. Were the Irish a dishonorable people, they could have then, with great advantage, repudiated the treaty, but the national honor was irrevocably plighted, and, consequently, there was an end of the struggle. Many honest Irish writers have blamed the precipitancy of Sarsfield and the other leaders in signing the articles of capitulation, and not without good cause. Lord Lucan should have court-martialed and shot the leaders of the peace-at-any-price traitors when they first showed their hands. Hugh O'Neill, Red Hugh O'Donnell, or Owen Roe O'Neill would have done so without hesitation, but, then, Sarsfield was only half a Celt, and had an unfortunate tenderness for his fellows of the Pale. It is regrettable that none of the French generals has left a clear statement of the events that led to the premature surrender of the town; but we know that King Louis, who subsequently honored Sarsfield, held D'Usson responsible, for Story tells us, on page 280 of his "Continuation of the History of the Wars in Ireland," that "the French king [Louis XIV] was so far from thanking him for it [the capitulation] that, after some public indignities, he sent him to the Bastile."

Viewed in the light of after events, the Treaty of Limerick, from the Irish standpoint, looks like a huge game of confidence, and is an ineradicable blot on English military and diplomatic honor. The civil articles were ignored, or trampled under foot, almost immediately. The military articles were better observed, except that provision which related to transportation to France, which was grossly violated and led to the drowning in Cork Harbor of a number of the wives of the Irish soldiery, who, unable to find room on board, owing to De Ginkel's alleged faithlessness, or the perfidy of his lieutenants, clung to the ropes, when the ships set sail, and were dragged beneath the waves to their death.

Mitchel, in his able "History of Ireland," page 3, writing of this painful incident, defends Sarsfield against an imputation cast upon that officer by Lord Macaulay, in his brilliant but unreliable "History of England," thus: "As to General Sarsfield's proclamation to the men 'that they should be permitted to carry their wives and families to France,' he made the statement on the faith of the First and several succeeding articles of the treaty, not yet being aware of any design to violate it.   But this is not all: The historian who could not let the hero go into his sorrowful exile without seeking to plunge his venomous sting into his reputation, had before him the 'Life of King William,' by Harris, and also Curry's 'Historical Review of the Civil Wars,' wherein he must have seen that the Lords Justices and General Ginkel are charged with endeavoring to defeat the execution of the First Article.   For, says Harris, 'as great numbers of the officers and soldiers had resolved to enter into the service of France, and to carry their families with them, Ginkel would not suffer their wives and children to be shipped off with the men, not doubting that by detaining the former he would have prevented many of the latter from going into that service.   This, I say, was confessedly an infringement of the articles.'

"To this we may add," continues Mitchel, "that no Irish officer or soldier in France attributed the cruel parting at Cork to any fault of Sarsfield, but always and only to a breach of the Treaty of Limerick.   And if he had deluded them in the manner represented by the English historian, they would not have followed him as enthusiastically [as they afterward did] on the fields of Steinkirk and Landen."

Mr. Mitchel did Lord Macaulay an unintentional injustice in attributing the original charge against Sarsfield to him. It originated with Chaplain Story, and can be found on pages 291-293 of his Continuation, in these words: "Those [of the Irish] who were now embarking had not much better usage on this side of the water [he had alluded to the alleged ill-treatment of the first contingent on its arrival in France], for a great many of them, having wives and children, they made what shift they could to desert, rather than leave their families behind to starve, which my Lord Lucan and Major-General Wauchop perceiving, they publish a declaration that as many of the Irish as had a mind to't should have liberty to transport their families along with themselves. And, accordingly, a vast rabble of all sorts were brought to the water-side, when the major-general [Wauchop], pretending to ship the soldiers in order, according to their lists, they first carried all the men on board; and many of the women, at the second return of the boats for the officers, catching hold to be carried on board, were dragged off, and, through fearfulness, losing their hold, were drowned; but others who held faster had their fingers cut off, and so perished in sight of their husbands or relatives, tho' those of them that did get over [to France], would make but a sad figure, if they were admitted to go to the late queen's court at St. Germain. . . . Lord Lucan finding he had ships enough for all the Irish that were likely to go with him, the number that went before and these shipped at this time, being, according to the best computation, 12,000 of all sorts [a palpable underestimate], he signs the following releasement:

" 'Whereas, by the Articles of Limerick, Lieutenant-General Ginkel, commander-in-chief of the English army, did engage himself to furnish 10,000 tons of shipping for the transporting of such of the Irish forces to France as were willing to go thither; and to facilitate their passage to add 4,000 tons more in case the French fleet did not come to this kingdom to take off some of these forces; and whereas the French fleet has been upon the coast and carried away some of the said forces, and the lieutenant-general has provided ships for as many of the rest as are willing to go as aforesaid, I do hereby declare that the said lieutenant-general is released from any obligation he lay under from the said articles, to provide vessels for that purpose, and do quit and renounce all farther claim and pretension on this account, etc. Witness my hand this 8th day of December, 1691. " 'LUCAN.

" '*Witnesses:*

MARK TALBOT,

F. H. DE LA FOREST, SUSANNEL.' "

From the same authority we learn that "on December 22, my Lord Lucan, and the rest of the Irish great officers, went on board the transport ships [bound for France], leaving hostages at Cork for the return of the said ships."

It is impossible to reconcile the circumstantial statement of the Williamite historian, Harris, in regard to Ginkel's faithlessness, with the official document, signed by Sarsfield, as Earl of Lucan, which practically exonerates the Dutch general. Would Sarsfield have signed such a release if Ginkel had been guilty of the treachery ascribed to him by Harris? Story's book was published a year before Lord Lucan fell in Flanders, and must have been read by that

general and the officers who served with him at Limerick.
One thing about the question is certain—if Sarsfield ever issued the proclamation, in conjunction with General Wauchop, ascribed to him by the English chaplain, he must have
been grossly deceived by somebody.   All writers of his own
times, and of after times, describe Sarsfield as the soul of
honor, but some have asserted that he was rather easy-going
in business affairs, and a little too ready to sign any document placed before him.

We have been unable to find any contemporary confirmation of the romantic Irish tradition that the Treaty of Limerick was signed on the historic bowlder, now preserved by
pedestal and railing near Thomond Bridge, on the Clare
bank of the Shannon.   But tradition is often more accurate
than written history.   Therefore, the Irish people having
accepted the story through more than six generations, we
accept with them the legend of "the Treaty Stone."

CHAPTER III

The Irish Troops, as a Majority, Enter the French Service—King
James Receives Them Cordially—His Testimony of Their
Devotion and Courage

IMMEDIATELY after the signing of the treaty, it was
fixed upon between De Ginkel and Sarsfield that, on October 6, the Irish infantry would march out of the King's
Island by Thomond Bridge, into the County Clare, and there
and then make a choice of service with England or France.
It was arranged that those who chose the former service
were to turn to the left at a certain point, where an English
flag was planted, while those who decided for France were
to march straight onward to a more distant point marked
by the French standard.   They were, in all, about 15,000

men, and, quite naturally, the respective leaders awaited the result with burning anxiety. They were not left long in doubt. The first body to march was the Royal Irish regiment of Foot Guards, fourteen hundred strong, of which Mr. Story remarks wofully, it "seemed to go all entire [for France] except seven men, which the general was much concerned at, then my Lord Iveagh's regiment of Ulster Irish came off entire to our side." In all a little over 1,000 officers and men ranged themselves under the flag of King William, while nearly 13,000 mustered under the Fleur-de-Lis. A few days afterward, the Irish horse, now much reduced, made choice in the same fashion, and with about the same proportionate result. The same privilege was granted the outlying bodies of King James's army, and all decided for France in the proportion of about ten to one. Of the Irish general officers, more or less under the suspicion of the army since the disasters of Aughrim and Annaghbeg, we find Generals Luttrell and Clifford, Baron Purcell, "and a great many more of the Irish nobility and gentry going toward Dublin," which means that they made terms with the enemy.

It was well along in the month of December before the Irish soldiers who had volunteered to go beyond the seas were entirely transported to France. The foot, for the most part, sailed from Limerick, many of them in the returning fleet of Chateau-Renaud, and the cavalry from Cork, where occurred the tragical event we have already related. In all —including the capitulated troops from every Irish garrison—20,000 men from Ireland landed in the French ports, and these, together with Mountcashel's Brigade, which had been in the French service since before the battle of the Boyne, made up a force of 25,000 veterans, who were mostly in the pay of King Louis, but all of whom were sworn to support King James in any effort he might put forth to recover his crown.

As much injustice has been done the memory of King James II by Irish writers, who have taken too much for granted on traditional "hearsay," we deem it only fair to place before the readers of this history the sentiments of the unfortunate monarch toward his Irish defenders. We quote from his Memoirs, Vol. II, pp. 465-467: "Thus was Ireland [he alluded to the fall of Limerick], after an obstinate resistance in three years' campaigns, by the power and riches of England, and the revolt of almost all its [Ireland's] own Protestant subjects torn from its natural sovereign, who, tho' he was divested of the country, was not wholly deprived of the people, for the greatest part of those who were then in arms for the defence of his right, not content with the service already rendered, got leave [as was said] to come and lose their lives, after having lost their estates, in defence of his title, and brought by that means such a body of men into France as by their generous comportment in accepting the pay of the country [much less than British or Irish pay] instead of that which is usually allowed there [in France] to strangers and their inimitable valor and service during the whole course of the war, might justly make their prince pass for an ally, rather than a pensioner, or burden, to his Most Christian Majesty, whose pay, indeed, they received, but acted by the king's, their master's, commission, according to the common method of other auxiliary troops. As soon as the king [James] heard of their arrival [in France] he writ to the commander [General Sheldon, who went with the first contingent] to assure him how well he was satisfied with the behavior and conduct of the officers, and the valor and fidelity of the soldiers, and how sensible he should ever be of their service, which he would not fail to reward when it should please God to put him in a capacity of doing it."

Following is the full text of the letter addressed to the Irish troops through their general by King James, as given in Story's Continuation, page 289:

"JAMES REX.

"Having been informed of the capitulation and surrender of Limerick, and the other places which remained to us in our Kingdom of Ireland, and of the necessities which forced the Lords Justices and general officers of our forces thereunto: we will not defer to let you know, and the rest of the officers that came along with you, that we are extremely satisfied with your and their conduct, and of the valor of the soldiers during the siege, but most particularly of your and their declaration and resolution to come and serve where we are. And we assure you, and order you to assure both officers and soldiers that are come along with you, that we shall never forget this act of loyalty, nor fail, when in a capacity to give them, above others, particular marks of our favor. In the meantime, you are to inform them that they are to serve under our command, and by our commissions; and if we find that a considerable number [of them] is come with the fleet, it will induce us to go personally to see them, and regiment them: Our brother, the King of France, hath already given orders to clothe them and furnish them with all necessaries, and to give them quarters of refreshment. So we bid you heartily farewell.

"Given at our Court at St. Germain the 27th of November [Dec. 7], 1691."

In pursuance of his promise, King James made two fatiguing trips from St. Germain to Bretagne and return, regimented the gallant exiles at Vannes, Brest, and other points, and in every possible way showed his marked appreciation of their devotion.   He was accompanied by his son, the Duke of Berwick.

In accepting French pay, the Irish soldiery exposed themselves almost to penury, and their officers submitted to be reduced in rank, almost without a murmur.   Major-generals became colonels; colonels, captains; captains, lieutenants, and many of the latter sergeants.   This was absolutely necessary, as there was room for only a certain number in the French establishment.   Many reduced officers served also as volunteers, without pay of any kind, waiting patiently for death or promotion.   The total amount of property sacrificed by these brave men in the Jacobite cause was 1,060,792 acres, and this new confiscation placed fully seven-eighths of the soil of Ireland in the hands of the supporters of the English interest.

William and Mary formally ratified the Articles of the Treaty of Limerick within the specified three months, but the English Parliament, influenced by motives of greed and bigotry, shamefully refused to acquiesce, and as William and Mary did not endanger their crown by offering a vigorous opposition, the civil articles of Limerick were, from that moment, a dead letter.   Then redescended on Ireland "the long, black night of the penal laws," and we gladly turn from it, for a period, to follow the brilliant but bloody fortunes of the Irish Brigade in the service of France.

CHAPTER IV

Early Exploits of the Irish Brigade in the Service of France—At Landen, Cremona, and Blenheim—Tribute Paid it by an English Historian

IN the preceding chapter we indicated that we would deal with the history of the Irish brigades in the French service, from 1692 to 1792, before touching on the terrible penal period in Ireland. Their services have won a fame so world-wide that no history of Europe is complete that omits them from its pages. They were prominently engaged in the reign of Louis XIV in the War of the League of Augsburg, which was hotly waged by nearly all Europe against him, from 1688 to the Peace of Ryswick, in 1697; in the War of the Spanish Succession—waged by Louis to support his grandson, Philip of Anjou, on the Spanish throne—commenced in 1700 and concluded by the Peace of Utrecht and Treaty of Rastadt in 1713-14, and under Louis XV in numerous minor wars with Germany, and especially in the War of the Austrian Succession— France supporting the claim of Charles VII, of Bavaria, against Maria Theresa, Queen of Hungary, daughter of the last Hapsburg Emperor of Germany, Charles VI. This war was begun in 1740. France took sides in 1743, and it was concluded by the Treaty of Aix-la-Chapelle, in 1748. In each of these contests France and England were on opposite sides—a circumstance favorable to the bloody development of Irish hatred. After the last of the wars specified, the Irish Brigade, having no warlike food on which to flourish, covered with laurels and "worn out with glory," faded from the fields of Europe.

In another place we have alluded to the campaign of Savoy, 1690-91, in which the ill-starred St. Ruth was chief in command. Mountcashel's, known as the "Old Brigade," scaled every Alpine fortress, drove the vengeful "Vaudois" from their rugged hills, and laid the country under fire and sword, leaving a reputation for military prowess fresh, at this day, amid the mountains of Savoy.

In Flanders, in 1692, under Sarsfield and Lord Clare, the "New" Brigade won great honor at Steinkirk, where Luxemburg routed King William. At Landen, or Neerwinden, in July, 1693, William held his ground desperately against the bravest efforts of the French. Luxemburg was in despair, when the fierce war-cry, "Remember Limerick!" rent the clouds, and the Royal Irish Foot Guards, led by Colonel John Barrett, shattered the English centre, broke into Neerwinden, opened a path to victory for the French Household, and William was hurled into the river Gette, while the Irish shout of victory shook the plain like a clap of thunder. Sarsfield, like the brave Barrett, received his death wound, but his dying gaze beheld the sight he most loved to see—the English flag in sullen flight.

This same year, in Italy, under Catinat, the "Old" Brigade made its mark at Marsaglia, where it defeated the Savoyard centre, drew the whole French army after it, and chased Victor Amadeus almost to the gates of Turin.

Thenceforth, Lord Mountcashel having died of his wounds, the two brigades were united as one. The younger Schomberg, son of the hero of the Boyne, fell before the Irish bayonets at Marsaglia. At the battle of Montgry, in Spain, fought in 1694, by the French against the Spanish, the "Brigade," under Marshal de Noailles, renewed its laurels, and the Irish charge proved potent in bringing the Spaniards to terms.

This war terminated gloriously for France by the Peace of Ryswick.

The War of the Spanish Succession broke out in 1700. England and Austria supported the Archduke Charles against Philip of Anjou, the Bourbon heir. This struggle brought upon the stage the Duke of Marlborough, for England, and Prince Eugene, of Savoy, for Austria, two of the greatest generals of modern times. Marshals, the Duke of Berwick, Catinat, Villeroy, Vendome, Villars, Boufflers, and Noailles, commanded the armies of France. In this frightful struggle, the Irish flag always blazed in the vanguard of victory, in the rearguard of defeat, and the Irish name became the synonym of valor.

In the winter of 1702, the citadel of Cremona, in northern Italy, was held for France by Marshal Villeroy, with a strong garrison. The French gave themselves up to revelry, and the walls were poorly guarded. Caissioli, an Italian, informed Prince Eugene, the Austrian commander, of the state of affairs. The traitor agreed to let in a portion of the enemy by means of a sewer running from outside the walls under his house. At the same time the French sentinels at the gate of St. Margaret, badly defended, were to be drawn off, so that Eugene himself, with a strong body of cuirassiers, might enter and join the other party. Count Merci was to attack the "Gate of the Po," defended by an Irish company, and Prince Vaudemont and Count Freiberg were to support the attack with the cavalry of their respective commands. The attack was made at midnight, and the plans were admirably executed. The Austrians were in

possession of the town before the garrison was alarmed.
Count Merci, however, met bad fortune at the "Gate of
the Po." The Irish guard, chatting over old times by the
Shannon, the Barrow, or the Suir, kept faithful watch. The
clatter of hoofs aroused them, as Merci, attended by several
regiments of dragoons, rode up to the gate and called upon
them to surrender. The Irish replied with a sharp volley,
which laid some of the Austrians out in the roadway. The
fire aroused the sleeping Irish regiments of Dillon and
Burke, who, in their shirts only, as they sprang from
bivouac, grasped their muskets and hastened to the rescue.
They were met in the square by Eugene's cuirassiers, who
charged them fiercely. Major O'Mahoney formed his Irish
into a square and let the Austrians have a fusillade. The
cuirassiers, urged by Eugene and Freiberg, dashed madly
at the Irish battalions, but, despite the bravest efforts of this
iron cavalry, the Irish actually routed them and slew their
leader, Baron Freiberg. Marshal Villeroy was made prisoner by Macdonald, an Irishman in the Austrian service,
and the French general second in command shared the same
fate. But the Irish still held out, fighting desperately and
losing half their men. This prolonged resistance alarmed
the French, who now, thoroughly aroused, gallantly seconded their Irish comrades, and, after a terrible carnage of
eight hours' duration, Prince Eugene, with all that remained
of the flower of the Austrian cavalry, gave up in despair, and
was hurled pell-mell through the gates of St. Margaret, by
the victorious garrison. This exploit of the Irish saved
northern Italy to the French monarch—the Austrians retreated to the Alps. All Europe rang applause. Louis
raised the pay of his Irish troops, and made O'Mahoney
a general. He also decreed that Irishmen, who deserved

the honor, should thenceforth be recognized as French citizens, without undergoing the form of naturalization.

At the first battle of Blenheim, Bavaria, in 1703, the Irish, under Marshal Tallard, contributed to that victory. The regiment of Clare, encountering the Austrian guards, was, for a moment, overpowered, but, immediately rallying, it counter-charged with such fury that it not alone recovered its own flag, but gained two colors from the enemy!

The second Blenheim, so disastrous to France, was fought in 1704. Marlborough commanded the English right, facing Marshal Tallard, and Eugene commanded the allied left, facing Marshal de Marcin, with whom was the Irish Brigade. Tallard was dreadfully beaten, and Marcin fared little better. The French suffered great slaughter, and were badly worsted. The Brigade, however, would not lose heart. Closing up its ranks, it made a superb charge on Prince Eugene's lines, broke through them—being one of the few corps in the French army that saved their colors that day— and covered the retreat of France to the Rhine!

The English professor, E. S. Creasy of Cambridge University, writing of the conduct of the Irish in this great battle, says, on page 318 of his "Fifteen Decisive Battles of the World": "The [French] centre was composed of fourteen battalions of infantry, including the celebrated Irish Brigade. These were posted in the little hamlet of Oberglau, which lies somewhat nearer to Lutzingen than to Blenheim." And, on page 320 of the same work, the professor continues: "The Prince of Holstein Beck had, with eleven Hanoverian battalions, passed the Nebel opposite to Oberglau when he was charged and utterly routed by the Irish Brigade, which held that village. The Irish drove the Hanoverians back with heavy slaughter, broke completely through the line of

the allies, and nearly achieved a success as brilliant as that
which the same Brigade afterward gained at Fontenoy. But
at Blenheim their ardor in pursuit led them too far. Marlborough came up in person and dashed in on the exposed
flank of the Brigade with some squadrons of British cavalry.
The Irish reeled back, and, as they strove to regain the
heights of Oberglau, their column was raked through and
through by the fire of three battalions of the allies, which
Marlborough had summoned up from the reserve." Competent military critics have observed that had the French
cavalry seconded the charge of the Irish infantry, Blenheim
would have been a French victory.

CHAPTER V

The Irish Brigade in the Campaigns of North Italy and Flanders—
Its Strength at Various Periods—Count Dillon's Reply to
King Louis XV

IN the summer of 1705, the Irish again, at the battle of
Cassano, where they fought under Marshal Vendome,
paid their respects to Prince Eugene. They fought with a
bravery that electrified the French and paralyzed the Austrians. Vendome's flank was badly annoyed by a hostile battery on the farther bank of the river Adda. The stream was
broad and deep, but two Irish regiments, under cover of
the smoke, swam across it, and, under the very nose of the
great Eugene, captured the Austrian cannon and turned
their fire upon the enemy! This intrepid action decided
the day, and France was once more triumphant, by her
Irish arm.

Conspicuous in this brilliant action, as also at Cremona,
was the famous "Regiment of Burke"—the last to yield

at Aughrim. Of it the Scotch-Canadian poet and novelist,
William McLennan, has written:

"Would you read your name on honor's roll?
    Look not for royal grant—
It is written in Cassano,
    Alcoy and Alicant!
Saragossa, Barcelona,
    Wherever dangers lurk,
You will find in the van the blue and the buff
    Of the Regiment of Burke!
All Spain and France and Italy
    Have echoed to our name—
The burning suns of Africa
    Have set our arms aflame!
But to-night we toast the morn that broke and
    wakened us to fame—
The day we beat Prince Eugene in Cremona!"

Marshal Villeroy, in May, 1706, allowed himself to be
cooped up by the Duke of Marlborough in the village of
Ramillies, in Flanders. The French were utterly over-
whelmed, and many thousands of prisoners were taken.
Lord Clare formed the Brigade into a column of attack and
broke through the victorious enemy. The regiment of
Clare, in this charge, met the English regiment of Churchill
—now the Third Buffs—full tilt, crushed it hopelessly, captured its battle-flags, and served a Scotch regiment, in the
Dutch service, which endeavored to support the British, in
the same manner. The Brigade then effected its retreat on
Ypres, where, in the convent of the Benedictine nuns, it
hung up the captured colors — "sole trophies of Ramillies' fray"—where they have waved, for many a generation,
a fitting memento of the faith and fame of the Irish exiles.

In April, 1707, the Brigade next distinguished itself, at the
battle of Almanza, in Spain, where it fought in the army of

Marshal the Duke of Berwick. The English and Austrians were commanded by Ruvigny—the Williamite Earl of Galway—who signalized himself at Aughrim. The Brigade paid him back that day. It charged with a fury never excelled in any fight. The allies were ovethrown, Ruvigny disgraced, and the crown of Spain was placed on the brow of Philip V.

In defeat, as in victory, the bayonets of the Brigade still opened up the road to honor. When the French retreated from Oudenarde, in July, 1708, Marlborough felt the Irish steel, as the gallant fellows hung doggedly behind the retiring French, kept the fierce pursuers at bay, and enabled Vendome to reorganize his beaten army. The battle of Malplaquet, fought September, 1709, was the bloodiest of this most sanguinary war. The French fought with unusual desperation, and the English ranks, led by Marlborough and seconded by Eugene, were decimated. It was an unmitigated slaughter. At length Marshal Villairs, who commanded the French, was wounded and Marshal Boufflers ordered a retreat. Again the Irish Birgade, which fought with its usual courage all through that dreadful day, had the honor of forming the French rearguard, and, although many flags, captured from France, were laid at the feet of the victor, no Irish color graced the trophies of Marlborough, who, with the ill-judged battle of Malplaquet, virtually ended his grand career as a soldier. After that fight the war was feebly waged—France being completely exhausted—until the Peace of Utrecht and Treaty of Rastadt, 1713-14, closed the bloody record.

It would be almost impossible to enumerate the sieges and minor actions in which the Irish Brigade of France participated within the limits of this history. The facts we have given, and are to give, rest on the authority of the French war records, and the testimony of English and other writers, carefully compiled by Matthew O'Conor, in his "Military History of the Irish People," and by John C. O'Callaghan in his invaluable "History of the Irish Brigades"—works which should ensure for their able and careful authors a literary immortality, and which people of the Irish race should treasure among their most precious heirlooms. It would be equally difficult to follow the career of those Irish soldiers who, at the peace, transferred their swords from France to Spain, because Louis XV, who succeeded his grandfather while yet a child, could not employ them all. In Spain, as in France, their swords were sharpest where the English were their foes, always, it must be admitted, worthy of their steel.

The subjoined statement of the strength of the Irish forces in the French service during the seventeenth and eighteenth centuries is taken from the authorities already quoted:

From 1690 to 1692, three regiments of foot; 1692 to 1698, thirteen regiments of infantry, three independent companies, two companies of cavalry, and two troops of horse guards; 1698 to 1714, eight regiments of infantry and one regiment of horse; 1714 to 1744, five regiments of infantry and one of cavalry; 1744 to 1762, six regiments of infantry and one of horse; 1762 to 1775, five regiments of infantry; 1775 to 1791—the period of the dissolution of the Brigade—three regiments of foot.

From the fall of Limerick, in 1691, to the French Revolution, according to the most reliable estimate, there fell in the field for France, or otherwise died in her service, 480,000 Irish soldiers. The Brigade was kept recruited by military emigrants, borne from Ireland—chiefly from the province of Munster—by French smugglers, under the romantic and significant title of "Wild Geese"—in poetical allusion to their eastward flight. By this name the Brigade is best remembered among the Irish peasantry.

After the death of Louis XIV, the Irish Brigade had comparatively little wholesale fighting to keep them occupied, until the War of the Austrian Succession, thirty years later. They made many expeditions to the smaller states on the Rhenish frontier, with which France was in a chronic state of war, under the Duke of Berwick. In every combat they served with honor, and always appeared to best advantage where the hail of death fell thickest. At times, like most of their countrymen, they were inclined to wildness, but the first drum-roll or bugle blast found them ready for the fray. On the march to attack Fort Kehl, in 1733, Marshal Berwick—who was killed two years afterward at the siege of Philipsburg—found fault with Dillon's regiment for some breach of discipline while en route. He sent the colonel with despatches to Louis XV, and, among other matters, in a paternal way—for Berwick loved his Irishmen—called the king's attention to the indiscreet battalion. The monarch, on reading the document, turned to the Irish officer, and, in the hearing of the whole court, petulantly exclaimed: "My Irish troops cause me more uneasiness than all the rest of my armies!" "Sire," immediately rejoined the noble Count Dillon—subsequently killed at Fontenoy—"all your Majesty's enemies make precisely the same complaint." Louis, pleased with the repartee, smiled, and, like a true Frenchman, wiped out his previous unkindness by complimenting the courage of the Brigade.

The great War of the Austrian Succession inaugurated the fateful campaigns of 1743 and 1745, respectively signalized by the battles of Dettingen and Fontenoy. The former was a day of dark disaster to France, and Fontenoy was a mortal blow to British arrogance.

At Dettingen the Earl of Stair commanded the English and Hanoverians, although George II and his son, Cumberland, were present on the field. Marshal de Noailles commanded the French, and was badly worsted, after a desperate engagement. The Irish Brigade, summoned from a long distance, arrived too late to restore the battle, and met the French army in full retreat, hotly pursued by the allies. The Brigade, under the orders of Lord Clare, opened their ranks and allowed the French to retire, and then, closing steadily up, they uttered their charging cry, and, with leveled bayonet, checked the fierce pursuers. Thus, once again, the Irish Brigade formed the French rearguard, as the Fleur-de-Lis retired from the plains of Germany.

CHAPTER VI

The Austrian Succession—Campaign of 1745—Magnificent Achievement of the Irish Brigade at Fontenoy—Prince Louis's Adieu to the Heroes

THE famous battle of Fontenoy was fought on the soil of Belgium, in the ancient province of Hainault, within some thirty miles of the memorable plains of Waterloo, on May 11, new style, 1745. France, as we have already noted, championed the cause of Charles of Bavaria, who laid claim to the Austrian throne, while England, Holland, Hanover, and Austria took the side of Maria Theresa, who eventually, owing to the unexpected death of Charles, won the fiercely disputed crown.

The French were besieging Tournay with 18,000 men. A corps of 6,000 guarded the bridges over the Scheldt, on the northern bank of which Marshal Saxe, accompanied by Louis XV and the Dauphin, having with him 45,000 men, including the Irish Brigade, took post, to cover the siege of Tournay, and prevent the march of the allies, English, Dutch, and Germans, under the Duke of Cumberland and Prince Waldeck, to its relief. The duke was a brave soldier, but fierce and cruel as a tiger. History knows him by the well-won title of "the butcher Cumberland." His business was to raise the siege of Tournay and open a road to Paris. He had under his command 55,000 veteran troops, including the English Household regiments.

The French lines extended from the village of Rhamecroix, behind De Barri's Wood, on the left, to the village of Fontenoy, in the centre, and from the latter position to

the intrenchments of Antoine, on the right.   This line of
defence was admirably guarded by "fort and flanking battery."   The Irish Brigade—composed that day of the infantry regiments of Clare, Dillon, Bulkeley, Roth, Berwick, and Lally—Fitz-James's horse being with the French
cavalry in advance—was stationed, in reserve, near the
wood, supported by the brigades of Normandie and De Vassieux.

Prince Waldeck commanded the allied left, in front of
Antoine.   Brigadier Ingoldsby commanded the British
right, facing the French redoubt at De Barri's Wood, while
Cumberland, chief in command, was with the allied centre,
confronting Fontenoy.

The battle opened with a furious cannonade, at 5 o'clock
in the morning.   After some hours spent in this manner,
Ingoldsby attempted to carry the redoubt, but was ignominiously repulsed, and could not be induced to renew the
attempt.   This refusal subsequently led to his dismissal
from the army on a charge of cowardice.   Prince Waldeck
fared no better at Antoine, being defeated in two attempts
to force the lines.   The Duke of Cumberland, grown impatient because of repeated failures, loaded the unfortunate
commanding officers with imprecations.   He took the resolve of beating the French at any cost by a concentrated
attack on their left centre, through a gap of about 700
yards, which occurred between the Fontenoy redoubts and
the work vainly attacked by Ingoldsby in the edge of the
wood of Barri.   For this purpose, he formed his reserves
and least battered active battalions, including the English
guards, several British line regiments, and a large body of
picked Hanoverian troops, into three columns, aggregating
16,000 men, preceded and flanked by twenty pieces of can-

non, all drawn by hand, to avoid the confusion incident on the killing and wounding of the battery horses. But subsequent developments compelled the Duke to change the original formation to one massive, solid oblong wedge, the British on the right and the Hanoverians on the left. Lord Charles Hay, the boldest soldier in the allied army, drew his sword and led the attacking column. Meanwhile, Cumberland renewed the attack all along the line, in order to cover the advance of his human battering-ram. Thus, the French were pressed hard at every point, but their batteries and battalions replied with spirit, and Antoine held out heroically in spite of all the efforts of Waldeck and his Dutch and Austrian troops against it. These latter were badly cut up by the fire of a French battery planted beyond the Scheldt. Up to this period, about the noon hour, everything had gone favorably for the French.

But the decisive moment had now arrived, and the great Anglo-Hanoverian column received the command—"Forward, march!" "In front of them, as it chanced," says Mitchel, "were four battalions of the French guards, with two battalions of Swiss on their left and two other French regiments on their right. The French officers seem to have been greatly surprised when they saw the English battery taking up position on the summit of the rising ground. 'English cannon!' they cried. 'Let us go and take them!' They mounted the slope with their grenadiers, but were astonished to find an army on their front. A heavy discharge, both of artillery and musketry, made them quickly recoil with heavy loss." On, then, swept the English column, with free and gallant stride, between Fontenoy and De Barri's wood, whose batteries plowed them from flank to flank at every step. But in the teeth of the artillery, the musketry and the bomb-shells which rose, circled and fell among them, killing and wounding scores at each explosion; charged by the cavalry of the royal household, and exposed to the iron hail of the French sharpshooters, that blue-and-scarlet wave of battle rolled proudly against the serried ranks of France. Falling by the hundred, they finally got beyond the cross-fire from the redoubts, crossed the slope and penetrated behind the village of Fontenoy—marching straight on the headquarters of the king! The column was quickly in the middle of the picked soldiers of France, tossing them haughtily aside with the ready bayonet, while the cheers of anticipated victory resounded from their ranks far over the bloody field. Marshal Saxe, ill, and pale with rage and vexation, sprang, unarmored, upon his horse, and seemed to think the battle lost, for he ordered the evacuation of Antoine, in order that the bridges across the Scheldt might be covered and the king's escape assured. At this moment, Count Lally, of the Irish Brigade, rode up to Duke Richelieu, Saxe's chief aide, and said to him: "We have still four field-pieces in reserve—they should batter the head of that column. The Irish Brigade has not yet been engaged. Order it to fall on the English flank. Let the whole army second it—let us fall on the English like foragers!" Richelieu, who, afterward, allowed the suggestion to appear as if coming from himself, went at once to Saxe and gave him the substance of Lally's proposal. The king and Dauphin, who were present, approved of it. The order to evacuate Antoine was countermanded, and aides immediately galloped to the rear of the wood of Barri to order up the Irish Brigade, commanded by Lord Clare, and its supporting regiments. These brave men, rendered excited and impatient by the noise of the battle, in which they had not yet been allowed to participate, received the command with loud demonstrations of joy. Their officers immediately led them toward the point of danger.

Meanwhile, the English column, marching and firing steadily—that "infernal, rolling fire," so characteristic of the British mode of fighting—kept on its terrible course, and crushed every French organization that stood in its path. Had the Dutch and Austrians succeeded in carrying Antoine at this moment, Cumberland must have been victorious and the French army could not have escaped. Already the column, still bleeding at every stride, was within sight of the royal tent. The English officers actually laid their canes along the barrels of the muskets to make the men fire low. Suddenly, the fire from the four reserve French cannon opened on the head of the column, and the foremost files went down. The English guns replied stoutly and the march was renewed. But now there came an ominous sound from the side of De Barri's wood that made Lord Hay, brave and bold as he was, start, pause, and listen. It swelled above the crash of artillery and the continuous rattle of musketry. "Nearer, clearer, deadlier than before," that fierce hurrah bursts upon the ear of battle! The English have heard that shout before and remember it to their cost. The crisis of the conflict has come, and the command, by voice and bugle, "Halt! halt!" rang from front to rear of the bleeding column. The ranks were dressed hastily, and the English prepared to meet the advancing enemy with a deadly volley from their front and long right flank. They looked anxiously in the direction of the wood and beheld long lines and bristling columns of men in blue and red— the uniform of the Irish Brigade—coming on at the charg-

ing step, with colors flying and "the generals and colonels
on horseback among the glittering bayonets." They did
not fire a single shot as they came on. Behind them were
masses of men in blue and white. These were the French
supports. Again the British officers laid their canes
across the barrels of the muskets, and, as the Brigade came within close range, a murderous volley
rolled out. Hundreds of the Irish fell, but the survivors,
leaping over the dead, dying, and wounded, never paused for
a moment. They closed the wide gaps in their ranks and
advanced at a run until they came within bayonet thrust or
butt-stroke of the front and right of the English column,
which they immediately crushed out of military shape; while
their fierce war-shout, uttered in the Irish tongue—"Revenge! Remember Limerick and English treachery!"
sounded the death-knell of Cumberland's heroic soldiers.
While the clubbed muskets of the Brigade beat down the English ranks, that furious war-cry rang even unto the walls
of old Tournay. The French regiments of Normandie and
Vassieux bravely seconded the Irish charge, and they and
other Gallic troops disposed of the Hanoverians. Within
ten minutes from the time when the Brigade came in contact with the English column, no British soldiers, except the
dead, wounded, and captured, remained on the slope of Fontenoy. Bulkeley's Irish regiment nearly annihilated the
Coldstream Guards and captured their colors.

This victory saved France from invasion, but it cost the
Irish dear. Count Dillon was slain, Lord Clare disabled,
while one-third of the officers and one-fourth of the men
were killed or wounded. King Louis, next morning, publicly thanked the Irish, made Lally a general, and Lord Clare
was, soon afterward, created a marshal of France. Eng-

land met retribution for her cruelty and faithlessness to Ireland, and King George vehemently cursed the laws which drove the Irish exiles to win glory and vengeance on that bloody day.

The losses in the battle were nearly equal—the French, Swiss, and Irish losing altogether 7,139 men killed, wounded, and missing; while the English, Hanoverians, Dutch, and Austrians acknowledged a total loss of 7,767 men, said by O'Callaghan to be an underestimate. Fontenoy was one of the greatest of French victories, and led, in the same campaign, to numerous other successes. Among the latter may be enumerated the triumph at Melle, the surprise of Ghent, the occupation of Bruges, and the capture of Oudenarde, Dendermonde, Ostend, Nieuport, and Ath.

Several officers of the Irish Brigade went with Prince Charles Edward Stuart to Scotland, when he made his gallant but ill-fated attempt to restore the fallen fortunes of his luckless father, called by the Jacobites James VIII of Scotland and James III of England and Ireland, in 1745-46. The Hanoverian interest called James the "Old" and Charles Edward the "Young" Pretender. The Irish officers formed "Prince Charles's" chosen bodyguard when he was a fugitive amid the Highlands and Western Isles after Culloden. One of the last great field exploits of the Irish Brigade was its victorious charge at Laffeldt, in Flanders, in 1747, when, for the second time, it humiliated Cumberland, and, in a measure, avenged his base massacre of the gallant Scottish Highland clans, in 1746. The victory of Laffeldt led to the Peace of Aix-la-Chapelle, which was favorable to France, in 1748. The Brigade took part in each succeeding war in which France was involved down to the period of the Revolution. Some of its regiments served also in

India and America. Under Count Dillon, several Irish battalions distinguished themselves in the dashing, but unsuccessful, attack on the British at Savannah, Ga., in 1779, when the brave Count Pulaski, who led the assault, was killed on the ramparts. By that time, however, the volume of recruits from Ireland had greatly diminished, owing to the gradual relaxation of the penal code, and a majority of the officers and soldiers of the Brigade were, although of Irish blood, French by birth. Some of the officers were French by both birth and blood, and, among them, in 1791, was the great-grandson of St. Ruth. The Brigade, as became it, remained faithful to the last to the Bourbon dynasty. Unfortunately this fidelity led the feeble remnant, under Colonel O'Connell, to take service in the West Indies, beneath the British flag, after the Revolution. In extenuation of their fault, it must be remembered that they were, to a man, monarchists; that the Stuart cause was hopelessly lost, and that both tradition and education made them the inevitable enemies of the new order of things in France. Still, an Irish historian may be pardoned for remarking that it were much better for the fame of the Brigade of Cremona and Fontenoy if its senile heir-at-law had refrained from accepting the pay of the country whose tyranny had driven the original organization into hopeless exile.

But the active career of the bold Brigade terminated in a blaze of glory. The hand of a prince, destined to be a monarch, inscribed its proud epitaph when, in 1792, the Comte de Provence, afterward Louis XVIII, presented to the surviving officers a drapeau d'adieu, or flag of farewell—a gold harp wreathed with shamrocks and fleur-de-lis, on a white ground, with the following touching words:

"Gentlemen: We acknowledge the inappreciable services that France has received from the Irish Brigade in the course of the last hundred years—services that we shall never forget, though under an impossibility of requiting them. Receive this standard as a pledge of our remembrance, a monument of our admiration and our respect, and, in future, generous Irishmen, this shall be the motto of your stainless flag—

"'1692-1792.'

"Semper et Ubique Fidelis!

("Ever, and everywhere, faithful.")

Never did military body receive a nobler discharge from service.

And yet, well might the haughty Bourbon prince so express himself. In defence of his house, there died beneath the golden lilies, in camp and breach and field, nearly 500,000 of Ireland's daring manhood. It is no wonder that with those heroes departed much of her warlike spirit and springing courage. Her "wild geese," as she fondly called them, will never fly again to her bosom across the waves that aided their flight to exile and to glory. The cannon of all Europe pealed above their gory graves, on many a stricken field, the soldier's requiem.

> "They fought as they reveled, fast, fiery, and true,
> And, tho' victors, they left on the field not a few;
> And they who survived fought and drank as of yore,
> But the land of their hearts' hope they saw nevermore:
> For, in far foreign fields, from Dunkirk to Belgrade,
> Lie the soldiers and chiefs of the Irish Brigade!"

Its successor in the French army was the Irish Legion, composed in the main of refugees who had participated in the "rebellion" of 1798 and the "rising" of 1803. This fine body of soldiers was organized by Napoleon himself, wore a distinctively Irish uniform of green and gold, and carried French and Irish colors. To it, also, was intrusted an eagle—the only foreign force that was so honored by the greatest of generals. The Legion fought for the Emperor, with splendid fidelity, from 1805 to 1815, participating in most of the great battles of that warlike period.

It was naturally expected that Louis XVIII, on his final restoration to the throne, would revive the old Irish Brigade, so highly praised by him, when Comte de Provence, in 1792, but he was under too many obligations to England, and, in fact, his treaty with that power, after the second exile of Napoleon, made it obligatory on him not to accept an Irish military contingent under any consideration. His acquiescence in this ignoble compact makes more emphatic the venerable adage, "Put not your trust in Princes."

BOOK VII

NARRATING THE MANY PENAL STATUTES AGAINST THE
CATHOLICS, AND CARRYING THE STORY DOWN TO THE
ACQUIREMENT OF A FREE COMMERCE BY THE IRISH PAR-
LIAMENT, UNDER THE LEADERSHIP OF GRATTAN, A.D. 1780

Anti-Catholic Penal Laws—Their Drastic, Brutal and Absurd Provisions—Professional Informers, Called "Priest-Hunters"

WE now approach a period of Irish history from which we would gladly escape, if we could; a period degrading to Ireland, disgraceful to England, and shocking to humanity. We are about to deal with the dark and bloody period of the revived penal code, in Ireland, following fast upon the capitulation of Limerick. Many writers have extolled the fair-mindedness and liberality of William III, but his course toward Ireland does not sustain the justice of their eulogies. That he was an indifferentist in matters of religion is not doubted, yet he permitted persecution for conscience' sake in his Irish dominion. That he was an able man has not been disputed, yet he permitted English jealousy to destroy the trade and industries of his own supporters in Ireland, thereby driving thousands on thousands of the Irish dissenters to the American colonies, which their descendants, in 1775-83, did so much to make "free and independent." We can find nothing to admire in the Irish policy of William III. Had he been an honest bigot, a fanatic on the subject of religion, we could understand his toleration of the legislative abominations which made the Irish Catholic a helot on his native soil. Had he been an imbecile we could understand how English plausibility might have imposed upon him in the matter of Irish Protestant commerce. However, not much of moral stamina could be expected from a man who estranged his wife and his sister-in-law, Anne, from their own father; or from a nephew, and son-in-law, that did not scruple to play the cuckoo and eject his own uncle and father-in-law from the royal nest of England. Add to this his heartless policy toward the Macdonalds of Glencoe, in Scotland, the order for whose massacre he countersigned himself, and we find ourselves utterly unable to give William of Orange credit for sincerity, liberality, or common humanity. He was personally courageous, a fair general, and a cautious statesman. These about summed up his good qualities. But he interposed no objection when, notwithstanding the solemn civil articles of Limerick, he permitted the estates of the adherents of King James, to whom his Lords Justices, by royal sanction, guaranteed immunity, to be confiscated.

Mitchel, a Protestant in belief, says in his "History of Ireland," page 3: "The first distinct breach of the Articles of Limerick was perpetrated by King William and his Parliament in England, just two months after those articles were signed. King William was in the Netherlands when he heard of the surrender of Limerick, and, at once, hastened to London. Three days later he summoned a Parliament. Very early in the session, the English House of Commons, exercising its customary power of binding Ireland by acts passed in London, sent up to the House of Lords a bill providing that no person should sit in the Irish Parliament, nor should hold any Irish office, civil, military, or ecclesiastical, nor should practice law or medicine in Ireland, till he had first taken the oaths of allegiance *and supremacy,* and subscribed to the declaration against transubstantiation. The law was passed, only reserving the right [of practice] to such lawyers and physicians as had been within the walls of Galway and Limerick when those towns capitulated."

Thenceforward there were repeated violations of the treaty, during the reign of William and Mary, although the penal laws did not reach the acme of their crushing severity until the reigns of their immediate successors, Queen Anne, George I, and George II. Lord Macaulay himself, who does not admit that William III was ever wrong, acknowledges, in his "History of England," that "the Irish Roman Catholics complained, and with but too much reason, that, at a later period, the Treaty of Limerick was violated." The main opposition to the confirmation of the treaty came, as might be expected, from the party of Protestant ascendency in Ireland, which had in view "the glory of God," and wholesale confiscation of Catholic property. Their horror of what they called "Popery" was strongly influenced by a pious greed for cheap real estate. There were, of course, many noble exceptions to this mercenary rule among the Protestants of Ireland, even in the blackest period of "the penal days." If there had not been, the Catholics must have been exterminated. It is only fair to say that the majority of the poorer Protestant Irish—particularly the Dissenters—had little or no part in framing the penal code, and that many members of the Irish House of Lords, including Protestant bishops, indignantly protested against the formal violation of the Articles of Limerick, contained in the act of the "Irish" Parliament, passed in 1695.

Lord Sydney, William's Lord Lieutenant in Ireland, summoned the first Irish Parliament of his master's reign, in 1692, and this was the only Parliament, except that called together by King James in 1689, which had met in Ireland in six-and-twenty years. No act of Catholic disqualification for Parliament existed in Ireland at that time, and, therefore, a few Catholic lords and commoners presented themselves, on summons, and took their seats. They had forgotten that the "paternal" English Parliament had, in 1691, provided for such an emergency, and were taken aback when the clerks of Parliament presented to them "the oath of supremacy, declaring the King of England to be head of the Church, and affirming the sacrifice of the Mass to be damnable." Mitchel says, further, of what followed: "The oath was put to each member of both Houses, and the few Catholics present at once retired, so that the Parliament, when it proceeded to business, was purely Protestant. Here, then, ended the last vestige of constitutional right for the Catholics; from this date, and for generations to come, they could no longer consider themselves a part of the existing body politic of their native land, and the division [of the Irish] into two nations became definite. There was the dominant nation, consisting of the British colony, and the subject nation, consisting of five-sixths of the population, who had, therefore, no more influence upon public affairs than have the red Indians of the United States." In order to more fully reduce the Catholics of Ireland to the condition described, an act was passed by the Irish Parliament in 1697 which provided that "a Protestant marrying a Catholic was disabled from sitting or voting in either House of Parliament." We may add that, following up this policy, the same Parliament, thirty years later, fearing that the Catholics were not even yet sufficiently effaced from political life, passed another bill by which it was enacted that "no Catholic shall be entitled, or admitted, to vote at the election of any member to serve in Parliament, as a knight, citizen, or burgess; or at the election of any magistrate for any city or other town corporate; any law, statute, or usage to the contrary notwithstanding."

Mitchel, commenting on the severity of the penal laws, presents a curiously contradictory situation in the Ireland of King William's time when he says: "But though the inhabitants of Ireland were now, counting from 1692, definitively divided into two castes, there arose immediately, strange to say, a strong sentiment of Irish nationality—not, indeed, among the depressed Catholics; they were done with national sentiment and aspiration for a time—but the Protestants of Ireland had lately grown numerous, wealthy, and strong. Their numbers had been largely increased by English settlers coming to enjoy the plunder of the forfeited estates, and very much by conversions, or pretended conversions, of Catholics, who had recanted their faith to save their property or their position in society, and who generally altered or disguised their family names when these had too Celtic a sound. The Irish Protestants also prided themselves on having saved the kingdom for William and the 'Ascendancy,' and having now totally put down the ancient nation under their feet, they aspired to take its place, to rise from a colony to a nation, and to assert the dignity of an independent kingdom."

Even the Irish Protestant Parliament of 1692 quarreled with Lord Lieutenant Sydney over a revenue bill, which originated in London, and which it rejected, although it passed another bill, having a like origin, on the ground of emergency. During the debate on these measures, several members denied the right of England to tax Ireland without her consent, and insisted that all revenue bills, which called for Irish taxation, should originate in Ireland, not in England. This bold spirit angered Lord Sydney, who immediately prorogued that Parliament, not, however, before he made an overbearing speech, in which he rebuked the action of the members and haughtily asserted the supremacy of the British Parliament over that of Ireland. His remarks left a sting in Protestant Ireland and served to strengthen, rather than weaken, the national sentiment alluded to by Mitchel.

In 1693, King James the Vacillating, then a pensioner of the King of France, at St. Germain, issued a declaration to his former subjects of England in which he made humiliating promises, at variance with his previous record, and in which, among other things, he promised if restored to the throne to keep inviolate the Act of Settlement, which deprived his Catholic supporters in Ireland of their estates! This perfidious document aroused great indignation among the Irish military exiles, and James, through his English advisers in France, attempted to smooth matters over by promising that, in the event of his success, he would recompense all who might suffer by his act, by giving them equivalents. Lord Middleton, a Scotch peer, is held chiefly responsible for having led King James into this disgraceful transaction—the most blameful of his unfortunate career. "There was no such promise [of recompense] in the declaration" (to the English), says the historian recently quoted, "but, in truth, the Irish troops in the army of King Louis were, at that time, too busy in camp and field, and too keenly desirous to meet the English in battle, to pay much attention to anything coming from King James. They had had enough of 'Righ Seamus' at the Boyne Water."

Lord Sydney, although inimical to the claim of Irish Parliamentary independence, was rather friendly to the persecuted Irish Catholics, and was, therefore, at the request of the "Ascendancy" faction, speedily recalled, not, however, before, after two proroguements, he had dissolved the Par-

liament convened in 1692.   Three Lords Justices—Lord
Capel, Sir Cyril Wyche, and Mr. Duncombe—were given the
government of Ireland in his stead, but, owing to serious dissensions among themselves, Capel was finally appointed Lord
Lieutenant, and, in 1695, summoned a new Parliament to
meet in Dublin.   This assembly was destined to be infamous.
Its first act was to bring up the articles of the Treaty of Limerick for "confirmation," and it "confirmed" them by vetoing all the important and agreeing to all the trivial provisions.   The enumeration of all the penal laws passed by
this Parliament would be tedious in the extreme, and a
bare outline will suffice to show their demoralizing tendency :
It was enacted that Catholic schoolmasters were forbidden
to teach, either publicly or privately, under severe penalty;
and the parents of Catholic children were prohibited from
sending them to be educated abroad.   All Catholics were required to surrender their arms, and, in order to enforce the
act more thoroughly, "right of search" was given to magis-
trates, so that Catholic householders could be disturbed at
any hour of the day or night, their bedrooms invaded, and
the women of their family subjected to exposure and insult.

   Notwithstanding the clause in the Treaty of Limerick
which was supposed to secure the Catholic landholders in
certain counties in the possession of their property, Parliament made a clean sweep by confiscating the property of all,
to the extent of over a million acres, so that now, at long
run, after three series of confiscations, there remained in
Catholic hands *less than one-seventh* of the entire surface
of the island.   The Protestant one-sixth owned all the
rest.

   It was agreed not to seriously disturb the parish priests,
who were incumbents at the time of the treaty, but no

curates were allowed them, and they were compelled to register their names, like ticket-of-leave men, in a book furnished by government. They had, also, to give security for their "good conduct," and there were other insulting exactions—the emanation of bitter hearts and narrow brains. All Catholic prelates, the Jesuits, monks, and "regular clergy," of whatever order, were peremptorily ordered to quit Ireland by May 1, 1698. If any returned after that date, they were to be arrested for high treason, "tried," and, of course, condemned and executed. The object was to leave the Catholic people without spiritual guides, except Protestants, after the "tolerated" parish priests had passed away; but, in spite of the penal enactment, a large number of devoted proscribed bishops and priests remained in Ireland, and the prelates administered holy orders to young clerical students, who, like themselves, had defied penalties and risked their lives for the service of God and the consolation of their suffering people.

In order to still further humiliate the unfortunate Irish Catholics, this Parliament of bigots decreed that no Catholic chapel should be furnished with either bell or belfry. Such smallness would seem incredible in our age, but the enactments stand out, in all their hideousness, in the old statutes of the Irish Parliament, still preserved in the government archives in Dublin and London. It was this Parliament that decreed, further, that no Catholic could possess a horse of or over the value of £5 sterling. On offering that sum, or anything over it, any Protestant could become owner of the animal.

The Irish peers who protested against this tyranny were Lords Londonderry, Tyrone, and Duncannon, the Barons Ossory, Limerick, Killaloe, Kerry, Howth, Kingston, and

Strabane, and the Protestant bishops of Kildare, Elphin, Derry, Clonfert, and Killala—to whom be eternal honor.

But the penal laws were not yet completed. They had just about begun. In 1704, when the Duke of Ormond, grandson of the Ormond of Cromwellian days, became viceroy for Queen Anne, another Irish Ascendancy Parliament enacted, among other things, that the eldest son of a Catholic, by becoming Protestant, could become the owner of his father's land, if he possessed any, and the father become only a life tenant. If any child, of any age above infancy, declared itself a Protestant, it was ordered placed under Protestant guardianship, and the father was compelled to pay for its education and support. If the wife of a Catholic turned Protestant, she could claim a third of his property and separate maintenance. Catholics were prohibited from being guardians of their own children, to the end that, when they died, the helpless ones might be brought up as Protestants.

Catholics were debarred from buying land, or taking a freehold lease for life, or a for a longer period than thirty-one years. No Catholic heir to a former owner was allowed to accept property that came to him by right of lineal descent, or by process of bequest. If any Protestant could prove that the profit on the farm of a Catholic exceeded one-third of the rent paid by the latter, the informer could take immediate possession of the land.

We have already alluded to the measures taken to exclude Catholics from civil and military service, by operation of the odious test oaths, which were also used to prevent them from entering Parliament, and from even voting for members of Parliament, although the latter had to be Protestants in order to be eligible. The Irish Dissenters—

Presbyterians and others—were also subjected to the test-oath indignity, which, together with the tyrannical restrictions on trade, imposed by the English and servile Irish Parliament, drove many thousands of them to America. The Irish Presbyterians, in particular, resented the "test" and "schism" acts, and refused to apply to Episcopal bishops for license to teach in schools; or to receive the sacrament after the fashion of the Church of England. Rewards were held out for all who would reveal to the government the names of Catholics, or others, who might violate the provisions of the barbaric laws summarized in this chapter. The scale of the rewards, as given by McGee and other authors, is a curious study. Thus, "for discovering an archbishop, bishop, vicar-general, or other person exercising any foreign ecclesiastical jurisdiction, £50; for discovering each 'regular' clergyman and each 'secular' clergyman, not registered, £20, and for discovering each 'Popish' schoolmaster, or usher, £10." If any person refused to give evidence of the residence of any proscribed person, he was fined £20, or else had to go to prison for a year. Many noble-hearted Protestants who, in spite of penal laws, loved their Catholic fellow-countrymen, suffered pains and penalties, under these enactments, and became objects of hatred to the more malignant section of their co-religionists, who were after the Catholic spoils. Thus, public distrust became epidemic, and the infamous "reward" policy begot, as a natural result, a host of professional informers, whose shocking avocation was mainly exercised in the spying out of the places of concealment of proscribed prelates and priests, and who are still remembered in Ireland as "priesthunters." These malignants also directed their efforts vigorously against the teachers of "hedge-schools"—that is to say, schools held in the open air, generally under the shelter of a tall hedge, or on the edge of a wood, and presided over by some wandering schoolmaster, who bravely risked liberty, and often life, in teaching the Catholic youth of Ireland the rudiments of education.

There existed a mean "toleration" of Catholic worship, in parishes whose priests were "registered," according to the provisions of the penal code, but, in parishes where the priests were not registered, and they were numerous, priests and people, who wished to celebrate and assist at the consoling sacrifice of the Mass, had to retire to ocean cave, or mountain summit, or rocky gorge, in order to guard against surprise and massacre. The English government of the day did not scruple to lend its soldiers to the priest-hunters, to enable the latter to more effectively accomplish their odious mission; just as in our day it has lent the military to the sheriffs to carry out those cruel evictions which the late Mr. Gladstone called "sentences of death." It was the custom to place sentinels around the places where Mass was being celebrated, but, despite of this precaution, the human sleuthhounds occasionally crept unobserved upon their unarmed victims—for then, as now, the Irish were systematically disarmed—and often slew priest and people at the rude altar stones, called still by the peasantry "Mass rocks."

So great was the enforced exodus of priests from Ireland, at this awful period of its history, that, says McGee, "in Rome 72,000 francs annually were allotted for the maintenance of the fugitive Irish clergy, and, during the first three months of 1699, three remittances from the Holy Father, amounting to 90,000 livres, were placed in the hands of the Nuncio at Paris for the temporary relief of the fugitives in France and Flanders. It may also be added here that, till the end of the eighteenth century, an annual charge of 1,000 crowns was borne by the Papal treasury for the encouragement of Catholic poor schools in Ireland."

Of the penal code which produced this dreadful condition of affairs, in and out of Ireland, Dr. Samuel Johnson, the great English scholar and philosopher, said, "They are more grievous than all the Ten Pagan persecutions of the Christians."

Edmund Burke, the illustrious Irish statesman, who passed most of his career in the British Parliament, and was, of course, a Protestant, or he could not have sat there, denounced them, substantially, as the most diabolical engine of oppression and demoralization ever used against a people or ever devised by "the perverted ingenuity of man."

And the Protestant and English historian, Godkin, who compiled Cassell's "History of Ireland," for English readers, says of the penal laws: "The eighteenth century was the era of persecution in which the law did the work of the sword, more effectually and more safely. There was established a code framed with almost diabolical ingenuity, to extinguish natural affection, to foster perfidy and hypocrisy, to petrify conscience, to perpetuate brutal ignorance, to facilitate the work of tyranny, by rendering the vices of slavery inherent and natural in the Irish character, and to make Protestantism almost irredeemably odious as the monstrous incarnation of all moral perversions." This honest Englishman grows indignant when he says, in continuation, "Too well did it accomplish its deadly work on the intellects, morals, and physical condition of a people, sinking in degeneracy from age to age, till all manly spirit, all virtuous sense of personal independence and responsibility, was nearly extinct, and the very features, vacant, timid, cunning, and unreflective, betrayed the crouching slave within . . . . Having no rights or franchises, no legal protection of life and property, disqualified to handle a gun, even as a common soldier or a gamekeeper, forbidden to acquire the elements of knowledge at home or abroad, forbidden even to render to God what conscience dictated as His due, what could the Irish be but abject serfs? What nation in their circumstances could have been otherwise? Is it not amazing that any social virtue could have survived such an ordeal?—that any seeds of good, any roots of national greatness, could have outlived such a long and tempestuous winter?"

But the seeds of good, although chilled, did not decay, and the manly spirit of the Old Irish race—the Celto-Norman stock, with the former element in preponderance—survived all its persecutions, and

> "—Exiled in those penal days,
> Its banners over Europe blaze!"

The great American orator and philanthropist, Wendell Phillips, lecturing on Ireland, and alluding to the enforced ignorance of a former period, said: "When the old-time ignorance of the Catholic Irish people is reproachfully alluded to by the thoughtless, or illiberal, it is not Ireland but England that should bow her head in the dust and put on sackcloth and ashes!"

CHAPTER II

Restrictions on Irish Trade and Manufactures—All Creeds Suffer—
Presbyterian Exodus to America—Death of Royal Personages
—Accession of George I

SINCE the days of Charles II, and probably before his reign, a contemptible jealousy of the growth of Irish commerce had taken possession of the commercial element in England. We have already said something about the crushing of the Irish cattle trade, while yet the "Merry Monarch" was on the throne; but a far deadlier blow was struck at Irish prosperity when, in 1698, the English manufacturers had the assurance to petition Parliament against the Irish woolen industry—then among the most prosperous in Europe. This petition was strongly indorsed by the English House of Lords, in an address to King William, wherein they, unconsciously, perhaps, paid a high tribute to Irish manufacturing genius. They virtually admitted that the superiority of Irish woolen fabrics made the English traders apprehensive that the farther growth of the Irish woolen industry "might greatly prejudice the said manufacture in his Majesty's Kingdom of England." Not content with this display of mean selfishness, the English fisheries' interest protested against Irish fishermen catching herrings on the eastern coast of their own island, "thereby coming into competition with them [the English]." The Colonial Parliament of Ireland basely yielded to English coercion, and, in 1699, actually stabbed the industries of their own country in the back, by placing ruinous export duties on fine Irish woolens, friezes, and flannels! And this hostile legislation was aimed, not against the Catholic Irish, who had no industries, but against the Protestant Irish, who possessed all of them!

The English Parliament, thus secured against effective opposition, immediately passed an act whereby the Irish people were forbidden to export either the raw material for making woolen goods, or the goods themselves, to any foreign port, except a few English ports, and only six of the numerous Irish seaports were allowed even this poor privilege. The natural result followed. Irish prices went up in England, and, in spite of the acknowledged excellence of Irish manufactures, the English people would not purchase them at an advanced cost. The Irish traders could not afford to sell them at a moderate price, and, within a few years, most of the latter were absolutely ruined. Dr. P. W. Joyce, in his "History of Ireland," estimates that "40,000 Irish Protestants—all prosperous working people —were immediately reduced to idleness and poverty—the Catholics, of course, sharing in the misery, so far as they were employed, and 20,000 Presbyterians and other Nonconformists left Ireland for New England. Then began the emigration, from want of employment, that continues to this day. But the English Parliament professed to encourage the Irish linen trade, for this could do no harm to English traders, as flax growing and linen manufacture had not taken much hold in England."

This, according to Dr. Joyce, was the beginning of that smuggling trade with France which Ireland carried on for more than a century, and a close acquaintance, therefore, sprang up between the French and Irish traders and sailors. Ireland could sell her surplus wool to great advantage in France, and received from that country many luxuries, which, otherwise, she could not have enjoyed. French wines became common at Irish tables, above those of the working-class, and French silks decorated the fair persons of Irish maids and matrons. Moreover, this adventurous trade developed a hardy race of Irish sailors, and, by means of the Irish smugglers and their French copartners, the Irish priests found a convenient avenue of transit to and from the Continent; and brave young Irish spirits, registered as "Wild Geese," found their way to the ranks of "the bold Brigade," whose fame was then a household word in Europe. But the Irish masses, both Catholic and Nonconformist, were reduced to abject poverty, and each succeeding year brought fresh commercial restrictions, until, finally, almost every Irish industry, except the linen, was totally extirpated in the island. The smuggling trade, alone, kept some vitality in the commercial veins of the ruined country, and, in defiance of English and Anglo-Irish enactments against it, it continued to flourish down to the beginning of the nineteenth century.

Well-meaning foreign writers, who did not make a study of Anglo-Irish relations in the sixteenth, seventeenth, and eighteenth centuries, have expressed astonishment at the paucity of Irish industries, outside of linen, and have ascribed it to Irish non-adaptability to manufacturing pursuits! Not alone did England compel Ireland to fine her own traders, by levying export duties on their output, but she also, as we have seen, by her own Parliament, limited such exports to the meanest possible proportions! Of course, at this slavish period of the old so-called Irish Parliament, duties to limit the importation of English goods and to foster home industries were not allowed. Ireland was stripped of everything but linen and "homespun," and then left a beggar. This is a most disgraceful chapter in the history of the political connection of Great Britain and Ireland—one that led to untold bitterness, and that caused the great orator, Grattan, in after years to exclaim, prophetically, in the Irish House of Commons: "What England tramples on in Ireland will rise to sting her in America!" He alluded to the Presbyterian and Catholic exodus, which so materially aided the American Revolution.

The last hope of King James again attaining the throne of the "Three Kingdoms" disappeared with the terrible defeat inflicted on the French fleet at the battle of La Hogue, 1692, and, thereafter, his life was passed sadly—for he had ample time to ruminate on his misfortunes—at St. Germain, until he died, in 1701. His rival, William III, whose wife, Queen Mary II, had preceded him to the grave, died from the effects of a horseback accident, in March, 1702. He was immediately succeeded by Queen Anne, the last of the Stuart line who occupied the throne of England. Her reign was one of glory for Great Britain and one of hate and horror for Ireland. We have already mentioned some of the penal laws passed while she held sway. Her ministers, of course, were responsible for her acts, because she herself possessed only moderate ability. Unlike most of the Stuart family, she swam with the current, and so got along smoothly with her English subjects. The most important domestic event of her reign was the legislative union of England with Scotland—which virtually extinguished Scotland as a nation. This event occurred in May, 1707, and was accompanied by acts of the most shameless political profligacy on the part of the English minister and the Scotch lords and commons. In fact, the independence of Scotland, like that of Ireland ninety-three years later, was sold for titles, offices, pensions, and cold cash. The masses of the people, to do them justice,

had little to do with this nefarious transaction, which was
subsequently satirized by the great Scottish poet, Robert
Burns, in his lyric, one verse of which runs thus:

> "What English force could not subdue
>   Through many warlike ages,
> Is sold now by a craven few
>   For hireling traitors' wages!
> The English steel we could disdain—
>   Secure in valor's station—
> But English gold has been our bane—
>   Such a parcel of rogues in a nation!"

The deeds in arms of Anne's great general, Marlborough,
who was a traitor to both King James and King William,
have been partially related in the chapters bearing on the
career of the Franco-Irish Brigade and need no farther mention in this history.

In the days of William III appeared a pamphlet called
"The Case of Ireland Stated," which was written by William Molyneux, a member of Parliament, for the Dublin
University.   It appeared in 1698, and made, at once, a
powerful impression on the public mind.   It, in brief, took
the ground that Ireland—that is, Protestant, colonial Ireland—was, of right, a separate and independent kingdom;
that England's original title of conquest, if she had any, was
abrogated by charters granted to Ireland from time to time,
and, finally, denied that the king and Parliament of England
had power to bind the kingdom and people of Ireland by
English-made laws.   The English Parliament was, of course,
greatly shocked and scandalized at the idea of a "mere Irishman" putting forth such theories, and solemnly ordered his
book to be burned, publicly, by "the common hangman"—
a functionary always in high favor when Ireland needs to
be "disciplined."   The book was burned accordingly, but
its spirit did not die then, nor is it yet dead, or likely to die,

while Ireland contains a population. King William, in replying to the English Parliament's address on the subject of Molyneux's utterance, assured its members that "he would enforce the laws securing the dependence of Ireland on the imperial crown of Great Britain."

In the chapter on the penal laws, many of the enactments of the reign of Anne have been summarized. Her sway was a moral nightmare over Ireland, and it is a remarkable historical coincidence that the Green Isle suffered more, materially and morally, under the English female than the male sovereigns. Under Elizabeth and Anne, the Irish Catholics were persecuted beyond belief. Under Victoria's rule, which the British statistician, Mulhall, has called "the deadliest since Elizabeth," they starved to death by the hundred thousand or emigrated by the million.

The régime of Queen Anne, like that of her predecessors and successors on the throne, gave the government of Ireland into the hands of Englishmen, who held all the important offices, from the viceroyalty downward, and who chose their sub-officers from among the least national element of the Irish people. This system, although somewhat modified, continues to the present day. In the Irish Parliament, there was an occasional faint display of sectarian nationality, but it proved of little advantage when the English wanted matters in that body to go as they wished. Ireland then, as a majority ruled by a minority, "stood on her smaller end," and so it is even in our own times, notwithstanding occasional "concessions" and "ameliorations."

But, from the day when the pamphlet, or book, of Molyneux saw the light, a Patriot party began to grow up in the Irish Parliament. The old Irish nation had, indeed, disappeared, for a period, but the new one soon began to manifest a spirit that roused the bitter hatred of England. Such infatuated Irish Protestants as still believed that they would be more gently treated on account of common creed with the stronger people were soon bitterly undeceived.

The death of Queen Anne, all of whose children by the Prince of Denmark had died before her, occurred in July, 1714. It is said that she secretly favored the succession of her half-brother, acknowledged by Louis XIV, and the Jacobite party in Great Britain, as James III of that realm, but the last Duke of Ormond, the Earl of Orrery, Bishop Atterbury, and Lord Bolingbroke, the Jacobite leaders in England, lost their nerve after the Queen's death and allowed the golden opportunity of proclaiming the exiled Stuart king to pass away. The Hanoverian faction, which called James "the Pretender," took advantage of their vacillation to proclaim the Elector of Hanover, who derived his claim from the Act of Succession or Settlement (which ignored the Stuart male line, or any of its Catholic collateral branches, and excluded them from the throne), under the title of George I. He derived his claim, such as it was, from James I, whose daughter, the Princess Elizabeth, had married the King of Bohemia. Her daughter, Sophia, married the Elector of Hanover and became mother of King George, who was a thorough German in speech, manner, and habit, although not in person or in manly characteristics. But he was a Protestant, and that sufficed for England. On August 1, 1714, he was proclaimed in London and Edinburgh, and on the 8th of that month in Dublin. The Scotch Jacobites ridiculed his accession in a racy "skit," which began with—

> "Oh, wha the deil hae we got for a king
> But a wee, wee German lairdie!"

Ireland, broken in spirit and disgusted by the memory of King James II, remained quiescent, but, in 1715, Scotland and a portion of the north of England rose in rebellion, the former under the Earl of Mar and the latter under young Lord Derwentwater. They were not heartily supported. Both met with defeat, and Derwentwater, together with several English and Scotch adherents of note, was captured, beheaded, and had his estates confiscated to the "crown." The English Parliament offered a reward of £50,000 ($250,-000) for the "apprehension" of "the Pretender," who had been previously "attainted," but there were no takers, "the Pretender" aforesaid being safely housed in Paris. This bloody episode ended Jacobite "risings" in Great Britain for a generation.

CHAPTER III

Further Commercial Restrictions—Continued Exodus of Working People—Jonathan Swift—"The Patriot Party"—Tyranny of Primate Boulter

SEEING that Ireland had taken no part in the attempted Stuart revolution at the beginning of his reign, it might be imagined that George I showed some favor to the Irish people, but he did nothing of the kind. On the contrary, the penal laws were enforced with greater virulence than ever, and several new enactments of a most oppressive character—chiefly bearing on the franchise—were passed. In 1719, the Patriot party in the Irish Parliament threw down a challenge to English supremacy. The Irish House of Lords annulled, on appeal, from the Dublin Court of Exchequer, a judgment in favor of one Annesley and gave it to the opposition litigant, Hester Sherlock. The former appealed to the English lords, who overrode the decision of the

Irish House, by reversing judgment in favor of Annesley. As the sheriff in whose jurisdiction (Kildare) the writ ran refused to obey the English decree, he was heavily fined. The Irish House retaliated by remitting the fine, applauding the sheriff and arresting the judges of the Dublin court who had decided for Annesley. The anger of England became boundless, as it usually does when Ireland asserts itself, and the English Parliament, without color of right, passed the drastic enactment, known as the 6th of George I, which definitively bound Ireland by English enactments, and took the right of appeal away from the Irish House of Peers. Thus was the chain begun by the Poynings' Law, in the reign of Henry VII, made complete, and, at one fell swoop, Ireland was reduced to a provincial status. Thenceforth, until 1780, the Irish Parliament was merely a machine for registering the will of England, in the matter of Irish government.

At the same time, England continued her war on the few remaining Irish industries—nothing seemed to satisfy the jealousy and covetousness of her merchants. The glaring outrages committed against the business of Ireland aroused the ire of the famous Jonathan Swift, Protestant Dean of St. Patrick's, who was the son of an Englishman. He wrote, anonymously, several bitter pamphlets against the selfish policy of England, and urged the Irish people to use nothing but native manufactures. In one of these fulminations, he used the memorable phrase: "Burn everything that comes from England, except the coal!" But his patriotic influence rose to the zenith when he attacked "Wood's halfpence"—base money coined to meet a financial emergency —in 1723. His philippics became known as the "Drapier's letters" from the signature attached to them, and, in the

end, he compelled the government to cancel the contract
with Wood. England foamed with rage, and had the printer
of the letters prosecuted. However, no judge or jury in
Dublin was found vile enough to convict him.

Swift, although an Irish patriot, was a Protestant bigot,
and detested the Celtic Catholics quite as much as he did the
English, whom, from a political standpoint, he hated. Yet,
he was the idol, during his long lifetime, of the Catholics,
because he had stood by Ireland against the common enemy.
This brilliant man, whose writings have made him immortal, and whose private sorrows can not be estimated, finally
"withered at the top," and died insane, after having willed
his property to be used for the building of a lunatic asylum.
In a poem written some time before his sad death, he alludes
to his bequest in the following lines:

> "He left what little wealth he had
> To build a house for fools and mad—
> To show, by one sarcastic touch,
> No nation needed one so much!"

No writer better knew how to enrage the English. He
took a savage delight in tormenting them, wounding their
vanity, and exposing their weaknesses. Neither did he
spare the Irish; and, as for the Scotch, he rivaled Dr. Samuel Johnson in his dislike of that people. In our day, the
average summer-up of merits and demerits would describe
Jonathan Swift as "a gifted crank."

Associated with him in the moral war against English
interference in Ireland's domestic concerns were such other
shining lights of the period as Dr. Sheridan, ancestor of
Richard Brinsley, and others of that brilliant "ilk"; Dr.
Stopford, the able Bishop of Cloyne, and Doctors Jackson,
Helsham, Delaney, and Walmsley, nearly all men of almost

pure English descent. McGee also credits "the three reverend brothers Grattan"—a name subsequently destined to
immortality—with good work in the same connection.

Whatever the private faults of Swift, Ireland must ever
hold his memory in reverence, with those of many other
Irish non-Catholic patriots, who, although they had little
or no Celtic blood in their veins, and were brought up under
English influences, nobly preferred the interests of their
unfortunate native country to the smiles and favors of her
oppressors. And so Ireland, considering these things,
blesses

> "—The men of patriot pen,
> Swift, Molyneux, and Lucas,"

as fervently as if they belonged to the race of the Hy-Niall
or Kinel-Conal.

Nor must it be supposed that the Patriot element, led by
Swift, escaped persecution at the hands of the Protestant oligarchy, although they, too, were of the Established Church.
Swift himself was discriminated against all his life, because
of his advocacy of Irish manufactures, his discrediting of
Wood's "brass money," and his defeat of the mischievous
national bank project, which was germane to it. As diocese
after diocese became vacant in Ireland, he saw dullards
promoted to the sees, while he was deliberately overlooked,
simply because he had advocated justice to Ireland! This
injustice afterward passed into a proverb. Said an Irish
orator, in after years, speaking of another great Irishman
who had also suffered from English resentment: "The
curse of Swift was upon him—to have been born an Irishman, to have been blessed with talents, and to have used
those talents for the benefit of his country!"

But Swift was not the only sufferer. There were other

distinguished offenders against English sentiment. It is true they had not provoked the government by their writings to offer a reward of £300 for their identity, as was Swift's fortune, but they had done enough to be made "horrible examples" of. Thus, Right Rev. Dr. Browne, Protestant Bishop of Cork, had been threatened with deprivation for protesting against the insulting language toward Catholics contained in the notorious Orange toast to the memory of William III; and Dr. Sheridan was deprived of his "living" in Munster, because, says McGee, "he accidentally chose for his text on the anniversary of King George's coronation: 'Sufficient for the day is the evil thereof!' Such," he continues, "was the intolerance of the oligarchy toward their own clergy. What must it have been to others!"

About this period, too, the differences between Episcopalians and Nonconformists—the latter having again repudiated the test oaths—became more bitter than ever. Swift took sides against the Dissenters, whom, as a fierce Church of England champion, he despised. "They were glad," he said, they or their fathers, "to leave their barren hills of Lochaber for the fruitful vales of Down and Antrim." He denied to them, with bitter scorn, the title they had assumed of "Brother Protestants," and as to the Papists they affected to contemn, they were, in his opinion, "as much superior to the Dissenters as a lion, though chained and clipped of its claws, is a stronger and nobler animal than an angry cat, at liberty to fly at the throats of true churchmen." Of course, the Church of England faction triumphed and the exodus of the Nonconformists from Ireland received a fresh impetus. "Outraged," says McGee, "in their dearest civil and religious rights, thousands of the

Scoto-Irish of Ulster, and the Milesian and Anglo-Irish of the other provinces, preferred to encounter the perils of the wild Atlantic rather than abide under the yoke and lash of such an oligarchy. In the year 1729, five thousand six hundred Irish landed at the single port of Philadelphia; in the next ten years they furnished to the Carolinas and Georgia the majority of their immigrants; before the end of this reign [George I] several thousands of heads of families, all bred and married in Ireland, were rearing up a free posterity along the slopes of the Blue Ridge in Virginia and Maryland, and even as far north as the valleys of the Hudson and the Merrimac. In the ranks of the thirteen United Colonies, the descendants of those Irish Nonconformists were to repeat, for the benefit of George III, the lesson and example their ancestors had taught to James II at Inniskillen and Derry."

We do not purpose entering into a chronological account of the several viceroys—most of them rather obscure—who represented English misgovernment in Ireland during the reigns of the early Georges. They simply followed out the old programme of oppression and repression with tiresome monotony. No matter who "held court" in Dublin Castle, the policy of England toward Ireland remained unchanged. If ever there came a lull in the course of systematic persecution, it followed immediately on some reverse of the English arms on the Continent of Europe. An English victory meant added taxes and further coercion for the Irish Catholics and Dissenters.

George I had died in 1727, leaving behind him an unsavory moral reputation, and regretted by nobody in England, except his Hanoverian mistresses, who were noted for their pinguid ugliness. He was succeeded without opposition by his son, who mounted the throne as George II. He, too, was small of stature, un-English in language and appearance, and inherited the vices of his father. He was not deficient in personal bravery, as he proved at Dettingen, and elsewhere, in after times, and he had the distinction of being the last king of England who appeared upon a field of battle.

The penal code was continued in full force during most of this reign, although it had lost favor among the English governing class in the time of the king's father, when the Protestant Ascendency party in the Irish Commons brazenly proposed to the English Privy Council the passage of an act whereby a proscribed prelate or priest arrested in Ireland would be made to suffer indecent mutilation. Bad as the English privy councilors generally were, where Ireland was concerned, they would not stomach such revolting savagery, and the hideous proposition was heard of no more. And yet England, knowing the ferocious character of the fanatics who proposed it, left Ireland virtually helpless in their hands! She could have, at any time, put an end to the intolerable persecutions visited upon the masses of the people by a heartless oligarchy, actuated about equally by cupidity and fierce intolerance. Had she done so, she might have won the Irish heart, as France won that of German Alsace and Italian Corsica, but she preferred to use one section of the Irish people against the other, in her lust of empire, and "Divide and Conquer" became, as in the Elizabethan times, the pith of her Irish policy.

The great English minister, Sir Robert Walpole, impressed by the necessity of breaking down the spirit of independence evoked by Swift and his able and patriotic colleagues, who had indeed "breathed a new soul" into the

Ireland of their day, appointed that inveterate politician and corrupt diplomat, Lord Carteret, viceroy. He also promoted the Right Rev. Hugh Boulter, Bishop of Bristol, also an Englishman of the virulent type, to the Archbishopric of Armagh—the primal see of Ireland. Boulter was Castlereagh's precursor in policy. Possessed of high office and vast wealth, he did not hesitate to use both prestige and money in the interests of England, and his corruption of many members of the Irish Parliament was so open and flagrant as to scandalize even the brazen chiefs of the atrocious "Court party"—the Prætorean guard of Lord Carteret. This unscrupulous churchman was the virtual head of the English interest in Ireland for eighteen years, and, within that period, overshadowing even viceregal authority, he made the English name more hated among not alone the Celtic, but the Scoto and Anglo-Irish than it had been for a century. He was the greatest persecutor of the Catholics that had appeared since the period of Cromwell, and he it was who manipulated the machinery of Parliament to deprive them of the last vestige of their civil and religious liberty in the closing days of the brutal reign, in Ireland, of George I. Nor did the Presbyterians and other dissenters fare much better at his hands. His black career terminated in 1742, and a weight of horror was lifted from Ireland's heart when the welcome news of his death spread rapidly, far and wide, over the persecuted country.

What made "Primate Boulter" particularly odious to the Catholic people of Ireland was his institution of the "Charter Schools"—used openly and insultingly for the perversion of the majority of the population from the Roman Catholic faith. Since that period, English politicians have not hesitated to use the influence of the Roman See, with more or less success, to curb political movements in Ireland. Even then, when England was enforcing the penal laws against the Irish Catholics with fire and sword, she was the ally of Catholic Austria against the French, and glibly advocated toleration for the Protestants of the Hapsburg empire, while her "priest-hunters" industriously earned their putrid "blood money" in unfortunate, Catholic Ireland. We may say, in passing, that Primate Boulter was succeeded in the primacy by another Englishman, Right Rev. George Stone, who proved himself worthy of his predecessor.

CHAPTER IV

Official Extravagance—Charles Lucas, Leader of Irish Opposition
—Chesterfield Viceroy—His Recall—Dorset's Vile
Administration

AN attempt made in 1729 to place an extortionate estimate on the public expenses, and which emanated from "the Castle of Dublin," had the effect of consolidating the Irish opposition in Parliament. These legislators protested in a dignified manner against extravagance in public expenditure. Under the administration of the Duke of Devonshire, in 1737, they set their faces against his method of corrupting the public conscience by a display of lavish generosity, which is always popular in a capital where trade depends to a great extent on courtly favor. The leaders in the House of Commons were Sir Edward O'Brien, of the House of Inchiquin; his son, Sir Lucius; the Speaker, Henry Boyle, and Mr. Anthony Malone, whose father had been an efficient ally of Sir Toby Butler, in defending Catholic rights under the articles of Limerick.

These gentlemen were ably assisted by Dr. Charles Lucas, who, although not a member of the House, possessed a vast outside influence, because of his great talent and moral worth. The doctor was also a druggist by profession, but could use a virile pen even better than he could a pestle and mortar. In 1741, he began hammering the government in public prints, on the lines of Molyneux and Swift, and with almost as great success. But "the Castle" censor came down upon him, and he was compelled to leave Ireland for a period. Like Swift, he was rather antagonistic to Catholic claims, but, as in the case of the great Dean, the Catholics forgave him because he was true to Ireland. After some years of exile, he returned to Dublin, was elected to Parliament, and became a leader of the Patriots in the House of Commons. In the House of Lords, the Earl of Kildare, afterward first Duke of Leinster, was the Patriot leader.

The famous Earl of Chesterfield became Viceroy of Ireland in 1745, and showed, from the first, a thorough disgust for the penal laws and the oligarchs who supported them. He connived at Catholic toleration to such an extent that he became an object of suspicion, if not of hatred, to the Ascendency faction. The government of England, with habitual cunning, had selected this finished courtier to rule in Ireland, because of disquieting rumors of an invasion of Great Britain contemplated by Charles Edward Stuart, son of "the Pretender," James III. Also, about the same time, came the stirring news of the victory of the Irish Brigade, in alliance with the French, over the Duke of Cumberland's column at glorious Fontenoy. "Accursed," old George II is said to have exclaimed, on being told of the Franco-Irish victory, "accursed be the laws that deprive *me* of such soldiers!" But Chesterfield was, in reality, friendly to the Irish. He liked their wit and esprit and took no pains to conceal the fact, greatly to the disgust of the Ascendency clique. But Charles Edward's attempt to recover the British crown utterly failed. Highland Scotland fought for him heroically. The Jacobites of England held, for the most part, aloof, and, beyond the officers of the Irish Brigade, who went with him from France, Ireland hardly furnished a man to aid his hardy and romantic enterprise—thus showing how completely her spirit was subdued during that momentous crisis. Charles Edward was a leader that, in the preceding century, the Irish would have been proud to follow. He was a great improvement on both his sire and grandsire, although he ended miserably, in his old age, a career begun so gloriously in his youth.

Chesterfield remained only eight months in his Irish office. He was recalled within ten days after the battle of Culloden. There was no further need, for the time being, to conciliate the Irish. The heir of the unhappy Stuarts was a houseless wanderer in the land over which his forefathers had reigned for centuries and their cause was hopelessly lost. The Earl and Countess of Chesterfield, on their departure from Dublin, received "a popular ovation." They walked on foot, arm in arm, from the viceregal residence to the wharf, where lay the vessel that was to bear them back to England, and the warm-hearted, "too easily deluded people" prayed loud and fervently for their speedy return. They came back no more, but Chesterfield was enabled to assure George II, when he reached London, that the only "dangerous Papist" he had seen in Ireland was the lovely Miss Ambrose, afterward Mrs. Palmer, Dublin's reigning beauty of the period. Chesterfield made much of her at "the Castle," and laughed po-

litely at the bigots who looked upon her as a species of De-
lilah. As Miss Ambrose enjoyed, also, the friendship of
Lady Chesterfield, her enemies could evoke no scandal from
the platonic intimacy. The earl's mild, insinuating system of
government had enabled him to spare four regiments from
Ireland for service in Scotland, during the Jacobite insurrection. His "Principles of Politeness," practically applied,
were much more effective in the cause of the House of Hanover than all the repressive enactments of the vicious bigots
of the party of Ascendency.

The last Jacobite expedition was organized in France, in
1759, and was under orders of an admiral named Con-
flans, who, when a short distance out from Brest, was encountered by an English fleet under Admiral Hawke and
totally defeated. A wing of this expedition, under Commodore Thurot, whose real name was O'Farrell, did not arrive
in time to take part in the battle, but succeeded in entering
the British Channel without interruption. A storm arose
which drove Thurot's five frigates to seek shelter in Norway
and the Orkney Islands, where they wintered. In the spring,
one frigate made its way back to France. Another sailed
with a similar object, but was never heard from afterward.
The remaining three, under Thurot, made for the Irish
coast and entered Lough Foyle, but made no attempt on
Londonderry. They soon headed for Belfast Lough, and
appeared before Carrickfergus about the end of February,
1760. Thurot demanded the surrender of the place, which
was stoutly refused by the military governor, Colonel Jen-
nings. The Franco-Irish sailor immediately landed his fighting men and took the town by a rapid and furious assault.
Then he levied on the place for supplies and again put to
sea. Off the Isle of Man he fell in with three newly com-

missioned ships of war under the English Commodore, Elliott. A sanguinary encounter followed. Thurot, alias O'Farrell, and three hundred of his marines and sailors were killed. The French vessels were fearful wrecks, and the victorious English towed them in a sinking condition into Ramsay. Thus terminated one of the most gallant naval episodes of the eighteenth century.

When the Earl of Harrington, afterward Duke of Devonshire, became Lord Lieutenant some time after the recall of Lord Chesterfield, the odious Primate Stone—accused both in England and Ireland of unspeakable immorality—ruled Ireland as completely as had his less filthy predecessor, Primate Boulter. Ireland, at the outset of the new régime, was astonished to find a respectable surplus in her treasury, and Lord Chesterfield, who always, while he lived, took a deep interest in Irish affairs, sent a congratulatory letter on the seeming prosperity of the country to his friend, the Bishop of Waterford. The Patriot party in the Commons, led by the sagacious and eloquent Malone, advocated the expenditure of the surplus on public works and needed public buildings throughout Ireland and in the capital. But Stone and the Castle ring fought the proposition bitterly, contending that the money belonged to the crown and could be drawn by royal order on the vice-treasurer, without regard to Parliament. When the Duke of Dorset succeeded Harrington as viceroy, in 1751, the question had reached an acute stage. Opposition to the royal claim on the Irish surplus had led to the expulsion of Dr. Lucas from Ireland. But Malone and Speaker Boyle kept up the fight in the Commons, and, after having sustained one defeat, on a full vote, finally came out victorious by having the supply bill, which covered all government service in the kingdom, thrown out by a vote of 122 to 117. Government showed its resentment by canceling Malone's patent of precedence as Prime Sergeant, and striking Speaker Boyle's name from the list of privy-councilors. This was outrageous enough, but what followed was still more so. The king (George II) by advice of Dorset, Stone, and their clique, overrode the action of the Irish Parliament and despotically, by operation of a king's letter, withdrew the long-disputed surplus from the Irish national treasury. This crowning infamy was consummated in 1753, and so great became public indignation that Stone and the obnoxious ministers were mobbed, and the Duke of Dorset could not appear on the streets of Dublin without being hooted at and otherwise insulted. Anglo-Ireland seemed on the brink of revolution, but the popular leaders took a conservative attitude and thus avoided a violent crisis. Dorset, alarmed by the tempest he had himself created, virtually fled from Dublin, followed by the execration of the multitude. He left the government in the hands of three Lords Justices, one of whom was Primate Stone, whose very name was hateful to the incensed people.

The viceroy was followed to England by the popular leader of the Irish House of Lords, James Fitz-Gerald, 20th Earl of Kildare, who had married the daughter of the Duke of Richmond, and, consequently, had a powerful English backing. Kildare presented to King George, in person, a memorial in which he strongly denounced the misgovernment of Ireland by Dorset, Stone, and Lord George Sackville, Dorset's intermeddling son. This memorial has been described as "the boldest ever addressed by a subject to a sovereign."

Although Lord Holderness, an English courtier, in a letter to Chancellor Jocelyn, says that the bold Geraldine "was but ill-received and very coolly dismissed" by the king, Kildare's policy soon prevailed in Ireland. Dorset was recalled in the succeeding year, and Primate Stone, with whom Kildare refused to act as Lord Justice, was removed from the ministry of Ireland.

The Duke of Devonshire, formerly Lord Harrington, or Hartington, succeeded Dorset, and immediately began the congenial work, to an English statesman, of breaking up, and rendering harmless, the Irish Patriot party. Boyle was made Chancellor of the Exchequer and was raised to the peerage as the Earl of Shannon, receiving also a pension of £2,000 per annum for thirty-one years. Malone would have accepted the Lord Chancellorship gladly, but was restrained by both private and public opinion from doing so openly. But Mitchel says that while Boyle remained nominal chancellor, Malone quietly pocketed the profits of the position, and his patriotic eloquence declined in proportion to the growth of his profits. Other leaders of the Patriot party were also "taken care of," and England managed to get rid of one of her most troublesome "Irish difficulties."

The purchased Patriots, however, may be fairly credited with having forced the beginning of the public works, such as canals and highways, in Ireland, and the construction of some of those splendid official edifices which still, even in their decay, "lend an Italian glory to the Irish metropolis."

Lord Kildare stands accused of having entered into the negotiations with the new viceroy for the "placation" of the Patriot party in the Commons. Such, however, were the political "morals" of the times, and the offices were, nominally at least, Irish and, therefore, quasi, not fully, national—seeing that Ireland was what might be called a semi-independent colonial province, distrustful of England, but without strength or resolution to snap her chains. The earl soon became Marquis of Kildare, and, subsequently, Duke of Leinster, but he is best remembered as the father of the gallant, unselfish, and devoted Lord Edward Fitzgerald, of 1798 fame.

An attempt made, in March, 1756, to pass a bill in the Irish Commons to vacate the seats of such members as should accept "any pension or civil office of profit from the crown," was defeated by a vote of 85 to 59—thus giving plain notice to the English viceroy that the Parliament was up for auction, and, within less than fifty years from that date, it was, accordingly, like that of Scotland, "knocked down to the highest bidder." How could it be otherwise? when, as Mitchel truly says in his Continuation of McGeoghegan's "History of Ireland," "The English Protestant colony in Ireland, which aspired to be a nation, amounted to something under half a million of souls, in 1754. It was out of the question that it should be united on a footing of equality with its potent mother country by 'the golden link of the crown,' because the wearer of that crown was sure to be guided in his policy by English ministers, in accordance with English interests; and, as the army was the king's army, he could always enforce that policy. The fatal weakness of the colony was that it would not amalgamate with the mass of the Irish people (*i.e.* the Catholics) so as to form a true nation, but set up the vain pretension to hold down a whole disfranchised people with one hand and defy all England with the other." And this insensate policy was pursued, with little modification, to the end, and in the end proved fatal to both "the colony" and the nation.

CHAPTER V

More Persecution of Catholics Under George II—Secret Committee
Formed—Snubbed by the Speaker—Received by the Viceroy—Anti-Union Riot in Dublin

THE Duke of Bedford became Lord Lieutenant of Ireland
in 1757, and came as a "conciliator," with a smile on
his face "and a bribe in his pocket." His mission was to
"soften" the penal laws, which had again become too scan-
dalous for the "liberal" and "civilized" reputation of England on the Continent. One Miss O'Toole, a Catholic, had
been pressed by some Protestant friends to "conform" to
the Established Church, so as to avoid persecution, and fled
to the house of a relative named Saul, who resided in Dublin, in order to escape disagreeable importunity. Mr. Saul
was prosecuted and convicted, under the penal code, and the
judge who "tried" the case said, in his charge, that "Papists
had no rights," because the "law" under which poor Saul
was punished "did not," in the language of the court, "pre-
sume a Papist to exist in the kingdom, nor could Papists
so much as breathe the air without the connivance of government!" This judge, harsh as his language may now seem,
did not misstate the case, for such, indeed, was the barbarous "law of the land" at that period, and for a considerable time afterward.

The bigots in the Irish Commons, soon after the arrival
of the Duke of Bedford in Dublin, had prepared a new and
even more drastic bill of penalties against Catholics than
already existed, and so intolerable were its proposals that
several leading Catholics among "the nobility, gentry, and

professional [clandestinely] classes" got together, and, after
a time, formed, in out-of-the-way meeting places, the first
"Catholic Committee" of Ireland—the precursor, by the
way, of the many similar organizations conducted by John
Keogh, Daniel O'Connell, and other Catholic leaders of succeeding generations.

The chief men of this committee were Charles O'Conor,
the Irish scholar and antiquary; Dr. Curry, the historical
reviewer; Mr. Wyse, a leading merchant of the city of
Waterford; Lords Fingal, Devlin, Taaffe, and some others
less known to fame. These amiable gentlemen were, at
first, frightened by the sound of their own voices, but they
gradually grew bolder, although they did not proceed far
enough to bring down upon their heads the full wrath of
"government." Indeed, they were, on most occasions, ob-
sequiously "loyal" to the "crown," which meant the English
king and connection. But the iron had entered their souls,
and the stain of its corrosion lingered long in their veins.
When the Duke of Bedford, by the instructions of the elder
Pitt (Chatham), who acted for King George, informed the
Irish Parliament that France contemplated a new invasion
and called upon the Irish people to show their loyalty to the
House of Hanover, Charles O'Conor drew up an abjectly
"loyal" address, which was signed by 300 leading Catholics, and had it presented at the bar of the House of Commons (Dublin) by Messrs. Antony MacDermott and John
Crump. The speaker, Mr. Ponsonby, received the document
in dead silence, laid it on the table in front of him, and coolly
bowed the delegation out. The Duke of Bedford, however,
took "gracious" notice of the address, and caused his answer
thereto, which was appreciative—England being then in
mortal terror of the French—to be printed in the Dublin

"Gazette," which was the "government's" official organ. And the poor Catholic gentlemen, who had signed the cringing document, went into convulsions of joy because of this "official recognition" of their slavish professions of "loyalty" to a foreign king, who cared less for them than for the blacks of the West Indies!

But Mitchel, the Protestant historian, who understood his country's sad story better, perhaps, than any writer who ever dealt with it, makes for the Catholic committee this ingenious apology: "We may feel indignant," says he, "at the extreme humility of the proceedings of the committee, and lament that the low condition of our countrymen at that time left no alternative but that of professing a hypocritical 'loyalty' to their oppressors; for the only other alternative was secret organization to prepare an insurrection for the total extirpation of the English colony in Ireland, and, carefully disarmed as the Catholics were [and still are], they, doubtless, felt this to be an impossible project. Yet, for the honor of human nature, it is necessary to state the fact that this profession of loyalty, to a king of England, was, in reality, insincere. Hypocrisy, in such a case, is less disgraceful than would have been a genuine canine attachment to the hand that smote and to the foot that kicked."

But Bedford, in his policy of conciliation, had even a deeper motive than fear of France. The statesmen of England, jealous of even the poor and almost impotent colonial Parliament of Ireland, so early as 1759, contemplated that "legislative union," which was to be effected in later times. Bedford's design was the truly English one of arraying the Irish Catholics against the Protestant nationalists, who had, with England's willing aid, so cruelly persecuted them.

When this project got mooted abroad, the Protestant mob of Dublin—the Catholics were too cowed at the time to act, and their leaders were committed to Bedford by their address—rose in their might, on December 3, 1759, surrounded the Houses of Parliament and uttered tumultuous shouts of "No Union! no Union!" They stopped every member of Parliament, as he approached to enter the House, and made him swear that he would oppose the union project. They violently assaulted the Lord Chancellor, whom they believed to be a Unionist, together with many other lords, spiritual and secular, and "ducked" one member of the Privy Council in the river Liffey. The Speaker and Secretary of the House of Commons had to appear in the portico of the House and solemnly assure the people that no union was contemplated. Even this assurance did not quell the tumult, and, finally, a fierce charge of dragoons and the bayonets of a numerous infantry, accompanied by a threat of using cannon, cleared the streets. Following up the policy of "conciliation," the Catholic leaders, with slavish haste, repudiated the actions of the Protestant mob, and thus produced a contemptuous bitterness in the Protestant mind, which aggravated the factious feeling in the unfortunate country. England's work was well done. She had planted, as a small seed, the idea of absorbing the Irish Parliament some day, and was willing to let it take its own time to ripen into Dead Sea fruit for Ireland. The Catholic helot had been cunningly played off against his Protestant oppressor, and thus the subject nation had been made the forger of its own fetters—at least in appearance, although England was the real artificer. Many Catholics in humble life may have joined in the Dublin anti-union riots, but the Catholic chiefs, who had their own axe to grind, were resolved to appear "loyal"—all the more so because some of the Protestant leaders in the late disorders sought to fasten the responsibility on the members of the proscribed faith. The outbreak, as was well known,. was mainly the work of the followers of Dr. Lucas, then in exile, but soon to be a Member of Parliament, and the fiercest opponent of a legislative union with Great Britain.

"It deserves remark," says a historian of the period, "that on this first occasion, when a project of a legislative union was really entertained by an English ministry, the Patriot party which opposed it was wholly and exclusively of the Protestant colony, and that the Catholics of Ireland were totally indifferent, and, indeed, they could not rationally be otherwise, as it was quite impossible for them to feel an attachment to a national legislature in which they were not represented, and for whose members they could not even cast a vote."

George II died of "rupture of the heart"—probably from the bursting of an arterial aneurism in that region—in 1760. He was never popular in England, because of his German ways and affections, and the Irish people regarded him with indifference. They had never seen him, and he was about as much of a stranger in his Irish realm as the Shah of Persia or the Khan of Tartary. His reign had lasted twenty-eight years, and, in all that period, the estimated population of Ireland—for there was no regular census—increased only 60,000. Presbyterian and Catholic emigration to the colonies—superinduced by the penal laws against both—was mainly the cause of this remarkable stagnation. There had been two famines also, and the victims of artificial scarcity—a condition produced by restrictions on trade and manufacture—were numerous.

CHAPTER VI

Accession of George III—His Character—Boasts of Being "a Briton"
—Death of Dr. Lucas—Lord Townsend's Novel Idea of Gov-
-erning Ireland—Septennial Parliament Refused

THE long reign of George III, grandson of the late
monarch, began in the month of October, 1760, when
he had attained the age of 22 years. His father, Frederick Louis, Prince of Wales, was a dissolute and almost
imbecile person, and was hated by his own father, George
II, with a most unnatural hatred. No doubt he, in great
measure, deserved it, for a member of his own family
described Frederick Louis as being "the greatest brute and
ass in Christendom." George III, when he mounted the
English throne, was a dull, commonplace young man, without pronounced personal vices, but exceedingly obstinate
and subject to spells of temper, when strongly opposed,
that gave assurance of future mental weakness. He was
not, by nature, cruel, but circumstances developed gross
cruelty under his régime, in India, in America, and in Ireland. He had enough of the Stuart blood in him to be a
stickler for "the right divine" of kings, and he was enough
of a Guelph to have his own way with even his most persuasive ministers. His father's politics, so far as he had
any, leaned toward Whiggery, but after that prince's death
his mother had placed him under the tutelage of the Marquis of Bute, who was an ardent Tory. Consequently, the
young king had had the advantage of being taught in the
two great English schools of policy, but, in the long run,
the Tory in his nature prevailed over the Whig, and George
III finally developed into a fierce and intolerant despot.

All that could be said in his favor was that, after he married—and he married young—his court became, at once, a model of propriety and dulness. The painted harlots, fostered by his grandfather and great-grandfather, were not succeeded by others of their kind, and the prudent mothers of England no longer feared to allow their handsome daughters to enter the precincts of the royal palace. The English masses were, at first, greatly astonished at the personal purity of their sovereign, but, after a while, became reconciled to the belief that a monarch need not, necessarily, be a libertine.

King George evidently borrowed a leaf from the book of Queen Anne when he assumed the crown. She had assured her subjects that hers was "an entirely English heart." George's first address from the throne opened with the words, "Born and educated in this country, I glory in the name of Briton." Coming from a king, this sentiment, addressed to a people in general so fervidly "loyal" as the English, produced a most favorable effect, and, to the end of his long reign, was never forgotten, even when his mule-like obstinacy wellnigh goaded them to desperation. George III, from first to last, in his love of domination, impatience of opposition, carelessness of the rights of other peoples, egotism, intolerance, and commercial greed, stood for John Bull. Behind John Bull stood England, very much as she still stands to-day. The address continued by declaring that the civil and religious rights of his "loving subjects" were equally dear to him with the most valuable prerogatives of the crown. It was his fixed purpose, he said, to countenance and encourage the practice of true religion and virtue. The eyes of all Europe, he declared, were on that Parliament and from it "the *Protestant* interest hoped for protection." At the end of the speech, King George intimated that the toleration of the Catholics—that is, connivance at their existence, particularly in Ireland—would not be interfered with. But the penal statutes remained unrepealed, and the Irish Catholics continued to be persecuted, although rather less brutally, particularly as regarded their religious observances, in their own country. They were not allowed to vote, or hold office, or have any say whatever in public affairs, although they were subject to taxes and fines. They could not be educated, and were debarred from practicing any profession under long-established penalties. In short, they were very little better off during the earlier years of George III's reign than under the sway of his two immediate predecessors.

The Irish Protestant mind, however, did not lose its patriotic impulse, because of the interested silence of Malone, Boyle, and the former leaders of the Patriot party. Members of Parliament had hitherto been elected to serve during the life of the sovereign, and, in the beginning of the reign of George III, the new Irish Parliament began an earnest agitation for octennial Parliaments. Among the able men—some of them destined to be famous—who were elected to the new body were Hussey Burgh, Dennis Bowes Daly, Henry Flood, and Dr. Lucas. It should have been stated that the original Irish demand was for a seven years' Parliament, and bills were passed, in 1761 and 1763, embodying the proposition, but the king and English Privy Council, to whom they had to be submitted, under the Poynings' Act, coolly "pocketed" them, and they were heard of no more. This arbitrary conduct of an alien monarch, and advisory body, aroused great public indignation, and the clamor became so loud, in 1767, that, finally, the bill was returned from England, changed to octennial, or eight years, and, with this amendment, it passed the Irish Parliament and received the royal sanction in February of the succeeding year. Under the new act, a Parliament was elected in 1768, and all the advocates of the new dispensation were re-elected. Where all did noble work, it is not detracting from their merit to remark that Dr. Lucas was the real leader of the movement, and was generally recognized as such. He lived only two years after his great triumph, and was almost universally mourned—the only exceptions being the members of the corrupt Court party. He was formally eulogized in the Irish House of Commons, and at his funeral the pall-bearers were Lord Kildare, Lord Charlemont, Henry Flood, Sir Lucius O'Brien, Hussey Burgh, and Speaker Ponsonby.

The Patriot party continued, in the new Parliament, under the administration of Lord Townsend, a vigorous opposition to unjust pension lists, and other evils which afflicted the nation. The Lord Lieutenant, who was jolly and persuasive, also corrupt, attempted to break up the opposition after the good old English fashion, but made no impression on the able phalanx led by Flood, who, after the death of Lucas, was looked upon as the chief of the Patriot element in the Commons. Kildare, notwithstanding his peculiar action in the days of Malone, *et al.,* continued to champion the popular cause in the House of Peers. Resistance to the supply bill, which changed the Irish military establishment from 12,000 to 15,000 men, brought about the prorogation of Parliament session after session for nearly two years. Meanwhile, the Castle was quietly "seeing" the members, and, in spite of Flood and Speaker Ponsonby, an address of confidence, carried by a bare majority, was passed by the

Commons. The Speaker refused to present it and resigned his post. A Mr. Perry was elected to succeed him, and, for a time, it looked as if the Patriots might be broken up. But Mr. Perry, in spite of his suspicious conduct in accepting the speakership, vacated by his friend, Mr. Ponsonby, remained faithful to Irish interests and the ranks of the opposition became even more formidable than before.

Lord Townsend, the jolly old corruptionist, became so unpopular that nearly every public print in Dublin was filled with lampoons upon him, and, finally, he requested retirement and was succeeded by Lord Harcourt, in 1772. He began well, but ended badly, as is usual with English viceroys in Ireland, who have seldom failed to fall eventually under Dublin Castle influences. He attempted to throw unjust burdens on Ireland, but was resisted at every point, particularly when he sought to make the supply bill extend over two years instead of one. Henry Flood delivered one of his best speeches in opposition to this dishonest innovation. Hussey Burgh promised that if any member in future brought in such a bill he would move his expulsion. But the climax was reached when the Hon. George Ogle, of Wexford, author of the well-known lyric, "Molly Astore," which has retained its popularity for more than a century, proposed that the bill, as introduced, be burned by the hangman. The Speaker reminded Mr. Ogle that the document was decorated with the great seal. "Then," replied the witty poet, "it will burn all the better!" Mr. Ogle's suggestion was not carried out, but the bill was subsequently modified to suit the ideas of the House of Commons.

CHAPTER VII

The Peace of Paris—Agrarian Warfare in Ireland—Judicial Murder
of Father Sheehy—All who Swore Against Him Die Violent
Deaths—Secret Societies

THE Peace of Paris, 1763, brought the Seven Years' War to a conclusion on the Continent of Europe. Frederick the Great retained Silesia, formerly an Austrian province, to which he had no just title; and there were other territorial changes of less importance. England had triumphed over the French interest in America; for Wolfe's victory of the Plains of Abraham, at Quebec, in September, 1759, decided the game of war in favor of the British, although other battles were fought by the opposing forces after that event.

Agrarian oppression in Ireland, particularly in the South, had caused the peasantry to organize themselves into secret societies for mutual protection. It was thus that the famous "White Boys" of the last century—so called from wearing linen shirts, or white woolen jackets, over their other clothes, so as to give them a uniform appearance— came into existence. Their methods were crude, wild, often fierce and sometimes cruel. They defied the law because they had found no element of protection in it. Rather had they found it, as administered by the landlord oligarchy, in whose hands it was placed by the evil genius of England, an instrument of intolerable oppression. No justice was to be obtained by any appeal they might make to their tyrants, and so they resorted to what an Irish orator has called "the wild justice of revenge." As usual, some naturally bad men found their way into these organizations, and often vented their malice on individuals in the name of the trampled people.   The landlords took advantage of the commission of crime to get up another "Popish plot" scare, and succeeded in making shallow and timid people accept the slander as truth.   The real object of the "White Boys" was to secure low rentals on tillage land, and to preserve "commonage rights"—that is, grazing lands in common at a nominal cost, or else free, something that had long been the usage—for their stock.   The landlords, not satisfied with levying exorbitant rents, and grown, if possible, harder and more greedy than ever, finally abolished and fenced in "the commons."   This action aroused the fury of the peasantry, particularly in the Munster counties, and they collected in large bodies and demolished the land-lords' fences.   This gave the tyrants an excuse to call for military aid—the argument being that the people were in arms against "the crown," which, of course, was false. The poor peasantry struck at their nearest and most visi-ble oppressors, and never thought about "the crown."   The king was, to them, very like a myth.   It would seem that many of the poorer Protestants joined with the Catholics in the demonstration against the inclosures, which, of course, showed the absurdity of the "Popish plot" story.   Still, the affair was not to terminate until it begot a cruel tragedy. The parish priest of Clogheen, County Tipperary, in 1765, was the Rev. Nicholas Sheehy, a high-minded and saintly man, whose heart was deeply touched by the sufferings of the poor tenants, whose ardent and eloquent champion he became.   The Cromwellian "aristocracy" of the county, headed by the Bagnals, the Maudes, the Bagwells, the Tolers, and a parson named Hewitson, resolved to get rid of Father Sheehy, and only waited for a good chance to insnare him in their toils.   Two years previous to the date already given, they had had the young priest arrested on a charge of swearing in "White Boys," but, because of insufficient evidence, he was acquitted.   Soon after he was released, one Bridge, who had been a principal witness against him, mysteriously disappeared.   The oligarchs had the priest arrested immediately on a charge of murder.   The witnesses employed to appear against him were a horse-stealer, named Toohey, a vagrant youth named Lonergan, and an immoral woman, named Dunlea.   He had lain in Clonmel jail, heavily ironed, for several months before he was brought to trial.   The prosecution did not have their witnesses fully instructed.   At last, March 12, 1765, Father Sheehy was brought up for trial.   He succeeded in proving an alibi, but that was of no avail.   His destruction was determined upon, and, on March 15, he suffered execution by hanging and subsequent decapitation.   This atrocious murder aroused the anger of the country.   Protestants and Catholics alike joined in execrating the crime.   Yet, he was not the only victim.   In May of the same year, Edward Sheehy, a cousin, and two other young farmers, were convicted and hanged on the same testimony that had sent Father Sheehy to his untimely grave.   McGee says: "The fate of their enemies is notorious; with a single exception, they met deaths violent, loathsome, and terrible.   Maude died insane, Bagwell in idiocy; one of the jury committed suicide, another was found dead in a privy, a third was killed by his horse, a fourth was drowned, a fifth shot, and so through the entire list.   Toohey was hanged for felony, the prostitute, Dunlea, fell into a cellar and was killed, and the lad, Lonergan, after enlisting as a soldier, died of a loathsome disease in a Dublin infirmary."

Another attempt at persecution of the priests was made in 1767, but Edmund Burke, the illustrious statesman, and other liberal Protestants, came to the rescue with funds for the defence of the accused, and the oligarchy were unable to secure the conviction of their intended victims. The fate of the perjured informers, who swore away the lives of Father Sheehy and his fellow-sufferers, was well known throughout the country, and, no doubt, had a wholesome effect on other wretches who might have been bribed into following their example.

The "White Boys" were not the only secret organization formed in Ireland at that period. Some were composed of Protestants, mostly of the Presbyterian sect, who combated in Ulster the exactions of the landlords. They bore such names as "Hearts of Steel," because they were supposed to show no mercy to "the petty tyrants of their fields"; "Oak Boys," because they carried oaken boughs, or wore oak leaves in their hats. The "Peep o' Day Boys" were political rather than agrarian, and professed the peculiar principles afterward adopted by the Orange Association. They confined themselves mainly to keeping up the anniversary of the Boyne and making occasional brutal attacks on defenceless Catholics. The respectable Protestant element kept scrupulously away from association with these rude fanatics. The successors of the "White Boys" in Munster were the equally dreaded "Terry Alts," who existed down to a very recent period, and belonged, mainly, to the County Tipperary. Like the "White Boys," they raided the houses of "the gentry" and their retainers for arms, and severe, often fatal, conflicts resulted from their midnight visitations. They also killed, from time to time, obnoxious landlords and their agents, and were hanged by the score in retaliation. The government was not over-particular regarding their guilt or innocence. The object was to avenge the slain land-grabbers, and also to "strike terror." As usual, many base informers were found to betray their fellows, but, in justice to the "White Boys" and "Terry Alts," it may be stated that the betrayers of their secrets were mostly Castle spies, or detectives, employed for the purpose of entrapping the unwary. Very few of the regular members, who lived among their own relatives, accepted blood money. In many cases, the peasantry committed unnecessary acts of violence, but, in general, they only visited with severe punishment landlords or their agents who were notorious evictors, or farmers who "took the land" over the heads of the evicted tenants.

The Catholic Church was the consistent opponent of the agrarian organizations, because of the mutual bloodshed between them and the landlord element, but, much as the Catholic peasants held their bishops and priests in reverence, the admonitions of the latter had small effect on the young men of their flocks while wholesale evictions were in progress. The "boys," with rough logic, would say, among themselves: "The clergy mean well, but we had better be hanged than starved to death, and, besides, revenge on our tyrants is sweet." There is hardly anything in Old World history more ghastly than the long, desultory, and deadly war of tenant against landlord in Ireland, from the days of George II to the latter part of Victoria's reign. It is a chapter we gladly turn away from, with the remark that the cruel oligarchy, who wantonly provoked a naturally humane people to crime, were infinitely more criminal than the poor, oppressed peasants they made desperate.

CHAPTER VIII

Flood and Grattan—Sudden Rise of the Latter—Speaks for a Free
Commerce—The Volunteer Movement—England Yields
to Irish Demand

IT was unfortunate for both America and Ireland that
Henry Grattan, who had entered Parliament in December, 1775, had not attained to the leadership of the Patriot
party when the colonies revolted against the tyranny of
George III. Flood held that position when hostilities appeared imminent, and his influence, somewhat ignorantly
exerted, had much to do with voting 4,000 troops from the
Irish establishment for service against the Americans. At
the time, the American case was not as well understood
in Ireland as it was later on, and, besides, an accommodation was hoped for. In the course of his speech supporting the policy of the government, Flood said that the troops
from Ireland were "armed negotiators"—a most unfortunate phrase, which Grattan, in after days, turned against
him to good effect, when he uttered that fierce philippic
against his quondam friend during an acrimonious debate
which arose soon after the Irish Parliamentary triumph over
England in 1782. It must be remembered by American
readers that the Irish Parliament which voted men to put
down the American revolutionists was Protestant in creed
and mainly English in blood. Not a Catholic sat in it, and
but few men of Celtic origin. The sympathies of the Catholic and dissenting masses were unmistakably with the
Americans, and Grattan in the Irish Legislature, and Burke
and Brinsley Sheridan in the English House of Commons,
were their eloquent champions. Flood, although a man of

fine intellect and an accomplished orator, soon found himself rather outclassed by Grattan, who was young, ardent, and animated by a "pentecostal fire," which prompted him to utter some of the most inspiring speeches that ever flowed from the lips of man. Flood, following the example of Malone at another period, had accepted office under the Harcourt administration, and it was openly charged by his enemies, and probably with some degree of truth, that he had been influenced in his action against America by the circumstance. He had also supported the embargo measure, imposed by order in council, which debarred Irish food products from exportation to the American colonies in revolt. Naturally, conduct of this kind produced dissatisfaction among his friends and followers, and his popularity immediately declined.

The decline of Flood as a Patriot leader left a free field for Grattan and his best-known competitors for oratorical honors, Hussey Burgh, Bowes Daly, and Yelverton. At first, Grattan was rather chary of speech in the House, but, gradually, he gained confidence in himself, and, although his gestures were awkward and his elocution generally faulty, the matter of his addresses was so full of fire, energy, and logic that he soon became the acknowledged chief of what Byron happily termed in his "Irish Avatar" the eloquent war. The restrictions on Irish commerce demanded his first attention, and his earlier utterances in Parliament were mostly devoted to that question. It has been erroneously stated that Henry Grattan was a "free trader" in the American and British sense of that term. On the contrary, he believed in a moderate tariff for the protection of Irish industries, and also for the accumulation of a revenue, and this was fully exemplified by the action of the Irish Parliament, when, from 1782 to 1800, it became virtually independent, in enacting tariff laws for the objects stated. It is true the tariff in regard to English imports was comparatively low, but still high enough to give the Irish manufacturer a good chance to compete with the manufactures of the richer country. What Grattan and his followers wanted was free commerce—an exemption from the export duties, which crippled Irish merchants; and freedom to export Irish goods, without hindrance from English customs officers, to any country of the world.

When the news of the battle of Saratoga and surrender of Burgoyne to the American army reached Ireland, in 1777, it produced a profound impression. Grattan, who always favored the American cause, moved an address to the throne in favor of retrenchment, which meant reduction of the military establishment, while Bowes Daly moved, and had carried, another address, which deplored the continuance of the American war, but professed fidelity to the royal person. As usual, when England got the worst of it abroad, small concessions were made to the Irish Catholics, and the Irish Parliament was permitted to pass a bill "authorizing Papists to loan money on mortgages, to lease lands for any period not exceeding 999 years, and to inherit and bequeath real property." This bill had "a rider" which abolished the test oath as regarded the Dissenters, and, no doubt, this provision had much to do with the success of the bill as a whole, which did not, however, pass without strenuous opposition.

An attempt made by Lord Nugent in the English Parliament to mitigate the severity of the navigation and embargo acts, as regarded Ireland, was howled down by the English manufacturers, merchants, and tradespeople generally. The knowledge of this action spurred on Grattan and his followers and, thenceforward, "Free Trade" became their rallying cry.

Protestant Ireland, since the year of Thurot's bold exploit, had lived in much terror of another French invasion, on a larger scale. When France, in 1778, became the ally of the United States of America, which had declared their independence on July 4, 1776, this feeling of alarm increased. Their leaders demanded military protection from the government, and were informed that the latter had none to give, unless they would accept invalids and dismounted cavalrymen. Henry Flood, seconded by Speaker Perry, had long advocated the formation of a national militia, and these gentlemen were cordially supported in the proposition by Grattan, Lord Charlemont, and other noted leaders of the Patriot party. A bill authorizing a volunteer militia passed the Irish Parliament in 1778. After a great deal of discussion, it was deemed more prudent to form the force from independent organizations of volunteers, armed by the state, but clothed and otherwise equipped by themselves. They were left free to elect their own officers. Immediately, a patriotic impulse permeated the nation, and the Protestant Irish, who were alone permitted to bear arms, rallied to the armories and parade-grounds by the thousand. Belfast and Strabane claimed the honor of having formed the first companies. The richer among the Catholics supplied money to the poor among their Protestant neighbors for the purchase of uniforms and other necessaries. This patriotic action on their part naturally resulted in an immediate mitigation of the penal discrimination against them and the entrance of hundreds of them into the ranks of the volunteers was, at first, connived at, and soon openly permitted. The result was that, by the spring of 1780, there were, at least, 65,000 men under arms for Ireland in her four provinces—Ulster leading in numbers and enthusiasm. The rank and file were artisans, farmers, and clerks, while the officers were, in general, selected from among the wealthy and aristocratic classes. Many of these officers equipped their companies, or regiments, at their own expense. The Earl of Charlemont —a weak but well-meaning nobleman—was elected commander by the Ulster volunteers, while the amiable Duke of Leinster—the second of that proud title—was chosen by those of Leinster. Munster and Connaught, not being quite as well organized as their sister provinces, deferred their selections. All English goods were tabooed by the volunteers, their families, and friends, and a favorite maxim of the period was that of Dean Swift, already quoted, "Burn everything coming from England, except the coal!"

The now feeble shadow of English government, holding court at Dublin Castle, viewed this formidable uprising with genuine alarm, and did its utmost to prevent the issuance of arms to the volunteers, but the Irish leaders were not to be cajoled or baffled, and, in the summer of 1779, the new Irish army was thoroughly armed, drilled and ready for any service that might be demanded from it. The leaders had now the weapon to enforce their rights in hand, and did not fail to make good use of it. They met and formed plans for the coming session of Parliament, and were delighted to receive assurances from Flood, and other officeholders, that they would support Grattan and his allies in the demand that Irish commerce have "free export and import."

An address, covering the points stated, with the amendment "free trade" substituted by Flood for the original phrase, passed the Houses, when they met, and on the succeeding day the House of Commons, with the Speaker at its head, proceeded to the Castle and presented the address to the viceroy. The volunteers, commanded by the Duke of Leinster, occupied both sides of the streets through which the members had to pass and presented arms to the nation's representatives, many of whom wore the diversified uniforms of the Patriot army. Dublin, in all its varied history, never witnessed a grander or more inspiring spectacle.

Alderman Horan, of Dublin, precipitated a crisis by demanding freedom of export for some Irish woolens to Amsterdam, and he filed his demand, in due form, at the custom house. This was in defiance of the prohibitory enactment of the reign of William III and an English man-of-war was stationed in Dublin Bay to enforce it. Mr. Horan, not being provided with a battleship, was fain to content himself with leaving his demand on file, but he had gained his point by directing public attention to an insulting grievance with a stern object lesson. Ireland saw, at once, that English monopoly would yield nothing, except to force, or the threat of force. Henry Grattan, in the Commons, replied to the shotted guns of the English frigate in the bay by introducing an amendment to the supply bill, which declared that "at this time, it is inexpedient to grant new taxes." This was carried overwhelmingly, and England began to think that, after all, Irish votes were a match for English guns. Grattan gained a further triumph over the government by causing the defeat of a bill providing duties for the support of the loan fund.

Lord North, when confronted with the ominous news from Ireland, remembering his unfortunate experience with the American patriots, determined to back down from his former despotic position. He brought in resolutions which gave Ireland the right to trade with British colonies in America and Africa, and granted free export to glass and woolens. The Irish Parliament adopted similar resolutions, and the main portion of Ireland's commercial grievances was, thereby, removed.

END OF VOLUME ONE